THE UNITED STATES AND
WESTERN EUROPE SINCE 1945

The United States and Western Europe since 1945

From "Empire" by Invitation to Transatlantic Drift

GEIR LUNDESTAD

OXFORD

UNIVERSITY PRESS

OXFORD
UNIVERSITY PRESS

Great Clarendon Street, Oxford OX2 6DP

Oxford University Press is a department of the University of Oxford.
It furthers the University's objective of excellence in research, scholarship,
and education by publishing worldwide in

Oxford New York

Auckland Bangkok Buenos Aires Cape Town Chennai
Dar es Salaam Delhi Hong Kong Istanbul Karachi Kolkata
Kuala Lumpur Madrid Melbourne Mexico City Mumbai Nairobi
São Paulo Shanghai Taipei Tokyo Toronto

Oxford is a registered trade mark of Oxford University Press
in the UK and in certain other countries

Published in the United States
by Oxford University Press Inc., New York

British Library Cataloguing in Publication Data

Data available

Library of Congress Cataloging in Publication Data

Data available

ISBN 0–19–926668–9

1 3 5 7 9 10 8 6 4 2

Typeset by Newgen Imaging Systems (P) Ltd., Chennai, India
Printed in Great Britain
on acid-free paper by
Biddles Ltd., Guildford and King's Lynn

PREFACE

Why another book on the American–Western European relationship? There are three main reasons why I decided to write this book. First, the American–Western European relationship was, and definitely still is, a crucial one. After the Second World War the United States clearly became the leading power in the world. Washington's most important allies were found in Western Europe (in addition to East Asia with Japan). The United States and the countries of Western Europe had many common interests, the most important one being the need to contain Soviet influence. Yet, there were also many divergent interests. With the end of the Cold War, many observers argued that NATO, the core of the American–European relationship, would break up. It did not. Now, however, many signs of tension can be seen in Atlantic relations, and clearly the balance between cooperation and conflict definitely shifted over time. This book tries to evaluate that balance in a crucial relationship during the past, in the present, and, with much less certainty, for the future.

Second, unbelievable as it may sound, there are actually very few research-based surveys of the entire American–Western European relationship since 1945, as opposed to the numerous detailed studies of various aspects of this relationship. The best ones and, depending on the definition of the topic, possibly the only ones, are Alfred Grosser's *The Western Alliance: European-American Relations Since 1945* and Richard J. Barnet's *The Alliance: America–Europe–Japan. Makers of the Postwar World*. Grosser's book was written in 1975. While containing a wealth of useful information, it is dated, and it is in many ways also poorly organized. Barnet's book is from 1983, but, as the subtitle indicates, it includes Japan, and is somewhat journalistic–biographical in its approach. So, there would indeed seem to be not only room, but also a great need for a new survey of the American–European relationship.

Third, in that I have already written many books and articles on various aspects of the American–European relationship, I felt that I had a good basis to write the present overview. My best-known article, " 'Empire' by Invitation? The United States and Western Europe, 1945–1952", presented a theory about the American–European relationship that has received a great deal of attention. Later I extended this theory both in time and scope. This book thus gave me the chance to do many things: draw together a great many relevant books and articles into a larger presentation; revisit my own earlier interpretations, keeping virtually unchanged what I still find useful, modifying the rest; and actually write a book on a crucial topic that could cover a surprisingly large hole in the existing literature. With reference to my own earlier work, I shall of course make explicit where I draw upon earlier presentations, but generally facts, figures, and statements that are documented there will not be documented again here.

A book on the American–European relationship can be written in many different ways. Since so little has really been done on the overall relationship, I quickly decided that although the book should be aimed at the general market, it should be written in such a way that it could be used also as a basic survey of the topic, even as a textbook.

Many believe that history textbooks should cover as much ground as possible in as few pages as possible and without revealing any sort of personal bias. This book is not for them. There is definitely nothing wrong in writing economically, and I have tried to do so, although some may feel that my success has been rather limited in that respect. I wanted to focus on the major developments. These would be covered in relative detail, while all kinds of information that might otherwise be relevant, but had little to do with the major story, would be left out. Thus, the many different countries in Western Europe would certainly not receive a more or less fixed number of pages, but be dealt with only where they were textually relevant. Still, in Western Europe the primary focus is, as one would expect, on Great Britain, France, and (West) Germany. The chapters on the early decades are longer than those on the most recent ones. That is because the sources available to historians are much more abundant for the early years and also because it is easier to develop perspectives on what is more distant.

In writing this book I have accumulated many debts. First, I am grateful to the Norwegian Nobel Committee who granted me a semi-sabbatical during the first half of 2002 and to the Nobel Institute's research director Olav Njølstad who filled in for me as director of the Nobel Institute during this period. Without this concentrated period of writing and reflection I would not have been able to finish this book in the period I did.

Second, I am pleased to recognize the assistance of my research assistant Dag Axel Kristoffersen. I realized early on that if this book were to have any merit I would have to deal with the French language literature in a serious way; Dag Axel went through much of this literature in an efficient and conscientious way, and his reports on French writings on the American–European relationship have added a new dimension to this book. Dag Axel was also of great assistance on certain other points too where he went through primary sources and literature in English.

Third, I owe a debt of gratitude to the research fellows at the Norwegian Nobel Institute in the spring term of 2002. They thought they came to Oslo to do their own serious writing and then I inflicted my draft of the present manuscript on them. They responded not only in a cheerful, but also a most useful way. My thanks go particularly to Beth Fischer, Leopoldo Nuti, Michael Cox, and Frédéric Bozo. I could not have had a better group of experts to save me from at least some of the mistakes that are inevitable in a book of this kind. For those that remain I am solely responsible.

At Oxford University Press I am particularly grateful to Chief Editor Dominic Byatt for his strong interest in my project and to Tom Chandler for his expert copy-editing. I also want to express my appreciation to Oxford's three anonymous reviewers who read my manuscript. Last, but certainly not least, the Nobel Institute library has, as always, been of immeasurable assistance. I do not even have to leave the Institute building to find the most wonderful collection of books, journals, and primary sources. For this I am eternally grateful. Bjørn Helge Vangen has been of special assistance in compiling relevant lists of literature, including the bibliography of this book, and in checking certain references.

Thanks, finally, to my wife Aase, who was against being acknowledged in the preface since this could not really make up for my many shortcomings and absences, physically and mentally. It cannot. But here is the acknowledgment, nevertheless.

As in my life, the shortcomings and mistakes in the book are all mine.

G.L.

March 2003

CONTENTS

ABBREVIATIONS

ABM	Anti-Ballistic Missile
ANZUS	Australia, New Zealand, and United States (Treaty)
CAP	Common Agricultural Policy (EC/EU)
CCF	Congress of Cultural Freedom
CDU	Christian Democratic Union (Germany)
CENTO	Central Treaty Organization
CFSP	Common Foreign and Security Policy
CFE	Conventional Forces in Europe
CIA	Central Intelligence Agency
CJTF	Combined Joint Task Forces
COB	Collocated Operations Bases
CoCom	Coordinating Committee (to regulate Western trade with the Soviet Union and its allies)
CSCE	Conference on Security and Cooperation in Europe
DC	Italian Christian Democrats
EC	European Community
ECA	Economic Cooperation Administration
ECE	Economic Commission for Europe
EDC	European Defense Community
EEC	European Economic Community
EEU	European Economic Union
EFTA	European Free Trade Association
EMS	European Monetary System
EMU	Economic and Monetary Union
EPC	European Political Cooperation
EPU	European Payments Union
ERP	European Recovery Program
ERW	Enhanced Radiation Weapon
ESDI	European Security and Defense Identity
ESDP	European Security and Defense Policy
EU	European Union
Euratom	European Atomic Energy Community
FDP	Free Democratic Party (German Liberal Party)
FLN	National Liberation Front (Algeria)
FRUS	*Foreign Relations of the United States*
GATT	General Agreement on Trade and Tariffs

GDR	German Democratic Republic
GNP	Gross National Product
ICBM	Intercontinental Ballistic Missile
ICC	International Criminal Court
IEA	International Energy Agency
IMF	International Monetary Fund
INF	Intermediate Nuclear Forces
IRBM	Intermediate Range Ballistic Missile
ITO	International Trade Organization
KLA	Kosovo Liberation Army
MBFR	Mutual and Balanced Force Reductions
MD	Missile Defense
MLF	Multilateral Nuclear Force
MFN	Most Favored Nation (trading status)
MSA	Mutual Security Agency
NAFTA	North Atlantic Free Trade Area
NATO	North Atlantic Treaty Organization
NLF	National Liberation Front (Viet Cong)
NSC	National Security Council
OECD	Organization for Economic Cooperation and Development
OEEC	Organization for European Economic Cooperation (became OECD)
OPEC	Organization of Petroleum Exporting Countries
OSS	Office of Strategic Services
PCF	French Communist Party
PCI	Italian Communist Party
PSI	Italian Socialist Party
SACEUR	Supreme Allied Commander Europe
SALT	Strategic Arms Limitation Talks
SDI	Strategic Defense Initiative
SDR	Special Drawing Rights
SEA	Single European Act
SEATO	South-East Asia Treaty Organization
SHAPE	Supreme Headquarters Allied Powers Europe
SIS	Secret Intelligence Service
SNF	Short-range Nuclear Forces
SPD	Social Democratic Party (Germany)
START	Strategic Arms Reduction Talks
TAFTA	Transatlantic Free Trade Area
UN	United Nations
WEU	Western Economic Union

Introduction

The Main Arguments

The basic arguments of this book are fairly simple. While focusing on the overall issue of cooperation versus conflict in American–European relations, the book represents an extension of my " 'Empire' by invitation" thesis as this has been presented in earlier works. While it would be ridiculous to claim that everything in Atlantic relations can be most usefully studied under this heading, it is remarkable how many elements there are that actually can be. This is therefore a theme that I shall be returning to frequently throughout the account.

The first argument deals with the position of the United States. This position was unique in 1945. No other Great Power had ever had such a vast lead over its potential competitors. On the basis of this strength American influence expanded in most parts of the world—certainly in Western Europe. In fact, so important was the American role there, that it could be argued that Western Europe became part of an American sphere of influence, even an American "empire". The term is meant to be descriptive.

To distinguish the American "empire" from traditional empires I have put the term in inverted commas. After all, in traditional empires most parts were ruled directly from the imperial capital, whereas American "empire" consisted mostly of independent countries. I could have used the word "hegemony", the term most frequently used by political scientists and political economists to describe the superior American role after 1945, but although the terms are different, in this case their meaning is largely the same. In my preference for "empire" I follow Zbigniew Brzezinski who has written that "I use the term 'empire' as morally neutral to describe a hierarchical system of political relationships, radiating from a center. Such an empire's morality is defined by how its imperial power is wielded, with what degree of consent on the part of those within its scope, and to what ends. This is where the distinctions between the American and Soviet imperial systems are the sharpest."[1]

The United States, like any other Great Power, could use its tremendous power for good or for bad. US efforts to control and dominate were based on American values, just as previously other Great Powers had tried to exercise control in ways based on their values. The American way of organizing its sphere, its "empire", left a great deal of room for flexibility, autonomy, and European self-organization; indeed, the United States even pushed hard for the integration of Western Europe. Yet, as we shall see, to a remarkable extent the US was able to secure its most important overall objectives in Western Europe: the Soviet Union was contained; West Germany was integrated into Western Europe; an Atlantic military alliance was established under America's firm leadership and with a comprehensive system of US bases; Communists, leftist socialists, and fascists were kept out of European governments; the European economies were integrated into an Atlantic framework; Europe was opened to America's mass culture. This was impressive indeed.

"Empire" could be interpreted to mean that the United States was able to dictate events in Western Europe. This would be wrong: the US had influence primarily on the overall global and Atlantic structure and on certain long-term developments. On the more practical level in the various national capitals many things happened that were clearly contrary to Washington's wishes. The Western European countries were well-established political units, most of them with a long history of independence. Some of them were still major powers. Western Europe was no *tabula rasa* on which the United States was free to make whatever imprint it wanted. In fact, one reason the United States could achieve as much as it did was that America's desires frequently coincided with those of Western Europe.

This book thus tries to strike a balance between the many successes and the things the United States could do and the fewer failures and what it could not do in Western Europe. While the Atlantic structure that was established in the first years after the Second World War proved remarkably stable, naturally this balance changed over time in favor of the Europeans, and, even in the early years, the United States suffered setbacks. Under the Marshall Plan Europe did not integrate as much as Washington wanted. In 1954 the French national assembly defeated the European Defense Community (EDC). Then Charles de Gaulle was to represent a dramatic threat to the American position in Europe. Britain was not admitted into the European Economic Community (EEC). Through *Ostpolitik* even West Germany was to chart a more independent course. In general the American role declined from the mid to late 1950s and again after the end of the Cold War. Yet, none of the setbacks mentioned was as dramatic as it seemed at the time, and even as late as the turn of the millennium the American role in Europe was surprisingly strong.

The second argument relates to the attitudes of the Western Europeans towards the United States. In the early years after 1945 the Western Europeans were so interested in involving the Americans in the affairs of their continent that it can be argued that they invited the Americans in. Western European governments needed, first, economic assistance for the reconstruction of their countries, then political support against the Communists and their supporters, and soon even military guarantees against the Soviet Union. Only the United States could provide these benefits in measure, and in the 1950s there were many references to the need for Atlantic integration. This was not really to be, at least not in any supranational sense: most Americans did not want any diminution in America's sovereignty; moreover, with the Americans in, complaints could increasingly be heard about US "interference" in the matters of Western Europe. Europe had to integrate and become stronger vis-à-vis the United States.

Amazingly, then, when at the end of the Cold War the United States reduced its presence in Europe, the Western Europeans actually reissued the old invitations, although in modified form compared to the early period. Despite growing assertiveness on the European side, the invitations were reissued since the United States could still fulfill important Western European needs. In liberated Central and Eastern Europe this was even more the case; here the invitations to the United States in fact very much resembled those issued by the Western Europeans in the first years after 1945. The European invitations were accepted by Washington because through the Atlantic structure the US was still achieving crucial objectives of its own.

Yet the Cold War was over. The United States had allegedly won. Triumphalism was rampant in America. The coming to power of George W. Bush, and especially the terrorist attacks on 11 September 2001, stimulated a more unilateralist approach to international relations. On the European side the European Union (EU) was expanding geographically and was also becoming increasingly deepened; more and more it defined its own identity even in its relations with the US. These basic facts, as well as a whole set of political–cultural factors, placed a definite question mark over the long-term future of the close American–European relationship that had existed from 1945 and until the turn of the millennium. In fact, in 2003 clear signs of transatlantic drift could be seen.

Perspective on and Literature about the United States and Western Europe after 1945[2]

The history of American–European relations after the Second World War appears to present itself as an endless series of conflicts. Even after the formation of NATO, when cooperation was supposedly the closest, the crises seemed almost continuous: the Korean War and West Germany's rearmament in the early 1950s, the latter including the defeat of the EDC in 1954; the Suez crisis in 1956; General de Gaulle's coming to power in France in 1958 and his rejection of British membership in the EEC, and the signing of the Franco-German treaty in January 1963; France's withdrawal from NATO's integrated command structure in 1966; the problems caused by America's war in Vietnam and by Germany's *Ostpolitik* in the late 1960s–early 1970s; the American–European bickering over Kissinger's Year of Europe initiative in 1973–4; in the Carter years there were the feuds over the neutron bomb and Afghanistan; in the Reagan years there were Poland, the Soviet pipeline, the Intermediate Nuclear Forces (INF) and the Strategic Defense Initiative (SDI), and Libya; under Bush there were problems involving the end of the Cold War, the unification of Germany, and the search for new missions for NATO. Under Clinton there were serious American–European disputes over Bosnia, over a whole array of trade issues, over NATO enlargement, and over a European Defense and Security Identity (ESDI). Under George W. Bush, on the one hand, there has been Washington's growing unilateralism, as seen in its plans for a (National) Missile Defense (MD), in its rejection of several important international agreements, and in many aspects of its response to the terrorist attacks on 11 September 2001, certainly including the war with Iraq. The Europeans, on the other hand, while divided, responded negatively to America's growing unilateralism and have become increasingly ambitious in their integration, seeing it also as a way to reduce their dependence on the United States. Finally, almost always, there were American–European quarrels over the Middle East: the creation of Israel, Suez, the Yom Kippur War, relations with the oil states, Europe's growing sympathy for the Palestinians while the United States remained Israel's primary supporter, etc.

It is no surprise, then, that the crisis perspective has dominated the literature on American–European relations. A librarian quickly collected nine full pages of relevant titles focusing on crisis or conflict. Just to take the titles of works by historians and political scientists in alphabetical order: Robert Art has written about *The United States and the NATO Alliance: Managing the Unsolvable*; C. Fred Bergsten about "America and Europe: Clash of Titans?"; Richard Betts about "NATO's Mid-Life Crisis"; Michael E. Brown about "Minimalist NATO: A Wise Alliance Knows When to Retrench"; Eliot Cohen about "The Long-Term Crisis of the Alliance"; Ivo Daalder about "Are the United States and Europe Heading for Divorce?"; Lawrence Freedman about "The Atlantic Crisis"; Walter Hahn and Robert Pfaltzgraff about the *Atlantic Community in Crisis*; Robert Jackson about *Continuity of Discord: Crises and Responses in the Atlantic Community*; Josef Joffe about "European-American Relations: The Enduring Crisis"; Karl Kaiser about "Die Krise der europäisch-amerikanischen Beziehungen"; Robert Kleiman about *Atlantic Crisis: American Diplomacy Confronts a Resurgent Europe*; Hans Morgenthau about "The Crisis of the Alliance"; John Palmer about *Europe without America?: The Crisis in Atlantic Relations*; William Pfaff about "The Coming Clash of Europe with America"; Elizabeth Sherwood about *Allies in Crisis*; Michael Smith about *Western Europe and the United States: The Uncertain Alliance*; Ronald Steel about *The End of Alliance: America and the Future of Europe*, a title which later forced him to write about "NATO's Afterlife"; Stephen Walt about "The Ties that Fray: Why Europe and America are Drifting Apart."[3]

Politicians and diplomats too have frequently written about American–European relations in general, and about NATO in particular, in a similar crisis vein, although they tend to combine analysis with exhortations about continued cooperation.[4] Henry Kissinger, still the academic, analyzed *The Troubled Partnership*, but even the politician argued that "Something is Deeply Wrong in the Atlantic Alliance."[5] Richard Nixon has warned of "The Time to Save NATO";[6] Sam Nunn has asked *NATO: Can the Alliance Be Saved?*[7] Jean François-Poncet has written about "Europe and the United States: The Lessons of a Crisis";[8] Robert Schaetzel about *The Unhinged Alliance: America and the European Community*;[9] and, finally, Paul-Henri Spaak about *The Crisis of the Atlantic Alliance*.[10]

Some historians, political scientists, politicians, and diplomats have of course written about cooperation between the United States and Western Europe. Yet, the list of titles stressing American–European cooperation comes to three short pages, and that includes ambiguous titles such as Beatrice Heuser's *Transatlantic Relations: Sharing Ideals and Costs*,[11] Michael Eliot Howard's "An Unhappy Successful Marriage: Security Means Knowing what to Expect",[12] and Gregory Treverton's *Making the Alliance Work: The United States and Western Europe*.[13] Even the NATO historian par excellence, Lawrence S. Kaplan, chose *The Long Entanglement* as the title of his most recent book on the organization.[14] Ronald Powaski called his account *The Entangling Alliance*;[15] Wallace Thies dealt with *Friendly Rivals*.[16]

On the less ambiguous side, Thomas Risse-Kappen has written about *Cooperation among Democracies: The European Influence on U.S. Foreign Policy*;[17] Robert Lieber about "No Transatlantic Divorce in the Offering";[18] Simon Serfaty about *Stay the Course: European Unity and Atlantic Solidarity*;[19] and Geoffrey Williams about *The Permanent Alliance: The European-American Partnership 1945–1984*.[20]

Beyond the titles of books and articles, many have stressed the important interests the United States and Western Europe had in common. The idea of a North Atlantic community was spelled out in the 1950s first by Karl Deutsch. To Deutsch the complementarity of common values and high levels of responsiveness to each other's needs were much more important for the cohesion of the Atlantic community than was the common security threat.[21] Similar approaches have been adopted by others, most explicitly by Thomas Risse-Kappen in his *Cooperation among Democracies*.

Whether one wants to emphasize conflict or cooperation does in large part depend on the standard of measurement. If the standard is some expectation of more or less perfect harmony between the United States and Western Europe, then the conflicts are indeed striking. If, on the other hand, the standard is the general nature of alliances in history, one is, I would argue, bound to emphasize the closeness of the American–European cooperation of which NATO was the most significant manifestation.

Thus, the Holy Alliance of 1815–48 was not really an alliance at all, but rather a misty understanding between Russia, Prussia, and Austria. The original document drawn up by the three countries' monarchs expressed their sympathies for religious idealism. Even the Austrian Foreign Minister Clemens von Metternich called it "a loud-sounding nothing," while English Foreign Secretary Robert Castlereagh described it as "a piece of sublime mysticism and nonsense."[22]

As even the name indicates, the triple entente between France, Russia, and Britain was an entente, not an alliance at all, at least until the outbreak of the First World War induced the three parties to pledge not to make a separate peace. The entente simply represented a settlement of certain important differences and a very gradual coming together to prevent German domination of the European continent.

The triple alliance between Germany, Austria-Hungary, and Italy was definitely more committing for the parties than was the entente. It was originally signed in 1882 and renewed at five-year intervals until 1915. However, the triple alliance was in direct contradiction to the league of the German, Austrian-Hungarian, and Russian emperors. Bismarck, the creator of this intricate system, although appreciating the importance of the alliance with Austria, disliked both the Austrians "from his days in Frankfurt to his death" and the Italians; he "scattered promises so as not to carry them out."[23] The triple alliance was primarily directed against France, but since France was not the aggressor in 1914 the Italians did not even feel themselves bound to support their allies. Eventually they joined the entente.

The Sino-Soviet alliance of 1950 was directed against Japan and states allied with Japan. The treaty was concluded for thirty years, but it only took about ten before the alliance had in reality collapsed due to the increasingly bitter ideological quarrel between the Soviet Union and China.[24] The Warsaw Pact lasted longer, but from its very beginning in 1955 it was rather obviously a Soviet-dominated treaty that most, if not all, the Eastern and Central European members would leave as soon as the people were given any say in the matter. This chance finally came with the revolutions of 1989.

The success of the Atlantic security system is also striking compared to the American alliance system in Asia. In Asia no NATO was possible; an elaborate system of alliances and bilateral treaties had to be created instead. Of these alliances, SEATO, created in 1954, had to be phased out towards the end of the Vietnam War; the Baghdad pact was changed into CENTO after the

Iraqi revolution of 1958, but even CENTO had to be dissolved after the 1979 revolution in Iran. In the more successful ANZUS from 1951, the American security obligations towards New Zealand were suspended from 1986 to 1990 due to differences over nuclear policy.

The North Atlantic treaty of 1949, on the other hand, has now lasted more than half a century, longer than any of the other alliances mentioned. NATO membership is much broader than the other alliances. With the partial exception of the French departure from the integrated military structure of NATO in 1966, no country has left NATO while Greece, Turkey, West Germany, and Spain joined during the Cold War. After that conflict ended Poland, the Czech Republic, and Hungary joined in 1999; in 2002 seven additional countries, including the Baltic states, were invited to join; more than twenty other countries cooperated with NATO, stretching across the Caucasus to Georgia and beyond to Tajikistan.

While virtually none of the other alliances mentioned even dreamed of consulting the general public, popular support for NATO has been strong in almost all the membership countries over the entire fifty-year period; as we shall see, only some of the countries on the southern flank represented at least temporary exceptions to this statement. Thus, the success of NATO would seem remarkable indeed.

The only somewhat similarly successful institution would seem to be not an alliance at all, but the European Union. NATO and the EU cover only partially overlapping geographical areas and they have different missions, but they have both prospered and developed over decades, combining geographical widening and, even in NATO's case, deepening of content. True, NATO is formally an alliance of sovereign states while the EU has developed increasingly strong supranational features; but this difference is smaller than it appears, in that NATO would never have functioned as effectively as it has if the members had had a real veto: they have simply refrained from exercising it. Yet, while NATO was an effective organization from its very first days, it has taken the EEC/EC/EU much longer to establish its credentials, particularly outside the economic area. Despite the EU's growing ambition, in the crucial security field NATO is still the dominant organization, with the EU being restricted both by NATO's role and by the national aspirations of its members.

Cooperation between the United States and Western Europe[25]

Thus, in a long-term historical perspective the American–European cooperation after the Second World War has been quite striking. This book will explore the vicissitudes of that cooperation, and the best starting point for any such discussion is probably still Lord Ismay's famous quip that NATO was formed to "keep the Russians out, the Germans down, and the Americans in" (Ismay was the first Secretary General of NATO).[26] As we shall see, in the years after 1945 the Soviet threat was the most important factor for the increasingly close cooperation between the United States and Western Europe. The perception of that threat reached a first climax in the spring crisis of 1948, a second in 1950 with the outbreak of the Korean War, a third in 1958–62 over Berlin and especially Cuba, and a fourth and final one over "the Second Cold War" in the early 1980s.

On the two sides of the Atlantic there was considerable stability from the late 1940s to the mid-1980s deriving from the fact that there was a Soviet threat. Thus, the French were as insistent as anyone else that the United States was needed to balance the Soviet Union. Its anti-American rhetoric notwithstanding, Paris basically never wavered from this conclusion, even after it withdrew from NATO's integrated military structure—in virtually every Cold War crisis Paris clearly supported the Western position, even including America's leadership. While, after 1966, American forces were not to be stationed on French soil, Paris regarded the American nuclear guarantee and the stationing of American forces elsewhere in Europe, particularly in Germany, as highly desirable. The French line of wanting military guarantees from the United States dated back to the aftermath of the First World War; it probably still exists in modified form, despite the Franco-American conflict over Washington's war with Iraq.

Within this overall consensus on the assessment of the Soviet threat, there were differences among the Western allies, differences which occasionally caused difficulties in Allied relations. The swings of the policy pendulum regarding the Soviet Union were somewhat wider, not to say wilder, in America: the considerable confidence in cooperation with the Soviets during the Second World War; the intensity of Washington's anti-Communism from the late 1940s until the 1960s; the high expectations for détente especially under Nixon–Kissinger; the backlash under Carter and, particularly, under Reagan; the later Reagan–Gorbachev lovefest; the initial caution under Bush, the close cooperation then between him and Gorbachev, between Clinton and Yeltsin, and, finally, at least initially, between George W. Bush and Vladimir Putin.

Swings could be found too in the policies of the European allies, but they did not always coincide with those on the American side. On the whole the British swings tended to be similar, but somewhat smaller than the American ones, with London in 1945–6 thus being more skeptical of the Soviet Union than was Washington and less hostile after 1948–9 and with smaller swings even in later periods. The German policy swung from rather fierce anti-Communism under Adenauer to cooperation with Moscow under Brandt, and later the Germans always insisted on protecting the benefits of *Ostpolitik*, even during periods of high East–West tension. The French naturally had their special pattern, flirting with certain middle positions both before and especially during de Gaulle's years in power; then in other periods the French could become surprisingly reserved about cooperating with the Soviets.[27]

Despite such differences, NATO was on the whole surprisingly able to coordinate the aspect of change with regard to the Soviet Union. Even after France had left NATO's military structure, in moving from confrontation to negotiation the allies walked in reasonable step. The Harmel report of 1967, which emphasized that "military security and a policy of détente are not contradictory but complementary," was unanimously adopted by NATO, including France. When the Soviet threat disappeared with the disappearance of the Soviet Union, many predicted the end of NATO. Allegedly, no alliance had survived the elimination of the threat against which it had been directed. Yet, NATO is not only alive; new countries still want to join it. Nevertheless, as we shall see in the final chapter, clear signs of transatlantic drift now exist.

The Americans and the Europeans also had a common interest in keeping the Germans "down". Despite the American-led policy of reconstructing the western zones of Germany, first economically, then politically, and, finally even militarily, Washington, like all the European capitals, long kept a watchful eye on the Germans. They had started two world wars and, despite the various precautions taken, one could never be entirely certain what they would be up to in the future. With their crucial geographical position, the rapid growth of their economy, and, perhaps most important, the division of their country, a division that might make Soviet proposals for new versions of Soviet–German cooperation quite tempting, the Germans might once again come to represent a serious challenge to peace and stability.

The Eisenhower administration and most Europeans generally trusted Konrad Adenauer, but could not know what would follow after *der Alte*. Toward the end of the Eisenhower years, and particularly under Kennedy, German–American relations deteriorated. Democracy had indeed taken new roots in a West Germany that was actually to behave in a less nationalistic way than virtually any other European country. Yet, the concern with Germany in allied capitals abated only slowly: British prime ministers Harold Macmillan and Margaret Thatcher both had strong aversions to Germany and the Germans. In the guarded response in Washington, London, and Paris to Brandt's *Ostpolitik*, a lingering fear of the "specter" of "classic German nationalism" could still be found. Then, suddenly, West Germany's good behavior in the 1970s and 1980s was almost overshadowed by British–French fears brought about by Germany's unification in 1989–90.

Initially, the concern about Germany was the single most important driving force behind European integration. Western Europe had to be integrated because West Germany had to be controlled, even after it had become formally free again. And with Germany unified, the need for further control of Germany in the form of deepened integration became obvious. This was a most important dimension behind the Maastricht treaty of 1991–2 with its projected Economic and Monetary Union (EMU) and Common Foreign and Security Policy (CFSP).

Still, European integration might not be sufficient to control Germany. This was where the United States and NATO came in. As we shall see, the United States was indeed the "pacifier" or "arbiter" of Western Europe. This was illustrated even after Germany's unification. When de Gaulle's vision had apparently come true, when the Cold War was over and Europe had in some ways become united "from the Atlantic to the Urals", at this very moment of possible Gaullist triumph, first François Mitterrand and then, more determinedly, new Gaullist president Jacques Chirac were bringing France closer to NATO's military structure again. Europe still needed America. Indications were that even Russia now saw advantages in American troops staying in Europe, since Moscow too had come to believe in the United States as the ultimate "arbiter" or "pacifier" in European affairs.[28]

As was the case with the Soviet threat, within the overall framework of cooperation in controlling Germany, there were significant differences between the United States and some of its European allies. After 1945 France wanted to detach the western parts of Germany and put them under varying forms of French influence and keep the rest of Germany as decentralized as possible. The next crisis occurred in 1954 when the French turned down the EDC proposal they themselves had been the strongest proponents of; the next again in 1963 when de Gaulle rejected British membership of the EEC and, even more important, concluded the Franco-German treaty with Adenauer. Allied skepticism to *Ostpolitik* has already been mentioned, as has the potential crisis over German unification in 1989–90.

Yet none of these crises developed into full crises: the French thesis on Germany was abandoned in 1947–8. West Germany joined NATO and the Western European Union (WEU) instead of the EDC; the meaning of the Franco-German treaty was modified to please the United States; *Ostpolitik* was not as dramatic as its opponents feared, and in 1989–90 the German–American understanding on unification quickly forced the British and the French into line.

The third element of Lord Ismay's famous quip was to "keep the Americans in." The Europeans had such a strong interest in keeping the Americans in that they actually "invited" them in. Once the Americans had clearly committed themselves, then cries of "interference" or "domination" could be heard even from the earlier supporters of the United States not only in France, but also in most other Western European countries. Now it was more widely argued that there should be fewer strings attached to the American economic and military assistance, that the American military presence ought to be circumscribed in various ways, that the Europeans be consulted on all important matters and some smaller ones too, etc.

Still, particularly in times of crisis, the need for America's involvement was underlined, even by the French. Most Europeans evidently thought it much better to have one clearly superior leader who was far away than two or more smaller European leaders very close at hand. Thus, the imbalance between the United States and the leading European powers, Britain, France, and West Germany, and the rivalry among the three, facilitated Atlantic cooperation. Even after the Cold War was over, European governments issued new invitations to the Americans to stay involved: in moderate form, but still clear enough from the Western Europeans; much more explicitly from the liberated Central and Eastern Europeans.

The Americans were generally happy to stay in Europe. America's dominating position in the world after 1945 depended in considerable part on its unique relationship with Western Europe and, increasingly, also with Japan. The Americans frequently underlined that they were involved because the Europeans wanted them to be; they would presumably pull out as soon as the Europeans suggested they do so. The truth was more complicated, as was obvious from Secretary of State Dean Rusk's comment in January 1963 that the United States was in Europe "because we believe our presence there is essential to the defense of the US"; Washington just could not permit de Gaulle "to force us out of Europe without the greatest effort to resist such a move."[29]

On a few occasions the United States used rather direct means to make the Europeans behave in the "right" way. Suez in 1956 was the most dramatic incident, when Washington forced London and Paris to stop their invasion of Egypt in the middle of the operation. This humiliating put-down had quite different long-term effects in London and Paris. London would repair relations by once again emphasizing the importance of the "special relationship" with the United States; in Paris the humiliation strengthened determination to pursue European integration, in part to make Europe stronger but also vis-à-vis the US. In 1963 the pressure Washington put upon West Germany led to the modification of the Franco-German treaty just signed; it also stimulated the fall of Adenauer and led to the selection of Atlanticist Ludwig Erhard as new Chancellor.

The Americans were all for *European* integration, but *American* sovereignty could not be limited. This was one important reason, but certainly not the only one, why Atlantic integration could never be an alternative to European integration. Those parts of NATO that were to be binding even on the US had to reflect rather exclusively American ideas. This was most clearly seen on the strategy side: when the Eisenhower administration adopted "massive retaliation", NATO did the same; when the Kennedy administration then changed to "flex- ible response", NATO, with some delay this time, did the same, although many Europeans were quite skeptical about this latter change.

As the economic, political, and military position of Western Europe improved in the 1950s and 1960s and as the United States began to experience balance of payments deficits and even trade deficits, the American–European relationship had to be redefined. The Europeans insisted on greater influence, the Americans on more burden-sharing. Such redefinitions of influence and burdens can break alliances; yet, in the larger picture it has to be said that even these disputes were usually well-contained. The much more dramatic redefini- tion of influence and burdens that will have to result after the end of the Cold War is going on right now. In the final chapter I shall be speculating about where this process could be taking the American–European relationship.

The importance of a common ideology and culture should also be stressed. In a global context, to start with the obvious, it certainly counted that both the United States and Western Europe were dominated by white, Christian males. This made understanding so much easier, as could be seen in America's and Europe's not so close relations with non-white, non-Christian leaders.[30] Under the influence of Cold War revisionism there was long a tendency to downplay the role of ideology, or, rather, to downplay the importance of a democratic tradition and instead play up anti-Communism as the bond that united Washington and most European capitals. Both elements clearly con- tributed. In recent Cold War history and even more in political science there has been a steady trend to upgrade the importance of ideology in general and of democratic rule in particular. The basic line of division during the Cold War was between Communism and democracy. Allegedly, democracies do not go to war, at least not against each other; democracies are better at pro- moting economic development and preventing hunger, better at protecting the environment, etc.; but, while correlations certainly appear to exist, more work is needed to explain the cause-and-effect relationships.

The common democratic heritage was greatly strengthened by the close personal bonds that were created during and immediately after the Second World War among many of the leading politicians on both sides of the Atlantic. In the 1940s, 1950s, and 1960s this inner circle included most of the key actors both on the American and the European side. Naturally, they were not all friends. Eden and Dulles did not get on very well in personal terms, and de Gaulle was clearly outside this circle of Atlantic friends, although he had very much been part of the joint war experience. Yet, the personal bonds that existed in the first decades after the war *were* special—meetings in the Trilateral Commission, significant as they were, could not compare with the fellowship and camaraderie formed during the war, the Marshall Plan, and the formation of NATO. However, even for the later decades the importance of the Atlantic organizational structure and ties, particularly in NATO, should not be underestimated. Many key politicians and bureaucrats, civil and military, were indeed part of a wider Atlantic complex.

On the more common level, American-dominated popular culture certainly brought people together, with American film, music, literature, and journalism influencing life in Europe more and more. There was resistance in Europe to certain aspects of America's mass culture, both on the radical left and on the nationalist, more elitist right, but even this did not prevent the adoption of significant parts of it. The exchange was rather one-sided, for only Britain could really make large, although somewhat occasional contributions to American mass culture; contributions from other countries were much smaller. On the high culture side the exchange was more evenly balanced.

The fact that the United States and Western Europe had so many basic interests in common made cooperation relatively easy. America's concentration on a few overall objectives and its willingness to compromise on most other matters did the same. The Europeans realized that the Atlantic community needed a leader and that there was no alternative to the United States.

Therefore, some of the procedures and standards that applied to national politics were actually transferred to the Atlantic level. To stretch a point, in some cases the Europeans could almost be said to have been added to the complicated federal process in the United States, since, in a way, the allies represented another layer of bodies and lobbies that had to be taken into account. Consultation became an influential norm on important matters, although a standard far from adhered to in every important matter, with Suez an obvious example of how the norm could break down. Sometimes transnational coalitions were formed where individuals and institutions in different countries cooperated against other individuals and institutions in the same countries.[31]

The economic side has normally been seen as divisive in American–European relations. True, there have been many economic quarrels between the United States and European countries: the bargaining under the Marshall Plan; the "chicken war" of 1962; the off-set negotiations with West Germany in the 1960s; the many quarrels about the Common Agricultural Policy (CAP) of the EC/EU; the Soviet pipeline dispute under Reagan; the differences concerning many of the directives of the Single European Act (SEA); fights in the various General Agreement on Trade and Tariffs (GATT) rounds; the American Helms–Burton and d'Amato Acts limiting trade with "rogue" states and the strong EU reactions to them; and, finally, the more recent feuds over Boeing–Airbus, bananas, hormones, genetically modified products, taxation, and last, but not least, steel. And the list rapidly keeps getting longer.

Still, even on the economic side cooperative aspects may be emphasized. During the Cold War the Marxists were clearly wrong. International relations were not determined by economic competition. The Soviet Union was not the primary economic competitor of the US; its closest allies, Western Europe and Japan, were. The United States, Western Europe, and Japan had common security interests in facing the Soviet–Communist challenge, but they also had important economic interests in common. On the whole these common interests counted for more than the disputes that would flare up from time to time. The United States and Western Europe were indeed woven together in one huge, increasingly interdependent market.

The European countries, with the United Kingdom and the Netherlands in the lead, were traditionally the major investors in the United States. Although slipping somewhat in recent years, with Japan challenging the United Kingdom as the leading investor, European countries still represent more than 60 per cent of total foreign investment in the US. American investment in Europe has been somewhat smaller percentage-wise, but Europe is still the single most important area for US investment abroad, with the United Kingdom and Germany the leading recipients. The French attempt in the 1960s, under the influence of de Gaulle primarily but also popular author Jean-Jacques Servan-Schreiber, to restrict American investment was quickly modified: soon the point was rather to attract as much American investment as possible.

On the trade side, in the years after 1945 the Western hemisphere with Canada was the largest partner for the United States, and thus more important than Europe. In recent years Canada, Japan, and Mexico have been the three most important trading partners for the United States, but the United Kingdom, Germany, France, and the Netherlands are still among the top ten purchasers of US exports, and Germany, the United Kingdom, France, and Italy are also among the top ten suppliers of US imports.

Conflict between the United States and Western Europe

Even if cooperation is emphasized, it is still true that there have always been strains, frequently even crises, in American–European relations. While, as we have just seen, the elements of cooperation have generally outweighed those of conflict with regard to the Soviet threat, the German problem, America's role and economic and cultural issues, elements of conflict were found along all these dimensions too. With regard to events outside the NATO area, primarily in Asia and Africa, the so-called out-of-area questions, the reverse was generally true: conflict outweighed cooperation.

The United States and France, the two countries with the strongest universalist aspirations, frequently clashed (Indochina, the Middle East, Northern

Africa, etc.), but they were far from the only ones to do so. Until the early 1960s the pattern was generally that the Europeans had colonial engagements for which they wanted American support, which they either did not get at all (Holland in Indonesia, France in Algeria) or they did not get as much or on as generous conditions as they wanted (the British in India and the Middle East, the French in Indochina, the Belgians in the Congo).

Even before 1960 there were occasions when American administrations complained that they were not getting the European support they hoped for in containing Communism in "the Third World." The recognition of "Red China" by Britain and several other Western European countries and the somewhat half-hearted support most Western European countries gave to the US during the Korean War would be examples of this.

From the 1960s the roles were generally reversed; Washington's complaints about Europe's lack of concern about Communist expansion in Asia and Africa gradually became the dominant pattern. Vietnam represented the climax, when the Johnson and the Nixon administrations were frustrated by Europe's lack of support, and this applied not only to France, although Britain and particularly West Germany attempted to minimize American–European fallout over Vietnam. When the United States, weakened by Vietnam, now encouraged the British to maintain a significant presence east of Suez the British felt economically unable to do so and withdrew after 1967–8.

Still, even the differences over out-of-area questions may be exaggerated. American support over the Falklands in 1982 was much more important for American–British relations than was the disagreement over the American invasion of Commonwealth member Grenada in 1983. In the Gulf War in 1991, the United States, Britain, and France cooperated surprisingly well. The feuds over the Middle East have been near constant, but generally contained by the fact that the Europeans too favored an Israel with secure borders, while the Americans not only had important oil interests in several Arab countries but also tried to mediate between Israelis and Arabs. In the 1990s, in the area of the former Yugoslavia the Europeans long felt that their efforts to establish peace were being undercut by Washington, but then reluctantly had to admit that this was not an area they could handle more or less on their own, but that, quite to the contrary, only the Americans possessed the resources necessary to bring about a diplomatic solution (in the form of the Dayton agreement) for Bosnia or a military victory in the later war over Kosovo. On the ground in Bosnia and Kosovo the American and European troops cooperated relatively well through established NATO procedures.

Beneath the concrete controversies, unmistakable strains of distrust could be observed between the United States and Western Europe in terms of their deeper political–psychological assessments of each other. On the European side, there were frequent doubts as to the maturity of the United States in international relations. US policy could swing dramatically and was unpredictable: there were the long-term fluctuations, from isolationism during the period between the two world wars to sending over half a million men to a relatively unimportant area such as Vietnam; the pendulum swung back and forth in terms of US evaluations of the Soviet Union. The same was true for the size of the defense budget; at certain times and in certain areas human rights were important, in others not at all.

The United States was free to pursue whatever policies it wanted, and, regardless of what the United States stood for, the leaders in Washington were at any given time convinced of the rightness of the policies they pursued. The European allies were always expected to follow America's lead, yet sometimes the Americans became skeptical even when the Europeans did so. Thus, while Nixon–Kissinger established détente, they were wary of the German version of this policy, *Ostpolitik*. When the Europeans really began to integrate their economies in the way Washington had pushed so hard for, then fears arose in Washington that Western Europe would become just too independent. Presidents such as Carter, Reagan, Clinton, and George W. Bush were almost completely lacking in foreign policy experience. Relations were not improved by the fact that there was almost always an intense struggle going on between different views within the various administrations in Washington. Sometimes, on top of it all, Congress would then modify the administration's policy. For the Europeans it could be quite frustrating; first you negotiated with the administration, then with Congress.

Finally, in the new millennium, the United States became more and more unilateralist in orientation. The European allies seemed to count for so much less as the US, so superior in its strength and so vulnerable after 11 September 2001, concentrated on the threats from many different kinds of rogue states and terrorist networks.

On the other hand, the Americans felt that the Europeans did not always know exactly what they wanted from the United States, so that, no matter what the United States did, to many Europeans it was wrong. If Washington cooperated closely with Moscow, the suspicion came creeping in that the two superpowers were trying to dictate developments ("a new Yalta" in de Gaulle's language). Only one thing seemed worse: when Washington did not cooperate with Moscow. If the United States did not consult Western Europe, that was definitely wrong; yet if emphasis was then placed on consultations with Europe, that would quickly be seen as a lack of US leadership. The Europeans protested when they were accused of being "regional" in their perspective; but if that was not the case, why did they care so relatively little about Soviet expansion in Africa and Asia and, later, about rogue states and terrorism? And if it was difficult to negotiate with the US, it was no easier to negotiate with the European Union: when the EU was finally able to agree on something, it was quite difficult to undertake the changes that all international negotiations involved.

In the military sphere many Europeans, but not necessarily their governments, were fond of criticizing NATO's emphasis on nuclear weapons, but repeated US attempts to strengthen conventional defense met with little success. European governments could request new US weapons for the defense of Western Europe, but when this gave rise to domestic controversy they sometimes withdrew, leaving the responsibility to the United States. In the new millennium the emphasis was all on European influence and European institutions, so little on burden-sharing and military capabilities. In the economic sphere complaints were heard when the dollar's exchange rate was low, for then European goods were not competitive. But if the exchange rate was high, that reflected high interest rates, with the result that European capital was attracted to the United States, and that was equally bad.

There were many reasons for such political–psychological tension between the United States and Western Europe. The media often placed primary emphasis on the persons in positions of authority in the United States and in the major Western European countries. Individual leaders could be important enough. The personal ties between the leaders in the 1970s and 1980s were never as close as those that had existed between the politicians who dominated Atlantic politics until the mid-1960s. For new generations of European leaders, Vietnam and ex-Yugoslavia took the place that the Second World War, the Marshall Plan, and the formation of NATO had held for the older one.

The geographic distance across the Atlantic increased to some extent, despite improved communications. In the United States the political center shifted to the west and south in line with population changes, and the influence of the more European-focused eastern and midwestern states was reduced, as was to some extent the level of interest in and knowledge about Europe; moreover, the population of the US was gradually becoming less and less European in its ethnic composition. In Europe, on the other hand, the focal point of leadership moved eastwards, with Britain's role diminishing as the post-war period progressed. At first France claimed a leadership role, then from the beginning of the 1970s West Germany became the leading power economically, and to a lesser extent even politically. After Germany's unification no European power could rival it, although it still took care to restrain itself. Yet France's and even Germany's relations with the United States were weaker than Britain's both historically and in terms of language, culture, and politics.

The dramatic shifts particularly in the relative economic strengths of the United States and Western Europe were bound to express themselves as tension within the Western alliance. As Western Europe prospered, the continent was becoming far more concerned about its voice being heard than before. The United States could no longer determine Western policy more or less on its own.

On the other side of the Atlantic, the Americans made it clear that Western Europe's new strength would have to express itself in greater contributions to Western defense. Why should the United States spend almost twice as much of its gross national product for defense as the Europeans did, when some European countries had actually become wealthier than the United States? It was easy enough for Europe and the United States to claim the advantages of their new status; it was much more difficult to relinquish the benefits of the past.

The United States became more and more global in its orientation, whereas the former European colonial powers became more regional than they had previously been, at least militarily, if not necessarily economically and culturally. Roughly speaking, it could be said that the Europeans came to fear a strong US involvement outside Europe while they were rarely afraid that the United States would commit itself too strongly in Europe. The United States on its part had been in favor of gradually dismantling the colonial empires, but later, particularly when pressed in Vietnam and elsewhere, and then by rogue states and terrorism, Washington would advocate a European military presence in parts of Asia and Africa.

In the final analysis, the controversies between the United States and Europe were the result of the fact that these two parts of the world have different histories and different geographic locations. The two continents' experiences of war and peace have differed. Western Europe's geographic location made it more vulnerable than the United States in the event of an East–West conflict, but it also offered the greatest advantages during periods of détente. The United States and Western Europe do not have the same view of essential political phenomena such as socialism and capitalism. They have different attitudes to many religious and moral questions. At the turn of the millennium it was becoming evident that many Europeans were criticizing the Americans for who they were, almost as much as for what the US did in foreign policy. Americans were what Europeans did not want to be (in caricature form: vulgar, gas-guzzling, hormone-eating supporters of the death penalty). As the number of Hispanics, Asians, and African-Americans increased, the United States, on the other hand, was becoming less and less of a "European" country. Many Americans were also getting sick and tired of being treated as brawny but somewhat ignorant human beings who supposedly had to be enlightened by sophisticated, but impotent, Europeans. More and more the talk on both sides of the Atlantic was about differences and drift.

Notes

1. Zbigniew Brzezinski, *Game Plan: How to Conduct the U.S.–Soviet Contest* (New York: Atlantic Monthly Press, 1986), 16. I also agree wholeheartedly with

G. John Ikenberry when he writes that: "If empires are coercive systems of domination, the American-centered world order is not an empire. If empires are inclusive systems of order organized around a dominant state—and its laws, economy, military, and political institutions—than (sic-GL) the United States has indeed constructed a world democratic-capitalist empire." For this, see his "American Power and the Empire of Capitalist Democracy," *Review of International Studies*, 27 (2001), 191–212, esp. 192.

I have also been influenced by Charles Maier on this point. For a recent contribution of his, see "Empires or Nations? 1918, 1945, 1989..." in Carl Levy and Mark Roseman (eds.), *Three Postwar Eras in Comparison: Western Europe 1918–1945–1989* (Houndmills: Palgrave, 2002), 41–66, where he defines empire in the following way: "By empire I refer to a form of territorial organization that groups different nations or ethnic communities around a sovereign centre which possesses preponderant resources of power and/or wealth" (48). Similarly, John Lewis Gaddis writes that by "empire" he means "a situation in which a single state shapes the behavior of others, whether directly or indirectly, partially or completely, by means that can range from the outright use of force through intimidation, dependency, inducements, and even inspiration." For this, see Gaddis's *We Now Know: Rethinking Cold War History* (Oxford: Oxford University Press, 1997), 27.

Even Arthur M. Schlesinger, Jr. refers to America's "informal empire." Washington did not directly run many parts of the world. Rather, the "informal empire" was one "richly equipped with imperial paraphernalia; troops, ships, planes, bases, proconsuls, local collaborators, all spread wide around the luckless planet." For this, see his "America and Empire" in *The Cycles of American History* (Boston: Houghton Mifflin, 1986), 141.

2. An early version of this section is found in my introduction to Geir Lundestad (ed.), *No End to Alliance. The United States and Western Europe: Past, Present, Future* (Houndmills: Macmillan, 1998), 3–7.

3. I am very grateful to Bjørn Helge Vangen, librarian at the Norwegian Nobel Institute, for having compiled the lists of books and articles on American–European conflict and cooperation. The full details of the works cited on conflict are as follows: Robert Art, "The United States and the NATO Alliance: Managing the Unsolvable," in *The 1980s: Decade of Confrontation?* The Eighth National Security Conference 1981. Proceedings (Washington, DC: National Defense University Press, 1981), 157–87; C. Fred Bergsten, "America and Europe: Clash of Titans?" *Foreign Affairs*, 78:2 (1999), 20–34; Richard Betts, *NATO's Mid-Life Crisis* (Washington, DC: Brookings Institute, 1989); Michael E. Brown, "Minimalist NATO: A Wise Alliance Knows When to Retrench," *Foreign Affairs*, 78:3 (1999), 204–18; Eliot Cohen, "The Long-Term Crisis of the Alliance," *Foreign Affairs*, 61:2 (1982), 325–43; Ivo H. Daalder, "Are the United States and Europe Heading for Divorce?" *International Affairs*, 77:3 (2001), 553–67; Lawrence Freedman, "The Atlantic Crisis," *International Affairs*, 58:3 (1983), 395–412; Walter F. Hahn and Robert Pfaltzgraff (eds.), *Atlantic Community in Crisis: A Redefinition of the Transatlantic Relationship* (New York: Pergamon Press, 1979); Robert J. Jackson, *Continuity of Discord: Crises and Responses in the Atlantic Community* (New York: Praeger, 1985); Josef Joffe,

"European–American Relations: The Enduring Crisis," *Foreign Affairs*, 59:4 (1980/1), 835–51; Karl Kaiser, "Die Krise der europäisch-amerikanischen Beziehungen", *Europa-Archiv*, 29:12 (1974), 387–98; Robert Kleiman, *Atlantic Crisis: America Confronts a Resurgent Europe* (New York: Norton, 1964); Hans Morgenthau, "The Crisis of the Alliance," in Karl H. Cerny and Henry W. Briefs (eds.), *NATO in Quest of Cohesion* (New York: Praeger, 1965), 125–7; John Palmer, *Europe without America? The Crisis in Atlantic Relations* (New York: Oxford University Press, 1987); William Pfaff, "The Coming Clash of Europe with America," *World Policy Journal*, 15:4 (1998/9), 1–9; Elizabeth D. Sherwood, *Allies in Crisis: Meeting the Global Challenges to Western Security* (New Haven: Yale University Press, 1990); Michael Smith, *Western Europe and the United States: The Uncertain Alliance* (London: Allen & Unwin, 1984); Ronald Steel, *The End of Alliance: America and the Future of Europe* (London: Viking, 1964), and "NATO's Afterlife," *The New Republic*, 2 Dec. 1991, 18–19; Stephen M. Walt, "The Ties that Fray: Why Europe and America are Drifting Apart," *National Interest*, 54 (1998/9), 3–11.

4. Thus, Stuart Eizenstat, "Are the US and EU Listening to Each Other?" *European Affairs*, 2:4 (2001), 35–43.

5. Henry Kissinger, *The Troubled Partnership: A Re-appraisal of the Atlantic Alliance* (New York: McGraw-Hill, 1965), and "Something is Deeply Wrong in the Atlantic Alliance," *The Washington Post*, 21 Dec. 1981, A21.

6. Richard M. Nixon, "The Time to Save NATO," *Atlantic Community Quarterly*, 6 (Winter 1968/9), 479–84.

7. Senate Committee on Armed Services, *NATO: Can the Alliance Be Saved?*, Report of Senator Sam Nunn, 97th Congress, 2nd Session, 1982.

8. Jean François-Poncet, "Europe and the United States: The Lessons of a Crisis," *Atlantic Quarterly*, 1:2 (1983), 105–15.

9. Robert J. Schaetzel, *The Unhinged Alliance: America and the European Community* (New York: Harper & Row, 1975).

10. Paul-Henri Spaak, *The Crisis of the Atlantic Alliance* (Columbus: Ohio State University Press, 1967).

11. Beatrice Heuser, *Transatlantic Relations: Sharing Ideals and Costs* (London: Royal Institute of International Affairs, 1996).

12. Michael Eliot Howard, "An Unhappy Successful Marriage: Security Means Knowing what to Expect," *Foreign Affairs*, 78:3 (1999), 164–75.

13. Gregory F. Treverton, *Making the Alliance Work: The United States and Western Europe* (Ithaca: Cornell University Press, 1985).

14. Lawrence S. Kaplan, *The Long Entanglement: NATO's First Fifty Years* (Westport: Praeger, 1999).

15. Ronald E. Powaski, *The Entangling Alliance: The United States and European Security, 1950–1993* (Westport: Greenwood Press, 1994).

16. Wallace J. Thies, *Friendly Rivals: Bargaining and Burden-Shifting in NATO* (Armonk: M. E. Sharpe, 2003).

17. Thomas Risse-Kappen, *Cooperation among Democracies: The European Influence on U.S. Foreign Policy* (Princeton: Princeton University Press, 1995).

18. Robert J. Lieber, "No Transatlantic Divorce in the Offering," *Orbis*, 44:4 (2000), 571–84.
19. Simon Serfaty, *Stay the Course: European Unity and Atlantic Solidarity* (New York: Praeger, 1997).
20. Geoffrey Williams, *The Permanent Alliance: The European-American Partnership 1945–1984* (Leyden: A.W. Sijthoff, 1977).
21. Karl W. Deutsch et al., *Political Community and the North Atlantic Area: International Organization in the Light of Historical Experience* (Princeton: Princeton University Press, 1957).
22. The quotations are from A. W. Palmer, *A Dictionary of Modern History 1789–1945* (Harmondsworth: Penguin Books, 1965), 155.
23. The quotations are from A. J. P. Taylor, *The Struggle for Mastery in Europe 1848–1918* (London: Oxford University Press, 1974), 278. Bismarck became a delegate to the assembly of the German Confederation in Frankfurt in 1851.
24. For the Sino-Soviet treaty, see for instance O. Edmund Club, *China and Russia: The Great Game* (New York: Columbia University Press, 1971), 383–4.
25. This section is in part based on my "American–European Cooperation and Conflict: Past, Present, and Future," in Lundestad (ed.), *No End to Alliance*, 245–54.
26. Apparently nobody has been able to locate the exact source of Ismay's alleged quip. Thus, it may not be entirely certain that he is the person behind it.
27. I have compared the swings in American and European foreign policy in "Uniqueness and Pendulum Swings in US Foreign Policy" in my *The American "Empire" and Other Studies of US Foreign Policy in a Comparative Perspective* (Oxford: Oxford University Press, 1990), 117–141.
28. I use both terms more or less interchangeably about the American role in Western Europe after 1945. "Arbiter's" connotation of "umpire" or "judge" may convey a meaning of too much objectivity on the part of the United States in Europe's affairs and a lack of enforcement powers, but its meaning of "one who has supreme control" seems to be just the right one. For the definitions, see *New Webster's Dictionary and Roget's Thesaurus* (New York: Basic Books, 1992), 30. The term "pacifier" has several useful connotations, but "pacify" also has the meaning of "appease" or "tranquilize", not the right meaning. For an excellent article using this term, see Josef Joffe, "Europe's American Pacifier", *Foreign Policy*, Spring 1984, 64–82. The most important way in which the United States kept the peace was by being the overall "balancer" in Europe, against the Soviet Union, but also vis-à-vis (West) Germany. The US thus became the "guarantor" of European security.
29. *Foreign Relations of the United States*, (hereafter *FRUS*), 1961–3, XIII, Summary Record of NSC Executive Committee, no. 39, 31 Jan. 1963, 158, 161.
30. See for instance Seth Jacobs, " 'Our System Demands the Supreme Being': The US Religious Revival and the 'Diem' Experiment, 1954–55," *Diplomatic History*, 25:4 (Fall 2000), 589–624.
31. These themes are most explicitly developed in Risse-Kappen, *Cooperation among Democracies*. For a summing-up of these factors, see 199–210.

1

The Historical Setting: The United States and Western Europe before 1945

The United States was born in rebellion against one European power, Great Britain, in cooperation with another, France, whose assistance was crucial in the winning of America's independence. In the war of 1812 the United States again fought against Britain and, since the British were at the same time heavily involved in the struggle against Napoleon, this war too actually brought the United States into cooperation with the French, although now more indirectly.

After these two wars, however, the United States came to heed the warnings against "foreign entanglements" that George Washington had presented in his farewell address. "Why," Washington had asked, "by interweaving our destiny with that of any part of Europe, entangle our peace and prosperity in the toils of European ambition, rivalship, interest, humor, or caprice?" There was no really good answer to this question. In the nineteenth century the United States concentrated on expanding its own territory, protecting it from breaking up through the Civil War, and developing its position in the Western hemisphere and in the Pacific.

Economically and culturally the bonds between the United States and Western Europe were close. The large-scale European immigration to the US was evidence of this; as were the millions of trips back and forth across the Atlantic with the many diverse impulses in both directions that flowed from this. The military–political isolation towards Europe lasted until 6 April 1917 when the United States declared war against Germany. Thus, the United States had become the ally of Britain, France, and, until the October Revolution, also of Russia in the last phase of the First World War. In his Fourteen Points of January 1918 President Woodrow Wilson presented an outline to prevent future wars, particularly in Europe, but, as we know, the Senate refused to go along with Wilson's ideas for the participation of the United States in the League of Nations and for the reorganization of Europe.

In the interwar years America's intervention in the First World War came to be seen as a mistake. The First World War did not become "the war to end future wars." America's involvement had apparently solved little or nothing. The Europeans had quarrelled in the past; they were soon at it again; they would probably continue in the same way in the future. There was, however, no reason for the United States ever again to involve itself in the wars of Europe.

In the 1930s isolationism hardened into the various Neutrality Acts, which were intended to keep the United States out of future European conflict, and also represented a criticism of the way in which the country had presumably become involved in the First World War. "Merchants of death," banks and munitions manufacturers in particular, had brought the US in; America's participation could not really have been the will of the people. In 1935, 95 per cent of the American people supported the view that in the event of another European war, the United States should stay out. As late as September 1941, when Washington had already taken very significant steps to support Great Britain, 87 per cent of the American people still replied in the negative when asked whether the United States should send troops to Europe to fight.[1]

Military–political isolationism towards Europe rested on two fundamental pillars. First, while the United States had more sympathy with some Great Powers than with others, the main dividing line still ran between the United States on the one hand and all the other Great Powers on the other. The US was special, representing the New World of democratic idealism as opposed to the Old World of special privilege and power politics. Thus, there was certainly no "special relationship" with Britain in the interwar years. In fact Anglophobia was quite strong in American politics, nourished by German and Irish immigration. In addition to the traditional political and cultural differences, Britain had allegedly "tricked" the United States into the First World War; financial and commercial rivalry between the two countries peaked in the 1930s; naval rivalry complicated relations even after the Washington treaties of 1922 limited competition in capital ships.

Second, the United States could not really be attacked, protected as it was by the Atlantic and the Pacific Oceans. Most military experts agreed that the development of faster and better aircraft and ships would only make an invasion of the United States, already very unlikely, more, not less, difficult for any European power. Why, then, should America involve itself in Europe's wars? (In the north there was Canada, in the south Mexico, but that was more of a problem for Canada and Mexico than for the United States.)

The Europeans, on the other hand, had much less of a desire to keep the Americans out of their affairs—on the contrary, they wanted to involve them. In March 1919 British Prime Minister David Lloyd George, in an effort to soften French revanchist desires towards Germany, had presented his idea for an American military guarantee to France against any new German threat in the future. Lloyd George had the guarantee phrased so that Britain would intervene *only* if the US did. Thus, the American guarantee was as much a guarantee to Britain as to France. In the end, the Senate did not vote on the

French treaty. Many Republicans actually supported it, but Wilson lost interest in it after the Senate voted down his much-cherished League. The French responded with "panic" and the British with "dismay" after Wilson let the French treaty suffer a somewhat mysterious death.[2]

After the First World War Europe's concern about involving the United States could be seen in many other ways as well. Both in Britain and in France there was strong interest in maintaining the many wartime inter-allied councils that during the war had regulated the supplies of armaments, raw materials, shipping, etc. The initiative appears to have come from France, but the British, as Michael Hogan has argued, wanted to "transform the economic agencies of the wartime coalition into semi-permanent reconstruction and relief councils." Again, the European invitations were rejected, not least because American business wanted to abandon regulation and return to normalcy as quickly as possible.

"Isolationism" was a relative term. Even with regard to Europe—and if "isolationism" was directed against any region it was against Europe—it applied rather exclusively towards the military–political area. On the economic side, involving anything from the Dawes and Young reparation settlements for Germany to investment, trade, and tourism, the United States became an important actor in Europe. Atlantic finance was to a large extent based on the triangle of the United States giving substantial loans to Germany; these were used by the Germans to pay their reparations to France and Britain; the reparations then formed the basis for the British–French repayments of the American loans that had financed such a significant part of their war efforts. American investment in Europe almost doubled, from 700 million dollars in 1919 to 1.3 billion in 1929. With the onset of the Great Depression investment fell, but less than one would have thought. Related to the size of the total economy, the United States was actually more dependent on foreign trade during the inter war years than it would be in the first decades after the Second World War, and Europe was by far the most important trading region for the US.[3]

On the cultural side, as early as 1901 British journalist William Stead had published his book *The Americanization of the World*, reflecting the early cultural influence of the US, while in his famous article in *Life* from February 1941, "The American Century," publisher Henry Luce referred to America's global cultural reach through "American jazz, Hollywood movies, American slang, American machines and patented products." These were "in fact the only things that every community in the world, from Zanzibar to Hamburg, recognizes in common."

The cultural Americanization of Europe really started in the interwar years. Between 60 and 95 per cent of the movies shown in the 1920s and 1930s in Britain, France, Italy, the Netherlands, and Germany (before 1933) were made in the United States. As Paul Claudel, French ambassador to Washington and himself a man of letters, told the Americans in 1930:

Your movies and talkies have soaked the French mind in American life, methods, and manners. American gasoline and American ideas have circulated throughout France, bringing a new vision of power and a new tempo of life. The place in French life and culture formerly held by Spain and Italy, in the nineteenth century by England, now belongs to America. More and more we follow the Americans.[4]

Yet, we should be careful not to exaggerate the American influence in Europe. European governments and publics remained wedded to their respective national interests. The United States was an interesting partner for most of them, but a rather distant one. In London, "Atlanticists" argued with "imperial isolationists" who stressed Britain's imperial role and who responded very negatively to the idea that the United States might be replacing Great Britain as the leading international power. The latter were particularly concerned about Anglo-American naval rivalry and economic competition. In Paris, the difficult question of French war debts to the United States dominated Franco-American relations in the 1920s. In Germany, as in so many other countries, there was certainly admiration for US technical and economic achievements, but also contempt for what the Germans called *Amerikanismus*, the American preoccupation with materialism over finer and nobler things.

American popular attitudes were surprisingly little influenced by the outbreak of the Second World War in 1939 and the early wartime events. What ended isolationism was the Japanese attack on Pearl Harbor on 7 December 1941, when the United States was attacked, albeit in a rather special part of its territory. It had also become increasingly obvious, at least to the Roosevelt administration, that Washington was closer in outlook to some European capitals than to others. Yet, even during the war it took time before most Americans warmed to Britain's cause, if they ever did. The United States was certainly not fighting to protect the British Empire, in fact, by way of its rapidly growing economic supremacy, the administration tried to modify Britain's imperial role. On the left many actually preferred the "democratic" and "peace-loving" Soviet Union of "Uncle Joe" to "imperialist" and "bellicose" Britain under Winston Churchill.[5]

Compared to America's late entry into the First World War, Pearl Harbor and Hitler's ensuing, but rather surprising, declaration of war on the United States meant that the US would be fully engaged in the Second World War relatively early on. Roosevelt made the decision to focus first on the war in Europe, since it was here everything could be lost. Only when Germany was defeated would the main focus shift to the Japanese threat in Asia and the Pacific.

In planning for the postwar world President Franklin D. Roosevelt consistently feared that he might become another Wilson, one who wished for and planned for America's involvement in Europe, but who had his plans defeated by the Senate and the public; but, although he was not to experience this himself, since he died on 12 April 1945, FDR's fears were to prove groundless. America was finally prepared to play the role that its economic power had for so long and its military power now so clearly indicated.

Notes

1. The literature on isolationism is vast. I have benefited particularly from Selig Adler, *The Isolationist Impulse: Its Twentieth-Century Reaction* (London: Collier-Macmillan, 1957); Manfred Jonas, *Isolationism in America, 1935–1941* (Ithaca: Cornell University Press, 1966); Wayne S. Cole, *Roosevelt and the Isolationists 1932–45* (Lincoln: University of Nebraska Press, 1983).
2. Most of this and the following paragraphs follow my "Empire by Invitation in the American Century," *Diplomatic History*, 23:2 (Spring 1999), 190–4.
3. US Department of Commerce, *Historical Statistics of the United States: Colonial Times to 1970* (Washington, DC, 1975), vol. 2, 870–1, 903, 906.
4. Lundestad, "Empire by Invitation in the American Century," 193.
5. In the vast literature on American–British relations during the Second World War I prefer Christopher Thorne, *Allies of a Kind: The United States, Britain, and the War Against Japan, 1941–1945* (Oxford: Oxford University Press, 1978). A stimulating recent article on the relationship is Robert Skidelsky, "Imbalance of Power," *Foreign Policy*, 129 (March/April 2002), 46–55.

2

Cooperation Established: "Empire" by Invitation, 1945–1950

America's Position of Strength[1]

In June 1947 British Foreign Secretary Ernest Bevin argued that the United States was in the position today where Britain was at the end of the Napoleonic wars. Historians have also argued that the American position in 1945 resembled that of the British in 1815. Both countries had completed a triumphant war; their technological revolutions had really taken off; their rivals were exhausted, and it seemed that they both could more or less control world markets.

In absolute as well as in relative terms, America's position after the Second World War was much stronger than Britain's had been at the height of *Pax Britannica*. It was certainly much stronger than the Soviet position after 1945. In fact, the United States was by far the strongest power the world had ever seen; true, its influence was limited by that of the Soviet Union, but even the Roman empire had been restricted largely to the Mediterranean world. Strong separate empires existed in China, India, and Iran. Harold Laski, British professor of political science, writer, and Labour politician, may have overdone it, but he was still closer to the mark than Bevin when, in November 1947, he wrote that:

America bestrides the world like a colossus; neither Rome at the height of its power nor Great Britain in the period of its economic supremacy enjoyed an influence so direct, so profound, or so pervasive...Today literally hundreds of millions of Europeans and Asiatics know that both the quality and the rhythm of their lives depend upon decisions made in Washington. On the wisdom of those decisions hangs the fate of the next generation.[2]

America's strength rested on four main pillars: its vast economic superiority, its substantial military lead, the broad domestic base for the foreign policy pursued, and America's strong international–ideological support. The economic base was the most impressive. In constant 1958 prices the American GNP had grown from 209.4 billion dollars in 1939 to 355.2 billion in 1945. Moreover, "only" 400,000 Americans had lost their lives during the war, whereas in the Soviet Union approximately 27 million had died and steel and agricultural production had been cut in half. Overall Soviet production figures are not known, but an earlier guess that in 1945 Soviet production may have been only one-fourth of that in the US is probably much too high.

In the nineteenth century Britain probably had the world's largest GNP for only a very short period around 1860, and although for much of the century Britain was the industrial leader, and also remained the commercial leader, at no time did it produce more than roughly one-third of the world's total manufacture. But in 1945 the United States produced almost as much as the rest of the world together, and its lead tended to be greater the more advanced the technology. In the decade 1940–50 the United States was behind 82 per cent of major inventions, discoveries, and innovations. The highest corresponding percentage for Britain had been 47 per cent in 1750–75. With 6 per cent of the world's population, the United States had 46 per cent of the world's electric power; its businesses controlled 59 per cent of the world's total oil reserves. America produced 100 times more cars than the Soviet Union and eight times as many as Germany, Britain, and France combined. In 1950 the US held 49.8 per cent of the world's monetary gold, reserve currencies, and IMF reserves.

There were some areas of economic life where Britain played a more important role in the nineteenth century than did the United States after the Second World War. Thus, British foreign trade constituted a higher percentage of world trade than American trade was ever to do. For example, in 1870 Britain had 24 per cent of world trade; in 1950 the corresponding US percentage was 18.4. But in the trade field it is difficult to know where economic and political leverage ends and vulnerability and dependence begin. The United States traded considerably less; the other side of the coin was that it was much more self-sufficient in manufactured goods and also in important strategic raw materials and food.

With the reconstruction after the Second World War and the rapid economic growth in most of the world in the 1950s, the US share of world production was bound to diminish. In 1950 the United States produced about 40 per cent of world GNP; in 1960 around 30 per cent. Yet, the United States continued to enjoy a lead over its chief rivals much bigger than Britain had ever done in the nineteenth century. In 1960 the United States had 59 per cent of world foreign investments. That was probably slightly more than Britain had at its highest (although, as for trade, in relation to the size of their economies foreign investment was much more important for Britain than for the United States). In the 1950s the US provided over half of global development assistance, an instrument that barely existed before the Second World War.

The interwar years had been a period of transition where the United States was beginning to replace Britain as the world's economic leader, but was doing so in a very half-hearted way. As Charles Kindleberger has argued, the lack of an international leader was probably an important factor in the

Depression of the 1930s.[3] After 1945 the international economic system was dominated by the United States to an even larger extent than Britain had dominated the system before the First World War, for, unlike Britain, whose main trading partners had been its political rivals, the United States had the advantage of trading primarily with its political allies, which strengthened America's role even further. The United States was the undisputed leader of the "free world." The political and economic arrangements set up after the Second World War, such as the United Nations (UN), the World Bank, the International Monetary Fund (IMF), the General Agreement on Tariffs and Trade (GATT), and even the Organization for European Economic Cooperation (OEEC), were all based on Washington's leadership. Despite this structure's imperfections, it still revealed America's supreme role.

The United States had rather clear-cut economic objectives, the most important of which had to do with the strengthening of economic multilateralism and, as the crucial point under this heading, the promotion of freer trade. The goal was for the market to be the invisible hand which guided international exchange (at least after a period of transition to correct the many imbalances created by the war and with some exceptions, such as for instance those few products where the US itself was not fully competitive). The unstated underlying premise for Britain earlier and for the United States now was that as the strongest economic power it would enjoy great advantages under a regime of freer trade.

The United States did have all the characteristics of an economic leader.[4] First, through the IMF and bilateral diplomacy it helped maintain the international structure of exchange rates. The dollar was tied to gold and all the other international currencies were tied to the dollar, in a way similar to what had been the case with the Classical Gold Standard (1870–1914) under British leadership. Due to the imbalance in trade between the United States and Western Europe, full convertibility with the dollar was only introduced in 1958, but the basic structure of the Bretton Woods system lasted from 1945 until 1971–3 when the dollar was taken off the gold standard and exchange rates were permitted to float.

Second, the United States maintained a flow of capital to borrowers in the same way the British had done in the nineteenth century. All in all the United States provided bilateral credits and grants to the tune of slightly more than 100 billion dollars in the years from 1945 to 1965. Practically every country in the world received some form of support and in most cases the United States was by far the most important source of outside support. In addition, the United States dominated the World Bank, as it did the IMF, both through economically weighted voting arrangements and in other ways.

America served as a lender of last resort in financial and economic crises, the clearest example of which is the 14 billion dollars provided to Western

Europe under the Marshall Plan. Both regular capital and crisis money would normally come with certain strings attached. The exact nature of the strings varied, but they all tended to strengthen Washington's influence. Under the Marshall Plan, as Theodore H. White wrote from France, the American "expert" "has become...as much a stock character as was the British traveler of the nineteenth century, as 2,000 years ago the Roman centurion must have been in conquered Greece."[5]

Third, the United States provided a market for distress goods from political friends. This was not so much of a need for the Western European countries, since their problem was not really to get rid of surplus production, although they certainly needed to export to the United States to earn hard currency. For the Japanese, however, who had difficulties finding markets for their goods well into the 1950s, the open American market was essential. Even more important, during critical shortages the United States could increase or share supplies. Thus, during the Iranian oil nationalization of 1951 and the Suez crisis of 1956 the United States could compensate for the shortages in the world's oil supplies more or less single-handed.

Fourth, Washington was the leader in coordinating international macroeconomic policies, particularly trade policies. Under America's leadership world trade moved steadily in a more liberal direction. The GATT system based on the Most Favored Nation principle was the key in this context. Reciprocity was basic. The stress on reciprocity also made the American position stronger than the British had been in the nineteenth century, in that the British tended to believe in free trade as a matter of faith, almost regardless of what others did.

Fifth, the United States dominated the international property regime. In the nineteenth century the British had established a property regime strongly biased in favor of the British investor. Expropriations of foreign investments were discouraged and if they nevertheless did take place, full compensation was expected. There were few challenges to this system and those that did arise were generally defeated through a combination of bondholder sanctions and use of the Royal Navy. After 1945 the United States was able to establish a similarly strong regime in the non-Communist world biased in favor of (American) multinationals. Until the late 1960s this system worked well, as seen from Washington, in part because US resources were sufficiently strong and concentrated to "punish threats to, absorb the costs of, and bribe medium powers into regime maintenance." Most challenges to the property regime were defeated, in a few cases by covert means (Iran, 1953; Guatemala,1954).[6]

The strong economy provided the basis for America's military strength. The dollar and the atomic bomb became not only the supreme symbols of America's strength; they also represented important realities of power in most parts of the world. Until 1949 the United States had a monopoly on the atomic bomb. The bomb was not as decisive a card in international relations as many

Truman administration policymakers had initially hoped, but it certainly strengthened America's role and many Americans and Europeans saw it as the main deterrent to Soviet aggression.

The United States had by far the strongest air force in the world. In 1944—at its highest—America's production of aircraft—95,000—surpassed that of Japan and Germany combined. Before the Second World War the Royal Navy was still slightly larger than the US Navy. The war changed that, so much so that the American Navy now had a control of the sea more absolute than was ever possessed by the British. The Soviet blue-water navy was quite small until the 1960s.

The only American weakness was the number of personnel, particularly on the army side. During the war the US and the Soviets both had about 12 million men under arms. Although the Soviets demobilized more than was recognized at the time and came down to 2.8 million in 1948, American strength was only about half of that. This number was more than doubled as a result of the outbreak of the Korean War, but the Soviets did remain far ahead in this one area.

Yet, the Second World War had given most dramatic evidence of how quickly the United States could shift from a civilian to a military economy. It is difficult to come up with good estimates of Soviet military spending, but there can be little doubt that overall the United States outspent the Soviet Union. In fact, by one estimate, as late as 1960 the US alone stood for 51 per cent of world military spending while it had 13 per cent of total personnel.

Before the war the United States had no allies and no US troops were stationed on territory it did not directly control; after it Washington entered into numerous alliances, and bases were established in the most disparate regions of the world. Geographically the postwar expansion was least noticeable in Latin America, because this had traditionally been the US backyard. The Monroe Doctrine had been Washington's unilateral proclamation of its special role in the Western hemisphere, and in 1940–1 Franklin D. Roosevelt extended the Doctrine hundreds of miles out to sea, implied that Canada fell under it, and even broadened it to cover Greenland (1940) and Iceland (1941). Privately the President believed that the Canaries, the Azores, and even West Africa should be covered too because of their strategic importance for the Western hemisphere.

In 1945–6 the Joint Chiefs' lists of essential bases illustrated how dramatically the war had expanded America's security requirements. The six most essential ones were found in widely scattered parts of the world: Greenland, Iceland, the Azores, Casablanca, the Galapagos, and Panama. There is no agreed definition of a "base," but, by one count, in 1955 the United States had 450 bases in thirty-six countries.

The domestic political side was the third pillar of America's strength. Since the Civil War the United States had probably had the largest GNP in the world; its economic lead was vast even before the Second World War. Yet, despite this economic basis, the US had rather limited military strength (in 1940 defense expenditures still stood at less than two billion dollars). Most important of all, politically the United States had little desire to be a world power. Thus, until the Second World War a vast discrepancy existed between the resources of the US on the one hand and its willingness to use these resources in Great Power politics on the other.

The events of the Second World War brought about a revolution in American attitudes. Isolationism in its traditional form was destroyed. After 1945 the United States joined the United Nations and took part in the occupations of Japan, Germany, Italy, and Austria. Defense spending, even in the low years from 1946 to 1950, was much higher than before the Second World War. In the course of 1946–7 a remarkable consensus developed on the main lines of America's foreign policy, particularly the containment policy toward the Soviet Union. Secretary of Commerce Henry Wallace's alternative on the left, which stressed a greater understanding for Soviet views, was not really seriously considered by the Truman administration, as was confirmed by Wallace's ouster from the Cabinet in the fall of 1946; his dismal showing in the 1948 presidential election ratified his defeat. Senator Robert Taft's unilateralist-isolationist alternative on the right had greater support, but even his partial opposition to the Marshall Plan and his more direct opposition to NATO was of limited importance. Taft's failure to win the Republican nomination in 1952 and his death soon thereafter signaled the decline of even this kind of right-wing criticism of containment.

First Germany and Japan had to be occupied. Then the Soviet Union had to be contained. To do all this the United States had to station forces abroad, and later enter into alliances—even outside the Western hemisphere, and in peacetime too; defense spending had to be much higher than in the past, although there was still disagreement as to exactly how high. Thus, almost all leading Democrats and most Republicans rallied around an ideology which could possibly be viewed, as Franz Schurman sees it, as a merger of internationalism and the nationalism which had formed such a strong part of the isolationist tradition. The isolationists had originally wanted to protect the uniqueness of America from the rest of the world, but, now the United States had become so strong, it could not only remain uncontaminated by the evils of the Old World, but even export America's own values to it.[7]

Institutionally America's policies were drawn up on the basis of strong executive leadership, but also presidential–congressional bipartisanship. The President and the executive branch had relatively firm control of the foreign policy process. Despite a Republican majority in Congress during 1947–8, all the major foreign policy initiatives taken by the Truman administration—the loan to Britain, the Truman Doctrine, the Marshall Plan, even the Vandenberg

Resolution leading to NATO—were in the end approved by Congress, although in most cases after months of persuasion. The Truman–Vandenberg model of bipartisanship was modified with Truman's reelection in 1948, the "loss of China," and senator Vandenberg's death, but much remained. In 1953, with internationalist Republican Dwight D. Eisenhower in the White House, bipartisanship was in great part restored. Most of Eisenhower's problems in fact came from his own Republican right.

Ideologically British imperialism had rested upon a sense of superiority. Great Britain stood for Christianity and "Western civilization," for material benefits and economic advancement. The crucial point was not that this belief was held by most Englishmen, but that for a long time it was also shared by most of the peoples subjected to their rule. In fact, so self-evident was this belief in the first half of the nineteenth century that it did not really have to be very actively promoted. Only with what could be seen as Britain's slow decline from the 1870s were these "truths" spelled out in any great detail through exhibitions, jubilees, the press, and the schools. The superiority was closely related to race. The white race was seen as superior to the yellow which in turn was superior to the black. (Within the white race Anglo-Saxons or Northern Europeans stood above Southern Europeans.) In this sense British colonialism was different from French, in that in theory at least the French came to stress culture over race. If you adopted French culture, you could also achieve the rights of a Frenchman.

In Marxism–Leninism the Soviet Union had an ideology with claims to historical inevitability and global validity. The class struggle could not be held back. The masses would prevail over the ruling capitalist classes. The world was bound to move from feudalism to capitalism, then to socialism, and finally, the highest stage, Communism. Thus, like the British, the Soviets possessed an ideology that could justify many forms of expansion.

To an ever larger extent the United States had an ideology that could not only unify the American people, but also justify expansion and serve to attract support abroad. True, there were elements in America's culture that were not particularly attractive to foreigners: the very strong sense of national mission, a definite hostility toward social revolutions, and a lingering racial classification of peoples. The Truman administration, and Secretary of State Dean Acheson in particular, in Dean Rusk's phrase, generally "overlooked the brown, black, and yellow peoples of the world." The Eisenhower administration was largely passive on the race issue, despite the rapidly growing number of Third World countries. Southerners, from Secretary of State James Byrnes to Senator William Fulbright, generally had to support the racism of their region if they wanted to maintain their political base.[8]

In the European context these elements were not so negative as in other parts of the world. The crucial point here was America's identification with democracy or, in its almost equally common negative version, its opposition to Soviet totalitarianism. On this overriding point agreement prevailed between most Western Europeans and virtually all Americans.

In its imperial heyday Britain faced opposition from many local sources, but it was not consistently challenged by any one Great Power. France was the primary colonial rival, but was occasionally overshadowed by Russia; in the early twentieth century the French threat was replaced by the German. But after 1945 the United States faced one consistent threat, the Soviet Union, which provided the American people with a unifying anti-Communist ideology. As we shall see, the perceived threat probably also provided the single most important reason for the many European invitations issued to the United States to increase its economic, political, and military role. And the United States could deliver; America's role rested on tremendous economic and military strength.

It was also very important that the United States represented a culture that was attractive to millions around the world. Its mass-based popular culture was to reach new and higher levels of influence in the years after the Second World War. This was the result of the enhanced position of the US in international relations in general, but it also reflected the weakening of more traditional elitist European culture. Anti-Americanism was strong within certain elites, which perceived American mass culture as vulgar. Since the experience of the Second World War stimulated the democratization of European societies, widening opportunities for the masses normally also meant the strengthening of America's cultural role.

The task of the administration in general and of the State Department in particular was to make the various countries open their borders so that America's culture could flow as freely as possible around the world. This was a standard objective in US bilateral negotiations with virtually every country, but not one always agreed to by the other party to those negotiations, for political, economic, or cultural reasons. In the occupied countries (Japan, Germany, and Italy) the United States tried to restructure entire societies in great part inspired by American ideals and practices.

Once the diplomats had provided the opening, American movies, music, and literature spread quickly in most Western European countries. Attempts for various reasons to ban American products were generally short-lived. Thus, the French ban on Coke in 1949–50, allegedly for health reasons, lasted little more than a year. A very important new instrument in the strengthening of America's cultural influence was the Fulbright program passed by Congress in 1946. Although in principle the program was a reciprocal arrangement between the United States and other countries, the most significant part was the bringing of large groups of foreign scholars and students to the United States. Other factors also helped make the United States "the educational capital in the world." In 1943–4 only 7,000 foreign students studied at American universities and colleges, in 1947–8 17,000 did, and in 1949–50 26,000. The passage of the Smith–Mundt Act in 1948 made it possible for the US government to use all its educational, information, and propaganda resources in the struggle against the Soviet Union. While Europeans could not be made into Americans, the attractiveness of American culture was such that over time Europeans became somewhat more like Americans.[9]

Interest, ideology, and concern for others flowed together in a seamless web. As Truman privately expressed it, "We are faced with the most terrible responsibility that any nation ever faced. From Darius I's Persia, Alexander's Greece, Hadrian's Rome, Victoria's Britain, no nation or group of nations has had our responsibilities." It was now America's task "to save the world from totalitarianism."[10]

While America was unique, it was at the same time allegedly upholding universal values such as international cooperation, democracy, and freer trade. The possible tension between uniqueness and universalism was rarely explored. Foreigners, particularly Europeans, often supported America's leadership and shared many of its values. In most countries support for the United States far exceeded that for the Soviet Union. This was certainly the case in the democratic European countries where public opinion could be most easily measured.

Yet, even friendly foreigners were bound to comment on the extent to which America's idealism coincided with rather ordinary national interests. In 1945 Winston Churchill, as close a friend of America as any, captured this skeptical note almost perfectly when, faced with yet another American lecture on the evils of power politics, he replied: "Is having a Navy twice as strong as any other power 'power politics'? Is having an overwhelming Air Force, with bases all over the world, 'power politics'? Is having all the gold in the world buried in a cavern 'power politics'? If not, what is 'power politics'?"[11]

The United States, the World, and Western Europe

Franklin Roosevelt's ambition had been to establish a global system based on American-inspired principles, an ambition strongly supported both by the State and the Treasury departments. The State Department focused on the political side, in the form of the United Nations. Hopes for the new organization were high at the founding conference in San Francisco in April–June 1945, in part stimulated by the guilt the United States felt for not having participated in the League of Nations. Soon, however, it became evident that the UN would not function in the way Washington had hoped, for although the United States had strongly supported the basic concept of the Great Powers—certainly including the US itself—having a veto in all matters of importance, when the Soviet Union started using its veto rather frequently, the Truman administration began to lose interest in the United Nations. Soon even Washington began to launch major initiatives with little regard for the position of the United Nations. The Truman Doctrine was to symbolize the new trend, although the negative response of an American public that had been taught and had then accepted much of the new UN ideology forced the administration to make some rhetorical connections between the new initiative and the UN. Despite these difficulties, the Korean War showed how useful the UN could be to the US.

On the economic side Washington and the Treasury Department were pinning their hopes first on the IMF and the World Bank, then on the International Trade Organization (ITO) and GATT. In the early negotiations on the international monetary system the British had considerable leverage, because of their traditional role in this field, the need for consensus between the two leading trading powers, and their negotiating skills. John Maynard Keynes, the British chief negotiator, put forward a radical plan for an international clearing union based on a world central bank. The hope was that this would guarantee deficit countries, as the United Kingdom was expected to be, plentiful liquidity while preventing surplus countries, primarily the United States, from pursuing policies that could lead to a global liquidity shortage.

The United States rejected the Keynes plan and instead made its own White plan, named after Treasury official Harry Dexter White, the basis of IMF. The White plan was an ambitious undertaking compared with earlier rudimentary arrangements, but fell short of Keynes's hopes. The IMF would thus be based on members' contributions of gold and foreign exchange. Countries would be able to borrow very limited amounts from the Fund on a conditional basis to finance temporary balance-of-payments problems. At the Bretton Woods Conference in 1944 the British were able to secure modifications in the White plan. Scarce currencies could be rationed and discriminatory trade and exchange conditions were to be permitted in an unspecified transition period after the end of the war, a greater degree of national sovereignty accepted for Britain over the exchange rate than had been initially envisaged. Despite these modifications, the IMF and the World Bank were to prove useful instruments in the US-dominated structure now established.

On the trade side the Roosevelt administration, particularly inspired by Secretary of State Cordell Hull, had worked to establish a global system of freer trade. This meant the dismantling of imperial preferences and other forms of discrimination. This ideology had been expressed before the war in the Reciprocal Trade Agreements Act of 1934 and the many bilateral agreements flowing from that act; during the war it had been manifested in important clauses in the Atlantic Charter of 1941 and in the various Lend-Lease agreements; after the war this ideology underpinned America's many bilateral loans. The United States was generally much more insistent on removing the trade barriers of other countries than on dismantling the still relatively high level of US tariffs.

In the December 1945 bilateral loan Britain agreed to eliminate imperial preferences. The US Treasury also pressed London to accept the convertibility of sterling within eighteen months. When London then introduced such convertibility in July 1947, a run on sterling immediately followed. This depleted British reserves so quickly that the United States had to agree to the suspension of convertibility. With Britain now permitted to continue imperial preferences, it became more difficult to persuade other countries to drop their various protectionist elements. In addition the United States itself had many products it wanted to protect. The protectionists were strengthened when the Republicans won control of Congress in the 1946 elections. The result was that the compromise-filled agreement on ITO was attacked both by free traders and protectionists. The Truman administration held it back from Senate ratification since it was obvious it would be voted down. With ITO dead in the water, interest quickly shifted to GATT. While the results of the first GATT rounds in 1948–49 were rather limited, the organization was to be essential in linking Western Europe to the wider Atlantic world.[12]

The outcome of these relative American disappointments as far as the UN, the IMF, ITO, and even GATT were concerned was that Washington had to shift from a relatively global approach to a more regional one. On the regional side, no region could compare in importance with Western Europe, economically, politically, and militarily.

The United States, Germany, and the Beginnings of European Integration[13]

The United States clearly organized its sphere of influence differently from the ways other Great Powers had done; for, while they had governed through a policy of divide-and-rule, Washington actually favored the creation of a supranational Europe with its own political bodies and, accordingly, at least the possible development of an alternative political center. As the "father" of European integration Jean Monnet put it, the American insistence on European integration "is the first time in history that a great power, instead of basing its policy on ruling by dividing, has consistently and resolutely backed the creation of a large Community uniting peoples previously apart."

Washington promoted European integration in three main ways. The first, and most obvious one, was by explicitly pushing the Europeans in the direction of integration. The second and even more important was by insisting, first, on the reconstruction and, then, on the equality of the western zones of Germany in European affairs. Nothing illustrated the crucial American role in Europe better than the fitting of emerging West Germany into the wider Western European context. How could Germany be both equal and controlled at the same time? European integration was the obvious solution. The third way in which the United States promoted European integration was through its role as Europe's ultimate arbiter or pacifier. The Europeans could undertake their integration on the premise that the United States was the ultimate pacifier in Europe in general and the guarantor against anything going seriously wrong in West Germany in particular.

Yet, at the same time, the United States clearly protected its own preeminent position, and this obvious fact was also reflected in its attitude on European integration. Two points are particularly important. First, while the United States was indeed different from other Great Powers, it did not pursue its pro-integrationist policy primarily for the sake of the West Europeans. Washington certainly thought its policy best also for them, but naturally it had its own motives for supporting an integrated Europe. None were more important than the "double" containment of Germany and the Soviet Union. Of the two, the Soviet threat was presented most explicitly—Washington's abiding concern about the role of Germany was kept much quieter, but was still striking.

Second, while the United States supported an integrated Western Europe, this was not to be an independent Europe in the sense of the "third force" often discussed, particularly on the European left. In the American perspective, the integrated Europe was always to be fitted into a wider Atlantic framework. Through this Atlantic framework, the United States would presumably be able to protect its leading role within the Western world, although this could not be absolutely guaranteed once a supranational Europe had been established. It would also be able to protect its substantial economic interests.

During and immediately after the Second World War the United States was actually largely skeptical toward European integration. The Roosevelt administration feared that such integration might lead to independent spheres of political influence and economic autarchy, and also that Germany might come to dominate an integrated Europe. When in late 1945 Washington began to modify this skepticism, the emphasis was at first on loose all-European integration in the form of the Economic Commission for Europe (ECE). The ECE included the Soviet Union and Eastern Europe and came to deal largely with minor practical matters.

With the Marshall Plan the United States came out firmly in support of Western European integration. This integration ought to be on as comprehensive a scale as possible. The Soviet Union and Communism had to be contained. The western zones of Germany had to be integrated with a revitalized Western Europe in general and with France in particular.

When the Europeans did not set up the kind of effective organization to administer the Marshall Plan assistance that the Truman administration had hoped for, they were pressured into making a new report, although even the new report proved rather disappointing from an American integrationist point of view. From 1947 to 1950 disappointment pretty much described the American reaction to what the Europeans were doing. No customs union was established, except the union between Belgium, the Netherlands, and Luxembourg (the Benelux countries), and this union was not really an American initiative. In any case, the OEEC was too weak, since the so-called free lists for trade among its members took too long to work out and there were too many reservations. Thus, although progress was made on integration, Washington thought this progress slow, much too slow.

The Truman administration clearly felt there was a lack of leadership on the European side. The natural leaders, the British, were holding back, as their relations with Western Europe had to be carefully balanced by their relations with the Commonwealth and with the United States. This applied both politically and economically. Britain's traditional distance toward the European continent was increased by the political distance between Labour ruling in Britain and more conservative forces dominating the governments on the continent. To many in Britain, not only on the left, the continent seemed to be dominated by "conservatives, capitalists, clerics, and cartels." The different war experiences were certainly relevant (with nationalism having been discredited in many quarters on the continent, but not in Britain). London's firm conclusion was that while it supported looser forms of European integration, it was entirely opposed to any form of European integration that smacked of supranationality.

At first it was even more difficult for the French than for the British to take any effective lead in promoting European integration. The temptation to exploit European integration to enhance France's international role, much damaged as a result of the Second World War, was there, but it was more than counterbalanced by other factors. French governments were many and weak, and the centrist forces that dominated these governments after 1947 in practice expected London to lead on European matters. On the crucial issue of Germany, Paris had difficulties in abandoning the course defined in 1945–6, which represented an evident continuation of the French policy after the First World War: the elimination of as much centralized power in Germany as possible, the separation of the Rhineland from the German state(s), the internationalization of the Ruhr, and the economic fusion of the Saar with France. The five-year Monnet plan for the economic modernization of France was based on German weakness in the form of inexpensive deliveries of coal from Germany to France and on France taking over traditional German markets. A poll from February 1947 revealed that only 3 per cent of the French felt "friendly" toward the German people as compared to 42 per cent in Britain and 45 per cent in the United States.

The French thesis on Germany collided increasingly with American and British policy. In Washington and London's opinion, Germany was to be maintained as one unit; it should not be divided up. If agreement could not be secured with the Soviets, the Western zones ought to unite. Slowly the Germans were to be given the right to determine their own political affairs, first locally, then regionally, and finally nationally. The US and Britain took less and less interest in German reparations and more and more in rebuilding German industry. Thus the Western zones were incorporated into the Marshall Plan; in 1948 a currency reform was undertaken despite the problems this would present vis-à-vis the Soviet Union. Gradually the German economy was to become self-sufficient in the sense that it would not depend on supplies from abroad. After the period of occupation was over, special restrictions on West Germany sooner or later had to be lifted. In this long-term perspective the right to self-determination presumably had to include even the right to defend itself. This whole process was speeded up enormously by the Cold War. Instead of punishing and retraining the Germans, the emphasis quickly shifted to seeking their loyalty in the confrontation with the Soviet Union.

In 1947–8, once reviving Germany economically and politically became an essential part of the integration problem, the French at first became even more paralyzed. If the traditional French course had to be abandoned and Germany treated more leniently, most Frenchmen felt it much too risky to balance Germany more or less on their own. Britain had to be brought in to help in the containment of Germany. Economically, France was still rather protectionist. That protectionism helped kill both the customs union with Italy that the two agreed upon in March 1949, and the loose schemes of cooperation with Italy and the Benelux countries (Fritalux) which were being discussed.

There matters long stood, despite the increasingly Western orientation of French policy in the form of the exclusion of the Communists from the government in May 1947 and the foreign policy shift towards Washington and London after the collapse of the Council of Foreign Ministers meeting in Moscow in March–April 1947. France could cooperate with Britain in the Dunkirk defense treaty of March 1947 between the two powers; for the French in particular the treaty was in large part still directed against Germany. In fact, France would not launch a major initiative on European integration without Britain being included, but Britain simply refused to take part in any form of supranational integration.

Still, slowly the French were moving on Germany: American pressure was making the French role more and more untenable, as was the Soviet position. The Soviet Union wanted a centralized Germany; France preferred as weak a Germany as possible. The partial Soviet blockade of West Berlin from April and the full blockade, with the exception of air corridors, from July 1948 further speeded up West Germany's rehabilitation. Washington, strongly supported by London, took the lead in organizing the response to the blockade in the form of the airlift to West Berlin. Paris played less of a role, but did support the Anglo-Saxon initiative. Clearly the West Germans had to become partners in the Cold War struggle against the Soviets; their role as the instigators of the Second World War in Europe was rapidly becoming part of history.[14]

In June 1948 the French national assembly accepted the London agreements which pointed the way to an independent West Germany. Prime Minister Georges Bidault persuaded the assembly that it had to choose between cooperation, including with the Western zones of Germany, and isolation. A French–American deal was clearly shaping up: France would accept the West German state if the United States committed itself more clearly to Europe. The Berlin blockade showed that the US was already doing so. Robert Schuman became French Foreign Minister in July 1948 and, with his background from Alsace-Lorraine, he had an obvious interest in Franco-German reconciliation. Schuman had strong backing from Jean Monnet who, starting in 1948, became a most ardent spokesman for European integration. Monnet was soon to become Washington's favorite European.

In part as a result of the political reconstruction of Western Germany, the French took the lead in the creation of a potentially supranational Council of Europe. But Britain, despite her strong opposition to any supranational features, was to be included in the European Council. This seemed like a vicious circle: really significant European integration could not be achieved with Britain and it could not be achieved without it. Washington was becoming increasingly frustrated by the lack of progress.

Yet, signs of change could be detected on the American side. In 1949 it was finally sinking in with the Truman administration that Britain simply would not take any lead on European integration. In fact, London became more and more Atlantic in its approach and Washington was at least in part accepting this, as illustrated most clearly by the close Anglo-American cooperation in the creation of NATO and in connection with the devaluation of the pound in September 1949. In its work to set up the European Payments Union (EPU) in 1949–50, Washington again cooperated closely with London. EPU was important in facilitating trade and exchange within Western Europe. Obviously a payments union without Britain would be much less valuable than one where it was included.

If, with the very partial exception of the EPU, Britain absolutely refused to take a constructive lead on supranational European integration, then the United States was now preparing to proceed without it. The reason for Washington's rapidly growing impatience was evident: developments in West Germany could not be put on hold. Germany had to be integrated into a European framework and if Britain would not take the lead in establishing such a framework, others had to do it. In May 1949 the West German state was formally established. The Truman administration was insisting that the controls on Germany had to be modified and eventually lifted, and on this point the British largely supported the Americans. European integration was the obvious solution for Washington and, to a lesser extent, even for London. Britain understood that French–German reconciliation was necessary, but was held back by the conviction that it could not itself join any supranational organization.

From the American point of view something now had to be accomplished. The alternatives of, on the one hand, continuing to hold Germany down and, on the other, giving it full freedom to act were simply not acceptable. France should agree to give the West Germans more independence in their political affairs and also take the lead in bringing Germany into all relevant international organizations. To do otherwise would be to weaken the democratic forces in Germany and strengthen extremism and the Soviet position there.

Washington's sympathy for London remained strong, however. In April 1950 a State Department position paper once again concluded that "No other country has the same qualifications for being our principal ally and partner as the UK." The US could find "its most important collaborators and allies in the UK and the Commonwealth, just as the UK and the Commonwealth are, in turn, dependent upon us." Partly on account of these very sympathies, American policymakers just could not bring themselves to give up entirely on Britain taking some sort of lead on European integration. The problem of course was that no British leadership was emerging. As we shall see in the next chapter, Paris finally responded in the form of the Schuman plan for a European Coal and Steel Community (ECSC).

"Empire" by Invitation: The Economic and Political Sides[15]

For centuries the European Great Powers had dominated international diplomacy. In 1945 their situation was dramatically different. Germany and Italy had been defeated; France was discredited because of its war record; Britain close to being bankrupt. The signs were strong that the European colonial empires would have to be reformed and, quite likely, scaled back. No one foresaw the pace that decolonization would actually come to take. The United States and the Soviet Union were emerging as the two leading powers, exerting overwhelming influence in their respective parts of Europe.

While the United States emerged as the world's main creditor after the First World War, both Britain and France were at that time still creditor states, but after the Second World War the United States was virtually the only major source of credit. (Canada and Sweden represented much smaller sources.) Practically every Western European country, certainly including Britain and France, wanted fresh economic assistance from the US, in this case from the government. (The more limited American credits extended after the First World War came largely from private banks.)

Britain was, as a matter of course, included as one of the world's three "superpowers." History certainly strengthened Britain's role; the fact that in 1945 Britain was still formally controlling almost 25 per cent of the world's population was important. So, most definitely, was Britain's distinguished war record, as was Winston Churchill's wartime leadership and his participation in the summits at Teheran, Yalta, and Potsdam.

But in July 1945 the British voters chose Clement Attlee's Labour over Churchill's Conservatives. The election symbolized a greater attention to domestic over foreign affairs. Britain's economic situation was difficult. Production was holding up surprisingly well; the balance of payments situation was critical, however. In 1945 Britain was spending abroad more than 2,000 million pounds and was earning about 350 million. The export trade had been halved and exports were paying for less than a fifth of imports. The income from foreign investment, which had meant so much for Britain's historic balance of payments, had been cut in half. Overseas assets of more than one billion pounds had been sold to finance the war or they had simply been lost.[16]

While the Attlee government understood that Britain was facing great economic and political challenges, it faced the future with surprising optimism. Britain had important assets; first, there was the Commonwealth; then Britain was seeing itself, and was being perceived by most West European governments, as the leader of Western Europe, and while Britain would not enter into any form of *supranational* European integration, it was prepared to promote institutions that were clearly based on *intergovernmental* cooperation. This was seen in the Dunkirk treaty with France, in the British fleshing out of the ideas presented on the American side with the Marshall Plan, in the establishment of the Western Union with France and the Benelux countries in 1948 and the Council of Europe in 1949, and in Foreign Office ideas about a European customs union, ideas which, however, were quickly shot down by the economic ministries in London.

Finally, there was the "special relationship" with the United States. The Attlee government was afraid of becoming too dependent on the US: the Americans were given to wild swings in their foreign policy, their judgement was not to be entirely trusted. When Britain in 1947 decided to develop its own atomic bomb, after Congress through the McMahon Act had abandoned the wartime understanding about a joint American–British development, this decision was in part meant to give Britain greater leverage, even vis-à-vis the United States.

Still, there could be no doubt about the British desire to involve the United States in the affairs of Western Europe. In fact, no country expressed Europe's attitude of inviting, even urging the Americans to abandon their isolationism and play an active part in Europe's affairs as clearly as did Britain. The invitations could be seen in many different ways: Whitehall expressed disappointment when wartime Lend-Lease was abruptly curtailed; hoped for a credit substantially larger than the 3.75 billion dollars it actually received; wanted to continue wartime cooperation in atomic energy and the existence of at least some of the combined Anglo-American boards, particularly the Combined Chiefs of Staff and encouraged the United States to carry a larger share of the expenses of the German Bizone (the unified US and UK zones).

The Europeans, and particularly the British, also played an important part in shaping the Marshall Plan. The crucial person here was Foreign Secretary Ernest Bevin. Although the Americans were skeptical of working through the ECE and thus of having the Soviets participate, Washington left much of the follow-up to Marshall's Harvard speech on 5 June 1947 to the British (and the French). In the ensuing British–French–Soviet conference in Paris, Bevin dominated the scene. The Soviet attempt to substitute a bilateral approach for the multilateral one favored by Washington was rejected. The ECE was to be bypassed and the Russians were to be left out.

Despite the initial optimism, in 1946–9 the British position was more or less collapsing in several different parts of the world. In most of these cases Britain wanted the United States to take up the British burden so that economic and political vacuums did not arise. The US was surprisingly willing to assume these new commitments. In May 1946 Bevin presented a paper to the Cabinet proposing that the British zone in Germany be consolidated with the other Western zones into a single economic unit. The paper was not formally adopted, being seen as somewhat too anti-Soviet. In addition, "the Americans are probably not ready for this" and "full American support would be essential." Britain was well ahead of the United States in reconstructing its zone in Germany economically and politically. London simply could not afford to be supporting Germany financially to avoid starvation and chaos there, when Britain itself was facing serious economic problems. The British "would be compelled to organize the British Zone...in such a manner that no further liability shall fall on the British taxpayer." So, when Secretary of State James Byrnes on 11 July offered to join the American zone with that of any other occupying power, Britain was more than ready.[17] The Bizone was established.

What really brought matters to a head was the extreme winter of 1947, the worst in Britain since 1881. In January 1947 manufacturing output declined well below production figures for the fall of 1946; in February output fell another 25 per cent. This immediate background, combined with the general perspective already outlined, led directly to the decision to abandon India and Palestine as quickly as possible and to terminate aid to Greece and Turkey.

India and Pakistan were to become fully independent, as had long been obvious. This was clearly in accordance with American desires. As Robinson and Louis have argued, the entire British approach to decolonization after the war was in considerable measure influenced by the American skepticism to colonialism.[18] In Palestine the British–American relationship was much more competitive and the British initially responded quite negatively to the American pressure to pull out. Still, facing the hostility of both Arabs and Jews, Britain's position was untenable, and in 1948 it pulled out of Palestine. Israel and Jordan were established (and numerous Palestinian refugee camps).

Greece and Turkey, like Germany, illustrated the invitational aspect of British policy. Throughout 1946 Washington had strengthened its role in the Eastern Mediterranean–Near East, from the decision to haul the Soviet Union before the UN Security Council for its failure to withdraw from Northern Iran to the increased presence of the American 6th Fleet in the Mediterranean. The British notes of 21 February 1947 to Washington really represented an invitation to have the US take over the traditional British role of protecting Greece and Turkey against Russia/the Soviet Union. The State Department officials who received the notes on Greece and Turkey realized at once "that Great Britain had within the hour handed the job of world leadership, with all its burdens and all its glory, to the United States."[19] The British financial situation was desperate. Still, the British decision to pull out was probably in part presented in the dramatic way it was to enhance the chance of the United States responding positively. Thus, some British troops actually stayed on in Greece beyond the announced deadline of 31 March by which they were to be withdrawn.

After it became evident that the British had to scale down their commitments to Greece and Turkey dramatically, these two countries were to press even harder than they had already done for the maximum American support available. The formal American reply finally came in the form of the Truman Doctrine, which concretely meant 400 million dollars in economic and military assistance to Greece and Turkey, 300 million going to Greece where both the economic and military needs were the most pressing.[20]

While Britain worked especially hard to involve the United States in the affairs of Europe, France actually did the same, but in a more indirect and implicit way. France's starting point in 1944–5 was that it had suffered a major defeat in 1940 and that its honor and prestige had to be resurrected as soon as possible. This goal was most clearly formulated by Charles de Gaulle, President of the provisional government, but it was taken over by later governments when he resigned in January 1946. During the war the relationship between de Gaulle and Washington had been strained. Only on 11 July 1944 in connection with his visit to Washington was de Gaulle's government recognized as the de facto government of France. De Gaulle returned convinced that Franklin Roosevelt's conceptions were "grandiose, as well as disquieting for Europe and France," since FDR obviously intended to relegate France from the league of Great Powers.[21]

France's weak position was somewhat improved by Britain's desire for a continental partner. It was largely thanks to Churchill's efforts at Yalta that France was granted a zone in Germany. The Franco-Soviet treaty of 10 December 1944 was an attempt to continue the traditional French policy of alliance-building in the east against Germany. The Soviet Union could also provide some leverage vis-à-vis "les Anglo-Saxons." It was even useful domestically since the Communist party (PCF) was strong and well organized. In fact, at its height in 1946, the PCF secured almost 29 per cent of the vote. The Franco-Soviet alliance proved a disappointment, however. The Soviet Union did not support the French position either on Rhineland-Ruhr or on central organs for Germany; Soviet policies in Eastern Europe quickly proved to be more suppressive than de Gaulle had foreseen; cooperation with the PCF became increasingly difficult until in May 1947 they were expelled from the government.

In the short run the emphasis was on American economic support to France. As in London, Paris quickly concluded that there was only one major source of credit and assistance, the United States. The Blum–Byrnes Accords of May 1946 effectively extinguished the French Lend-Lease debt of over 2 billion dollars and gave the French credits of more than 750 million dollars. In the wake of Marshall's June 1947 initiative Foreign Minister Georges Bidault provided surprisingly strong support to the firm line Bevin was taking against Soviet ideas of how to organize the Marshall Plan. Since the plan would only be effective from April 1948, France, like Germany, Italy, and Austria, was granted interim aid to help it through the short-term crisis. France received 284 million dollars in such assistance. These three programs of economic assistance were all important for the implementation of the Monnet plan for France's modernization, based as it was on support from the United States and a break with traditional French protectionism. Paris's major complaint was that the support was just too limited. At his most optimistic Monnet had even dreamed of a 3.5 billion dollar credit.

In 1944–5 the United States had emphasized the need for broad coalitions in Western Europe to tackle the huge economic and political problems facing the continent. These coalitions might well include the Communist party. In 1946–7 Washington's attitude changed; it became obvious that Washington wanted the Communist parties out of these coalitions. This change of attitude coincided with rapidly rising tension within the coalitions themselves. In some countries, Italy being the best example, Washington actively encouraged the non-Communists to break with the Communists. Secretary Marshall made it clear that an Italian government without Communists would meet with a more positive response financially than one with Communists. In France the parallel resignation of the Communists appears to have been largely domestically driven, but again it was obvious that the reformed government would meet with a positive response in Washington. In 1947–8 the newly founded Central Intelligence Agency (CIA) cooperated with the American Federation of Labor in forming alternatives to the Communist-led unions in France and Italy. In the crucial Italian elections in April 1948 the CIA spent at least ten million dollars in a successful effort to defeat the Communist party. Most of the money went to the Christian Democrats, less to the Republicans and the Social Democrats.

The US not only wanted to keep the Communists and socialist leftists, like the Nenni Socialists in Italy, out; it was also skeptical about the inclusion of the far right, both in the form of fascism and even of de Gaulle's rightist nationalism. It was another matter that once the United States started to promote centrist governments, these in turn had considerable leverage with the US since the alternatives were so clearly disagreeable to Washington. In fact, the weaker they were, the more leverage they sometimes had.

Elsewhere on the European continent, from the wartime years to the signing of the North Atlantic treaty, the Dutch in particular followed a consistently Atlanticist policy emphasizing the role of the United States, and they did so despite the bitter American–Dutch feud over Indonesia.[22] The Italian governments, particularly under Christian Democrat Alcide de Gasperi, were pressing hard for American assistance—from the negotiations over the terms of Italy's peace treaty to humanitarian assistance and the Marshall Plan and interim aid. It was another matter that particularly in the early years the United States did not deliver in the way the Italians had hoped: like London and Paris, Rome received much less credit than it had dreamed of, 100 million dollars as opposed to the 940 million initially requested. Italy had after all been on the Axis side during most of the Second World War. Even the intense efforts of the Italian government, the Catholic Church, and the Italian–American lobby could not entirely overcome this embarrassing fact of history.[23]

In the period from July 1945 through June 1947 Western Europe in fact on a yearly average received a slightly larger amount of assistance than it did through the Marshall Plan, 8.3 billion dollars from 1945 to 1947 in bilateral form versus 14.1 billion through the four-year multilateral Marshall Plan. And this does not take into account the more than three billion dollars that the Western Europeans received in humanitarian aid in the first two years after the war. All other forms added up, in 1945–7 Britain's share alone was 4.4 billion dollars. France received 1.9 billion, Italy 330 million, the Benelux countries

430 million. In this period Eastern Europe got a total of 546 million. The Eastern Europeans, certainly including the Soviets, were interested in much more, but for political and economic reasons Washington refused. Cold War considerations were rapidly becoming decisive.

Under the Marshall Plan the Europeans first requested 28 billion dollars from the United States. This was much more than Washington was willing to give. The Truman administration cut this down to 17 billion and Congress in turn appropriated 14 billion. Most European countries fought long and hard for as large grants and loans as possible. Socialist Norway was probably the only country that consciously limited the amount it applied for, in an effort to reduce dependence on "capitalist" America. It soon reversed its policy, however. Only Moscow's opposition prevented Finland, Czechoslovakia, Poland, and even other Eastern European countries from taking part in the Marshall Plan. Washington's own attitude blocked the participation of Franco's Spain, the only country formally excluded from the very beginning. So, at least on the economic side, there can be no doubt that the Europeans were most interested in involving the United States closely in Europe's affairs.

"Empire" by Invitation: The Military Side[24]

Contrary to what especially revisionist historians on the American side of the Atlantic have so frequently written, most of the initiatives leading to the creation of NATO were taken in Western Europe, not in Washington. In late 1947 to early 1948 the European interest in any "third force" standing between the United States and the Soviet Union was rapidly disappearing. The international climate in particular, but also the domestic situation in many countries, forced governments to make a clear choice between the two emerging blocs, East and West.

In fact, in 1945–6 the main antagonists were Britain and the Soviet Union, not the United States and the Soviet Union. In this respect it made virtually no difference that in the middle of the Potsdam Conference power in London was transferred from Churchill and the Conservatives to Attlee and Labour. In 1944–5 the British chiefs of staff and even the Foreign Office were clearly less optimistic that their American counterparts about the possibilities of continued cooperation with the Soviet Union once the Second World War was over. At Yalta Roosevelt repeatedly made comments at Churchill's expense in an effort to establish himself in some sort of middle position between the two antagonists; Truman did less of this at Potsdam, but the political distance was still even greater between London and Moscow than between Washington and Moscow. At the Council of Foreign Ministers meetings in London and Moscow in late 1945, Secretary of State James Byrnes was the one trying to find the compromises, although he met with a negative reaction from Truman after Moscow. Soviet propaganda clearly distinguished between Britain, with its "reactionary" social democratic government as the chief obstacle to "peace," and the United States. British imperialism, not American capitalism, was primary the target of attacks from the Kremlin.

Only gradually in 1946 did British and American policies become more unified. By the end of 1946 the Foreign Office was finally happy. The main reason for this happiness was

the reaction of the United States . . . to the continued expansionist policy pursued by the Soviet Union . . . a movement in American public opinion which by the end of the year had substituted for any previous tendency to appease the Soviet Union a determination to oppose her further advance and the extension of Communist influence at every point on the borderland between the Soviet and the Anglo-American zones of influence.[25]

Many forms of military and intelligence cooperation actually did continue between the United States and Britain after the war. The British would have preferred such cooperation to have been undertaken openly, but that was deemed politically impossible in Washington. When the Truman administration balked at certain forms of intelligence cooperation, the Attlee government still continued to provide intelligence unilaterally to the US until Washington in 1946–7 again decided to reciprocate fully. For a short while it was even possible to continue the joint wartime effort in the nuclear field, until Congress decided to put a stop to this, much to Britain's chagrin.

In Britain Bevin conducted a virtual campaign to involve the United States in an Atlantic security system. He made his first presentation to Marshall after the meeting of the Council of Foreign Ministers in December 1947. The emphasis was still on defense cooperation between Britain, France, and the Benelux countries, but this group had to be linked to the United States. Bevin presented these ideas in a letter to Marshall before he made his public presentation in the House of Commons on 22 January 1948. On 27 January Bevin requested informal talks between the United States and Britain on the topic of Western security. His objective was obvious: the Western European treaties that were being proposed "cannot be fully effective nor be relied upon when a crisis arises unless there is assurance of American support for the defense of Western Europe. The plain truth is that Western Europe cannot yet stand on its own feet without assurance of support."

Washington was receptive to Bevin's objective of organizing Europe's defense, but remained non-committal on the ways in which the United States would support this system. Bevin felt that a vicious circle was being created. The United States would not define its position before the European arrangement had been agreed upon. The British argued that an arrangement could not be worked out at all without American participation since the Western Europeans would see little point in a purely European approach.

There matters remained until 12 March when Marshall notified London that "we are prepared to proceed at once in the joint discussions on the estab-lishment of an Atlantic security system." Thus, negotiations could be started right away, and the security system was to be *Atlantic*; no longer was the emphasis on the United States simply supporting a Western European treaty.

I have argued elsewhere that a series of events explain this dramatic change of attitude in Washington: the crisis in Czechoslovakia which led to the full control of Soviet-oriented elements; the Soviet proposal to Finland for a defense agreement between the two countries; General Lucius Clay's warn-ing from Germany about Soviet intentions there; but, most of all and largely neglected in the later literature, the rumors that the Soviets might be present-ing a pact proposal not only to Finland, but even to Norway. On 11 March Bevin again used dramatic language to attract the attention of the Americans:

all possible steps should be taken to forestall a Norwegian defection at this time, which would involve the appearance of Russia on the Atlantic and the collapse of the whole Scandinavian system. This would in turn prejudice the chance of calling any halt to the relentless advance of Russia into Western Europe.[26]

Although de Gaulle's and other French governments in 1945–7 refused pub-licly to take sides in the emerging Cold War and instead stressed France's independent role, privately it was obvious that they had an active interest in strengthening the American presence in Europe. In a note written as early as April 1945 the general insisted that one should "link in the future the United States with the security of the European continent and establish through their presence the conditions of a necessary balance of power in Europe." The French General Staff soon started secret planning for a Western European defense with American support.[27]

In 1946–7 the French soundings for America's support in case of a crisis were tied to the name of Pierre Billotte, first deputy chief of staff, then a member of the French delegation at the UN, and with excellent connections both to de Gaulle and Bidault. The ultimate ambition of those behind Billotte was to establish some sort of joint American–French defense against the Soviet Union, but since this objective was not shared by the neutralists and the Communists in the government the soundings could only go so far.

With the Communists out of the government, the defeat of the French thesis in Germany, and the growing East–West tension, in December 1947 Atlanticist Foreign Minister Georges Bidault received the authorization of the Cabinet to start talks with the United States, Great Britain, and the Benelux countries to achieve some sort of joint military organization. The objective was to get the Americans to conclude a secret military agreement for the defense of Western Europe. This led to clandestine conversations near New York between generals Billotte, Ridgway (US), and Morgan (UK).[28]

On 4 March 1948 Bidault requested Washington "to strengthen in the political field, and as soon as possible in the military one, the collaboration between the old and the new worlds, both so jointly responsible for the preservation of the only valuable civilization." The British and the French perspectives were somewhat at a variance, with London emphasizing the wider Atlantic structure and Paris primarily military assistance and a security guarantee directly to France. In any wider set-up Paris wanted a leadership role on a par with Washington and London. With France not being represented in the US–UK–Canada talks on Atlantic security in March–April, this was to lead to considerable confusion. Yet, the result of London and Paris's policies was the same: strong invitations to the United States to become more involved in Europe, even militarily.

Similar invitations were issued also by other Western European countries. None had contacts with the United States as close as those of Britain; few combined clear-cut realism about the true state of affairs with such public skepticism towards the United States as did France. The Netherlands was also Atlanticist in its military approach and wanted American involvement to be strong and direct. Belgium preferred a dumb-bell-like relationship, with roughly equal partners on both sides of the Atlantic, and not a Western Europe dominated by the United States. This was not to be. The dumb-bell concept had support only from a minority in Washington; the British were instrumental in concluding the Brussels treaty of March 1948 which created the Western Union, but more and more the point had become to bring the Americans in as strongly as possible; even the French were ambivalent since a European organization would be led by Britain and could thereby limit direct French contacts with the United States.

For the United States it was important to widen membership in the Atlantic security system beyond the Brussels treaty members Britain, France, and the Benelux countries, in addition to the United States and Canada. (Canada played an important and frequently overlooked role in creating the Atlantic system that was to be NATO.) The "stepping-stones" for communication between North America and Europe were particularly important strategically. Thus, Washington pushed strongly for the membership of Portugal (the Azores), Iceland, Denmark (Greenland), and Norway.

Norway, Denmark, and Iceland would actually have preferred their military ties with the United States to have been more limited than they became. In the summer of 1947 they had all joined the Marshall Plan together with Sweden, Norway rather reluctantly. In 1948 their overall orientation was becoming increasingly Western, but there was still the urge to see whether a Scandinavian military solution could not be found. Norway and Denmark negotiated with

Sweden to set up a security system with only modest ties with the US. The major issue between increasingly Western-leaning Norway and neutralist Sweden, with Denmark in the middle, was exactly what these ties were to be. When a Scandinavian system with minimal ties to the West could not be agreed among the three, Norway chose NATO. Its decision in turn influenced Denmark and Iceland to do the same.[29]

Scandinavia's hesitation was not typical for Western Europe, however. In Italy, despite the opposition of the left—and even of the right—the predominant center, strongly urged on by Ambassador Tarchiani in Washington, pushed for membership. Membership would show that the country had become a fully accepted part of the West. The United States and Britain were rather skeptical about the inclusion of a former Axis country unwashed by the Atlantic Ocean, but in the end the French were able to bring Italy in, in part to compensate for the American insistence on the three Nordic states in the north.[30] Authoritarian Portugal, with the crucial base in the Azores, was very pleased to be accepted into such good company. Spain, Greece, and Turkey all wanted to join NATO, but they were not permitted to do so in this round. Ireland would have been welcome as a member, but the conflict with Britain over Northern Ireland prevented any such development.

In the negotiations to set up NATO virtually every European country wanted to make the American military commitment to Europe as automatic as possible. For many that was the whole point of NATO. The State Department thus had to mediate between the Western Europeans on the one hand and a Congress on the other that under no circumstances would give the Europeans the right to declare war on behalf of the United States. In the end the crucial Article 5 of the treaty simply stated that in the case of an attack each of the parties would take "such action as it deems necessary, including the use of armed force, to restore and maintain the security of the North Atlantic area."

Western Europe's pressure for closer American involvement in its military affairs did not end with the setting up of NATO. Thus, at the first session of the Council of the North Atlantic Treaty Organization in September 1949 the question of NATO's further organization was discussed. A Defense Committee, a Military Committee, and a Standing Group, the last composed of one representative each of the US, the UK, and France, were established. Five Regional Planning Groups were also created. Crucial in this context was pressure from practically all the European states to have the United States as a member of their particular regional group. This was the case within the Western Europe group consisting of the Brussels treaty countries, the Northern Europe group of Norway, Denmark, and Britain, and the Southern Europe group of France, Italy, and Britain. The result was that the United States became a full member of the North Atlantic Ocean Regional Planning Group and the Canada–United States Regional Planning Group and only a "consulting member" of the other three. As the report of the NATO Council stated with regard to the three regional groups, "The United States had been requested and has agreed to participate actively in the defense planning as appropriate."

The European pressure was to a large extent continued also after the outbreak of the Korean War, but the definition of what was "appropriate" changed dramatically. Now the Europeans worked hard to establish an integrated NATO force in Europe commanded by an American general. The Europeans were unanimous in their preference for General Dwight D. Eisenhower, who was duly selected by Truman. Four additional US divisions were sent to Europe to reduce European fears that the outbreak of the Korean War might be only the prelude to a much bigger conflict in Europe. While the number of US military personnel in Europe stood at 80,000 in 1950, the lowest number after 1945, it increased to 244,000 in 1953.[31] American military assistance to Europe also increased greatly. Even Norway, which did not permit the stationing of foreign troops on its soil, worked hard and with some success to "nail" the US to Northern Europe and particularly to get "a hook in the nose of the US Air Force."[32]

As we shall see, the Europeans in return had to agree to West German rearmament. They also agreed to increase their own military forces and defense budgets considerably, but here we come to one element that was to trouble the alliance time and again: once the Americans had increased their commitment to NATO, this tended to reduce the inducement for the Europeans to do their part. The American objective of increasing Europe's own defense efforts therefore met with only partial success.

Invitations and the State of Public Opinion[33]

Thus, the pressure from European governments was undoubtedly in the direction of more, not less, American attention to Europe. The question should be raised about the extent to which the governments represented their peoples on this point.

It is difficult to give one clear answer. The situation varied from country to country and polls are not available for all of them, entirely satisfactory polls for hardly any of them. In occupied Germany, Italy, and Austria, in dictatorships such as Spain and Portugal, in civil war-plagued Greece, and in Turkey as well it was difficult to talk about public opinion. The growing American support to all these countries, from 1950 to 1951 even including Spain, clearly showed that in the containment of the Soviet Union Washington was not afraid of cooperating with undemocratic forces. Conversely, the popular basis of the Czechoslovak government did not prevent the Truman administration from breaking with it in the fall of 1946. Increasingly anti-Communism counted even more than democratic sympathies, although a combination of both was naturally to be preferred. In Western Europe, different from so many other parts of the world, Washington could frequently have the best of both worlds.

Britain, France, and West Germany were the most important countries. In Britain, the Attlee government received the support of strong majorities for its US policies. In January 1946, 70 per cent thought Britain should accept a loan from America, while 17 per cent said no. In April 1948, 63 per cent favored the government's general attitude toward the US, while 19 per cent disapproved of it. In July 1947, 22 per cent had stated that they thought the United States wanted to dominate the world, but this declined to 14 per cent in July 1948 and to 4 per cent in August 1950. (The corresponding percentages for Soviet domination were 78, 70, and 63.) It is a different matter that the British, not surprisingly, did not want the United States to run British affairs and that strong minorities disliked certain aspects of America's foreign policy. The basic feeling was that the two countries should act together, but that Britain should definitely remain independent of the United States.

The picture was more ambiguous in France, although there too sympathy for the United States prevailed. In July 1945 the United States was only favored 43 to 41 per cent over the Soviet Union in reply to the question of what country would have the greatest influence after the war. Yet, the US was picked by 47 to 23 per cent for the Soviet Union when it came to whom the French would *prefer* to see in this influential position. The doubt as to who would actually dominate lingered on until the spring of 1947, but there was less doubt about popular preferences. Pluralities supported the American loan of 1946, French participation in the Marshall Plan, and France joining the Atlantic pact, although the number of uncommitted/uninformed persons was frequently surprisingly high.

In West Germany much criticism could be found of various aspects of the occupation, but at least in the American zone the sympathy for the United States was much stronger than for the other occupying powers. In October 1947, 63 per cent trusted the US to treat Germany fairly, 45 per cent placed such trust in Britain, 4 per cent in France, and 0 per cent in the Soviet Union. The support for the Marshall Plan was pronounced; the same was true for the creation of a government for the three Western zones. The West German population sustained America's actions, but the United States did not pursue the policies it did primarily for the sake of public opinion. The relationship was succinctly expressed by the editors of the official OMGUS (Office of the Military Government in the US Zone) Survey: "The existence of a population that was receptive to reorientation ... enhanced the Allies' opportunity to help shape German history."

In comparative polls from August 1947 and February 1948, no country showed such skepticism toward the United States as did Norway. Here, in

February, 23 per cent thought the US would go to war to achieve its goals and not only to defend itself against attack. (37 per cent responded that the Soviet Union would do so.) This was higher than in France (20 per cent), Holland (16), Italy (16), Sweden (13), Canada (13), Brazil (9), and the United States itself (5). This reflected traditional Norwegian feelings of distance to virtually all Great Powers. Yet, only two months later 61 per cent thought Norway should join a Western bloc (the US role in this bloc was not clear), 2 per cent favored an Eastern bloc, while 37 per cent thought Norway ought to remain uncommitted. A majority also supported the decision to join NATO, at least after it had been made. The perception of a dramatic increase in the threat from the Soviet Union and the strong campaign of the Gerhardsen Labor government for Norway to join NATO changed Norwegian public opinion dramatically.

Thus, little indicates that the European political leaders did not receive the tacit or even explicit support of their peoples when they brought their countries into closer economic, political, and military cooperation with the United States.

Why the European Invitations? Did They Determine US policy?

It is no mystery why the Europeans invited the Americans in. In fact, the reasons were rather obvious. First, as we have seen, Western Europe needed economic assistance and only the United States could provide it substantially. Second, the forces of the political center in most Western European countries wanted American support to strengthen their position, both domestically vis-à-vis the more extreme forces on the left and right and often also internationally vis-à-vis other countries. The challenge from the left was strongest in France and Italy where the Communists and their allies regularly polled 25–30 per cent of the vote. The challenge from the right was also strongest in France, although the Gaullist vote fluctuated a great deal. Internationally, Alessandro Brogi has demonstrated how a complicated mixture of cooperation with the United States and independence from it characterized both France's constant search for *grandeur* and even Italy's for *grandezza*. Washington had it in its power to promote or relegate countries in their constant struggle for prestige and status.[34] Third, the Europeans wanted as much military support and as strong military guarantees as possible to guard against Soviet-Communist expansion. Although Washington had no particular desire to give Europe billions of dollars in assistance, it definitely shared its desire to contain the Soviet-Communist threat.

The Western Europeans invited the Americans into Europe despite the conditions set by Washington, whether in the form of currency convertibility, as in the December 1945 loan to Britain; the freer import of Hollywood movies, as in the Blum–Byrnes Accords; or special shipping clauses, as in most

American loans to Western Europe. Under the Marshall Plan the Europeans had to agree to a stronger OEEC organization than some of them had wanted, to a more restrictive level of trade between Western and Eastern Europe, etc.

On the military side most European governments wanted a substantial American military presence. This presence could certainly expose them to risks. Yet, even when the initiative came from Washington, as with the US B-29 bombers stationed in Britain in response to the Berlin crisis in 1948, the British agreed so quickly and uncompromisingly that Marshall had to check with Bevin if London had actually fully considered the implications. (Only later did it become publicly known that the aircraft had not yet been modified to carry nuclear weapons.)[35]

For the Europeans there was always the possibility that they would be overwhelmed by the formidable power of the United States. However, one reason why they so confidently invited the Americans in was that the Europeans were consistently able to transform US initiatives into something less threatening than they might have seemed at first. True, the price might still be high, as in the American–British loan negotiations; but if it were too high, reality would interfere, as when the collapse of the pound led to the suspension of the convertibility London had promised.

In the Marshall Plan negotiations the British fairly successfully opposed the American efforts to make the OEEC truly supranational; they could not be forced to take part in European integration, then or later. Britain was simply too strong, too important, and too highly considered in Washington to be directly pushed into such responsibilities. The Scandinavians and other lukewarm integrationists could then hide behind the British.

Under the Marshall Plan the counterpart funds seemingly provided the best leverage for the Truman administration. Each government had to deposit local currency funds equal to the amount of dollar assistance received, and these counterpart funds could only be used with the consent of the United States. In Germany, Austria, Turkey, and Greece the Missions of the Economic Cooperation Administration (ECA) did exert a great deal of authority. But too much should not be made of this: Germany and Austria were occupied countries where naturally the occupying power would exert a great deal of authority; in Greece and Turkey local administrations had broken down to such an extent that here too the US would be rather directly involved in running the countries. These were rather different circumstances from those prevailing in most other Marshall Plan countries.

In Britain and Norway the counterpart funds were generally used for debt retirement, a fact that obviously gave the ECA little influence on where the money was invested. Certain concessions were gradually made to the ECA representatives' wish for a more investment-oriented policy, but the two countries were still able to continue their basic policies. In Italy the government also invested too little, in the opinion of ECA; thus, counterpart funds were held back to make the Italians perform better with some, albeit limited, success. In France ECA's complaints were the opposite: the Monnet plan was too ambitious. In addition, fiscal reform was consistently postponed, Communists not purged, etc. Elaborate plans were drawn up to make Paris follow American desires, again with only limited success. In the end the Truman administration was caught between a rock and a hard place: if it did not push hard, the French, and the Italians, would do little or nothing; if it pushed hard, weak centrist governments might fall and that was clearly even less acceptable to the US. In the flood of new American ideas and proposals to reform the European economies, the Europeans were frequently able to pick those they liked and reject those they liked less.[36]

The story was rather similar when it came to American efforts to limit trade with the Soviet Union and Eastern Europe. In December 1947 the Truman administration initiated a strategic embargo on trade in certain products with these countries (the A-1 list composed of military commodities and the B-1 list containing semi-strategic or "dual purpose" goods). In the summer of 1948 Washington started work on having these lists adopted by the ERP countries. A permanent coordinating committee (CoCom) was set up to monitor trade with the Communist countries. The American position was soon strengthened by the increased international tension as a result of the Communist victory in the Chinese civil war, the Soviet explosion of the atomic bomb, and the outbreak of the Korean War. Nevertheless, with Britain in the lead, egged on especially by Denmark and Norway, the Western Europeans were able to substantially modify both the A-1 and, particularly, the B-1 list to take account of European economic interests. One reason they succeeded as well as they did was that after 1952 president Dwight D. Eisenhower clearly saw himself in a middle position between most Europeans on the one hand and Congress in particular on the other.[37]

On the military side, the increases in European defense spending were generally smaller than Washington would have preferred. The European governments had their own interest in increasing defense expenditures, but the optimal combination was one of the Americans spending rather more and the Europeans rather less. Those countries that were skeptical toward an explicit American presence, such as exposed Norway and Denmark, could pursue their policy of no allied bases on their territory (except in crucial Greenland in Denmark's case). Initially, at least, this was done with considerable sympathy from a Washington that understood their special needs. Thus, all European governments seemingly had some leverage with the United States: strong governments had this because they were strong; weak governments had it exactly because they were weak, often so weak that they risked being replaced by alternatives considerably less to Washington's liking.

It is arguments such as these that have made Alan Milward and others argue not only that the Marshall Plan was not particularly important for the recovery of Western Europe, but also that the American design for Western Europe was largely defeated.[38] Similar comments have been made about some of the other American initiatives discussed.

Yet, these arguments go only so far. To take the Marshall Plan, for example, Milward probably underestimates the economic importance of the Plan somewhat, for, with the exception of agriculture, the ERP actually reached or surpassed all its major production targets. The direct economic significance of the Marshall Plan was considerable, although it certainly did not "save" Western Europe single-handedly: Marshall funds accounted for 10 to 20 per cent of capital formation in the European countries in 1948–9 and less than 10 per cent in 1950–1.[39]

Milward definitely underestimates the Plan's political and psychological importance. Many actually believed it had saved Western Europe. Then this belief developed a reality of its own. The Marshall Plan also changed European perceptions of the United States in a more positive direction. George Kennan may have gone too far, but he was certainly on to something when he stated that "The psychological success at the outset was so amazing that we felt that the psychological effect was four-fifths accomplished before the first supplies arrived."[40] Even more important in this context is the point that, although the Truman administration definitely did not reach its maximum objectives, European governments always had to keep at least one eye on Washington's response to the policies they pursued. Thus, in May 1949 the British Cabinet even feared that "increased investments in the social services might influence Congress in their appropriations from Marshall aid."[41]

At the more structural level, despite certain shortcomings the political success of the ERP was still spectacular. It helped achieve political stabilization in Western Europe, externally vis-à-vis the Soviet Union and internally vis-à-vis local Communists; it promoted some measure of European integration; it made the Western zones of Germany part of this stabilization and integration; it changed European perceptions of the United States dramatically for the better, from Washington's point of view; it mobilized the American public around a comprehensive US role in Europe. On this level the success of the Truman administration could be seen as astounding. The same basic argument can be made with relevance to NATO.

Naturally, for the Europeans nothing beat having the United States involved without the Americans exerting much influence on national policies. Yet, eating one's cake and having it too is an impossible combination, in international politics as in any other area of life. The United States would not have become involved in European politics after 1945 to the extent it did unless

Washington had had its own reasons to do so *and* the Europeans had wanted this to happen. Agreements between free governments presuppose a mutuality of interests: otherwise the agreements presumably would not have been concluded.

On the invitation side, it has been argued that the invitations did not really *determine* US foreign policy. America's foreign policy was determined primarily by America's own interests, not by the invitations from the outside. This point is obviously true, so true in fact that I have made this explicitly clear myself: "I just take it for granted that the United States had important strategic, political, and economic motives of its own for taking on such a comprehensive world role."[42] Indeed, the invitations had to be combined with America's own interests. After 1945 the European invitations were extended to a United States disposed to respond in a much more affirmative way than it had done in 1918–20.

At the same time, however, it should be stressed that the European invitations after the Second World War were definitely more insistent, lasted longer, and came from many more countries than on the earlier occasion. While little is really known about the state of public opinion in Europe after the First World War, if we are to generalize about public opinion after the Second, we may say that the invitations extended to the United States by most Western European governments clearly came to receive the basic support of the populations involved.

In the perspective of American–European relations it is certainly crucial to study the European response to the new role for the United States after 1945, even if the response had little or no effect on America's actions. Yet, the invitations definitely did have an effect. Obviously there would not have been any economic assistance if the Europeans had not wanted it. Considering Washington's initially lukewarm response to Bevin's pleas for an Atlantic security system, it seems likely that the setting up of NATO would at least have been substantially delayed if it had not been for the European invitations. The heart of NATO, Article 5, would probably not have had even its semi-automatic form if the Europeans had not pushed as hard as they did for an even more automatic American response to potential Soviet aggression.

The experience after the First World War indicates that European invitations alone were not enough to change America's attitude, although it is not really possible to tell what would have happened if the invitations then had been as insistent, lasted as long, and come from as many countries as they did after the Second World War. After 1945, with the United States determined to play a much more active role, the invitations did not force the Americans to do anything they did not really want to do, but they certainly influenced at least the timing and scope of America's actions toward Western Europe.

Notes

1. This section largely follows my *The American Empire and Other Studies of US Foreign Policy in a Comparative Perspective* (Oxford: Oxford University Press, 1990), 39–46.
2. Laski is quoted in Norman Graebner, *America as a World Power: A Realist Appraisal from Wilson to Reagan* (Wilmington: Scholarly Resources, 1984), 275.
3. Charles P. Kindleberger, *The World in Depression, 1929–1939* (Berkeley: University of California Press, 1973).
4. These characteristics are largely derived from Charles P. Kindleberger, "Hierarchy versus Inertial Cooperation," *International Organization*, 40 (Autumn 1986), 841.
5. Theodore H. White, *Fire in the Ashes* (New York: Harper & Row, 1953), 359. See also White's *In Search of History: A Personal Adventure* (New York: Harper & Row, 1978), 273–318.
6. For two fine accounts of the international property regime, see Charles Lipson, *Standing Guard: Protecting Foreign Capital in the Nineteenth and Twentieth Centuries* (Berkeley: University of California Press, 1985); Kenneth A. Rodman, *Sanctity versus Sovereignty: The United States and the Nationalization of Natural Resource Investments* (New York: Columbia University Press, 1988). The quotation is from Rodman, 325–6.
7. Franz Schurman, *The Logic of World Power: An Inquiry into the Origins, Currents, and Contradictions of World Power* (New York: Pantheon, 1974), 46–8.
8. Thomas J. Schoenbaum, *Waging Peace and War: Dean Rusk in the Truman, Kennedy and Johnson Years* (New York: Simon and Schuster, 1988), 193. For good accounts of the race issue in American foreign policy during the Cold War, see Mary L. Dudziak, *Cold War Civil Rights: Race and the Image of American Democracy* (Princeton: Princeton University Press, 2000) and Thomas Borstelmann, *The Cold War and the Color Line: American Race Relations in the Global Arena* (Cambridge, Mass.: Harvard University Press, 2001).
9. Richard Pells, *Not Like Us: How Europeans have Loved, Hated, and Transformed American Culture since World War II* (New York: Basic Books, 1997), 37–63; Frank A. Ninkovich, *The Diplomacy of Ideas: US Foreign Policy and Cultural Relations 1938–1950* (Cambridge: Cambridge University Press, 1981), 139–83. The number of students is found on 139. For the ban on Coke, see Richard Kuisel, *Seducing the French: The Dilemma of Americanization* (Berkeley: University of California Press, 1993), 38, 64.
10. Walter Millis, ed., *The Forrestal Diaries* (New York: Viking, 1951), 281.
11. Quoted from Thorne, *Allies of a Kind*, 515.
12. For the short version of this story, see Andrew Wyatt-Walter, "The United States and Western Europe: The Theory of Hegemonic Stability,"in Ngaire Woods, *Explaining International Relations Since 1945* (Oxford: Oxford University Press, 1996), 134–7. For a longer version, see Thomas W. Zeiler, *Free Trade. Free World: The Advent of GATT* (Chapel Hill: University of North Carolina Press, 1999).

13. This section builds in very large part on chapter 4 in my *"Empire" by Integration: The United States and European Integration, 1945–1997* (Oxford: Oxford University Press, 1998), 29–39.

14. A good account of the Western response to the blockade is found in Avi Shlaim, *The United States and the Berlin Blockade, 1948–49: A Study in Crisis Decision-Making* (Berkeley: University of California Press, 1983).

15. For earlier drafts of this section, see my "Empire by Invitation? The United States and Western Europe, 1945–1952," *Journal of Peace Research*, 23:3 (Sept. 1986), 263–77, particularly 268–9, and *The American "Empire"*, 54–62.

16. Peter Calvocoressi, *The British Experience 1945–1975* (Harmondsworth: Pelican, 1979), 10–13.

17. David Reynolds, "Britain," in Reynolds (ed.), *The Origins of the Cold War in Europe: International Perspectives* (New Haven: Yale University Press, 1994), 81–3.

18. Wm. Roger Louis and Ronald Robinson, "The United States and the Liquidation of the British Empire in Tropical Africa, 1941–1951," in Prosser Gifford and William Roger Louis (eds), *The Transfer of Power in Africa: Decolonization 1940–1960* (New Haven: Yale University Press, 1982), 31–55.

19. Joseph M. Jones, *The Fifteen Weeks: An Inside Account of the Genesis of the Marshall Plan* (New York: Harcourt, Brace & World, 1955), 7.

20. For Turkey's many invitations to the United States, see Ekavi Athanassopoulou, *Turkey: Anglo-American Security Interests 1945–1952* (London: Frank Cass, 1999).

21. F. Roy Willis, *France, Germany, and the New Europe 1945–1967* (Oxford: Oxford University Press, 1968), 8–12.

22. Cees Wiebes and Bert Zeeman, "Benelux," in Reynolds, *The Origins of the Cold War in Europe*, 167–93.

23. Good accounts of the Italian–American relationship are found in James Edward Miller, *The United States and Italy 1940–1950: The Politics of Diplomacy and Stabilization* (Chapel Hill: University of North Carolina Press, 1986); Ilaria Poggiolini, "Italy," in Reynolds, *The Origins of the Cold War in Europe*, 121–43; Christopher Duggan and Christopher Wagstaff (eds), *Italy in the Cold War: Politics, Culture & Society 1948–58* (Oxford: Berg, 1995).

24. See the references under n. 15.

25. The quotation is from D. Cameron Watt, "Britain, the United States and the Opening of the Cold War," in Ritchie Ovendale (ed.), *The Foreign Policy of the British Labour Governments, 1945–1951* (Leicester: Leicester University Press, 1984), 58. See also Alan Bullock, *Ernest Bevin: Foreign Secretary, 1945–1951* (London: Heinemann, 1983); Reynolds, "Britain," in Reynolds, *The Origins of the Cold War in Europe*, 77–95; Lawrence Aronsen and Martin Kitchen, *The Origins of the Cold War in Comparative Perspective: American, British and Canadian Relations with the Soviet Union, 1941–48* (Houndmills: Macmillan, 1988); Victor Rothwell, *Britain and the Cold War 1941–1947* (London: Jonathan Cape, 1982).

26. My version of the founding of NATO, a version I still basically adhere to, is found in my *America, Scandinavia, and the Cold War, 1945–1949* (New York: Columbia University Press, 1980), 167–97. The quotations are from 175, 179.

27. Georges-Henri Soutou, "France," in Reynolds, *The Origins of the Cold War in Europe*, 100.
28. This analysis of developments in France is based primarily on Soutou, "France" in Reynolds, *The Origins of the Cold War in Europe*, 96–120, and Charles Cogan, *Forced to Choose. France, the Atlantic Alliance, and NATO: Then and Now* (Westport: Praeger, 1997), 17–51.
29. Lundestad, *America, Scandinavia and the Cold War*, 290–328.
30. Miller, *The United States and Italy 1940–1950*, 266–71; Poggiolini, "Italy," in Reynolds, *The Origins of the Cold War in Europe*, 130–6.
31. Daniel J. Nelson, *A History of US Military Forces in Germany* (Boulder: Westview, 1987), 45.
32. Rolf Tamnes, *The United States and the Cold War in the High North* (Oslo: Ad Notam, 1991), 79–85.
33. This section follows closely my original "'Empire' by Invitation" argument in "Empire by Invitation?", *Journal of Peace Research*, 272–3.
34. Alessandro Brogi, *A Question of Self-Esteem: The United States and the Cold War Choices in France and Italy, 1944–1958* (Westport: Praeger, 2002).
35. Septimus H. Paul, *Nuclear Rivals: Anglo-American Atomic Relations, 1944–1952* (Columbus: Ohio State University Press, 2000), 141.
36. For a useful summing up of the most recent literature on the Marshall Plan, see Kathleen Burk, "The Marshall Plan: Filling in Some of the Blanks," *Contemporary European History*, 10:2 (2001), 267–94. See also Martin Schein (ed.), *The Marshall Plan: Fifty Years After* (New York: Palgrave, 2001).
37. The literature on CoCom is increasing. For a recent, convincing study, see Ian Jackson, "'Rival Desirabilities': Britain, East–West Trade and the Cold War, 1948–51," *European History Quarterly*, 31:2 (2001), 265–87.
38. See Alan S. Milward *The Reconstruction of Western Europe, 1945–51* (Berkeley: University of California Press, 1984) and also his *The European Rescue of the Nation-State* (London: Routledge, 1992).
39. For the Marshall Plan numbers, see Charles S. Maier, "The Two Post-war Eras and the Conditions for Stability in Twentieth-Century Western Europe," *The American Historical Review*, 86:2 (1981), 342.
40. Charles L. Mee, Jr., *The Marshall Plan: The Launching of the Pax Americana* (New York: Simon and Schuster, 1984), 246.
41. The quotation is from Cabinet Papers, EPC 5 (49), 23.5.49, Cab.134/192 found in Teddy Brett, Steve Gilliat, and Andrew Pople, "Planned Trade, Labour Party Policy and US Intervention: The Successes and Failures of Post-War Reconstruction," *History Workshop*, Spring 1982, 138.
42. Lundestad, "Empire by Invitation?", 268. In *The American "Empire"* I strengthened this formulation further and wrote that "Neither the Europeans nor any other foreigners could determine US foreign policy. This was done in Washington largely on the basis of America's own interests" (56).

3

The Atlantic Community, Germany's Role, and Western Europe's Integration, 1950–1962

America's Domination and Europe's Centrality

After the uncertainties of the very first years after 1945, the US had gradually developed clear-cut objectives for Western Europe. On the whole, it was able to secure these objectives, by far the single most important of which was to limit Soviet expansion. After the "fall" of Czechoslovakia in 1948, no European country joined the Soviet bloc. To fight "Soviet Communism" the resources of the United States and Western Europe had to be coordinated. To Washington this meant that Western Europe had to be fitted into an Atlantic framework. NATO was the most important part of this framework; originally set up on European initiative, once, in March 1948, London had persuaded Washington to commit itself to the idea of an Atlantic security organization, the United States was to heavily influence, sometimes to decide more or less on its own, the policies of this organization: who the members were to be, its military strategy, its overall attitude towards the Soviet Union, and, to a much lesser extent, the level of defense spending in the member countries. With the American system of domination went a comprehensive system of US bases including virtually every allied country, from the wide network of such bases in West Germany and Britain and to the "facilities" to be used in times of crisis in Denmark and Norway.[1]

From 1950 it also became essential for the United States to have the larger part of Germany, West Germany, on its side even militarily, either directly in the form of West Germany's membership in NATO or, more indirectly, by its membership in a European defense organization which in turn was linked to NATO. European integration was under no circumstance to lead to an independent "third force," but was to be part of the Atlantic structure under America's leadership.

On the domestic side, America's overriding goal was to keep the Communists and their "fellow-travellers" out of power. On the right, fascists and extreme nationalists were also to be excluded. With the small exception of Iceland in 1956–8, where a leftist bloc including Communists actually participated in the government, the United States was able to fulfill this objective in all the NATO countries until the revolution in Portugal in 1974. Iceland was such a special country that this limited the fear of the example spreading to other countries; due to the events in Hungary in October–November 1956 the same leftist government in Reykjavik that had asked for the abrogation of the defense treaty with the US actually ended up negotiating a new agreement for the American air base at Keflavik; measures were taken to keep particularly sensitive documents out of Communist hands.[2]

On the economic side, the Atlantic framework was constituted primarily by the OEEC, GATT, and CoCom. The OEEC had not become as strong an organization as the United States had wanted, but it still played a prominent role in administering American economic assistance and in coordinating the overall economic policies of its members, and though not a direct member the US still exerted great influence on the organization, particularly during the Marshall Plan years. When the OEEC in 1961 was transformed into the Organization for Economic Cooperation and Development (OECD), the United States was brought directly in (together with Canada). Through GATT Washington could fit Europe's efforts at economic integration into the Atlantic framework in such a way that the integration did not hurt America's economic interests too much, although the GATT rounds of the 1940s and 1950s were rather modest affairs. CoCom regulated the trade of the NATO members, and to some extent even of the neutral European states, with the Soviet Union and its Eastern European allies. The US had been directly instrumental in setting up CoCom, but could not prevent a significant reduction in the number of embargoed goods, particularly after Stalin's death in 1953.[3]

On the cultural side, the United States wanted to keep Western Europe, and the rest of the world for that matter, open to American culture. On this point too the US was quite successful. American movies, literature, music, and other forms of expression steadily widened their distribution. The United States became the country to visit, for aspiring politicians, businessmen, scholars, and to some extent even artists.

These were all very significant American successes. Within the Atlantic community everybody took it for granted that the United States was the leader. Whenever something important happened, the other countries looked to the US for guidance. By acting first, so to speak, Washington was normally able to set the parameters within which the other capitals determined their course of action. Even when it did not speak first, the allies always had to figure America's response into their actions. This defining function was crucial. When capitals disagreed with the United States, they had to justify their actions to the administration in Washington. On the whole America secured its objectives through close cooperation with the Europeans and, when the two sides of the Atlantic had strong common interests, there was little need for Washington to use sharper instruments of influence. Yet the Suez conflict of 1956 showed that the US was indeed able to use very direct pressure on even two of its most important allies, Britain and France, in a matter of great significance to these allies.

Still, the United States could rarely dictate to the Europeans what they were to do, and suffered significant, although relatively few, defeats in the 1950s. The rejection of the European Defense Community by the French national assembly in 1954 was the most notewothy one. France could defeat the EDC, but it could not stop the rearmament of West Germany, now done through NATO and the Western European Union (WEU). More defeats for the US were to follow after the coming to power in France of de Gaulle in 1958, but in the first few years after he had taken over American–French relations were actually relatively good.

After the Japanese attack on Pearl Harbor in 1941, Roosevelt had decided to focus primarily on the war in Europe against Germany, only secondarily on the war in the Pacific against Japan. Then, in the late 1940s, Truman had given a very determined and successful response to the Communist challenge in Europe. But in the civil war in China he did considerably less. China was "lost." Similarly, the strongest response to the outbreak of the Korean War came not in Korea and Japan, but in fact in Europe. The United States sent four new divisions to Europe; West Germany was to be rearmed; defense spending in Europe greatly increased.[4]

Thus, in the 1950s and early 1960s American–European cooperation was based on the shared assumption that Europe was the area of the world that mattered most. The struggle between East and West was primarily a struggle over Europe. It was only natural that the Europeans wanted Europe to be at the center of attention, but they had the full assent of Washington. The Cold War, just like the Second World War, would be won or lost in Europe.

The Atlantic Community

The close relationship between North America and Western Europe in the 1950s–early 1960s can be explained in many different ways. Realists will emphasize traditional balance of power or, better, balance of threat considerations. Western Europe did not balance against the strongest power (since the United States was clearly the strongest), but rather against the greatest perceived threat in the form of Soviet Communism.[5] To this could be added the domestic threat from Communists and other anti-democratic groups. A watchful eye was certainly also kept on the potential future threat from Germany.

Liberals will point to the centrality of ideology, institutions, and communication. In 1957 Karl Deutsch and his collaborators published *Political Community and the North Atlantic Area,* clearly an attack on the dominant realism. Here Deutsch developed the concept of a "security community," defined as a group of people that had become integrated to the point that there is a "real assurance that the members of that community will not fight each other physically, but will settle their disputes in some other way." In this sense the NATO area definitely constituted a security community, no mean achievement in the light of Western Europe's preceding 100-year history.

A "pluralistic security community" such as the North Atlantic area possessed a compatibility of core values derived from common institutions and mutual responsiveness and developed a sense of "we-ness" to the point that the members of the community entertained "dependable expectations of peaceful change." Through communication in the form of trade, migration, tourism, and cultural and educational exchanges, contacts were established not only among the elites, but to some extent also among the masses, instilling even in them a certain sense of community.[6] It is easy to list the quarrels and the differences within the North Atlantic area, yet these should not make the observer overlook the very strong bonds that were developing particularly after the creation and integration of NATO in 1949–50. The term "Atlantic Community" itself was increasingly used in the late 1950s–early 1960s.[7]

There is every reason to view realism and liberalism not primarily as competitive theories, as is normally done by political scientists, but as complementary ones. They are not mutually exclusive, except in their purest form. As will be amply illustrated throughout this chapter, they both help explain the nature of cooperation between the United States and Western Europe.

Just as the Second World War had brought the United States and Western Europe together, the threat from the Soviet Union was to hold them together even when the task of defeating Germany had been completed. After an initial period of some confusion, perceptions of the Soviet threat were on the whole quite similar in most NATO capitals as long as Stalin was alive. After Stalin's death in March 1953, London, once again under Churchill's leadership, was soon to take an active interest in establishing closer contact with the Kremlin. This was to be done in the form of bilateral or multilateral summits that, in addition to potentially improving the East–West climate, would definitely enhance Britain's faltering international position. Some of the same considerations applied to Paris, although the French were even more absorbed than the British in matters outside of Europe (first Vietnam, then Algeria).

Eisenhower disliked the idea of an early East–West summit; it would only serve to strenghten the Soviet position. Bonn was also skeptical of such summits and insisted that a solution to the German problem be uppermost in the minds of allied leaders. Even the Foreign Office in London did not really like Churchill's summit idea. In this context, too, the United States held the upper hand not only because of its superior strength, but also its middle position between London and Bonn. Only in 1955, after Moscow had provided various concrete proofs of its seriousness, Adenauer had visited Moscow, and the EDC had been replaced by West Germany's membership in NATO, did Prime Minister Anthony Eden—Churchill had finally been forced to let him take over—meet Khruschev, Bulganin, Eisenhower, and French premier Edgar Faure in Geneva.[8] The summit led to "the spirit of Geneva," but few substantive results.

The "spirit of Geneva" disappeared in 1956 with the uprising in Hungary and the Suez crisis, and in 1958 the Soviet ultimatum concerning Germany and West Berlin led to new tension. Such tension brought the allies together, but also revealed fissures between them. Now, somewhat unlike the situation in Berlin ten years earlier, no one stood as fast as France, for de Gaulle wanted to impress on Adenauer that he was Germany's truest friend. The United States was willing to explore solutions, even solutions that Adenauer disliked, while Britain was now the country pushing hardest for agreement. No solution was found; the crisis was only gradually to calm down after the erection of the Berlin Wall in August 1961.[9]

NATO was clearly dominated by the United States. The primary point in establishing NATO had been to commit the US to the defense of Europe. The combination of America's atomic weapons and the American conventional trip-wire in Germany was to provide the deterrent against a Soviet attack. The Europeans wanted the American nuclear guarantee to be as firm as possible, so that the threat to unleash America's atomic weapons would make the Soviets think twice about attacking Western Europe. Under such circumstances it was more or less inevitable that US strategy became NATO strategy. It helped that the Western Europeans were relatively satisfied with this strategy as it was finally explicitly formulated under Eisenhower in the form of the New Look's emphasis on massive retaliation. The Europeans particularly liked the part about American deterrence, less so the planned conventional European contribution. In fact, in 1952 London had already formulated a similar strategy, in the form of the Global Strategy Paper, although the British influence on the New Look can easily be overstated.[10] In 1960 the French went the same route once their *force de frappe* was available. Both the British and the French wanted to underline the importance of their new weapons as much as possible.

In 1948, during the Berlin crisis, the United States had given the appearance of deploying aircraft with atomic bombs in Britain, but in reality some of the nuclear components were still missing in the B-29s. In 1954 Eisenhower authorized the deployment of complete weapons to Morocco (initial moves had apparently been made without informing the French government) and to Britain. From 1955 to 1963 US atomic weapons were stationed in West Germany (1955), Italy (1957), Turkey (1959), the Netherlands (1960), Greece

(1960), and Belgium (1963). Plans had been made to station such weapons even in France, plans that had evidently not been implemented when de Gaulle came to power and reversed course. US atomic weapons had also long been stationed on Greenland, although the island was in principle covered by Denmark's no nuclear weapons policy. Denmark's very top leaders had actually given their consent, without involving the Danish Parliament, a fact that caused a great deal of confusion when an American B-52 with nuclear weapons crashed in 1968 near the American base of Thule in northern Greenland.[11]

The deployment of American intermediate range missiles (IRBMs) in Western Europe showed how complex the interplay between the two sides of the Atlantic could be. As such missiles were under development in 1955, the US wanted to station them in Western Europe to strengthen both deterrence against the Soviet Union and the overall relationship with its European allies. For both political and military reasons Britain quickly expressed an interest and such weapons were then stationed on British soil.

Moscow's launching of *Sputnik* in October 1957 made the stationing of such weapons in Europe more urgent. At the NATO meeting in December of that year, Eisenhower offered IRBMs to the European allies. The response was somewhat disappointing to Washington, but no one could be forced to accept weapons they did not want. Turkey was enthusiastically in favor of the offer since IRBMs would strengthen its position vis-à-vis the Soviet Union. Italy was also favorable, as the weapon would elevate its status and relationship with the US, though the Italian public was skeptical. France was interested too, but only on British terms of considerable national control, which was impossible because of restrictions laid down by Congress; in any case, de Gaulle's coming to power ended further French interest on this point. In West Germany Adenauer was secretly interested, but public opinion was against and in the end both the US and the NATO allies felt it was too controversial to station missiles there. Denmark and Norway were strongly against IRBMs not only on their own territories, but preferably also in other countries, certainly including West Germany. In the end the missiles were stationed only in Italy and Turkey, in addition to Britain.

The missiles were largely obsolete by the time they were finally deployed. The Kennedy administration expressed an interest in removing them, and finally agreed to take them out of Turkey as part of the resolution of the Cuban missile crisis in October 1962. Turkey was not informed about this Cuban context, a context that would have caused an uproar inside NATO, and would clearly illustrate de Gaulle's point about the United States being willing to make concessions at Europe's expense. As Under Secretary of State George Ball argued before the secret deal was made, "If we talked to the Turks, they would take it up in NATO. The thing would be all over Western

Europe, and our position would have been undermined." Since the context remained secret for many years, little harm was done to NATO as such. Less related to Cuba, the missiles were also to be taken out of Italy. As to the reality, Turkey and Italy agreed to the pull-out only after having been offered abundant military compensation; Turkey, however, even then only consented after lengthy objections.[12]

To a very large extent the United States decided what would be the borders, the *limes*, of Western defense and who would be the members of NATO. In 1948–9 Truman had decided, first, that West Berlin was to be defended during the Soviet blockade of the city, despite some French and even British hesitation. Then, Washington made it perfectly clear that the "stepping stones"— Norway, Denmark, Iceland, and Portugal—were to be included in NATO. In 1950, as we shall see, the United States took the lead in insisting that West Germany become part of Western defense. In 1951–2 the US lead was even clearer when Greece and Turkey became members of NATO. Britain wanted the two countries to join a Middle East arrangement where Britain could more easily hold its own with the United States, but this was not to be. Most other NATO members were lukewarm about their accession, but gave up when the Greeks and Turks themselves so strongly supported Washington's determination. It helped that Turkey had established a democratic government in 1950 which was as interested as its authoritarian predecessors in getting Western, primarily American, support against its old enemy, Russia/the Soviet Union. The ending of the Greek civil war in 1949 facilitated Greek membership.[13] When the European opposition was even broader and more determined, as in the case of NATO membership for Franco's Spain, the United States gave up on direct membership, but secured the reality of military cooperation in the form of the Spanish–American base agreement of 1953.

NATO was one comprehensive alliance, bound together primarily by the overall American guarantee in Article 5 of the treaty. Yet, as James Kurth has argued, the degree of integration varied widely. On the Central Front there was "High NATO" with the fullest degree of integration (West Germany, Britain, Holland, Belgium, Luxembourg, Italy, and until de Gaulle even France), where American nuclear weapons and troops were generally stationed and integrated with significant local forces. On the Northern Flank there was "Low NATO" (Denmark and Norway). Here American nuclear weapons were never stationed and US troops were permitted only for exercises. In Denmark defense spending was rather low. In Norway it was somewhat higher, but still relatively low compared to the size of the territory and the common border with the Soviet Union. On the Southern Flank there was "Pseudo NATO" (Greece and Turkey). Although US nuclear weapons were occasionally stationed in these two countries, nuclear deterrence did not apply in the same explicit way as on the Central Front. While the US Navy had considerable port rights, only US air forces were permanently stationed on Greek and Turkish soil. Defense budgets were high, as was American military assistance. Local forces were large, but hardly integrated with American units. In fact, to a considerable extent these local forces were directed against each other.[14]

NATO meant that a Great Power extended protection to lesser powers strategically located. Historically there was little new in this, yet, as Ernest R. May has argued, "For protection—and money—the great power expected troops. So Britain had managed its affairs for three centuries. So other empires had trafficked with client states from at least the time of Cyrus the Great." What happened on NATO's part was a surpise: the American guarantee was given and considerable US military assistance extended. Still the continental allies—the Europeans—provided fewer soldiers than expected.[15]

The Europeans wanted to move NATO's defense line east. Initial American war plans in case of a Soviet attack had been based on giving up virtually the entire European continent and then staging the counter-attack from Britain and Spain. Even after the founding of NATO, Washington saw a defense line at the Rhine as too difficult to hold. In 1950, however, under European pressure NATO extended the line of defense to the Elbe. The idea of even initially giving up NATO territory was simply impossible to present to the European public, particularly in crucial West Germany.

Roosevelt had told Stalin at Yalta that American troops in Europe would have to be withdrawn within two years. In Stuttgart in September 1946 Secretary of State Byrnes had proclaimed that the American troops would remain in Europe as long as the German occupation lasted. After the outbreak of the Korean War the United States sent four additional divisions to Europe to be placed alongside the American forces already there under General Eisenhower's integrated NATO command. As President, Eisenhower frequently expressed his hope that the American forces could be brought back from Europe, but this was not to be; somehow conditions were never right.

After the outbreak of the Korean War and the decision to move the defense line to the Elbe, it was obvious that Europe's conventional contribution had to be increased substantially. The rearmament of West Germany had to be seen in this perspective. The most ambitious force goals were established at the Lisbon NATO meeting in February 1952. At that meeting the alliance committed itself to having fifty divisions in 1952, seventy-five in 1953, and ninety-six in 1954.

The United States also pushed for mechanisms to supervise and coordinate European defense spending. In 1951 a high-level Temporary Council Committee (TCC) was established with a three-member Executive Bureau under the leadership of the US delegate, Averell Harriman. European defense spending more than doubled during the Korean War, from 5.3 billion to approximately 12 billion dollars. US defense spending increased from about

15 to 50 billion, or 13.8 per cent of GNP. Britain, the country that spent the most on the European side, used on average 9.75 per cent of its GNP on defense in the years from 1946 to 1957.[16] From 1950 to 1962 Western Europe received about 15 billion dollars in military assistance directly from the United States. (From 1963 to 1970 it was to receive only about 1.5 billion in such assistance.) As a case in point, it has been estimated that from 1950 to 1965 Norway covered only 60 per cent of its own defense expenditures. The remaining 40 per cent came largely from the United States and NATO infra-structure funds (even much of the latter paid for by the US).[17] Similar per-centages must have applied to other NATO allies as well, particularly the smaller ones. Thousands and thousands of European officers were educated in the United States.

Washington was still to be disappointed. The Lisbon force levels were never met: instead of ninety-six divisions, in 1954 NATO in fact had twenty-five, with an additional twenty-five in reserve. The TCC recommendations for the various NATO countries were not adhered to. There were many reasons for this: the death of Stalin changed the Cold War climate and took away much of the incentive for drastic increases; the defense spending actually undertaken seriously overextended European economies; the Eisenhower administration gave up Truman's idea of a year of maximum danger and instead wanted to work for "the long haul"; finally, by shifting the emphasis to tactical nuclear weapons NATO could seemingly rather easily compensate for the shortfall in conventional forces.

With the American forces in place in Europe, many Europeans felt the European contribution would be of secondary importance anyway. Only the US forces provided the link with America's nuclear weapons. Western European governments were pleased to have the American troops in place. At their highest, in the late 1950s, the number of US troops in Europe was around 400,000. Two-thirds of these troops were located in West Germany, a country the size of the state of Oregon. The West Germans readily accepted that a large part of their national territory was covered by a network of US bases and training facilities. In fact, in some countries, Italy being the best example, there was an interest in increasing the number of US troops further. Any hint, as in the so-called Redford plan in 1956, that the United States would reduce its number of troops in Europe led to uneasiness and protests from the European allies.[18]

Eisenhower was frustrated; he definitely felt that the United States was doing too much and Western Europe too little:

I get weary of the European habit of taking our money, resenting any slight hint as to what they should do, and then assuming, in addition, full right to criticize us as bitterly as they may desire. In fact, it sometimes appears that their indulgence in this kind of criticism varies in direct ratio to the amount of help we give them.[19]

Yet, there was some compensation for Washington, even in disappointment. The added emphasis on nuclear weapons meant that America's influence on NATO's strategy would be even greater than it would have been with a larger European conventional role.

On the political side, it was obvious that the many meetings in the various Atlantic organizations and the establishment of permanent bureaucratic structures for these organizations had to encourage the creation of transnational elites. In addition to the ever-growing permanent NATO staff in Paris and the politicians, military, and diplomats involved in NATO on a more or less daily basis, there were broad-based new institutions such as the North Atlantic Assembly (founded in 1955) with its 188 members and as many alternate members who met twice a year. Although formally independent of NATO, it constituted a strong link between the national parliaments and the Alliance officials. The Atlantic Treaty Association was founded in 1954 based on national branches in the member countries set up to promote the activities and objectives of NATO.

Corporatist historians, such as Charles Maier and Michael Hogan, have particularly emphasized the importance of these elites, with Maier even referring to "the elites superintending Western society" over half a century.[20] The creation of such elites far from ended conflicts among the participating nations, but it must have made the chances of resolving conflicts somewhat greater. The effect was significantly heightened by the fact that many of the members of these transnational elites had worked together for as long as they had under the most challenging of circumstances. Huge events such as the Second World War and/or the start of the Cold War had to bring the various personalities together, particularly since the outcomes of these events were perceived as favorably as they were.

On the American side the names of these key persons are well known and have already figured or will figure in the present text: Eisenhower, Marshall, Acheson, Dulles, Robert Lovett, John McCloy, David Bruce, Robert Bowie, George Ball, Walt Rostow. Their opposite numbers on the European side are equally well known: Winston Churchill, Anthony Eden, Clement Attlee, Ernest Bevin, and Harold Macmillan in Britain; Paul Henri Spaak in Belgium; Joseph Luns and Dirk Stikker in the Netherlands; Georges Bidault, Jean Monnet, and Robert Marjolin in France; Halvard Lange in Norway; Konrad Adenauer and somewhat later Willy Brandt in Germany; Alcide de Gasperi and Count Sforza in Italy. In 1948–52 the relationship between Acheson and British Ambassador Oliver Franks was so close that Franks was seen virtually as a trusted member of the Truman administration. Walter Hallstein, another German member of the postwar network, used the verb to "co-conspire" about the activities of these Americans and Europeans, particularly in their promotion of European integration. As Helmut Schmidt has written, until the years of the Vietnam War not only did the members of the rather small foreign policy elites in the United States and in Western Europe meet frequently, but they also tended to have the same overall approach to international relations. Even for the younger generation, such as Schmidt himself and Helmut Kohl, memories of the early Cold War years were crucial. Both were to speak repeatedly of the impression American Care packages made on them after the Second World War. To them America represented generosity.[21]

Of course, to have been in contact during the Second World War and the initial years of the Cold War did not guarantee personal friendship. Meeting each other did not necessarily mean liking each other—some became personal enemies instead. Charles de Gaulle had spent the war years in London, where apparently he made few really close Anglo-Saxon friends, although the respect he developed for Eisenhower and Churchill may still have restrained the general during his years in power. The rather tense relationship between Dulles and Eden is well known. And the makers of foreign policy were kept in check by the majority of national politicians who were not really part of such transnational elites.

In the 1950s cooperation between the two sides of the Atlantic was helped by the fact that politically both the United States and the leading European countries were all moving in a conservative direction. The 1952 election in the United States made Republican Dwight D. Eisenhower President after twenty years of Democrats Roosevelt and Truman. The Italian election of 1948 introduced a fifty-year period of domination by the Christian Democrats; the 1949 election in West Germany brought conservative Konrad Adenauer to power and his rule was to last for fourteen years; the 1951 elections in France weakened the left and strenghtened the center and the right; in Britain Labour lost the elections of 1950–1 and in succession Winston Churchill, Anthony Eden, and Harold Macmillan became Conservative prime ministers. Although Conservatism did not necessarily mean the same thing on the two sides of the Atlantic or even from one European country to another, the politicians mentioned generally had many political elements in common: anti-Communism, democracy, capitalism combined with at least some social welfare and religion in the form of Christianity.

While politically the 1950s were a conservative decade indeed, it should be emphasized that the emerging Atlantic community had a wide political basis. The narrowest basis was found in France where the center-left, the center, and the center-right in the form of the Socialists, the MRP, and the Republicans were sandwiched between the Communists and the neutralist left on the one side and the Gaullists and nationalist right on the other. In France the highest period of true Atlanticism was probably in 1950–2 with the Pleven and Pinay governments. The election in 1951 strengthened the right, a fact that was to influence the outcome of the EDC negatively.[22] In West Germany the Socialist SPD, while strongly anti-Communist and anti-fascist, was long determined to avoid a repetition of the Weimar years when the party had been perceived as the upholder of the unpopular Versailles treaty and therefore seen as insufficiently nationalist. Now they emphasized the need to unify Germany and opposed West Germany's membership of NATO and even of the ECSC and EEC. *Bündnislosigkeit*, non-alliance, was the slogan. The losses to the CDU in the 1953 and particularly in the 1957 elections changed this: in 1959 the domestic program was reformed in a more centrist direction; in 1960 NATO was fully accepted. In Italy the Socialists, under Pietro Nenni, worked closely with the Communists and Nenni even received the Stalin Peace Prize; the party's movement first away from the Communists and then toward acceptance of NATO started only after the events in Hungary in 1956, but in Italy, unlike in France, the center and the right were almost solidly behind NATO. In Britain both main parties were strongly Atlanticist in their orientation; the new generation coming up in the Labour party was even more so than the older one.

On the American side a whole array of measures was undertaken in the 1950s to strengthen Atlantic solidarity further. The CIA set up a comprehensive covert cultural program of conferences, lectures, magazines, exchange programs, etc. administered through the Congress for Cultural Freedom (CCF). The journals *Encounter* in Britain and *Der Monat* in Germany were perhaps the most successful part of this program. The private Ford and Rockefeller Foundations cooperated with the CIA in some of these efforts. The European federalist movement was to a large extent financed from these sources. The Dutch-inspired Bilderberg group, where members of the Atlantic elite met, was also supported. The group took its name from the hotel, owned by Prince Bernhard of the Netherlands, where its first meeting was held in May 1954. Bernhard was actually to remain its chairman until 1976, when he was forced to resign by the Lockheed bribery scandal.[23]

Education of future Atlantic leaders was particularly emphasized by many different governments and institutions, and many American universities ran programs especially aimed at such individuals. As Henry Kissinger explained in 1950 about the Harvard Summer School, where he taught, it could give "inwardly alive, intelligent Europeans an opportunity to study the deeper meaning of US democracy." Seminars "can provide the antidote to the spirit of nihilism rampant among the European youth and achieve an understanding of the meaning of personal responsibility." At the high school level, the American Field Service was particularly active in student exchanges. Essay contests were held to promote the Atlantic framework. In 1954 the assignment was the following: "Why it is important for America and Europe to remain friends and how may this friendship best be promoted?" The winner came from Norway; the runners-up were from France and Britain. First prize was a trip to the United States and a likely scholarship to study at an American university. In Germany a network of America Houses was set up. To an amazing extent intellectual debate in the United States and in Western Europe became "Atlantic" in the sense that many of the same texts were frequently read and discussed on both sides of the ocean. Some of the key names in this context were John Kenneth Galbraith, Arthur Schlesinger, Daniel Bell, and even the early Henry Kissinger in the United States and Anthony Crosland, Arthur Koestler, Raymond Aron, and even Gunnar Myrdal on the European side.[24]

As far as public opinion was concerned, the pattern from the years 1945–52 was reinforced. American–European cooperation was not limited to the elites, as is at least implied by corporatist historians. While of course no identity of interest was perceived between the home country and the United States, public opinion in Britain, West Germany, and Italy on the whole remained quite friendly to the United States while French opinion was clearly more ambivalent. Thus, in polls from the years 1956 to 1963 more than 70 per cent in Britain consistently answered that "the basic interests of Britain and those of the United States" were either "very much in agreement" or "fairly much in agreement" as opposed to "rather different," "very different," or "no answer." In West Germany the corresponding percentage varied more but the average was about 70. The percentage for Italy also varied, with a somewhat lower average of about 55 per cent. In France the percentage fluctuated from a high of 53 to a low of 27 with an average of about 40 per cent.[25]

On the cultural side, as Richard Pells has argued, what was new to Europeans about American mass culture after the Second World War "was not its presence—they had been going to American movies and hearing American music since the 1920s—but its pervasiveness." Everywhere the symbols of American culture were found: Walt Disney cartoons, American jazz and pop records, the American movies with their many movie stars, American food from Coke to burgers and fries, the T-shirts and the jeans, even the language was being invaded by American phrases.

Opposition to American politics and culture was voiced in many parts of Europe. Politically, McCarthyism was the most damaging issue for the United States, and in country after country US embassies reported the very negative effects the anti-Communist witch-hunt and President Eisenhower's very low public profile on this important matter had on America's standing. The discrepancy between America's insistence on being the strongest promoter of democracy while at the same time not giving political rights to blacks in the South was also frequently and negatively commented upon.

At the same time, many on the left disliked American culture, while on the right too there was opposition. In almost every country conservatives criticized the vulgarity of America's culture, its lack of standards, how it undermined much of the best of what Europe stood for. While in its cultural programs Washington wanted to show that the United States did indeed have something to offer even in high culture, the basic point was still to promote an understanding of the legitimacy of mass culture as such. Some of America's finest intellectuals, such as Schlesinger, Galbraith, and Bell, were brought into service in this cause.[26]

On the whole Washington was very successful in this area: American movies illustrated the trend. Despite various national attempts to reduce the American influence through quotas and taxes, by 1951, 61 per cent of the movies playing on any given day in Western Europe were American. The figures in certain individual countries were striking indeed: Ireland 85 per cent, Belgium, Luxembourg, and Denmark 75, Britain, Finland, Greece, and the Netherlands 70, Italy and Portugal 65, Norway 63, Sweden 60, France and Switzerland 50. By 1958, nearly 50 per cent of Hollywood's profits came from abroad, compared to 40 per cent in 1937. The Hollywood expansion did not necessarily spell doom for the European film industry. In fact, in the 1950s and 1960s the film industries of Britain, France, Italy, and Sweden were enjoying good years both artistically and economically, so good in fact that European exports to the United States set new records.[27]

In country after country English became the first foreign language, and increasingly this English was Americanized. This was a product of America's status after 1945, particularly in the field of culture, and the massive decline of German as a result of the Second World War. The status of American English was strengthened by the many scholars who spent some time in the United States; indeed, in many fields of academic work it was considered almost a *sine qua non* to have visited universities in the United States. In Norway, where the American cultural influence was probably stronger than in most countries, by 1968, 60 per cent of Norwegian social scientists and 50 per cent of natural scientists had spent at least half a year in the US.[28]

On the economic side, the American dollar continued to set the standard against which all other currencies were measured, even though Washington's economic assistance diminished rapidly in the 1950s with the end of the Marshall Plan. From 1946 to 1955 Western Europe had received more than 33 billion dollars in grants and credits from the United States; from 1956 to 1965 the corresponding amount was 6.7 billion, with Italy, Spain, and Yugoslavia now receving the largest amounts.[29]

Starting with the Marshall Plan, American influences were to change European economies in many ways. The emphasis on growth, productivity, stability, and consumption was certainly strengthened, in great part at the expense of traditional class aspects. Naturally this varied from country to country, as did the specific forms of such broad processes that were related to the American influence, with France perhaps being the most skeptical in principle while still enjoying more rapid growth than many other European countries.[30] American–European trade continued to grow in absolute numbers, although the relative importance of this trade declined somewhat compared to the 1940s. This was to be expected as Western Europe recovered economically after the Second World War and the Europeans would once again be able to trade more with each other and less with the United States. US investment in Western Europe increased rapidly as did European investment in the United States. In 1950 US investment in Western Europe stood at 1.7 billion dollars, only slightly higher than in 1929 (1.3 billion): about one-seventh of total US investment abroad. By 1962 such investment had increased to 8.9 billion dollars, almost one-fourth of total US investment, much of the new investment coming from large oil and car companies. European investment in the United States started higher, but increased more slowly, from 2.2 billion dollars in 1950 to 5.2 billion in 1962.[31]

In the 1950s there was much talk about Atlantic integration and how it could be further strengthened, particularly after various crises in the Atlantic relationship. After the Suez debacle NATO appointed a group of "three wise men" (Foreign Ministers Pearson of Canada, Martino of Italy, and Lange of Norway) to come up with proposals to strengthen unity within NATO. Their report recommended a considerable degree of pooling of sovereignty: "Our ultimate aim is to reach harmonization of policy and unity which comes only as a result of a long process of consultation."

Some suggested that a formal Atlantic Community, politically and economically integrated, be formed, but this was not to be since the United States was fiercely opposed to anything that meant a reduction in America's sovereignty. Foreigners could not possibly be allowed to help determine US policies; both the United States and Western Europe agreed that the emphasis was to be on Europe's integration; too strong an insistence on Atlantic integration would harm, possibly even kill these efforts entirely.[32]

European Integration and the Atlantic Framework, 1950–1962[33]

The fear of Germany dominating Europe was the primary reason why the United States had intervened in two world wars. In the Cold War the United States intervened again in Europe, this time to contain the Soviet Union, though it was still quite concerned about Germany's role. The United States was obviously opposed to the integration of Europe if this took place under the leadership of a hostile power. Therefore, the American support for European integration was clearly premised on certain conditions being fulfilled, by far the most important of which was that a more united Europe should remain friendly to the United States. To make certain that this happened, the new Europe had to be fitted into a wider Atlantic framework. To a large extent this "Atlantic framework" was a code phrase for overall American leadership—there was never any real doubt that Western Europe belonged to America's sphere of influence.

Emphasis on the Atlantic framework in the 1950s should not be carried too far, however; in historical perspective the Eisenhower administration was remarkable not for its largely implicit emphasis on this framework, but rather for the strong and direct support it gave to European integration. The British kept pushing for unambiguously Atlantic solutions, whether in the form of German rearmament in NATO, an OEEC approach to cooperation in atomic energy, an Atlantic free trade area to "dilute" the European Economic Community, or even putting all the European institutions—the European Coal and Steel Community, Euratom, and the EEC—into some sort of Atlantic setting. All these efforts were opposed in Washington. While favoring a wider Atlantic framework for European integration, with this framework already in place the United States, unlike Britain, insisted that the "six should increasingly act as a unit within Atlantic organization, and that integrity of developing institutions of six-country Community should be safeguarded."

As we have already seen, Washington pursued European integration with considerably more fervor than the six ECSC/EEC countries themselves. From 1949 to 1960 the United States apparently channeled a total of 4 million dollars into supporting various federalist activities in Europe, much of this through intelligence contacts. In 1950 Washington helped bring about a change of leadership in the European Movement, away from Churchill's cautious British attitude to Belgian Foreign Minister Paul-Henri Spaak's Continental approach.[34] European federalists had excellent connections on the American side, and none more so than Jean Monnet, who had easy access to the highest American officials throughout most of the 1960s.

In the negotiations leading to the European Coal and Steel Community, the United States did not stress the Atlantic framework at all; in fact, no such framework was even foreseen, except for the ECSC's loose connections with the OEEC. Washington made little or no effort to bring Britain in, since the Labour government there clearly did not want to join, and any further talk of British membership might therefore come to obstruct the whole project. An explicit Atlantic emphasis would have run directly counter to the objective of getting the French–German integration process started. As under the Marshall Plan, the Truman administration stressed greater European self-sufficiency, in part to reduce American costs. Finally, the ECSC would not represent any challenge anyway to the crucial part of the Atlantic framework in the form of NATO.

As we have seen in the previous chapter, in 1949–50 the American eagerness to build up Germany economically and politically was rapidly increasing, to the extent that even Germany's military reconstruction could clearly be foreseen on the horizon. Washington made it perfectly evident that Germany not only had to be reconstructed but also eventually be treated as an equal partner, and if the French did not come up with ideas on how this was to be done, the United States would have to involve itself much more directly than it already had. Although Washington had presented no definite idea on how to proceed, it had repeatedly indicated that some form of Western European integration was the best, probably the only, way out.

On the French side, as early as September 1949 Foreign Minister Schuman had referred to a "mandate" from the United States to lead on the German question. Long Paris had hesitated, hoping that somehow the United States could solve the German problem for it. One way would indeed be to transform the Atlantic alliance into an economic as well as a military organization, but since Paris was strongly opposed to anything that would mean letting Germany indirectly into NATO, not much could be done there. For its part, Washington did not want to become too intimately involved in Europe's affairs, and, in the end, all that could be agreed on was a certain strengthening of the American role in the OEEC. This then became part of the framework for the dramatic initiative Paris was about to take.

Paris had to act if it was not to lose control entirely over developments in Germany. On 15 May 1950 the NATO Council was to open its meeting in London, to be preceded by a meeting of the Foreign Ministers of the US, the UK, and France. Although the question of Germany's contribution to the strength of the West was difficult to handle in the formal NATO context, it was obvious that the Americans would again be concerned about "speeding up the integration of Western Germany with the West, and, if possible, to relax our controls in Western Germany."

The crucial French initiative, the Schuman plan for a European Coal and Steel Community, was taken on 9 May 1950 against this rather complex background. The idea of a coal and steel community already existed, and was already familiar to the American side as could be seen from statements by High Commissioner John McCloy in Bonn; indeed, Ambassador David Bruce in Paris had even discussed the concept in advance with Jean Monnet. The more specific forms were worked out in Paris. The technical work was done by Monnet and his group, and they received the political support of Robert Schuman and the French Foreign Office and, later, Premier Bidault and the Cabinet.

After Washington's initial doubts about the cartel aspects of the Schuman plan had been resolved at least in part, the Truman administration was to give the plan full backing. This was, finally, the initiative that Washington had been searching for at least since the formation of the West German state, or even earlier. As John Foster Dulles commented after Schuman had launched his plan, this was what he and Marshall had talked about as early as the

Council of Foreign Ministers meeting in Moscow in March–April 1947, "but we did not believe the French would ever accept."

Although economic issues were obviously of the highest importance, the defense area was at the core of the Atlantic framework. After the outbreak of the Korean War, Truman soon concluded that German resources were needed also on the military side. This conclusion was presented to the NATO foreign ministers' meeting in New York in September 1950. Again the Americans underlined what had to be done, in this case that West Germany had to be rearmed, but exactly how this was to be done was to be decided later. Clearly rearmament within NATO was the solution favored by Washington. In the negotiations on West Germany's rearmament flowing from the NATO meeting in September, Washington openly stressed the Atlantic or NATO framework, not least because at first it seemed unlikely that German rearmament could be undertaken in any other context.

In October 1950 French Defense Minister (Prime Minister August 1951– January 1952) René Pleven came to insist on a European context for West Germany's rearmament in the form of the European Defense Community. Again, Monnet played an important role in the preparations on the French side. He feared that bringing West Germany directly into NATO could destroy his ECSC. At first the Truman administration disliked this European approach, seeing it as militarily unsound, as discriminating strongly against Germany, and as reducing the role of NATO too much. The French were allegedly trying to have it both ways, at one and the same time promoting the integration of and maintaining the discrimination against Germany; at worst, the French proposal could be seen as a way of postponing, even defeating West German rearmament. But, despite the fact that the other NATO countries also preferred the NATO to the EDC approach, the French view could not simply be overlooked. And it was after all Washington's policy even in the defense area to encourage further unity on the Continent and particularly Franco-German rapprochement. Some sort of compromise between the American and the French proposals had to be found.

This was accomplished by December 1950. The so-called Spofford compromise, named after Charles M. Spofford, US deputy representative on the NATO Council, stressed the complementary rather than the competitive nature of the American and French plans. It clearly suggested that NATO was the immediate answer and a European army a longer-term one. In commenting upon this compromise, Acheson reiterated: "We favor this solution as long as it is clearly a part of and under NATO umbrella." The details would have to be worked out later, but in any European army within NATO the most obvious forms of discrimination against Germany had to be ended.

In July 1951 High Commissioner McCloy, Ambassador Bruce, and NATO Commander Eisenhower, at least indirectly assisted by Jean Monnet, persuaded the Truman administration that the United States should basically accept the French EDC plan. In their opinion, it was really the only way to get the French to accept German rearmament. They also saw it as "a major, and probably decisive, step toward European political federation." In his diary Eisenhower wrote that a satisfactory solution to the European security problem could be found only in "a US of Europe—to include all countries now in NATO" as well as West Germany, and some neutrals which he later left out. "If *necessary*, U.K. could be omitted [emphasis in original]."

The Truman administration, at first somewhat grudgingly, and the Eisenhower administration, quite wholeheartedly, supported the EDC approach. So complete was the conversion that the two administrations in fact did so despite the French soon beginning to display a curious lack of faith in their own plan. In Washington's new analysis, not only had France to be brought along—and the best way to do so would appear to be by supporting its plan—but the more West Germany would be bound up with France, the better, and the more difficult it would be for Moscow to tempt the Germans with neutrality. The Eisenhower administration invested so much prestige in the EDC that Dulles, supported by the President, threatened "an agonizing reappraisal" if the French national assembly did not pass the proposal. It was indeed remarkable that the administration went as far as it did in trying to promote European defense cooperation through the EDC.

Yet, even the EDC was to be tied to NATO. With the exception of West Germany, where most of the US troops in Europe were stationed anyway, the members of the EDC would all be members also of NATO. American troops would remain in Europe, although both the Truman and the Eisenhower administration refused to give any guarantees of permanence on this point. The American nuclear umbrella would apply. Especially in time of war the EDC's governing bodies would fall under the NATO supreme commander, who was an American. As Dulles pointed out to the NATO Council in December 1953, an integrated European Community and the wider Atlantic Community would depend on each other: "These two structures will differ but they must be built together. Each is vital to the success of the other and each today, happily, is in fact being built."

In a paradoxical twist, Washington was soon being pressured by Paris to modify an EDC project that only the French had initially favored. The truth was that support for the EDC was never that strong in France. The Communists and the Gaullists opposed the idea all along. The latter were considerably strengthened in the 1951 elections. Many Socialists in particular were disappointed that Britain would not join and that ties with NATO were not even stronger than they actually were. Others in the political center used the EDC to attract American support for the French position in Indochina. The implication was that if Washington supported Paris in Indochina, Paris would return the favor by approving the EDC. After France's position had collapsed at Dien Bien Phu, the French assembly on 30 August 1954, turned the EDC down.

The Eisenhower administration was at first somewhat unwilling to give up the project and considered "punishing" the French for their behavior. London had actually favored a NATO solution all along, and Europe's expectations that the Conservatives under Churchill would pursue a more pro-European course than had Attlee's Labour government were largely unfulfilled. As Churchill himself stated, "We are with Europe but not of it." The old man described the EDC as a "sludgy amalgam" and now told Eisenhower that "I do not blame the French for rejecting EDC but only for inventing it." But even after Washington came to support the NATO course which London was finally pushing openly, Dulles was still unhappy to see European suprana-tionality go: "This was always to me the most important aspect of EDC."

The initial reason why the EDC road had been chosen was that the French had refused to let West Germany directly into NATO. But after first having rejected the EDC and then on Christmas Eve rejecting even the entry of Germany into NATO, the French national assembly on 30 December 1954 finally approved the new agreements in their entirety. Britain under Eden had taken the lead in working out the new arrangement, whereby West Germany was to be admitted into NATO, as well as into a strengthened Western Union together with Italy, now renamed the Western European Union (WEU). In the end the French felt they had little choice after having created such a crisis in the alliance, fearing that if they rejected even NATO membership, a separate treaty between the United States, Britain, and West Germany seemed most likely, hardly an enticing idea for them; indeed, French public opinion seems all along to have disliked the NATO option the least. But the WEU was to be no big success. Its most important function was already fulfilled when it had served as the framework for West Germany's integration into NATO, rather in the same way that the most significant task of the Western Union in 1948 had been to help bring the United States into NATO.

Though Dulles still felt that there was just too little supranationality in the NATO solution, he had had no specific alternative prepared in case the EDC failed, and therefore in the end had no choice but to praise British Foreign Secretary Anthony Eden's conception as "brilliant and statesmanlike." The British initiative "at least avoided the disaster of a neutralized Germany, an isolated France, and Soviet domination of Europe." Militarily Dulles saw it as an advantage to have British troops tied more closely to the Continent—and this was part of the new solution—but politically it involved a country, the United Kingdom, "which is not as ready to develop supra-national agencies. This was something of a disadvantage."

After the dramatic failure of the EDC, European integration quickly came to focus on two new projects. The first was Euratom, which was an extension of the so-called functionalist or sectoral approach supported by Monnet in particular. Monnet argued that it was logical to move from one energy field, coal and steel, to another, atomic energy, especially when this new field appeared to be highly promising technologically and without too many vested interests. The second project was the more comprehensive common market approach supported by the Benelux countries in general, and by Dutch Foreign Minister Johan Willem Beyen in particular. This was a more ambitious project, so ambitious in fact that it had been discussed earlier without much success. The two projects were soon linked, also in the sense that Monnet and Beyen supported each other's ideas.

The United States adopted a lower profile after the failure of the EDC, since their heavy pressure during the EDC debate was seen to have backfired; but there could be no doubt about Washington's continued support for the most comprehensive forms of European integration.

The Eisenhower administration clearly had it in its powers to make or break Euratom, for in the nuclear field Western Europe was quite dependent on the United States both for technical expertise and for uranium. Washington could cooperate with European states either through Euratom or bilaterally. Although some bilateral agreements were concluded with member countries, it generally preferred the first course, since to have concluded only bilateral agreements would, in the words of Monnet, have made the European countries the "atomic satellite" of the United States. However, the US Atomic Energy Commission and the American atomic energy industry, the former being especially concerned about laxness of security, the latter being eager to obtain quick bilateral deals with the various European countries, and both worrying about the "socialist" nature of Euratom, favored the bilateral route. Eisenhower supported the State Department in its preference for the supranationality of Euratom.

The most ambitious American ideas of 1947–9 for a customs union under the OEEC had been rather similar to the European common market project of the 1950s, so in principle Washington was a strong supporter of the common market concept. Tactically, however, it was now afraid that the concept was simply too ambitious, and thus could easily lead to failure again. The project was seen as rather general and unlikely to meet with any speedy response, particularly from protectionist France. The British, who agreed to send an observer to the Spaak committee set up after the Messina meeting of the continental six in June 1955, quickly excused themselves from further efforts. In the alleged words of a Foreign Office observer: "The future treaty which you are discussing has no chance of being agreed; if it was agreed, it would have no chance of being ratified; and if it were ratified, it would have no chance of being applied. And if it was applied, it would be totally unacceptable to Britain."[35]

Before the meeting of the six ECSC countries in Venice in May 1956 Dulles therefore cabled the US embassies that he certainly hoped that the approval of the Euratom treaty, which was of such immediate importance, "would not be held up until complex and doubtless lengthy Common Market negotiations concluded." Still, there was no doubt that the United States strongly favored the common market and that Washington wanted the French to take the lead even on these matters.

Paris was long holding back, however. The centrist governments of France still preferred to move in some sort of cooperation with Britain, fearing to be left so exposed vis-à-vis the Germans. Yet, gradually the French showed a more favorable attitude to the common market than had been expected. First, they wanted to counteract the negative impression they had created of themselves as a result of the EDC failure; second, they also had a strong interest in the Euratom since the French nuclear industry was the most advanced on the continent; third, and perhaps most important, Suez gave a very strong impetus to the French process of committing itself decisively to Europe. In fact, when Prime Minister Eden called his French counterpart Guy Mollett to announce that the British–French invasion of Egypt had to end, Mollett was shocked. The French premier was at that very moment engaged in conversation with Konrad Adenauer who immediately used the occasion to push the case of European integration: "Now is the time to build Europe." This marked the beginning of increased French–German cooperation.[36]

The process therefore soon moved surprisingly quickly. In drawing up a more definite US position on the market, and British (counter)plans for a wider OEEC free trade area within which the common market could be fitted, Eisenhower simply joined the two together and publicly stated that nothing had been more heartening than the recent announcement of the two new proposals that would advance further the economic integration of Europe. In early 1957, as further progress was made on the common market, Eisenhower praised the project in the highest of terms.[37]

On 25 March 1957 Belgium, France, Italy, Luxembourg, the Netherlands, and the Federal Republic of Germany signed the treaties of Rome that established the EEC and Euratom. New members would in principle be required to adhere to the terms of these treaties, which were ratified by the six countries surprisingly quickly. Dulles sent his warm congratulations to key politicians in France and Germany.

The United States gave priority to the plans of the Six over the British Atlantic schemes. The Common Market had to be established before the six countries entered into negotiations with the British. In the 1950s few Americans believed more strongly in the good cause of European integration than did Eisenhower and Dulles. In fact, Britain should be encouraged to join the Six only if it was prepared to accept supranationality and the ultimate goal of some sort of European federation. Otherwise it could come to ruin this historic development.

Despite its opposition to Britain's explicit Atlanticism, the Eisenhower administration continued to take the wider Atlantic framework for granted. The Six would operate within the NATO structure. Until de Gaulle came to power, no one in NATO really disputed American preeminence. However, the founding of the EEC created a need to fit the new organization into a reformed Atlantic economic framework. As we shall see, first, America's balance of payments problems and, then, the evolution of de Gaulle's policies both strenghtened Washington's emphasis on the Atlantic framework considerably. While this framework had been largely implicit until 1958–9, thereafter it became a constant and explicit part of US policy. The fact that John Foster Dulles—who combined such strong support for both European and Atlantic integration—became ill and had to leave office in April 1959 and was replaced by the more Atlantic-oriented Christian Herter helped smooth this transition.

In 1958–9 Washington took two important initiatives aimed at strengthening the economic part of the Atlantic framework. The first was the proposal of October 1958 to launch a new GATT round. This fifth such round—which became known as the Dillon round (1958–62) after Under Secretary of State for Economic Affairs Douglas Dillon—was aimed, like the previous four rounds, at establishing lower tariffs among the industrialized countries. This was a general objective that the Truman and Eisenhower administrations had both been pursuing, with rather lukewarm support from Congress. There was no doubt that the creation of the EEC added a special dimension to this effort.

When the EEC proposed a 20 per cent cut in most of its common external tariffs, the US could respond to this offer only after strong presidential leadership had been exerted over both Congress and a Department of Agriculture which was disappointed that reductions could not also be secured in the Community's rather protectionist Common Agricultural Policy (CAP).

The second initiative the Eisenhower administration took led to the transformation of the OEEC into the Organization for Economic Cooperation and Development (OECD). Again this was an initiative that emerged only gradually. The OEEC might well have been reformed anyway, but the formation of the EEC speeded up the process. In the new organization the United States and Canada would become direct members, with the US presumably playing the leading role; the OECD could also provide a most useful setting for upcoming negotiations between the EEC and the British-led European Free Trade Association (EFTA), a setting which could help Washington avert the danger of the two organizations reaching a free trade agreement at the economic expense of the United States. Finally, the new organization also aimed at increasing the role of the Europeans in development assistance. The OECD convention went into effect on 30 September 1961, but in reality it came to represent no dramatic change compared to its predecessor.

With this kind of Atlantic framework, rather implicit at first, then more explicit, it was evident that Washington did not really see Western Europe as an independent actor. Europe might occasionally come to have positions different from those of the United States, but the assumption was nearly always that the two sides of the Atlantic would continue to share the most basic interests.

Although under Eisenhower and even under Kennedy references could be found to an integrated Europe representing a "third force," most of these references simply meant that a united Europe would be a third important actor in international politics, after the United States and the Soviet Union. There was rarely any implication that Europe would be an independent unit standing in the middle between the two existing superpowers; it was just an additional one, and the expectation was almost always that it would be standing rather close to the United States.

Eisenhower repeatedly talked about Western Europe as a "third force", but always in this context of the united Europe cooperating with the United States. Thus, in February 1956 the President referred to the industrial capacity of a united Europe and then expressed his belief that "such a 'third force' *working with the rest of the free world* [my italics] would change the whole complexion of present circumstances and insure peace." Earlier he had even talked about "developing in Western Europe a third great power bloc, after which development the United States would be permitted to sit back and relax somewhat."

The Kennedy administration, however, rarely used the expression "third force", probably because General de Gaulle was now the spokesman of a more truly independent Europe. Washington certainly did not want to express any support for his kind of "third force." Instead, the Atlantic framework was to be stressed more explicitly than ever. Thus, Secretary of State Dean Rusk told French ambassador Herve Alphand that the "third force" issue touched a very sensitive nerve. "The concept that Europe could be the arbiter between the US and the Soviets was basically fallacious. Europe was the key issue outstanding between the US and USSR." Rusk even vaguely threatened that if Europe ever decided to play an independent role, "issues between the US and the USSR would be greatly reduced." If Europe did not behave, Rusk thus threatened to reach some sort of deal with Moscow.

The Motives for America's Support of European Integration[38]

The American policy of supporting European integration flowed from many different sources. Yet, without simplifying matters too much, these sources, or motives, may be arranged in ascending order of importance in five different clusters which we may refer to respectively as the American model, a more rational and efficient Europe, a reduced American burden, the containment of the Soviet Union, and, finally, the containment even of Germany. These motives were found in their purest form in the 1950s–early 1960s, but in modified form they have exerted their force until the present.

The American Model. As numerous observers have noted, Americans tend to see many features of the American model as universal, as something that the rest of the world should emulate. This was certainly the case with the American federal system, political democracy, and free and open markets. Many congressmen long had rather simplistic notions about the ease with which Europe could develop along the pattern of the thirteen original American colonies and they frequently lectured Europeans on the importance of the American lesson, usually with somewhat ambiguous results at best. Such statements were not, however, limited to congressmen. Some prominent officials spoke in similar ways, with the speech of 31 October 1949 by ECA head Paul Hoffman perhaps offering the most striking example.

A More Efficient Europe. Closely related to the importance of the American model was Washington's emphasis on an integrated Europe being a more rational and efficient Europe. The economic side was obvious. As NATO commanding general Dwight D. Eisenhower stated in July 1951, Europe could not solve its problems as long as it was "divided by patchwork territorial fences": "Once united, the farms and factories of France and Belgium, the foundries of Germany, the rich farmlands of Holland and Denmark, the skilled labor of Italy, will produce miracles for the common good." On the political side, integration would allegedly not only do away with old-fashioned European nationalism and war, but also make it easier for the United States to deal with Western Europe. America would have one effective partner in Europe instead of a complicated network of bigger and smaller states. As Kissinger would later ask, "When I want to talk with Europe, who do I then call?"

A Reduced American Burden. In many different ways European integration could also lighten the heavy burden put upon the United States after the Second World War. Probably the main reason why the United States insisted on the Europeans working out an integrated four-year economic plan—a measure which was unthinkable in the US itself—to implement Marshall's words at Harvard was to make sure that the Europeans would not come back and ask for more money at the end of the four years.

Eisenhower kept insisting that European unity "would mean early independence from aid from America and other Atlantic countries." He very much wanted to reduce US federal spending, and that certainly included a reduction in defense spending. Time and again Eisenhower returned to the need to "bring the boys home" as soon as possible. He kept hoping that this would be possible "in a few years' time," which he generally estimated to be four to ten years. Dulles similarly argued that complete sovereignty for the many nations of Europe was "a luxury which European countries can no longer afford at US expense."

It was another matter that this motive of reducing the US burden and, particularly, "bringing the boys home" did not go over well with most Europeans. They strongly favored American financial assistance and military guarantees in the form of American troops stationed in Europe. Eisenhower's firm support for the EDC was undoubtedly in part related to his desire to reduce the American troop presence in Europe. To communicate this motive openly, however, could easily undermine support in Europe for the EDC. This situation led to rather confusing statements in Washington about the effect EDC ratification would have on American troop levels. Dulles tried to square the circle by arguing that defeat of the EDC would give an even stronger impetus to a US withdrawal from Europe.

Kennedy was not so afraid of federal expenditures as his Republican predecessor, but he was the more concerned about America's growing negative balance of payments and shared the view that, if the United States were to do less, Europe had to do more. A united Europe would be capable of playing a greater role in the common defense, of doing more for the poorer nations, of joining with the United States and others in lowering trade barriers and resolving commercial and financial problems, and even "developing coordinated policies in all economic, political, and diplomatic areas."

Starting in the late 1950s American policymakers had begun to worry about the balance of payments situation. Increasing concern was being expressed about the EEC keeping American goods out. To the American preoccupation with what Europeans themselves could do to relieve the American burden in Europe and elsewhere was soon added the basic question of whether the EEC would actually benefit the United States economically. Although the answer to this question was quite complicated and involved difficult calculations, most administrations concluded that the creation of new trade between the United States and Western Europe outweighed the relative diversion of American trade away from Western Europe (and vice versa) which had to be expected from a customs union like the EEC.

Containment of the Soviet Union. While some policymakers might still feel somewhat ambivalent about the economic benefits to the United States of a more united Europe, Washington's faith in the contribution such a Europe could make to the containment of the Soviet Union remained constant for forty-five years. Although the Marshall Plan was not formally directed against any one, in reality the containment of the Soviet Union and of Communism was crucial.

Throughout the many years of the Cold War, NATO was similarly directed against the Soviet–Communist threat. In the Truman administration, but more frequently in that of Eisenhower, it was also argued that European integration could do more than simply contain the Soviet threat. Eisenhower himself thus expressed the hope that "A solid power mass in Western Europe would ultimately attract to it all the Soviet satellites, and the threat to peace would disappear." A united Europe could wean Eastern Europe away from Soviet control.

Containment of Germany. A final, but crucial motive for the American promotion of European integration was the need to integrate Germany with Western Europe in general and with France in particular. To rebuild western Germany without giving economic aid to the French as well was politically explosive in France. This necessity to support both countries at the same time formed an important part of the background for the Marshall Plan. The further reconstruction of Germany also strengthened the case for the American security guarantee to Western Europe, certainly including France, which formed the backbone of NATO.

In Washington, as in most European capitals, the reconstruction of western Germany was seen as necessary, but it was still undertaken with considerable uneasiness. What policies would the new Germany pursue? If the new Federal Republic of Germany was to achieve equality, and it had to if a nationalistic reaction was to be prevented, then integration was really the only alternative to full independence. Such independence, practically everybody agreed, was just not possible. In the combination of Germany's need for equality and of Europe's need to contain Germany lay probably the deepest roots of European integration. The French had to take the lead in integrating Germany since the British had clearly demonstrated their unwillingness to do so. And in 1950 the French finally did take the plunge.

In the crucial case of Germany, neutrality was out of the question for Washington as well as for London and Paris. The Soviet note of March 1952 promoted the idea of a united and neutral Germany. Both prospects were actively discouraged by the Western powers. A united Germany had to be committed to the West; few things frightened Western policymakers more than a neutral Germany free to throw its weight around. While this could be stated fairly openly, it was impossible to reject outright a united Germany as such. Yet, clearly the Western capitals, and even Adenauer in Bonn, were quite happy with the status quo in Germany. Considering the problems involved in fitting the western part into a European and Atlantic framework, one could only imagine how much more difficult it would have been to do this with a united Germany. British Minister of State Selwyn Lloyd probably came closer than anybody to expressing the feelings of the West, and possibly even of the Soviet Union, in mid-1953:

Germany is the key to the peace of Europe. A divided Europe has meant a divided Germany. To unite Germany while Europe is divided, even if practicable, is fraught with danger to all. Therefore everybody—Dr. Adenauer, the Russians, the Americans, the French and ourselves—feel in our hearts that a divided Germany is safer for the time being. But none of us dare say so openly because of the effect on German public opinion. Therefore we all publicly support a united Germany, each on his own terms.[39]

In the discussions on the European Defense Community, Eisenhower could become quite alarmist about Germany's future. In his talks with Churchill in July 1954, before the French vote on the EDC, he underlined that "we could not afford to lose Germany even though we were to lose France." He raised the question "as to the point at which action to preserve Germany would be required on our part." In June 1961 Kennedy told de Gaulle that in addition to the economic and political strengthening of Europe, there was also another reason why the US favored the European Economic Community: "It is because it contributes to tie West Germany to Europe. It is not clear what will happen in Germany after Adenauer and, therefore, every tie which links Germany to Europe should be welcome."

In the period of maximum concern with Germany, in the 1940s and 1950s, the ultimate fear was that Germany would side with the Soviet Union. European integration was thus to contain both the Soviet Union and Germany. (This was "double containment." In some respects Washington felt that even France and other Western European allies of the United States had to be contained—"triple containment.")

Again and again, members of the Eisenhower administration returned to this horror among horror scenarios. After the French national assembly had rejected the EDC, Dulles thus told the National Security Council that the heart of the matter was whether or not the US would be able to preserve NATO. Moscow "could dangle the possibility of unification of Germany, rectification of the Polish frontier, and economic advantages" before the Germans. The Soviets held strong cards, and if they played them cleverly, Washington's consuming fear was that the Germans would be tempted by the siren songs of neutrality. Adenauer held them in place and rejected Soviet overtures; but, again, what would happen after him?

While Eisenhower and especially Dulles had a very close relationship with Adenauer, in 1960 the President was clearly becoming frustrated with the German Chancellor's "increasingly confirmed...rigidity" and his "growing senility." The young Kennedy quickly came to feel that the old Adenauer was much too rigid on East–West matters, including the status of Berlin and even of East Germany. Despite this, even the Kennedy administration was quite concerned about post-Adenauer Germany becoming a loose cannon. Adenauer was too rigid, but the good thing about him was that he was a guarantor against any form of Soviet–German deal. Washington's drawn-out support for the Multilateral Nuclear Force (MLF) in NATO illustrated America's fear that if the Germans were discriminated against, even in the nuclear field, they could come to respond in dangerously nationalistic ways. Germany could not be discriminated against, but neither could it be set free. Again, integration appeared to be the obvious answer.

The European Economic Challenge to the Atlantic Framework, 1950–1962[40]

De Gaulle came to represent the major political challenge to the primacy of the Atlantic or, more directly expressed, the American-dominated framework. The second challenge was economic, in the sense that European integration could discriminate against certain American economic interests. This European challenge was, however, long tempered by two considerations: first, and most important, was the fact that political objectives clearly took precedence over economic ones; second, most key policymakers concluded that however harmful European integration might be to some American interests, on the whole such integration was beneficial to the US even economically.

This pattern was displayed as early as under the Marshall Plan. Here political considerations, in the form of the containment of the Soviet Union and of Communism, the integration of West Germany, etc. were seen as justifying a certain overall discrimination against US economic interests. If Europe's acute dollar problem was to be solved, the remedy appeared simple: the Western European countries had to import relatively less from the dollar area and more from each other. Yet, this general conclusion did not prevent the Truman administration and Congress from instituting privileges for specific American business interests, with shipping and certain agricultural products providing the most striking examples.

When the Truman administration supported the creation of the European Coal and Steel Community, this was again done primarily for political reasons and, more particularly, to bring about French–German reconciliation and integrate West Germany firmly with the West. The American coal and steel industries tended to fear the consequences of strengthening their European competitors and certainly did not push for the creation of the ECSC. On the economic side Washington was also concerned about the cartel aspects of the community, even after Monnet and others had tried hard to calm American fears on this point.

Business interests were represented both in the Truman and in the Eisenhower administrations, more strongly in the latter than in the former. Thus, in December 1953 Secretary of the Treasury George Humphrey argued that Congress and business were "going to strenuously object to our using their tax money to finance additional steel competition from abroad." However, even these objections could not stop the administration from supporting Monnet or from pushing particularly the Germans to implement the ECSC. Neither did they stop Washington from giving a 100 million dollar loan to the ECSC, but the objections were probably instrumental in making the loan considerably smaller than it would otherwise have been. 400–500 million dollars had actually been considered.

The strong American support for the European Payments Union was also based in part on political considerations. The State Department and the Economic Cooperation Administration (later the Mutual Security Agency) saw even the EPU in the light of containment, but also as a step on the long road towards multilateralism. The more negative Treasury saw the EPU as another postponement of convertibility and multilateralism. Various lobbies objected to the EPU's discrimination against American goods, but again the State Department prevailed. On Euratom, although the US atomic industry generally favored the bilateral route, it had few problems in accepting Euratom once Washington for political reasons had adopted the supranational approach.

With the proposals for a general common market advancing in 1955–6, Washington had to go beyond general political statements and analyze the whole spectrum of economic interests. European economic integration certainly presented challenges for the United States. At the working level in the Eisenhower administration, the European proposals were seen as having to be harmonized with the general promotion of multilateral trade, the ultimate attainment of general currency convertibility, and the avoidance of large-scale discrimination against US goods or even those of certain other countries. Agriculture was quickly identified as particularly problematic, because here heavy European protectionist elements would be most likely to injure a major and growing American export interest. Despite the overall positive emphasis, concrete American economic interests were not to be neglected.

American industry as such was divided over the pros and cons of the market. The conclusion from a meeting of some forty of the major companies was that a common market would discourage US exports since the whole arrangement was based on preferences for member countries. On the other hand, the vast integrated new market would clearly have a positive effect on US investment in Europe: one big market was much better than many small ones. For the big American oil and car companies already present in Western Europe the latter point was an important one.

The State Department decided that while the economic concerns were to be mentioned to the countries involved, more concrete negotiations should take place only *after* the Six had ratified the treaties of Rome. Earlier action "could seriously interfere with favorable parliamentary action" in the six member countries. Nothing should be done that could slow down the establisment of the EEC.

After the treaties of Rome had been negotiated and, to Washington's surprise, even quickly ratified by the Six, the administration kept up the general political encouragement. While the free trade area promoted by Britain could alleviate some of the economic problems for the United States involved in the creation of the EEC, these negotations should not delay the implementation of the common market. The State Department instructed the relevant embassies that the political importance of European integration, "looking to permanent solution of age-old Franco-German problems", had committed the US to "the success of the European Common Market."

Alan Milward and Federico Romero have argued that starting in 1958 the American policy toward European integration became much more negative. In this respect Romero points out that it was very fortunate that the EEC came about in 1955–7, because "if it had come about just two years later the common market would have certainly received very different treatment in Washington."[41]

The United States had run its first post-war balance of payments deficit in 1950, and this was actually repeated in most years in the 1950s, but the deficit was still relatively small and not really seen as representing a major problem, since the US was after all running a substantial surplus in its balance of trade. The payments deficit also meant that Europe was receiving much needed dollars. In 1958–9 the payments deficit increased considerably. (The trade surplus lasted until 1971.) Military expenditures and private investment abroad were seen as the main culprits.

Although economic considerations became more important in 1958–9, the Milward–Romero interpretation seems considerably overstated. In fact, while there were some changes in US policy toward the EEC, these were smaller than one could have expected. The explanation was obvious: political considerations, as interpreted by the State Department, continued to dominate the American policy towards the EEC well after 1958. In addition, for the US the economic side included more than simply the balance of payments problem, however serious this was becoming.

Even after the EEC came into operation in 1958, Washington hesitated to press its economic grievances. At first it was hoped that a combination of the long-awaited introduction of currency convertibility, a lowering of the EEC tariffs to the outside world, and increased European military and development spending would improve the US payments situation. In any case, it took time to change established policies.

Largely in response to the formation of the EEC, Britain, Denmark, Sweden, Norway, Switzerland, Austria, and Portugal in 1959–60 etablished the European Free Trade Association (EFTA). Washington was rather lukewarm about EFTA. While at first it primarily underlined that the new organization had to be compatible with GATT rules, the Eisenhower administration became increasingly skeptical, though in October 1959 Secretary Herter nevertheless told the relevant embassies that since the EFTA convention would be signed soon, "it would be counter-productive for US even to imply that it is attempting to bring influence to bear against signature."

But no such negative feelings were expressed toward the EEC. In November 1959 Herter wrote the President that the United States had "strongly supported" the EEC "for political as well as economic reasons." Although admittedly some economic reasons were seen to exist for the United States to back the EEC, most of the American support clearly flowed from political sources. In August 1960 the State Department underlined that the basic point was still that the United States continued to feel that European integration was of vital importance both for the member countries and for the overall strength of the Atlantic alliance. While a more open and liberal Community was definitely to be encouraged, primarily through new GATT negotiations, such measures should not have the effect of weakening the EEC. To sum up: the worsening balance of payments situation made Washington increasingly skeptical toward the British plan for a free trade area and later toward EFTA, but not toward the EEC. Unlike the EEC, the other two represented economic discrimination against the United States with no overall political advantage.

With the coming of Kennedy, the concern about the balance of payments situation was to increase significantly. The first run on the dollar took place in November 1960 during the elections; foreign dollar holdings for the first time exceeded US gold reserves. Even before he took office, Kennedy appointed a task force, headed by George Ball, to look into the foreign economic policy of the United States, with emphasis on the balance of payments situation. The task force recommended a growth strategy, combining an opening of foreign markets with expansive policies in general. The US was to export its way out of the payments problem.

In April 1961 Kennedy told Secretary of the Treasury Douglas Dillon that the two things that worried him the most were "nuclear war and the payments deficit." The new President was to return to the problem of the payments deficit again and again. Ball thought JFK's concern was related to his closeness to his businessman father. "Every weekend he went up to Hyannis Port," Ball recalled, "he came back absolutely obsessed with the balance of payments." Ball, emphasizing the political side, tried to get Kennedy to decide on these issues in for him (Ball) more favorable settings.

Washington began pushing West Germany to support the American troops there in the form of so-called offset payments. (This meant that the Germans would pay for, or offset, the extra costs Washington had in maintaining troops in Germany.) Kennedy adviser John Kenneth Galbraith argued that it was foolish for the United States to increase its own balance of payments problems by promoting a strong high-tariff bloc like the EEC. Matters would (allegedly) become even worse with British membership. Galbraith received some support in his rather dramatic opposition to a well-established policy and he was to repeat his views later. Thus on 21 August 1961 Kennedy sent Ball a memorandum stating that he was concerned about the economic effect upon the United States if Britain joined the EEC. "I have been informed that the effect will be extremely serious."

Despite such pressure, there was to be no basic change in Washington's encouragement of European integration. Even in the August memorandum the President confirmed about past US policy that "We have been in the position, of course, of encouraging the expansion of the common market for political reasons." The political reasons for the American attitude had repeatedly been underlined, and they were strongly expressed even under Kennedy.

For these same political reasons the Kennedy administration was in fact pushing more directly than its predecessor for British membership of the EEC, but, as we have seen, Washington was clearly against a simply commercial arrangement between the Six and Britain. As Kennedy told Macmillan in May 1961, it was because of this political conviction that the US had been willing "to face the prospect of significant—although we hope temporary—economic disadvantage to the United States in the spread of the Common Market." A customs union alone for the EEC, Britain, and possibly other EFTA countries would be an economic challenge to the US, without compensating political advantages, and "we should be most reluctant to see such a result." Similarly, Washington did not want the neutral EFTA countries as members of the EEC because that too would mean further economic discrimination against the US without any political compensation.

Kennedy had expressed to Macmillan the hope that the disadvantage to the United States in a European common market would be temporary. But Ball's quick response to Kennedy's memorandum of 21 August was again to present even the economic side in an optimistic light. The Under Secretary of State argued that it was inherent in a European common market that it would discriminate, at least relatively, against American goods, but, in his analysis, the common market would also lead to higher overall growth. This growth would in turn stimulate higher imports also from the United States. With only a quarter of 1 per cent higher growth than would otherwise have been the case, this trade creation would compensate for the trade diversion. Thus, the United States would benefit both politically *and* economically from a highly integrated common market.

The best of all worlds was of course to have as much political integration as possible with as little economic discrimination against the US as possible, and all this with British membership in the EEC and a strong NATO–GATT

framework. Two related economic areas were regarded as particularly difficult for the United States. As was to be expected, the first one was agriculture,
which in 1958 constituted one-third of total US exports to the EEC. Although
agricultural exports to the EEC were going up in absolute numbers, they were
declining relatively, and thus helped less than had been hoped in stemming
the growing balance of payments deficit. Agricultural interests were also
extremely well organized and well represented in Congress. Washington was
therefore quite concerned about the signs of the EEC working out a rather
protectionist agricultural policy.

The preferences extended by the EEC to the member countries' former
colonies represented the second main area of controversy. This point had
particular relevance in connection with British membership. If commercial
privileges were extended to the entire Commonwealth, not only to the
colonies producing tropical products, this would mean a very substantial relative discrimination not only against the United States, but also against Latin
America. Considering the products involved, the latter would be even more
directly affected than the former. While trying to hold direct discrimination to
a minimum, the most promising approach for Washington seemed to be to
work for a general reduction of protectionism through the upcoming Kennedy
round in GATT.

Special Relationships

The term "special relationship" has most frequently been applied to the
US–British relationship after the Second World War. As such the term seems
to have been used first by Winston Churchill in his famous Fulton speech of
5 March 1946. There was no special relationship between the United States
and the United Kingdom before the Second World War. Quite on the contrary,
the disagreements between the two countries at that time were many. As
Robert Skidelsky has argued, the relationship only became special when the
United States clearly became superior to the United Kingdom. In other words,
only "as British power declined and the Soviet threat became paramount" was
a special relationship established. In that relationship the United States led
from a position of strength.[42]

During the Second World War Washington and London frequently disagreed. The two capitals had different views on Britain's imperial role, on the
conditions for America's economic assistance during and after the war, on
military strategy, and on the postwar order. Still, in fighting the war the two
countries cooperated more closely than any other Great Powers in modern
history. Even those historians who later came to doubt the existence of any
such "special relationship" generally accept that during the Second World

War and the first decades after the war the American–British relationship was indeed special. No doubt "special relationship" was a term used much more frequently by British politicians and observers than by American ones.[43] Still, even leading American politicians, if they did not use the term itself, referred at least to the reality behind it. Eisenhower thus wrote a friend that "Britain has not only been, but must be, our best friend in the world." Similarly, Theodore Sorensen, Kennedy's very close special counsel, has stated that "The Western leader whom he [Kennedy] saw first, liked best and saw most often...was British Prime Minister Harold Macmillan."[44]

British thinking was stated with admirable clarity in January 1949 by senior officials from four departments:

Since post-war planning began, our policy has been to secure close political, military and economic co-operation with USA. This has been necessary to get economic aid. It will always be decisive for our security.... We hope to secure a special relationship with USA.... for in the last resort we cannot rely upon the European countries.[45]

For its part, Washington did not want to underline the special nature of the relationship with London too much, since the term could easily imply that something was missing in Washington's relations with capitals other than London. And many prominent American politicians felt that the UK took the notion of an American–British special relationship just too far, using it, for instance, as an excuse to stay out of Europe. The Kennedy administration declared in National Security Action Memorandum 20 April of 20, 1961, that "the UK should not be encouraged to oppose or stay apart from that move-ment [European integration] by doubts as to the US attitude or by hopes of a 'special' relation with the US...and over the long run, it would be desirable if the British decided to phase out the nuclear deterrent."[46]

In some fields the United States undoubtedly cooperated more closely with Britain than with any other power. Atomic weapons illustrated both the strength and the limitations of the relationship. After Congress ended the intim-ate nuclear cooperation of the Second World War, London developed atomic weapons largely on its own, but certainly with Washington in mind. The decision to develop the H-bomb in 1954 and the tests in 1957 also had the United States in mind. The purpose was twofold, to increase independence from the US and to encourage it in the direction of resuming cooperation with Britain. Eisenhower had long wanted to cooperate with Britain, and when in 1958 he was finally able to persuade Congress to modify the McMahon Act of 1946, nuclear cooperation between Washington and London did resume. Similarly, after Britain had to cancel its own Blue Streak project for financial reasons, it came to rely on the United States even for the means of delivery for its nuclear weapons. Despite the Kennedy administration's attitude, as reflected in the NSA Memorandum, at Nassau in December 1962

Kennedy promised Macmillan to provide Britain with Polaris when the Skybolt missile, promised earlier, was cancelled by the administration.

Cooperation was also extremely close with regard to bases. Starting in 1948 the United States wanted to establish new bases in Britain, and in the early years British supervision of these bases was kept to an absolute minimum. So, in view of the already large number of such bases, it was somewhat paradoxical that the stationing of American Polaris submarines in Scotland following the Nassau agreement caused as much public controversy as it did. This probably had to do partly with the openness of the agreement, partly with its explicitly nuclear nature, and partly with the English–Scottish relationship.

In the intelligence field American–British cooperation was far more extensive than that between any other major powers. Here the relationship was somewhat more balanced than in the rather one-sided nuclear field. Intelligence cooperation never stopped entirely after the Second World War. Immediately after the war London gave more than it got, simply to encourage the Americans to resume cooperation; only gradually did Washington reciprocate.[47] In 1947 intelligence cooperation was expanded to include Canada, Australia, and New Zealand (the so-called CAZAB link), a most useful association that has been lasting to this very day, and in recent years has become known as Echelon.[48] Later the two countries cooperated about U-2 flights, where British pilots flew some of the missions, and the "running" of the leading Soviet spy in this period, Oleg Penkovsky. There were also joint covert operations. CIA and Secret Intelligence Service (SIS, also MI6) thus cooperated in the successful overthrow of Mossadeq in Iran in 1953 and in the less successful effort to assassinate Congolese Prime Minister Patrice Lumumba in 1960. (Lumumba was indeed killed, but probably not by the CIA–SIS.)

When Macmillan in December 1959 asked his Foreign Secretary, Selwyn Lloyd, precisely what the "special relationship" amounted to, Lloyd answered that "It means preferential treatment for us in the discussion and in certain types of knowledge (nuclear, intelligence, etc.). It certainly gives us considerable influence on United States policy." There was little doubt about the privileged arrangements in the nuclear and intelligence fields. The answer to the question of Britain's influence on US policy is more uncertain.

In the 1950s and 1960s the standard examples of British influence referred to by British politicians and observers are:

1. a moderating impact on the United States during the Korean War;
2. the promotion of some trade with the Soviet Union and Eastern Europe and the nudging of the Americans towards summit meetings with the Soviet leaders;
3. Eden's solution to the German rearmament problem;
4. the test-ban treaty of 1963;
5. finally, the demise of the NATO mulilateral force in 1964–5.

With the exception of the German rearmament problem where, as we have seen, Eden did indeed play a crucial role, none of these examples is particularly striking. In Korea, Washington was firmly in the driver's seat; American insistence probably made Britain's involvement much larger than it otherwise would have been. On the other hand, Attlee's views did strengthen US forces of moderation in the non-use of atomic weapons, in limiting actions directed against China, and in Truman's ultimate firing of US general Douglas MacArthur as commander of the UN troops, although it can hardly be argued that Britain's attitude actually determined any of these outcomes.[49] London's work to cut down on embargoed items in trade with the East was important enough, but of relatively limited importance after all. Churchill's early summit efforts largely failed. The British worked hard to bring about a test-ban treaty and tried to promote compromise on the crucial question of verification, but the treaty was only concluded, and then rather rapidly, when the Soviets accepted a limited treaty with limited verification instead of the comprehensive one that had been their alternative for so long. By 1964–5 the MLF had so many enemies in Washington that the British opposition added little extra.

With no other country did the United States have such deep, broad, and lasting relations as with Britain, yet there were countries that cooperated particularly closely with the United States for more limited periods of time and/or in specific fields. In Germany, at the elite level, Chancellor Adenauer's policies were quite pro-American up to the late 1950s, and the rapport between Adenauer and Dulles was certainly far better than between Dulles and Eden. Most of the American troops in Europe were stationed in Germany, with the huge troop presence causing amazingly little controversy there. The need for protection against the Soviet Union clearly overshadowed the incidents that almost always follow from such a presence. Despite the dislike felt by some conservative circles, American culture was readily accepted in Germany, in part because Washington put much effort into spreading it, but primarily because defeated Germans were so ready to receive it. At the level of public opinion the German image of the United States was, after a surprisingly short period of transition, idealized to an extent witnessed in few European countries.

Still, the overall German–American relationship could not compare with the British–American one. The legacy of the two world wars alone prevented that. In the late 1950s Washington increasingly came to see *der Alte* as too old and dogmatic. This was to be even more noticeable under Kennedy. The American troops were to remain, but there was no nuclear cooperation between Washington and Bonn. Little is known about intelligence cooperation between the United States and West Germany, but, despite the use the Truman administration made of the German Gehlen organization remaining from the war, it is quite unlikely that this relationship was as close as the American–British one. For obvious reasons the differences between American and German culture were much larger than those between American and British culture.

In the case of Norway intelligence cooperation gradually became very close. Due to Norway's geographical position, it had great potential as a listening post directed toward the Soviet Union. The cooperation in intelligence in a way compensated for Norway's reluctance to have American troops and nuclear weapons stationed on Norwegian soil, although there were periods, such as after the shooting down of the U-2 plane on its way to Bodø in northern Norway in May 1960, when Norwegian politicians tightened even intelligence guidelines. While an open American presence on Norwegian soil would not have been acceptable to the Soviet Union or to large segments of the Norwegian public, the very extensive, but partly covert intelligence cooperation with the United States met with few protests from either side.[50] Norwegian military and scientists gradually became almost exclusively oriented towards the United States. On the cultural side few countries were as open to American culture as was Norway. The traditional barriers to such culture, the left together with the Communists and the more "high culture" right, were both weak in Norway.

Yet, these were rather specific fields. Norwegian political, as opposed to military, authorities remained firm in their opposition to foreign troops and atomic weapons on Norwegian soil. In the 1950s Scandinavian social democrats and American Republicans frequently viewed each other with considerable suspicion, as was obvious from Scandinavian denunciations of McCarthyism and of American racial practices and from Eisenhower's sweeping denunciation of the welfare state in 1960. Although Sweden was his primary target, Norway was affected too.[51] On the domestic side, Scandinavians, as other European leftists, definitely felt more comfortable with Democrats than with Republicans in charge in Washington.

The United States also developed interesting relations with some neutral countries and even with one pro-Communist one. Since the most important criterion to fulfill to become a member of the Atlantic community was to stand up to the Soviet Union and to Communism, in allied countries Communists and leftist Socialists thus were unacceptable. Neutral countries represented a special challenge in this context, as in virtually all of them all the major parties supported neutrality. One category consisted of those countries like Switzerland, Austria, and Ireland that were committed to neutrality by treaty or history. Switzerland's special neutrality was widely accepted. In the Austrian case the state treaty of 1955 represented a victory for the West, in that the Soviet Union was finally willing to pull out of its zone of the country, so that neutrality was thus an acceptable concession for the Soviet move. Ireland had its historic problems with Britain in the North. Little or nothing was done to induce these three counties to become members of NATO, nor did Washington want them as members of the

EEC since that would only weaken the political dimension of the European integration effort. Culturally, however, they were clearly Western oriented, and were included in several of the American cultural programs to make sure they stayed that way.

Sweden was a different case. In 1948–9 Washington clearly wanted Sweden to become a member of NATO, while London showed somewhat greater understanding for the Swedish position, particularly its role in relation to exposed Finland. In the early 1950s Washington softened its position. With Norway, Denmark, and Iceland in NATO, the US could relax a bit. Sweden had been unable to persuade its strategically more important neighbors to remain neutral. Now it made effective use of the argument that its weapons were pointed in one direction only, against a possible Soviet invasion. It could indeed contribute to the effective defense of Scandinavia, and secretly Stockholm developed considerable military ties not only with Oslo and Copenhagen, but also with Washington. Intelligence about the Soviet Union was shared; plans were developed for the use of Swedish airfields in wartime; weapons systems and military technology exchanged, beginning with a "private" agreement between Truman and Swedish Prime Minister Tage Erlander in 1952. While staying out of CoCom, Sweden to a large extent complied with the embargo on export of strategic goods to the Soviet Union and Eastern Europe. As for culture, Sweden was very Western indeed in its orientation.[52]

Washington's appraisal of Finland moved somewhat in the opposite direction. In the first years after 1945 Finland was unique in the sense that developments there were acceptable to Moscow as well as to Washington and London. On the basis of the country's history and geography, the Truman administration encouraged Finland to follow a foreign policy primarily oriented towards the Soviet Union. The Finns were seen as pursuing such a policy largely for pragmatic reasons, not for reasons of conviction as in the Czechoslovak case. In the 1948 crisis Helsinki was admired for the firm way in which it had handled a most difficult situation with the Soviet Union. In the 1950s, however, Washington came to feel that Helsinki carried its cooperation with Moscow a bit far and that it had become too good at determining whatever signals that might be coming from the Kremlin. There was too much conviction and too little pragmatism.[53]

Only in the very special case of Tito's Yugoslavia was Washington, like other Western capitals, prepared to cooperate with a Communist state. In Western Europe it was out of the question to work with Communists, but since Tito had been a particularly activist Communist with whom Stalin had then broken in 1948, the situation was clearly different here. In the years 1948–50 the Truman administration was still trying to understand what had actually happened in Yugoslavia and what Tito's new role would be. After 1950 Washington was to support Tito in many different ways. It had become evident that Tito's survival would represent a defeat for Stalin and could encourage diversity in Eastern Europe. Yet, the American–Yugoslav relationship was one of convenience, not of shared ideals.[54]

The United States and Western Europe: If So Strong, Why So Many Concessions?[55]

America was the undisputed leader of the "free world." It exerted great power over the military, political, and economic structure within which all America's allies had to operate. America's overall design was rather loose and flexible. Washington's basic objectives were all largely fulfilled, although most countries went rather shorter on the road to economic multilateralism than Washington desired. In this most comprehensive perspective much of the rest could be seen as details which did not really warrant all-out stands. The United States had tremendous influence in the occupied countries, and this influence continued in somewhat modified form even after West Germany became formally independent. Frequently Washington had a very significant impact also on matters in non-occupied countries. This was particularly true when Washington had considerable local suppport for its position, as was almost always the case.

Yet, the United States was far from omnipotent. The wartime planners' dream of an effective world organization came to nothing. Instead of "one world" there would be two, East and West. In the East the United States had very little influence indeed. In the West, despite its tremendous strength, the United States frequently compromised. There were American half-successes such as the increasing cooperation and integration of Western European countries, the introduction of full currency convertibility in 1958, the imposition of restrictions on trade with Eastern Europe, and the increased defense expenditures in Western Europe. These were only half-successes in that Britain, and the smaller countries that still followed Britain in such matters, refused to join any supranational European grouping, be this the European Coal and Steel Community, Euratom, or the European Common Market; and full currency convertibility came at least ten years later than the Americans had hoped. As soon as the Cold War subsided somewhat, particularly after Stalin's death and the end of the Korean War, the European trade restrictions and defense increases were modified more than Washington would have liked. The different countries simply followed different policies, although some deference was naturally shown to what the Americans wanted.

Then there were the outright refusals to heed America's advice. The French national assembly refused to ratify the plans for the EDC despite Dulles's threat of "an agonizing reappraisal" of America's attitude to Europe. The troop issue was quite problematic: Eisenhower insisted that the American troops were in Europe only as a temporary measure, that the Europeans ought to handle the long-term problem by themselves. As early as the end of his first year, the President was nevertheless forced to conclude that "Unhappily, however, the European nations have been slow in building up their military forces and have now come to expect our forces to remain in Europe indefinitely." In the nuclear field first the British and then the French built their own forces, generally to Washington's dislike, particularly under Kennedy.

However, America's defeats were not as dramatic as they sounded. The EDC lost out, but West Germany was brought into NATO; the Europeans did increase the number of troops, and their failure to do even more had the somewhat redeeming effect of further strengthening America's domination of NATO; the British did not join Europe, but worked closely with Washington and integrated their deterrent with America's; de Gaulle's first years in power were actually seen by Washington as relatively positive. When America felt its overall position was threatened, it could act swiftly and directly. Suez in 1956 and the Franco-German treaty in 1963 were to provide the clearest evidence of Washington's ability to put even the largest allies in their place.

Yet, there *was* a discrepancy between America's vast strength and the more limited influence it frequently exerted over its allies and friends. Many reasons can be found for this discrepancy. One set of reasons had to do with the ways in which Washington more or less directly weakened its own leverage.

First, sometimes the United States consciously promoted arrangements that reduced its role because it recognized its own strength as excessive. As William Borden has argued, "the sheer economic supremacy of the United States...caused a tremendous imbalance in the world economy that threatened both the prosperity of the United States and its foreign policy objectives." Western Europe (and Japan) had to be rebuilt and integrated, within limits discrimination against US goods was even encouraged, etc. Yet, there was nothing automatic here. In the interwar period the United States had shown that it was quite possible to pursue policies far less enlightened than it did after the Second World War.

Second, American leverage was limited by the official ideology, by the right any country had to choose its own government and policies. (This applied especially to the democratic governments in Western Europe.) Cold War revisionists are fond of quoting William Clayton, the negotiator of the 1945 loan to Britain, when in response to criticism that he had not done enough to stop socialism, he stated that "We loaded the British loan negotiations with all the conditions that the traffic would bear." He went on to say, however, and this part is less frequently quoted:

I don't know of anything that we could or should do to prevent England or other countries from socializing certain of their industries if that is the policy they wish to follow. The attempt to force such countries to adopt policies with respect to their domestic economies contrary to their wishes would, in my opinion, be an unwarranted interference in their domestic affairs.

Similarly, as we shall see, in France Washington certainly came to regret de Gaulle's anti-NATO and anti-US policies, but there was very little it could do as long as the French people had expressed their preference as clearly as they had.

On many occasions Washington actually circumscribed its own influence quite directly. Thus, the European Recovery Program, which undoubtedly represented the single strongest American lever, was to be worked out primarily by the Europeans themselves. Although the American role clearly exceeded the "friendly advice" foreseen, much was indeed left to the Europeans. For instance, to a large extent they decided how the American aid was to be divided up among the participating countries. In a rather paradoxical twist, Belgian leader Paul-Henri Spaak in 1954 blamed the United States for the lack of unification in Western Europe. The alleged reason was Washington's "over-generous policy": the Americans "had missed a golden opportunity when at the outset of the Marshall Plan they did not make all Marshall aid contingent upon the creation of a unified political community in Europe."

Third, occasionally the American political system was an obstacle to strong and concerted action. America was strong, but in many ways weakly organized to exert this strength. The system's many checks and balances frequently made decisionmaking a rather cumbersome process. The divided nature of the American political system, in addition to its openness, also gave foreigners a rather unique access and chance to influence the outcome. Within the executive branch there would almost always be some who defended the position others wanted to modify. For example, the Treasury Department on the whole favored a relatively pure multilateral world open to American business while the State Department showed much greater sympathy for political considerations, including the views of foreigners; the State Department tended to receive the support of both Presidents Truman and Eisenhower; "localitis," in the form of strong sympathy for a foreign country, was widespread within the geographical offices of the State Department and most local US embassies.

Then, there was another related set of reasons that served to weaken the bargaining power of the US and strengthen that of the allies. These were not, like the first set, primarily products of America's political system or of its own decisions, but instead either flowed from more indirect circumstances or had to do with the nature of America's partners.

First, since the Europeans well realized that Washington had essential reasons of its own for pursuing the policies it did, American threats to back out of Europe tended to lack credibility. This is another way of saying that before the United States was really committed to Europe, it had great leverage. Once the commitment had been made, the leverage became smaller. Whatever leverage remained after the formation of NATO and the build-up of American strength in 1950–1 was significantly reduced with Eisenhower's election in 1952 and the gradual disappearance of the unilateralist–isolationist alternative. This point was well illustrated in the French EDC debate. Dulles's threat of an "agonizing reappraisal" of the American role in Europe was quite simply not credible. Even before the negative vote in the French assembly, the key American ambassadors in Europe reported that "the agonizing reappraisal had not in general been taken seriously." The Americans would not withdraw. Then, the alternative of bringing West Germany directly into NATO was well known in advance and was seen by quite a few on both sides of the Atlantic as at least as satisfactory as the EDC solution itself, although this was rarely explicitly stated because so much prestige had been committed to the EDC and because it was feared that to suggest alternatives would only prolong the French process further.

More generally, whenever Washington reflected on the possibility of threatening to "bring the boys home," four main reasons strongly discouraged this course. First, such threats would, even if they were not actually carried out, strengthen the Soviet Union in its competition with the West, definitely not the image of allied relations that Washington wanted to project. If carried out, Moscow would achieve one of its main objectives and the risk of war might even increase. Second, the threats would also stimulate Adenauer and West Germany's "neurotic fears regarding US disengagement from Europe." At worst they might even encourage West Germany to develop its own nuclear weapons to compensate for the American withdrawals. Third, after de Gaulle had come to power, the threats would play directly into the general's hands in that they seemed to confirm his warnings about the unreliability of the United States. Finally, as just mentioned, threats lacked credibility because the US had its own reasons for staying in Europe.[56]

With the US in, Washington was bound to dominate NATO. Political economists have made us realize that public or collective goods theory applies to alliances as well as to national and local matters. One aspect of the domination was that since the hegemon—the United States—would provide the good in question (for instance security) largely on its own, there was less of an incentive for the allies to come up with substantial contributions, particularly if these were as controversial domestically as they often were. The temptation was then great for the allies to take America's role for granted and pursue policies that demanded less of themselves.

Second, some countries were so strong and so insistent on certain points that if the United States were to achieve its will, this would at best be only after a bitter struggle. Britain was America's closest ally, but on some questions also its main challenge. It was financially weak, but it still carried considerable political weight. When, in 1947, the British were forced to make sterling convertible and this led to the collapse of Britain's foreign exchange position, Washington could not very well drive Britain into bankruptcy. Britain also simply refused to join continental schemes that would dilute its sovereignty. Here too Washington eventually adjusted. Finally, the Attlee government had established a comprehensive system of social welfare and economic regulations. Many US policymakers thought this system went too far, but could do little to change it, and once it was "permitted" in Britain it had to be accepted in the smaller Western European countries as well. In this respect the protection offered by the British was a prominent element in the policies of, especially, the Scandinavians.

There is also the phenomenon referred to as "the tyranny of the weak." Attempts to apply pressure on the Europeans might, as one official put it, be a "successful operation, but the patient would be dead." This was the primary reason why, for instance, the many ways of using Marshall Plan counterpart funds to pressure various centrist governments in France so often failed. The alternatives, the Communists on the left and the Gaullists on the right, were simply unpalatable to Washington. In the EDC debate both Eisenhower and Churchill referred to what they called "the tyrannical weakness of the French Chamber."

Even occupied West Germany had considerable leverage in its dealings with the United States, for while Adenauer was dependent on the United States, the US in turn became dependent on Adenauer. If the "Allied" Chancellor did not do well, Kurt Schumacher and the SPD would probably take over. Initially Washington had preferred a CDU–SPD coalition government, but with the SPD coming out so strongly against NATO, support for Adenauer's party was stepped up. In a longer perspective, to hold Germany down could lead to new nationalism, possibly even to a new Hitler, or, more likely, bring about its increased cooperation with the Soviet Union, another Rapallo. Thus, one State Department memorandum concluded that Adenauer was "bargaining with us from what is essentially a position of strength."

Notes

1. For an extensive survey of the American system of bases, see C. T. Sanders, *America's Overseas Garrisons: The Leasehold Empire* (Oxford: Oxford University Press, 2000).
2. Valur Ingimundarson, *The Struggle for Western Integration: Iceland, the United States, and NATO during the First Cold War* (Oslo: Institute for Defense Studies, no. 3, 1999), 46–59.
3. Ian Jackson, *The Economic Cold War: America, Britain and East–West Trade, 1948–63* (Houndmills: Palgrave, 2001).
4. For the centrality of Europe in American strategy, see for instance Robert Osgood's still useful *NATO: The Entangling Alliance* (Chicago: University of Chicago Press, 1962).

5. This important distinction within realism between the threat itself and the perception of the threat is made in Stephen M. Walt, *Origins of Alliances* (Ithaca: Cornell University Press, 1987).

6. Karl W. Deutsch et al., *Political Community and the North Atlantic Area: International Organization in the Light of Historical Experience* (Princeton: Princeton University Press, 1957). See also Emanuel Adler and Michael Barnett (eds.), *Security Communities* (Cambridge: Cambridge University Press, 1988), 6–7; John Duffield, "The North Atlantic Treaty Organization: Alliance Theory," in Ngaire Woods (ed.), *Explaining International Relations Since 1945* (Oxford: Oxford University Press, 1996), 337–54.

7. Jeffrey Glen Giauque, *Grand Designs & Visions of Unity: The Atlantic Powers and the Reorganizaton of Western Europe, 1955–1963* (Chapel Hill: University of North Carolina Press, 2002), 98–103.

8. The story about the preparations for the Geneva summit and the summit itself is told in Günter Bischof and Saki Dockrill (eds.), *Cold War Respite: Geneva 1955* (Baton Rouge: Louisiana University Press, 2000). For Churchill's plans, see also Klaus Larres, *Churchill's Cold War: The Politics of Personal Diplomacy* (New Haven: Yale University Press, 2002), chs. 11–16.

9. See e.g. John P. S. Gearson, *Harold Macmillan and the Berlin Wall Crisis, 1958–62: The Limits of Interest and Force* (Basingstoke: Macmillan, 1998).

10. Andrew M. Johnston, "Mr. Slessor Goes to Washington: The Influence of the British Global Strategy Paper on the Eisenhower New Look," *Diplomatic History*, 22:3 (1989), 361–98.

11. Robert S. Norris, William M. Arkin, and William Burr, "Where They Were," *The Bulletin of Atomic Scientists*, 55:6 (Nov./Dec. 1999), 26–35.

12. The account of the IRBMs is based largely on Philip Nash, *The Other Missiles of October: Eisenhower, Kennedy, and the Jupiters 1957–1963* (Chapel Hill: University of North Carolina Press, 1997). For Ball's comment, see Elisabeth D. Sherwood, *Allies in Crisis: Meeting Global Challenges to Western Security* (New Haven: Yale University Press, 1990), 122.

13. Mark Smith, *NATO Enlargement During the Cold War: Strategy and System in the Western Alliance* (Basingstoke: Palgrave, 2000); Athanassopoulou, *Turkey: Anglo-American Security Interests, 1945–1952*, 183–230.

14. James Kurth, "The Next NATO: Building an American Commonwealth of Nations," *The National Interest*, 65 (Fall 2001), 10–11.

15. Ernest R. May, "The American Commitment to Germany, 1949–1955," in Lawrence S. Kaplan (ed.), *American Historians and the Atlantic Alliance* (Kent: Kent State University Press, 1991), 53.

16. Alan P. Dobson, "The USA, Britain, and the Question of Hegemony," in Geir Lundestad (ed.), *No End to Alliance. The United States and Western Europe: Past, Present and Future* (Houndmills: Macmillan, 1998), 157.

17. Bureau of the Census, *Historical Statistics of the United States: Colonial Times to 1970* (Washington, DC: Government Printing Office, 1975), 872–4; Knut Eriksen and Helge Pharo, *Kald krig og internasjonalisering 1949–1965. Norsk utenrikspolitikks historie*, bind 5 (Cold War and Internationalization 1949–1965.

The History of Norwegian Foreign Policy, vol. 5) (Oslo: Universitetsforlaget, 1997), 74–5.

18. Simon Duke and Wolfgang Krieger (eds.), *US Military Forces in Europe: The Early Years, 1945–1970* (Boulder: Westview, 1993), 3–10, 269–72; Hubert Zimmermann, *Money and Security: Troops, Monetary Policy, and West Germany's Realtions with the United States and Britain, 1950–1971* (Cambridge: Cambridge University Press, 2002), 87–95.

19. The quotation is from Stephen Ambrose, *Eisenhower: The President* (New York: Simon & Schuster, 1984), 143–4. For a general presentation of the questions of conventional forces and defense budgets, see John S. Duffield, *Power Rules: The Evolution of NATO's Conventional Force Posture* (Stanford: Stanford University Press, 1995), 28–111.

20. Charles S. Maier, "The Two Postwar Eras and the Conditions for Stability in Twentieth-Century Western Europe," *American Historical Review*, 86:2 (1981), 333–4; Michael Hogan, *The Marshall Plan: America, Britain and the Reconstruction of Western Europe, 1947–1952* (Cambridge: Cambridge University Press, 1987). I have discussed their corporatist views in "The United States, the Marshall Plan and Corporatism," in *Maktpolitik och Husfrid: Studier i internationell och svensk historia tilägnade Gøran Rystad* (Power Politics and Domestic Peace: Studies in International and Swedish History Dedicated to Gøran Rystad) (Lund: Lund University Press, 1991), 279–94.

21. Many studies exist of these elites, particularly on the American side. See, for instance, Walter Isaacson and Evan Thomas, *The Wise Men: Six Friends and the World They Made* (New York: Simon and Schuster, 1986); David Halberstam, *The Best and the Brightest* (New York: Random House, 1972). For a recent study with a more transatlantic perspective, see Klaus Schwabe, "Do Personalities Make a Difference," in Kathleen Burke and Melvyn Stokes (eds.), *The United States and the European Alliance since 1945* (Oxford: Berg, 1999), 239–67. For Helmut Schmidt, see his *Menschen und Mächte* (Men and Powers) (Berlin: Siedler, 1987), 159–71, 265–8.

22. Georges-Henri Soutou, "France and the Cold War, 1944–63," *Diplomacy and Statecraft*, 12:4 (Dec. 2001), 42–3.

23. Volker R. Berghahn, *America and the Intellectual Cold Wars in Europe* (Princeton: Princeton University Press, 2001). For information on Bilderberg, see www.bilderberg.org.

24. The CIA story is told in many places, most recently in Richard J. Aldrich, *The Hidden Hand: Britain, America and Cold War Secret Intelligence* (London: John Murray, 2001), 447–63. The Ford Foundation story is well told in Berghahn, *America and the Intellectual Cold Wars in Europe*. The Kissinger quotations are from W. Scott Lucas, "Mobilizing Culture: The State–Private Network and the CIA in the Early Cold War," in Dale Carter and Robin Clifton (eds.), *War and Cold War in American Foreign Policy* (Houndmills: Palgrave, 2002), 92–4. The story about the essay competition is told in Dagfinn Stenseth, *Vitne til historien* (Witness to History) (Oslo: Damm, 2001), 34–40. The argument about the common texts is made in Eric Hobsbawm, *Age of Extremes: The Short Twentieth Century 1914–1991* (London: Michael Joseph, 1994), 283–6.

25. Richard L. Merrit and Donald J. Puchala (eds.), *Western European Perspectives on International Affairs* (New York: Praeger, 1968), 254–5.

26. This story is well told in Berghahn, *America and the Intellectual Cold Wars in Europe*.

27. Richard Pells, *Not Like Us: How Europeans have Loved, Hated, and Transformed American Culture since World War II* (New York: Basic Books, 1997), esp. 205, 219, 220–5.

28. Johan Galtung and Nils Petter Gleditsch, "Norge i verdenssamfunnet" (Norway in the World Community), in Natalie Rogoff Ramsøy and Mariken Vaa (eds.), *Det norske samfunn* (Norwegian Society) (Oslo: Gyldendal, 1975), 782.

29. Bureau of the Census, *Statistical Abstract of the United States, 1989* (Washington, DC: Government Printing Office, 1989), 781.

30. For the American influence in general, see David W. Ellwood, *Rebuilding Europe. Western Europe, America and Postwar Reconstruction* (London: Longman, 1992), 222–40. For France in particular, see Kuisel, *Seducing the French*, 154–71, 176–84.

31. Bureau of the Census, *Historical Statistics of the United States: Colonial Times to 1970*, 870–1.

32. The question of Atlantic integration is further dicussed in my *"Empire" by Integration*, 147–53.

33. This section builds on chs. 4 and 5 in my *"Empire" by Integration*, 38–57.

34. Aldrich, *The Hidden Hand*, 342–70. See also *FRUS*, 1955–7, IX, NSC 5720: Status of United States programs for national security as of June 30, 1957, September 11, 1957, 605.

35. Like Lord Ismay's famous comment about NATO, Russell Bretherton's about the EEC cannot be properly located. Thus, although it certainly expresses a dominant view at the time, it may not even have been uttered. For this, see Hugo Young, *This Blessed Plot: Britain and Europe from Churchill to Blair* (Houndmills: Macmillan, 1998), 92–4.

36. William I. Hitchcock, *The Struggle for Europe: The History of the Continent since 1945* (London: Profile Books, 2003), 181.

37. Giauque, *Grand Designs & Visions of Unity*, 17–34.

38. This section largely follows chapter 3 in my *"Empire" by Integration*, 13–28.

39. Memorandum of Selwyn Lloyd to Prime Minister Churchill, PM/MS/53/254, 22 June 1953, in Public Record Office, London, U.K. PREM 11/673. Here quoted from Klaus Larres's review of Thomas Banchoff, "The German Problem Transformed," *Journal of Cold War Studies*, 4:2 (Spring 2002), 116.

40. This section largely follows ch. 7 in my *"Empire" by Invitation*, 83–98.

41. Federico Romero, "Interdependence and Integration in American Eyes: From the Marshall Plan to Currency Convertibility," in Alan S. Milward et al., *The Frontier of National Sovereignty: History and Theory 1945–1992* (London: Routledge, 1993), 155–81. The quotation is from 179. See also Milward's contribution, "Conclusions. The Value of History," particularly 198–200 and Romero, "US Attitudes to Integration and Interdependence: The 1950s," 103–21, particularly 116.

42. Robert Skidelsky, "Imbalance of power," *Foreign Policy*, 129 (March/April 2002), 46–55.

43. For a good collection of essays on the relationship, see Wm. Roger Louis and Hedley Bull (eds.), *The "Special Relationship": Anglo-American Relations Since 1945* (Oxford: Clarendon Press, 1986). See also John Dumbrell, *A Special Relationship: Anglo-American Relations in the Cold War and After* (Houndmills: Macmillan, 2001).

44. Geoffrey Warner, "De Gaulle and the Anglo-American 'Special Relationship' 1958–1966: Perceptions and Realities," in Pierre Melandri, Maurice Vaisse, and Frederic Bozo (eds.), *La France et l'OTAN 1949–1996* (Bruxelles: Complexe, 1996), 247–52.

45. Kathleen Burk, "War and Anglo-American Financial Relations in the Twentieth Century," in Fred M. Leventhal and Roland Quinault (eds.), *Anglo-American Attitudes From Revolution to Partnership* (Aldershot: Ashgate, 2000), 254.

46. *FRUS*, 1961–3, XIII, Policy Directive, NATO and the Atlantic Nations, 20 April 1961, 286–7.

47. Aldrich, *The Hidden Hand*, 83–8.

48. Stella Rimington, *Open Secret: The Autobiography of the Former Director-General of MI5* (London: Hutchinson, 2001), 205–9; Dumbrell, *A Special Relationship*, 132–4.

49. For a summing-up of Britain's role during the Korean War, see Peter Lowe, "Waging Limited Conflict: The Impact of the Korean War on Anglo-American Relations, 1950–1953," in Dale Carter and Robin Clifton (eds.), *War and Cold War in American Foreign Policy, 1942–62* (New York: Palgrave Macmillan, 2002), 133–55.

50. Olav Riste, *Norway's Foreign Relations—A History* (Oslo: Universitetsforlaget, 2001), 217–25.

51. See for instance Jussi M. Hanhimäki, *Scandinavia and the United States: An Insecure Friendship* (New York: Twayne, 1997), 70–102.

52. Commission on Neutrality Policy, *Had There Been a War...: Preparations for the Reception of Military Assistance 1949–1969* (Stockholm: Fritzes, 1994). For short accounts of Sweden's situation, see Mikael af Malmborg, "Sweden—NATO's Neutral 'Ally'? A Post-Revisionist Account," in Gustav Schmidt (ed.), *A History of NATO: The First Fifty Years* (Houndmills: Palgrave, 2001), vol. 3, 295–303; Simon Moores, " 'Neutrals on our Side': US Policy towards Sweden during the Eisenhower Administration," *Cold War History*, 2:3 (April 2002), 29–62.

53. A good account of the Finnish case is found in Jussi M. Hanhimäki, *Containing Coexistence: America, Russia, and the "Finnish Solution," 1945–1956* (Kent: Kent State University Press, 1997).

54. See for instance Lorraine M. Lees, *Keeping Tito Afloat: the United States, Tito, and the Cold War* (University Park: Penn State University Press, 1997).

55. With some revisions, this section largely follows my *The American "Empire,"* 70–81.

56. NA, Record Group 59, The Papers of Charles E. Bohlen, Box 26, Memorandum for the President: Answers to Eight Questions, 17 June 1962.

4

De Gaulle's Challenge to America's Hegemony, 1962–1969

A Period of Transition

Sometimes it is difficult for a historian to decide where one chapter should end and the next one begin. Thus it may seem awkward to begin a chapter on de Gaulle's challenge to America's hegemony in 1962, as I have decided to do, when the general in fact came to power in 1958, but there are two sound reasons for doing this. First, as we shall see shortly, Washington was initially quite favorable to de Gaulle's coming to power in France, seeing him as an improvement on the weak governments of the Fourth Republic, and not until 1962 did the Kennedy administration reverse the positive judgement formed by Eisenhower. Second, although in many ways the celebration of the United States in Western Europe reached its climax in 1963 with President Kennedy's trip to Europe, it would be wrong to let the previous chapter on the Atlantic Community run to 1963, because by then the feud between Washington and Paris was very bitter indeed.

Kennedy's trip to Europe (West Germany, Ireland, Britain, and Italy) in June 1963 was undertaken in direct response to de Gaulle's challenge to the United States in January of that year in the form of vetoing Britain's membership of the EEC and of concluding the Franco-German treaty. The trip was a huge success. Everywhere the President went he was met with huge crowds. The climax was reached in Berlin when he declared that "All free men, wherever they live, are citizens of Berlin, and, therefore, as a free man, I take pride in the words '*Ich bin ein Berliner*'." In particular the trip began to improve relations between the United States and the Western European left, not only in the countries Kennedy visited, but also elsewhere. The moderate left definitely preferred the young liberal American president to his old conservative predecessor. In Italy the new administration and the President's visit to Italy produced in December 1963 that *apertura a sinistra* (opening to the left) that had been so long anticipated, when the reformed Nenni Socialists finally joined the Italian government that had been firmly controlled by the Christian Democrats since 1948. But not until Nenni moved toward support for NATO did he win the acceptance of both Washington and Rome that was needed for such a significant change. In Germany Kennedy met an admirer in the young SPD leader Willy Brandt. In Britain Labour leader Hugh Gaitskell and Kennedy took a liking to each other. Even in France many came to admire JFK, but here the scene was entirely dominated by de Gaulle.[1]

The Atlantic structure that had been created in the first years after 1945 was to prove remarkably stable. NATO received the broad support both of governments and the general public; American troops remained in Western Europe, with little or no pressure in Europe to have them leave. On the economic side, while American economic assistance tapered off in the 1950s, the 16.7 billion dollars that Western Europe received in military assistance from 1950 to 1970 was most welcome.[2] US investment in Western Europe increased rapidly. While in 1950 such investment stood at 1.7 billion dollars, about one-seventh of total US investment abroad, by 1970 it had grown to 24.5 billion— about one-third of total US investment abroad. European governments virtually competed to attract American capital.[3] On the cultural side, new generations of Europeans were welcoming the American mass culture for which they were a fast-expanding market.

Yet, it was inevitable that friction existed between the United States and Western Europe. Even in the formative years from 1945 to 1950, when the European emphasis had been on invitations to the United States, there had been extensive bargaining about the conditions under which the Americans were to come in. Naturally, there were almost always conditions attached to the American presence: defense budgets had to be increased, Communists and "fellow-travellers" had to be kept out of governments, West Germany had to be integrated into the Atlantic structure, trade with the Soviet Union and Eastern Europe curtailed, barriers to US trade and investment and to the flow of American culture dismantled.

For Europeans who had been used to playing the leading roles on the international stage, it could be difficult now to pass the torch on to Washington. In 1957 French historian Amaury de Riencourt described the "American expert, adviser, army officer, proconsul, diplomat, and businessman" as "the Roman of our times." André Visson, a European-born American writer, agreed that the United States had a duty to "maintain order," just as the Romans once did, but although Europe had to follow the American lead, Europeans refused to concede that the United States had also become the cultural center of the world. "And so they were free to scorn America, much as the Greeks had condescended to Rome."[4]

The temptation was great to take the welcome American economic, political, and military presence for granted and then to complain about the many ways in which the Americans influenced various national priorities. This was what happened in France under de Gaulle, though the change was gradual in that France had presented problems for the United States even before de Gaulle came to power in 1958 and at first the general was seen as a definite improvement on his predecessors.

Although the French President came to want NATO as such to continue, and definitely favored both the American nuclear guarantee to Western Europe and American troops in Europe (but not in France!), he took strong exception to Washington's views on many important foreign policy issues. De Gaulle's emphasis on the French role was to present a serious challenge to the American-defined Atlantic structure, with Germany the primary battleground for the French–American conflict. West Germany had been the most loyal of America's NATO partners, but in the 1960s signs were multiplying that it too was beginning to stake out a more independent course.

Other factors than de Gaulle and France were also to challenge Atlantic stability. The war in Vietnam was to have an even greater impact on the general public than on the governments of Europe. The growing détente between East and West after the Cuban missile crisis threatened to modify the very foundation of an Atlantic unity that had been forged to face the Soviet threat. Then there were aspects of American influence, not to say interference, which, though acceptable enough in the first years after the Second World War, were no longer so. The Atlantic relationship had to be redefined in the light of Europe's renewed strength. Such redefinitions are always difficult. The Americans insisted that the Europeans now do more to defend themselves and to support the West in general; the Europeans emphasized that now they had to be heard and respected to a much greater degree than previously.

Therefore, with the jealousies and the differences that existed between the two sides of the Atlantic it was remarkable that de Gaulle gained as little support as he did outside of France. True, even the countries that remained loyal to the United States soon charted a more independent course, including West Germany; yet, in the face of the strong challenge from de Gaulle, all the other NATO allies were determined to show that they stood together under America's leadership.

France and the United States before 1962

The governments of the Fourth Republic definitely wanted the United States to commit itself to the defense of Europe in the form of the nuclear guarantee and an American troop presence in Europe, including France. In NATO's early years, deterrence rested primarily on America's nuclear weapons and the Washington's strategy of "massive retaliation" was firmly supported by European capitals, including Paris; this insistence on massive retaliation created a heavy dependence on the US, with Europe's defense left largely to the Americans. Although American tactical nuclear weapons were not stationed on French soil because Washington and Paris could not agree on the control arrangements for them, the French forces in Germany accepted nuclear weapons even when they remained under formal US control; indeed, in 1957–8 the French government was very tempted to accept the American offer from the NATO summit in Paris in December 1957 to station intermediate range ballistic missiles in France itself, but again no agreement was reached on the thorny issue of control before de Gaulle came to power. Moreover, the French had long been hoping for the modification of the McMahon Act so that it could receive some form of nuclear assistance from the United States; and by wanting NATO to provide cover even for the French colonies, Paris was actually giving the United States an opening to influence its colonial policies. The American troop build-up had been rapid during the Korean War from 6,000 US troops in France at the end of 1951 to 38,000 a year later,[5] so there was clearly little doubt in Paris about the essential role of the United States in the defense of Western Europe.

Yet, the signs of a more independent profile had always been there. The idea of a triumvirate of the United States, Britain, and France leading NATO, which de Gaulle was to make so much of, really dated from the very beginning of NATO in 1948–9. Washington had rejected the idea in its most political form, although on the military–technical side it could be said to lie behind the creation of NATO's Standing Group. The decision to develop French nuclear weapons was taken in December 1954. In 1957–8 France had been flirting with the idea of French–German–Italian nuclear cooperation so as to strengthen the French position, but in the end little had come of this, in great part because none of the three partners was willing to strain relations with the United States,[6] but the frustration over the McMahon Act remaining in force was considerable.

Three developments greatly strengthened the French yearning for more independence. First, Paris wanted to see colonial defense as part of NATO's defense, the implication being that NATO was committed to supporting the French effort to hold on to its colonies. Washington disagreed: the French colonies did not formally fall under NATO, and in any case the United States saw itself as an anti-colonial power. Paris was particularly disappointed at the lack of support it received from the United States over Algeria, which it regarded as a part of France; but, despite the fact that Algeria actually fell under the NATO treaty, Washington viewed it as an area that, like other colonial areas, had to receive its independence sooner rather than later. Washington was especially insistent on this since the Algerian Front de Libération Nationale (FLN) was clearly non-Communist and had no special ties with the Soviet Union.[7]

Second, the failure of the Suez expedition in 1956 was to lead to dramatically different conclusions in Britain and in France. Whereas the British decided that never again would they undertake an operation that could lead to such conflict with the United States, the French concluded that even in vital matters they could not really trust the US, and therefore had to become less dependent on it.

Finally, and more subtly, the shift within American and NATO strategy toward reliance on tactical nuclear weapons was interpreted in Paris as a sign that the United States might become a less credible defender of Western Europe against a Soviet invasion. While the US saw the tactical weapons as necessary in part because Europe's planned conventional build-up had not really materialized, Paris feared that they signaled America's retreat from the use of strategic weapons against a Soviet attack. Would the US actually risk its cities for the defense of Europe? Such French fears were to become particularly acute after the Soviets in 1957 had demonstrated that they had intercontinental ballistic missiles (ICBMs) that could reach the US itself.

A revolt of right-wing elements in Algiers led to Charles de Gaulle coming to power in France on 1 June 1958, and the fall of the Fourth Republic. Within a few months de Gaulle created a constitution for the new Fifth Republic based on the strong presidential powers he had first sought in 1945–6: his main objective was to restore the position and "grandeur" of France as much as possible; France had to be accepted into the highest Western circles alongside the United States and Great Britain; France's control over its own territory had to be reasserted at the expense of American base rights; the development of French nuclear weapons had to be speeded up.

De Gaulle had been somewhat skeptical toward the United States even before the Second World War—his upper-class Catholic background probably reduced the attraction of a democratic–popular country dominated by mass production and mass culture. He had been disappointed too by America's military–political withdrawal from Europe after the First World War, as a result of which nothing became of the planned American–British guarantee to France against Germany. To a person like de Gaulle, who was thinking in very long-term historical perspectives, the American withdrawal proved that the United States was not all that firmly committed to Europe.

After the fall of France in June 1940 it immediately became clear to de Gaulle that the future of the West and of France depended on the United States. Yet, even amidst the worst trials of the Second World War, his fears that the United States would undermine France's position, first in the colonies, then in Europe, began to predominate. De Gaulle's skepticism toward the United States was greatly enhanced when President Franklin D. Roosevelt made it so abundantly clear that he did not like him, and indeed regarded the Frenchman as pompous, nationalist, and unrepresentative. Until the invasion of North Africa in 1942 Washington had recognized the Vichy government; then it had tried to work out deals with General Giraud and even Admiral Darlan. Only when all these efforts had failed did Washington, in October 1944, recognize de Gaulle as the legitimate ruler of France. Even in the liberation of France in 1944–5 there had been numerous episodes that illustrated Washington's dislike for what it saw as the arrogance and nationalism of de Gaulle.[8]

Having returned to power in 1958, de Gaulle did not wait long in announcing his desire for major change in allied relations. In September 1958 he presented his dramatic ideas for a world triumvirate, "a world-wide organization" to be created of the United States, the United Kingdom, and France. This organization should, on the one hand, "take common decisions in political questions affecting world security" and, on the other, "draw up and, if necessary, implement plans of strategic action, particularly where the use of nuclear weapons is concerned." In other words, a directorate of the three was to run the Western world, not simply to decide on NATO matters.

Although the memorandum reflected deep elements in de Gaulle's thinking and showed the impact of Algeria, Suez, and Sputnik, its immediate background was constituted by events in Lebanon, Jordan, and Iraq, and in Quemoy–Matsu in 1958. In the Middle East the United States and Britain had intervened in traditionally French-dominated Lebanon without consulting the French; indeed, American bases on French soil had been used without consultation. In China too Washington was apparently willing to risk a major war, again without consulting the French. Time and again de Gaulle was to argue that America's unilaterally determined actions outside the NATO area could result in the involvement of the NATO allies.[9]

The memorandum illustrated the nature of de Gaulle's ambitions; such tripartite cooperation would have far exceeded the nature of American–British cooperation. It is unlikely that de Gaulle actually thought Washington would agree to such an ambitious proposal, but it represented a sign of the kind of change he wanted. In fact, in January 1963 de Gaulle told one of his ministers, Alain Peyrefitte, that the 1958 memorandum was intended as a diplomatic instrument. "I had to find a way to leave NATO, to take back the liberty which the Fourth Republic had given up. So therefore I asked for the moon." When the United States and Britain refused to give him the impossible, de Gaulle was free to draw his own conclusions.[10]

In the near future, some of his rhetoric notwithstanding, de Gaulle did not actually want to push the United States out of Europe; in the somewhat more distant future he hoped that Western Europe under French leadership would become sufficiently strong to take over the functions now performed by the United States—in any case there was always the uncertainty that for their own reasons the Americans would one day simply decide to leave Europe militarily. Despite their early opposition to the EDC, de Gaulle and his Gaullists had in fact supported a German contribution to NATO, a point the general apparently made in a letter to Washington in January 1951.[11]

De Gaulle was a conservative politician and his anti-Communism was evident, particularly in his early years as President. This anti-Communism he shared with Washington; but de Gaulle saw himself as the staunch protector of West Germany against the Soviet Union and resisted Soviet ideas on Berlin so firmly that in the Berlin crisis of 1958–61 he came to feel that Washington was just too willing to negotiate with Moscow. His determination on Berlin was to strengthen his relationship with German Chancellor Konrad Adenauer. Later, in October 1962, de Gaulle was to back Kennedy in his firm response to the Soviet installation of missiles in Cuba, although the French President felt that the Cuban events again underlined the extent to which the United States acted alone in situations that could come to involve its NATO allies in crucial ways.[12]

Yet, in de Gaulle's opinion, since the European countries had become so much stronger than they had been in the early years of NATO, and the United States had become increasingly concerned with events outside of Europe, the American–European relationship had to be redefined; the United States was to constitute a "reserve" or an "arsenal" that the Europeans could draw upon in case of need. This was made explicit by de Gaulle in his conversation with President Kennedy on 1 June 1961, when the French President stated that European defense should be handled by the European powers, not without the US, but "not exclusively through the U.S. … Germany being the vanguard, France the second line of defense, Britain covering the northern flank and insuring communication by sea, and Italy covering the southeast in the Alps. As for the U.S., it would be the reserve to be committed fully but not at the first moment.… the part of the U.S. is to be the arsenal of democracy." De Gaulle made it clear that "the smaller countries count for very little."[13]

To de Gaulle the American threat to France was primarily economic and cultural, although he supported the Marshall Plan; he saw the American role in Europe as a form of hegemony that he called a "protective hegemony." The security threat of course came from the Soviet Union, and while in good times the need for the American presence declined, at those times when the Soviet threat was most evident de Gaulle clearly stressed the importance of the American role in Europe. This had been the case in 1945–6 when the Soviet domination of Eastern Europe became much more direct than he had expected, and it was to happen again, in somewhat milder form, after the Soviet invasion of Czechoslovakia in 1968.[14]

Even with the benefit of hindsight, it is not always easy to reconcile the different strands in de Gaulle's foreign policy thinking. Apparently he wanted the United States to be the guarantor of last resort for Western Europe while limiting its influence as much as possible. It was bad if the United States dominated Europe; but it was probably even worse if it withdrew from Europe, as it had done after the First World War and as de Gaulle thought it would do again, sooner or later. De Gaulle's ambassador to the United States, Herve Alphand, stated in his notebook in August 1963: "De Gaulle is filled with the deepest mistrust because he fears both the hegemony of the US and its disengagement."[15] The balance between these fears certainly fluctuated over time.

In opposition the general had been against a supranational European Economic Community, but only a few days after he took over in 1958 he signalled that he would respect the agreements which France had already signed,[16] including the treaties of Rome. In fact de Gaulle soon came to promote the development of a common foreign and defense policy for the EEC, but, like his policy toward the EEC in general, this was to be based on a combination of French leadership and respect for national, particularly French, sovereignty.

Irving Wall has argued that the United States was largely behind the fall of the Fourth Republic, the coming to power of de Gaulle, and de Gaulle's decision to give up Algeria.[17] This represents a vast overestimation of the American role in France, but it is true that during de Gaulle's first years in power Washington did in fact see him as an improvement on his predecesors; he might be more nationalistic, but would also be much more forceful. De Gaulle could well be the person to alleviate France's "tyrannical weakness," a person with whom it might be possible to reach some sort of agreement that would actually stick, instead of the ever-dragged-out negotiations that had characterized the Fourth Republic.

Early American reactions to de Gaulle were therefore quite favorable, influenced as they were by the analysis that he had saved France from a deep political crisis. For at least two years before de Gaulle came to power, President Eisenhower had actually told anyone interested that "only de Gaulle's accession to power could save France." France's twelve-year history of "chronic instability" under the Fourth Republic "almost demanded the presence of a 'strong man'—in the person of de Gaulle."[18] A National Intelligence Estimate of 29 July 1958 concluded that if de Gaulle should fail, his most probable successor would come from the authoritarian right, and "there would be a prolonged period of serious unrest and possible civil strife with far-reaching consequences for France's position in Europe and NATO." Even in late 1959 the National Security Council concluded that:

There is little question as to France's importance to the Western Alliance, or that the Gaullist experiment offers the best hope in decades of rejuvenating France as a strong ally. Nor is there any argument that a strong if nationalistic France is so important to long-run US interests that, to the extent compatible with US interests, we should do all we reasonably can to accommodate De Gaulle.

So, the full challenge from de Gaulle developed only gradually. What was remarkable about French opinion on NATO was the high percentage of those who were uninformed or refused to answer questions asked by the pollsters. Thus, in polls from 1957 and 1960 respectively 40 and 39 per cent in France answered that they had not even heard about NATO.[19] Yet, even by 1960 it had become obvious that the general would represent a challenge to traditional American leadership in NATO. In 1959 France withdrew its Mediterranean fleet from NATO's command. Moreover, Washington was opposed to de Gaulle's proposal of a triumvirate running NATO or even the (Western) world. No such formal arrangement could be permitted to develop. It gave the wrong impression of Washington's policies and the Eisenhower administration resented the implication in de Gaulle's idea that France would be speaking on Germany's behalf.

Eisenhower still wondered if there were not some way in which the US could get from the so-called Standing Group of the Military Committee already existing in NATO, made up of the US, the UK, and France, to "a real tripartite discussion of strategic and military questions *in return for which de Gaulle would get on with NATO* [emphasis in original]." This search for a compromise that could give de Gaulle some of the substance of tripartite leadership in less direct ways than he had proposed actually continued well into the Kennedy administration. Kennedy was prepared to offer France the position of SACEUR (Supreme Allied Commander, Europe); Ambassador James Gavin in Paris and the Pentagon were advocating the exploration of nuclear cooperation with the French; but in the end these efforts came to nothing. De Gaulle wanted the new status for France to be explicitly recognized, and various indirect offers were therefore not sufficient; Washington was divided on how much to give him, but the skeptics there held the upper hand; Britain and the other NATO allies were reluctant to give France much at all.[20]

The meeting between Presidents Kennedy and de Gaulle in June 1961 (their first and their last) went relatively well, although the disagreement on NATO, particularly on nuclear strategy, was obvious. The United States was strongly opposed to France developing its own nuclear weapons, even after the first French test detonation had taken place in 1960. On the EEC the two did agree, however, that the tying down of Germany was perhaps the most profound reason in its favor.

But even on the EEC the split between France and the United States kept growing: where de Gaulle favored a French-led, slightly protectionist confederation based on the nation-state, Kennedy advocated a supranational group with open borders to the outside world, particularly to the Atlantic community, and to this end he wanted Britain to join the EEC.

The Eisenhower administration had been afraid that British membership of the EEC could not be accomplished without diluting it, and so had really done little to encourage the British to apply. Always optimistic and believing that all good things could be achieved at the same time, Kennedy decided to work more actively to bring Britain in, but again without this having the effect of diluting the EEC significantly: in other words, Britain should accept the full conditions for membership and not insist on solutions also for the EFTA and Commonwealth countries. British membership was necessary to strengthen the EEC's Atlantic orientation, and it could also serve to neutralize America's growing feud with de Gaulle. Washington clearly played down the significance of the so-called "special relationship" between the United States and Britain. The UK should not be encouraged to oppose or stay apart from European integration "by doubts as to the US attitude or by hopes of a 'special' relation with the US." Instead, as a senior member of the administration formulated it, "We hoped that if England went into Europe, it would take a sense of 'special relationship' with it, and that we would then have a 'special relationship' with Europe." On the other hand, the hope was that the integration process in the EEC might have reached the "point of no return" and that the community might therefore be somewhat more flexible now than earlier.

On 31 July 1961 Britain applied for membership in the EEC, a decision which reflected the growing importance of Western Europe in Britain's economic and foreign policy and the declining role of the Commonwealth. The EEC, unlike EFTA, quickly proved a success and Britain had to relate to it—in short, the EEC quite simply showed greater political and economic strength than London had foreseen.[21]

Although official historian Alan Milward is somewhat ambivalent on this point, it appears that America's preference for the EEC and its pressure on Britain to join played an important role in the British decision to apply. Milward concludes that "The British decision to seek membership would have been taken even if the USA had not expressed the wish that it should do so, even though the decision was reactive to the general changes in US policy towards western Europe as a whole." The "special relationship" with the United States now had to be maintained inside the EEC, if there were to be any such relationship at all.[22]

The Crisis Years: The United States, France, Germany, and Britain 1962–1967[23]

Since the United States had long favored the integration of Western Europe, both the Eisenhower and the Kennedy administration also supported de Gaulle's early efforts to have this integration include foreign relations and defense. A Fouchet group, named after French chairman Christian Fouchet, was set up among the six EEC members and produced a preliminary report in October 1961. Its aim was to develop a "Union of States," and its most striking proposal was for a common foreign and security policy based on regular consultations at the highest level among the six member countries. The Kennedy administration supported this idea. It opposed Dutch efforts to stop the initiative; it also opposed suggestions that Britain was to take part in these negotiations even before joining the EEC. In November 1961 the State Department told the relevant American embassies that the administration saw "no more inherent inconsistency between Six role in defense field and NATO than there is between Six role in economic field and OECD."

As de Gaulle became increasingly independent, Washington counted on the other five members of the EEC and later on Britain to control him. This was too optimistic. In January 1962 de Gaulle concluded that his diplomats had been too conciliatory and hardened the French position by having all references to NATO in the Fouchet Plan deleted. Only now did Washington come out against the proposal. But the negotiations broke down primarily because of disagreement between the five (with the partial exception of West Germany) and France, rather than because of the American opposition to de Gaulle's ideas.[24]

Now the American–French relationship was rapidly becoming more strained. The Atlantic approach was very much the cornerstone of Kennedy's Grand Design as presented in Philadelphia on 4 July 1962. The United States was prepared "to discuss with a united Europe the ways and means of forming a concrete Atlantic partnership, a mutually beneficial partnership between the new union now emerging in Europe and the old American Union founded here 175 years ago." Or, as the President put it more succinctly half a year later, the United States wanted "an outward-looking Europe with a strong American connection."

De Gaulle's vision was clearly different from Kennedy's, and the resulting trend was of US relations with France becoming ever more strained. When in early May 1962 Rusk drew up a long list of grievances against the French, stressing their differences on NATO and nuclear weapons, President Kennedy still tried to calm his Secretary of State. At the same time, however, Kennedy himself strongly disliked de Gaulle's "notion that we should stay out of all of Europe's affairs while remaining ready to defend her if war should come."

Well into 1962 the administration nevertheless remained reasonably optimistic about the possibilities of coming to some sort of understanding with Paris. The US objective should be not to attack or isolate de Gaulle publicly, but to let him draw for himself the conclusion that he could not bring the Germans along with him on his European conception; once he recognized how isolated he really was, he would presumably adjust his course.

After the State Department received reports that Adenauer was actually moving closer to de Gaulle, instead of the other way around, Kennedy tried to warn Adenauer that if the British were not admitted to the EEC, this could bring Labour to power in Britain and that "the Labor party did not have any position on Berlin." Adenauer was told that a widened EEC would create economic difficulties for the United States, but political considerations had to prevail. There were three massive power blocs in the Atlantic area, the US, the Six, and then Britain and the Commonwealth. "It was absolutely necessary to join these three blocs more closely together into one Atlantic Community."

In Washington evaluations about the likelihood of Britain actually being able to join the EEC fluctuated somewhat but, the whole, the atmosphere was optimistic. In early December 1962 the State Department concluded that despite serious difficulties with de Gaulle, "His ultimate aims are not irreconcilable with the interests of the West." As Under-Secretary Ball, the person in the Kennedy administration largely responsible for European integration, was to state after the negotiations had failed, the administration "recognized the possibility—although not the probability—that these negotiations [UK–EEC] would break down."

One important tactic in working with de Gaulle was to avoid any image of an Anglo-Saxon bloc. In Washington's analysis, de Gaulle's doubts as to British membership appeared to be based on his fear that Britain would challenge French hegemony and become a permanent spokesman for American interests within the EEC; therefore the United States should not be seen as sponsoring Britain's membership. To this end Washington repeatedly stressed that it was not a party to the negotiations; undue attention should be avoided on the special US–UK relationship in the nuclear field.

This strategy failed. The United States *was* seen as the sponsor of Britain in the negotiations with the EEC. And Washington recognized that a relationship existed between nuclear weapons and European integration, as was reflected in the administration's October instructions to new ambassador to France Charles E. Bohlen. His position on nuclear weapons "should reflect US confidence that movement toward greater unity in Europe and toward a closer US–European partnership will eventually make itself felt in the nuclear field, as elsewhere." The US had to be willing to cooperate with Europe even in the nuclear field. The MLF was the recommended route, however. A different form of partnership already existed in relations with Britain, and Macmillan, who understood the importance of the nuclear issue in the EEC negotiations, encouraged even de Gaulle to approach the Americans.

After Washington had simply cancelled the US–UK Skybolt missile project, at Nassau in December 1962 Kennedy offered Macmillan the American Polaris missile instead. Although Polaris was to be packaged as part of a NATO multilateral force, it was ultimately to be under British control. Kennedy was prepared to give France a similar arrangement, but the administration was too divided to make it explicitly clear to de Gaulle that in actual fact he might now have French nuclear weapons in cooperation with Washington. For de Gaulle no vagueness was acceptable on this point. The

French nuclear project was also considerably behind the British one and thus required even more assistance than London received—France had neither the warheads nor the submarines that Britain already had. The outcome was that in the nuclear field Britain was maintaining its superiority while becoming more dependent than ever on the United States, while France continued its independent role and lagged behind. De Gaulle became furious and denounced Britain for "betraying Europe."[25]

De Gaulle may well have vetoed British membership in the EEC even without the Nassau agreement. After the end of the war in Algeria and his victory in the referendum on direct election of the French President, de Gaulle's position was extremely strong, as was his self-confidence. Britain in the EEC would mean a fundamentally altered structure. The President's famous press conference on 14 January 1963, where he shut the door on Britain, clearly suggested that the differences were fundamental. He likened British participation to the entry of an American Trojan horse, claiming that the EEC "would seem like a colossal Atlantic community under American dependence and direction, and that is not at all what France wanted to do and is doing, which is a strictly European construction." Still, Nassau provided important additional evidence, if that was needed, that Britain was closer to the United States than to Europe, at least in the overall strategic matters that so concerned the general.[26]

De Gaulle's veto on Britain led to a feeling of "distress" in Washington. Still, the State Department did not want to enter into a public discussion with the general, preferring to express to Adenauer the strong hope that the Chancellor could make his leadership felt to prevent a downward turn of events which "could have most serious consequences for all of us." If the other five countries held firm in opposing de Gaulle and the Germans made it absolutely clear that they would accept nothing else, then "de Gaulle may be induced to yield." German firmness was the key in this situation.

When, however, de Gaulle's veto was followed on 22 January with a Franco-German treaty, Washington went into a state of "shock". The treaty aimed at establishing common policies in foreign affairs, defense, education, and youth matters through an extensive system of bilateral meetings. In fact it had been in preparation for some time and the United States had actually supported the treaty early on, considering that as long as it did not develop into "a Bonn–Paris axis" at the expense of NATO and the Atlantic community, French–German reconciliation was highly desirable.

In the new context of what seemed like a direct contest between the American concept of an Atlantic Europe and de Gaulle's European one, Washington's positive position was immediately reversed. Now it disliked the timing of the treaty, the atmosphere in which it was signed, and the fact that it was a formal treaty instead of the set of protocols that had been anticipated.[27] George Ball made it clear that West Germany might soon have "to make a difficult choice between its relationship with France and its ties with the rest of Europe and the US." President Kennedy called the treaty "an unfriendly act" and lectured German ambassador in Washington Heinrich Knappstein on the evils of concluding "a directorate with France" after the United States had tried to protect Germany by refusing to agree to the French idea of a tripartite directorate. Old-time luminaries Acheson, McCloy, and Clay from the days of the Berlin blockade used very strong language in their communications with German officials. Clay was the most dramatic when he told Knappstein that if the treaty was ratified "bedeutet dies das Ende Berlins" (this means the end of Berlin).

Kennedy's strongest fear was that the French would attempt to strike a deal with the Soviets that would also include the Germans. He directed that "we should concentrate our intelligence resources on finding out everything we can about discussions and negotiations between the French and the Russians." (Moscow was in fact strongly against the Franco-German treaty since it feared that Germany could become dominant in the relationship.) The President's language became almost warlike: the United States might not get into "an across-the-board battle with de Gaulle," but Kennedy wanted to be certain that "if de Gaulle continued to harass us, we would be in a position to defend ourselves. The US military position is good but our financial position is vulnerable." Rusk commented that the United States was in Europe not because the Europeans wanted "us there but because we believe our presence there is essential to the defense of the US;" Washington just could not permit de Gaulle "to force us out of Europe without the greatest effort to resist such a move."[28]

The focus was on Germany—for de Gaulle had in a way done no more than could realistically have been feared from him. Washington was bitterly disappointed by Germany and Adenauer. Kennedy stressed that he wanted a strong letter sent to Adenauer, since the United States must not give the Chancellor the impression that he could "have it both ways," close cooperation with Paris as well as with Washington. The President's letter of 1 February appealed for a common front against the Soviet challenge "in Berlin, in the Caribbean, and elsewhere around the world." Germany had to confirm that it belonged to the West, while "Those who feel that 45 billion dollars and 16 years of continuous economic and military assistance have earned us nothing but the hostility of certain European leaders and newspapers" were likely to press for "concepts that would end Western unity." Adenauer simply responded that de Gaulle was a staunch friend of the United States, and was clearly at a loss to understand why the US had responded so dramatically to a treaty it had favored earlier.

Washington's short-term objective now became to have the Franco-German treaty modified by expressions of German loyalty to the United States and to

NATO. With the partial exception of Adenauer, whose fall from power had already started and who wanted to be remembered by his reconciliation with France, the German government quickly agreed to make amends. Most of its key members alleged they had indeed been shocked, first, by the circumstances leading to the treaty and, then, by the strong American reaction to it.

Faced with a choice between Washington and Paris, Bonn was quite explicit: it would choose the former. The outcome of all this was that the declaration of loyalty was included in a preamble to the treaty. The German government also confirmed its preliminary decision to stop the planned delivery of steel pipes to a Soviet project to export gas to Western Europe, deliveries that German industry had been strongly pushing for and 700,000 tons of which had actually already been sold.[29] After Bonn had bowed to Washington in these ways, the State Department could again point out that it really agreed with the basic idea of French–German reconciliation even in the form of a separate treaty.

In a logical, if not in a political, sense the preamble tended to make the treaty meaningless, but despite a strong annoyance, especially on the part of Adenauer, over the Kennedy administration's signals of a more flexible policy on Berlin, the Oder-Neisse border, and even on the existence of East Germany, Bonn had to side with the United States.[30] The US was the primary guarantor of Germany's security, and on a fundamental security issue was clearly more important than France. Kennedy also decided to go on a trip to Europe, including Berlin and Germany, in great part to counter an earlier visit by de Gaulle, and, once again, the Germans were to choose—now between Kennedy and de Gaulle. As we have already seen, Kennedy's visit proved a big success—even bigger than de Gaulle's earlier one—not only in Germany, but in most of Western Europe as well. While Kennedy proclaimed himself a Berliner, for some reason de Gaulle never visited Berlin officially.

De Gaulle's rapidly growing independence and the sympathies he had aroused in Germany did not lead the United States to abandon the goal of European integration, the case for which was still seen as sound and the traditional reasons for US support still existed. At the same time, the alarm over the Franco-German treaty was to have important consequences for American policy. Although Washington's support for him had clearly waned under Kennedy, Adenauer seemed to be a fixture on the German scene, whereas Vice Chancellor and Minister of Economic Affairs Ludwig Erhard had been seen as rather weak and, especially on integration, as too much oriented towards a free trade area at the expense of the cohesion of the Six. After the Franco-German treaty, however, the Kennedy administration became more favorable to Erhard, who himself made it clear to the Americans that he had at best been lukewarm to the treaty. His emphasis on the Atlantic framework was now viewed more sympathetically than previously, and he thus became

Washington's choice; he was clearly encouraged to make a move against Adenauer. London too had become angry at the Chancellor's behavior. American, British, and, most important, widespread German dissatisfaction, both inside and outside his own CDU, with *der Alte's* stubbornness in general and his growing friendship with de Gaulle in particular constituted important factors in Adenauer's resignation and Erhard's taking over as Chancellor in October 1963. And Adenauer had after all reached the advanced age of 87. Still, he complained that "the third dismissal was the worst" (the other two had been by Hitler in 1933 and by the British in 1945).

Britain's membership of the EEC had been seen as the single most important element in strengthening the Atlantic framework. With that element now defeated, or at least long delayed, Washington concentrated on a series of other initiatives, most of which had been developed earlier, but which were now reinvigorated to contain de Gaulle and to buttress the American position in general.

Kennedy had long been pushing the Trade Expansion Act, in part for overall trade purposes, but also to soften the impact on the United States of the EEC outer trade wall and to strengthen basic relations between the two sides of the Atlantic. The Act was clearly framed with the purpose in mind of encouraging British membership in the EEC. In his message to Congress, the President had told the lawmakers that "The two great Atlantic markets will either grow together or they will grow apart." That decision would "either mark the beginning of a new chapter in the alliance of free nations—or a threat to Western unity." The Act passed the House of Representatives in June and the Senate in September 1962, laying the foundation for the Kennedy round in GATT. De Gaulle's veto added urgency to the GATT discussions. Thus, on 30 January 1963 Rusk instructed the key embassies in Europe that the US should be moving ahead as rapidly as possible with negotiations under the Trade Expansion Act. "Progress along this line will tend to minimize the damage that the French veto will cause for all of us."

In trying to strengthen the Atlantic framework, Washington now also put renewed emphasis on the MLF. The idea for this force had originated in the Eisenhower administration in 1960 and was expressed in the form of a fleet of surface ships, or possibly submarines, manned by mixed crews from NATO countries under NATO command. The project was developed in part to counter the growing deployment of Soviet intermediate-range missiles directed at Western Europe. Initially the idea had been to use land-based missiles, but this had proved politically difficult in most European countries and the sea-based MLF was therefore put together.

Even more importantly, the MLF was developed to provide Germany and to some extent Italy with a sense of equality with atomic powers Britain and France, but without giving the Germans direct access to nuclear arms. The underlying analysis was that while France might be the most troublesome ally at the moment, the Federal Republic was in the longer run more threatening. The Germans "will reach point of despair as to their hopes of ever getting their hands on nuclear weapons by multilateral route and will therefore move, surreptitiously at first and then openly, to create their own nuclear force."

Kennedy himself seems to have held a more realistic view of the MLF's limited potential than the many State Department "theologians" on this issue. On 31 January the President did remark, however, that the US had narrowly averted a disaster which would have occurred if the British had decided to join with de Gaulle in a separate European nuclear arrangement. The even bigger fear, that Germany would join with France in some sort of nuclear cooperation, seemed to be only partially relieved by the French insistence that they had absolutely no desire to see a German finger on the French nuclear trigger.

After the Kennedy administration cooled off on the MLF from the summer of 1963, in the spring of 1964 Johnson began to push the idea again. In November 1964 National Security Adviser McGeorge Bundy told the President that all his top advisers still believed that the MLF, although not an end in itself, was the least unsatisfactory means of keeping the Germans well tied into NATO. The CIA apparently feared that Bonn would turn to Paris for nuclear assistance if Washington did not continue to push the MLF. But with Britain and France not really interested; with West Germany divided and some in Bonn supporting the idea because the United States pushed it; with Bundy, Secretary of Defense Robert McNamara, the Pentagon, and the Senate increasingly lukewarm at best; and with the Soviet Union opposed, the scheme was more or less dropped in December, although it formally remained on the table until 1966.

Since the Germans now clearly preferred Washington to Paris, the sense of crisis that de Gaulle had created subsided, and there was less of a need to satisfy the Germans through measures such as the MLF. The German and even the Italian disappointment at the fate of MLF was to show in their rather guarded support for the Non-Proliferation Treaty of 1968, which neither country ratified until 1975, just in time to participate in the first review conference. In the end they had no choice, however. Neither country could openly proclaim any nuclear ambition, but they still disliked having the nuclear option so explicitly taken away from them without obtaining much in return.[31]

The US continued to support the idea of British membership of the EEC. Again, however, the British should be prepared to make concessions to its supranational nature. Washington was still against the EFTA neutrals joining the EEC either as full members or even as associate members, since this would easily come to mean a "lowest common denominator" approach to integration and thereby slow the desired process toward supranationalism.

Thus, membership for the neutrals continued to be negative politically for the US and would also harm its economic interests.

Ever since the defeat of the EDC the various administrations in Washington had underlined that the forms European integration were to take had to be decided primarily by the Europeans themselves. As we have seen, this formal position never stopped Washington from making its views clear, and although under Johnson the United States was actually becoming a less central actor than before, this had at least as much to do with the growing preoccupation with the war in Vietnam as with any change of position on European integration as such.

De Gaulle's independence from the United States and NATO had been growing since he came to power in 1958, as was made abundantly clear by the events of 1962–3. Yet, more was to follow, for many different factors now made it possible for the general to play an increasingly independent role:

- The Western position had been strengthened by the outcome of the Cuban missile crisis, making it less necessary for the West to stand firmly together.
- The tense situation over Berlin had in a way been resolved with the building of the wall between East and West Berlin in August 1961.
- The split between the Soviet Union and China had weakened the Soviet side a great deal.
- Over a long period of time Western Europe had been getting stronger, and was much less dependent on the United States than it had been earlier, both economically and even militarily.
- France had developed its own nuclear force. The first test detonation took place in 1960; the *force de frappe* was operational in 1969.
- In 1962 the Algerian war finally ended. It had been difficult to foresee a dramatic change in France's position in NATO as long as a substantial part of its forces was tied down in Algeria. The French troops that were now pulled back from that country were put under French national control, and not integrated into NATO.
- In 1965 de Gaulle was reelected as President for another seven-year period.
- In January 1966 the crisis in the EEC over supranationality and the funding of the Common Agricultural Policy that in 1965 had led France to boycott the EEC Council of Ministers was resolved and France once again resumed its representation on the Council.

In 1963 the growing independence was seen in the rejection of British membership of the EEC, in the French–German Elysée treaty, and also in the French rejection of the Limited Test Ban treaty; in 1964 it was seen in the French recognition of Communist China; in 1965 in the growing rhetoric about creating a Europe stretching "from the Atlantic to the Urals," where in other words the role of the United States was rather unclear, and in the increasingly bitter denunciation of the role of the dollar in international finance; in 1966 in de Gaulle's withdrawal from the military integration in NATO, in his trip to Moscow, and in his statement that the United States bore sole responsibility for the war in Vietnam; in 1967 in the continued anti-dollar campaign, in the speech about a free Quebec, and in American–French differences over the Six-Day War in the Middle East.

By far the most important of these issues for the American–French relationship was the withdrawal from military integration in NATO. The expectation in Washington had been that de Gaulle would wait until the NATO treaty came up for renewal in 1969 to redefine the overall relationship. This he did not do. On the other hand he did not take France out of the alliance as such, as some had feared, he only removed it from military integration. In fact, *le général* distinguished clearly between the North Atlantic treaty and the alliance as such, which he favored, and the military integration in NATO, which he was against. Thus, in his letter to President Johnson of 7 March 1966 where he announced that France intended "to recover the entire exercise of her sovereignty over her territory, presently impaired by the permanent presence of allied military elements or by constant utilization which is made of her airspace," de Gaulle also reaffirmed that France would remain part of the alliance as such. France would be "in 1969 and thereafter determined even as today to fight at the side of her allies in case one of them will be the object of unprovoked aggression."[32]

The official American response to de Gaulle's action was relatively calm. Although there were many, particularly Rusk, Ball, and the NATO old-timers, who wanted to give a firm, public response to de Gaulle's move—and Ball and Acheson actually did—President Johnson instructed Rusk and McNamara:

I would be grateful if you would make it known that I wish the articulation of our position with respect to NATO to be in constructive terms. I see no benefit to ourselves or our allies in debating the position of the French government. ... we shall develop ... proposals which would bind the Atlantic nations closer together; support, as best we can, the long term movement towards unity in Western Europe; and exploit the possibilities of easing East–West tensions.[33]

Johnson's NSC advisers (Robert Komer, Francis Bator) prevailed against the hardliners. Johnson also stopped an idea to propose a transfer of the latest in American science and engineering, provided, as in the Marshall Plan, Europe developed an integrated framework to put this knowledge to good use. There was to be no ganging up against de Gaulle—LBJ's focus was now definitely on Vietnam and de Gaulle's move had not exactly come as a shock, since he had already withdrawn, in 1959, the French Mediterranean fleet and, in 1963, the Atlantic fleet from NATO control. The Americans had also started to scale down the number of troops in France even before de Gaulle made his announcement, reducing the total number of Americans at the bases there, including civilian dependants, from 57,400 in 1962 to 28,700 in 1965.[34]

Again, much of the concern was with what Germany would do. As Acting National Security Adviser Robert Komer told the President, "The real problem, as always, is not France but Germany." Once again, various ideas for nuclear sharing with Germany were trotted out, but once again led to little of substance. Seven years of trying to contain Germany's nuclear ambition had ended. If nothing else, the whole affair at least illustrated the crucial role of Germany in American policy.

France had after all decided to remain in the alliance, thus proving entirely wrong the intelligence reports that de Gaulle would choose to leave the organization. As the general explained to ambassador Bohlen, the Soviet Union did not appear bellicose any more, but since this could change, France would remain in the alliance.[35] The military consequences of the French withdrawal were also considerably smaller than one could have feared. Thus, the French troops in West Germany remained, although they too were removed from the integrated structure. Strong forces both in Bonn and particularly in Washington wanted to insist on these troops staying integrated in NATO, but again Johnson chose the soft option. The most important thing was after all that the troops were kept in Germany.[36] Under certain conditions US tactical nuclear weapons even remained at their disposal.

The American response to de Gaulle's withdrawal was softened by the fact that not only West Germany, but also all the other members of NATO now reaffirmed their commitment to the alliance, a measure of their determination to show that de Gaulle's challenge in no way represented a threat to NATO as such. De Gaulle's France was isolated. Somewhat surprisingly, the departure of France from NATO's military structure was therefore to make cooperation among the remaining members easier. In December 1966 NATO set up a Nuclear Planning Group where the US could more informally discuss nuclear strategy with its allies, including some of the smaller ones. Not only were the cumbersome disputes about the status of France now ended, but, with the French out, NATO could finally adopt the strategy of flexible response. Although most Europeans were not initially happy to see what could be perceived as a weakening of the American nuclear guarantee to Europe, they accepted that massive retaliation had become outdated. Again Britain had taken the lead on the European side.[37] As we shall shortly see, the United States and West Germany agreed on new offset payments to pay for the costs of the US military presence there. The NATO machinery was streamlined. On top of all this, NATO and Paris were able to reach agreement on close military cooperation in case of war. Secretary of Defense McNamara was in fact so pleased with some of the new arrangements that SACEUR Lyman

Lemnitzer was to complain that "one more benefit of this sort and we will be out of business."[38]

The Harmel Report of December 1967, named after Belgian Foreign Minister Pierre Harmel, was to be the key document in redefining NATO's role in a period of détente. The report underlined that the alliance had two functions. The first was the traditional one, "to maintain adequate military strength and political solidarity to deter aggression and other forms of pressure and to defend the territory of member countries if aggression should occur." In the relationship with the Soviet Union, the second one was new: "to pursue the search for progress towards a more stable relationship in which underlying issues can be solved."[39]

The Harmel Report and the thinking behind it had considerable support within NATO, particularly from Britain, Italy, Canada, Belgium, Norway, and Denmark, and, though a Belgian initiative, it could still be seen as a victory for the United States, to a large extent at the expense of France. For different reasons France, West Germany, Greece, and Turkey were on the skeptical side. The report not only ratified the process of détente, but also gave the organization an important role in the process. NATO was strengthened; US leadership was renewed, and this in a period when France wanted a reduction in the importance of the military blocs. Nevertheless, France approved the report, although reluctantly. There was little else it could do. On the substance side, de Gaulle liked to underline his leadership role in the process of détente. His visit to Moscow in June 1966 was to signal Franco-Soviet rapprochement. He could not now be seen as coming out against détente. On the tactical side, when Washington agreed to leave military matters largely out of the report and underlined the political side, it became difficult for Paris to argue that the report was contrary to its policy of withdrawal from NATO's military structure.

In the wider historical context, de Gaulle was deeply disappointed with the Soviet response to his anti-bloc policies. This response, or rather lack of such, made Washington's task in managing the threat from de Gaulle much easier than it would otherwise have been. The French President had clearly hoped that his NATO move would be reciprocated in the East and that this could then, at least in the long run, be a step on the road to uniting Europe from "the Atlantic to the Urals." But this was not to happen, for although Moscow appreciated France's independent stance, it showed no interest in reducing its own role in Eastern Europe. Soviet leader Leonid Brezhnev made this clear to the French President when de Gaulle visited Moscow just weeks after he had left NATO's military organization. In 1967 the Poles were also to inform *le général* rather bluntly about the realities of power in Eastern Europe, and in the following year the Soviet invasion of Czechoslovakia in August 1968 provided concrete evidence of what limited freedom of action Moscow's allies in Eastern Europe really had. There is no doubt that this lack of a response in the East seriously limited the effects of de Gaulle's policies inside NATO too.[40]

The US Economy, France, Germany, and the EC[41]

When de Gaulle turned down British membership of the Community, this was seen by the US as an unmitigated disaster politically. Economically, however, in an otherwise gloomy National Security Council meeting on 31 January 1963 George Ball noted that the Common Agricultural Policy would probably not now go into effect, and that the colonial problems would also be reduced, in part because Britain remained outside, in part because the other five EEC countries might now reject a deal even for the French colonies. Even this more optimistic analysis soon proved wrong: the EEC *did* work out a common agricultural policy and preferential agreements *were* established for the former colonies.

In March 1962 President Kennedy, with reference to the balance of payments problems, raised American duties on carpets and glass, which in turn led the EEC to suspend concessions it had already made to the US on imports of polystyrene, polyethylene, synthetic and artificial clothing, and varnishes and paint. Protectionist sentiment in Congress then led Washington to new measures regarding wool and chemicals, and to these the EEC responded on the poultry front. The first serious trade war had broken out between the United States and the EEC. Many were to follow later.

On the monetary side too there was an increasing conflict between the United States and France. As we have seen, the international monetary structure set up after the Second World War was based on America's leadership and the preeminence of the dollar. The dollar was, as the only currency, tied directly to gold and acted as the international reserve currency. While this had been entirely natural in the 1940s when the dominance of the US economy was unchallenged and the US was running balance of payments surpluses, once Western Europe was in recovery and the United States was beginning to run balance of payments deficits, then some began to argue that the monetary system had to be modified.

Nobody argued this harder than de Gaulle and his monetary adviser Jacques Rueff. Soon after becoming President of the new Fifth Republic, de Gaulle, inspired by Rueff, had made a whole series of important economic decisions. While he would bring negotiations on an Atlantic free trade area to an end, de Gaulle would still proceed down the liberalist road by accepting not only the existence of the EEC, which he had originally been against, but also the liberalization program of the OEEC and the convertibility of the franc into the dollar. The franc would be devauled 17.5 per cent, taxes would be raised, and public expenditures cut. The end of the free trade negotiations was strongly criticized by France's allies in the EEC, but the economic program initiated a period of significant economic growth in France.[42]

With the United States running deficits while at the same time unilaterally controlling the supply of the currency in which its debt was denoted, it was the only country in the world that enjoyed the option of using the printing press to pay its debts. Paris argued that gold ought to play a larger role in a reformed monetary system. The French could do more than simply argue. They could exchange their considerable dollar-holdings for gold. During the crisis following the dramatic events of January 1963, Washington was afraid that Paris would use its Eurodollars against the United States. In the Kennedy administration there was disagreement about exactly how vulnerable the United States was to French financial pressure. Treasury Secretary Douglas Dillon and head of the State Department's policy planning staff Walt Rostow argued that the American position was stronger than many financial experts believed.[43]

So concerned was Kennedy himself about this situation that in the fall of 1963 he was on the verge of deciding that a substantial number of US troops should be withdrawn from Western Europe. Within the administration the Treasury Department had long been arguing that such withdrawals would solve the payments problem, while the State Department consistently argued against this option. Far more remarkable was the fact that, under Kennedy and even more under Johnson, Robert McNamara and the Defense Department were prepared to go along with a decision to reduce troops. The United States ought to focus on nuclear forces and the Navy and the Air Force in Europe. The Europeans should then carry more of the army burden; if necessary the American troops could be lifted back to Europe on short notice.

About 50,000 US troops were actually withdrawn from Europe from 1962 to 1964, leaving some 370,000 or 320,000 in place (the numbers apparently vary a great deal).[44] Still, the basic decision was to keep the troops stationed in Europe. In December 1963 the new Erhard government in West Germany signed a generous offset agreement covering most of the costs of the American troop presence in Germany; it also more or less promised not to exchange dollars into gold; in its security policy it aligned itself firmly with Washington and abandoned the pro-French course that Adenauer had been following in his last years in power.[45]

The war in Vietnam, America's balance of payments problems, the improved East–West climate, and de Gaulle's policies all helped increase pressure in Congress to reduce the number of US troops in Europe. The pressure for reductions was even greater in financially troubled London, which made some withdrawals from West Germany. But the Johnson, as the

Kennedy, administration was opposed to any substantial weakening of the American, or even the British role, preferring instead, together with London, to negotiate with the ever more affluent Germans to have them make new payments to offset the extra American and British costs involved in deploying troops in Germany. In 1967, after complicated negotiations, an agreement was signed whereby the American troop level was reduced only marginally, while the German payments again increased significantly. For Erhard the price was high. The American and British demands were tough, and this in a period of economic recession. The leadership of this American favorite proved weak. He was replaced as Chancellor by Kurt Georg Kiesinger.[46]

France's position was strengthened by the strong economic growth that it experienced in the 1950s and 1960s. It was also building up its gold reserves more or less as a matter of policy. In 1957 these reserves stood at 500 tons of gold; in 1967 they stood at 4,650 tons. In 1964 France proposed to do away with the gold exchange standard and to introduce instead the classical gold standard, and in 1965 the Banque de France started to exchange dollars for gold, despite Washington's request that they refrain from doing this. France also wanted to weaken the role of the IMF since this was seen as dominated by the United States; thus, while in the 1950s the French had worked to attract foreign capital, in the early 1960s this attitude changed, as in great part American investment in France was seen as undermining French sovereignty. As a result, American investment now declined in France while it increased in Germany and Britain. By the time author Jean-Jacques Servan-Schreiber's *Le Défi américain* (the American challenge) was published in 1967, however, the French government had already concluded that the restrictions had been taken too far. In the steadily growing technological competition France in fact punished itself by limiting the influx of US capital.[47]

In the Johnson administration the United States continued to support European integration, but it was increasingly concerned that the EEC was not becoming the outward-looking institution Washington favored. Secretary of the Treasury Henry H. Fowler repeatedly expressed his worries about the balance of payments situation. With reference to the EEC, at a NSC meeting on 3 May 1967 he rhetorically asked whether the US could halt a process which during the last eight years had led to American reserves going down and the EEC's going up. Fowler was also agitated about French measures to restrict US investment: "France is trying either to expel us completely from Europe or at least to diminish our power there." Again, it was assumed that the balance of payments situation would become even worse if Britain joined the EEC and/or devalued the pound. In fact London had to do the latter in November 1967, setting off a wave of speculation against the dollar which in turn forced Johnson to increase taxes, cut spending, and regulate American foreign investment.

Still, Washington's conclusion remained the same as it had always been. While the United States would work hard to open up the EEC to American agricultural exports and to reduce US foreign spending by making the Europeans pay more in offset military outlays, in development assistance, etc. Washington would continue to support the EEC's further expansion, which continued to include membership for Britain. The fact that the United States was still running a surplus in its balance of trade reduced the economic worries somewhat. The problem was thus not primarily trade, but all the "extra" expenses involved in being a Great Power with global commitments.

In July 1967 the Wilson government renewed Britain's application for membership of the EEC. The United States would maintain a low profile in this matter, but as early as November 1966 President Johnson had told Prime Minister Wilson that "if you find on the way that there is anything we might do to smooth the path, I hope you will let me know." Low profile or not, de Gaulle had not changed his mind. On November 27 he informed the world that before he could agree to Britain's entry, it would have to make "very vast and deep changes." "What France cannot do is to enter into a negotiation with the British and their associates which could lead to the destruction of the European structure of which she is part."

The internal disputes in the Kennedy–Johnson administrations about America's economic response to the EEC/EC, despite growing, were softened by four factors. First, although the economic issues were important and becoming only more so, they were still generally seen as less important than the political ones. Second, the economic picture was far from one-dimensional. On the positive side, the conclusion that trade creation was more important than trade diversion was still widespread. This presumably applied even to agriculture, as total US farm sales to the EEC countries increased, although they declined as a percentage of EEC imports. Only exports of certain products, particularly those affected by protectionist levies, such as for instance chicken, fell dramatically. The number of American corporations establishing themselves inside the EEC increased rapidly, and these corporations on the whole had a very positive attitude to the Common Market. An integrated market obviously made their operations much easier than did a fragmented one.

Third, the United States and the EEC were making good progress in establishing that multilateral framework so strongly desired by Washington. The Kennedy round negotiations in GATT (1964–7), greatly facilitated by the Trade Expansion Act, were the crucial element in this context. Naturally, the final agreement represented a compromise, and the EEC, which for the first time negotiated as one unit, played a substantial role in shaping this compromise. Nevertheless, again with the exception of agriculture, the GATT compromise was certainly acceptable also to the United States.

Fourth, related particularly to the first factor mentioned, American foreign policy was still formulated primarily by the State Department. The economic departments, primarily Treasury, Commerce, and Agriculture, naturally paid much more attention to domestic economic interests than did State. But Presidents, normally backed by their National Security Advisers, still tended to support State, particularly since the economic departments often were divided. Agriculture took the narrow view which the name suggests; Commerce supported broader American business interests, especially those of an industrial nature; Treasury was primarily interested in promoting multilateral trade.

De Gaulle: Final Years

Through (first) agreements of 1960 concerning the Mediterranean and of 1964 about the Atlantic and the Channel and (then) the Ailleret–Lemnitzer agreement of 22 August 1967, France and NATO were able to establish a pattern of close cooperation for what would happen if a war broke out and France then made the expected decision to put its forces at the disposal of NATO. While the French role was dramatically changed in peacetime, the changes could thus be much smaller in wartime if France, as expected, chose to support NATO's military response. NATO was also permitted to continue the operation of the important oil pipeline through France to Germany; later de Gaulle even permitted flights of allied aircraft from Britain to Southern Europe in French airspace. In return the French were given access to NATO's new sophisticated air alert system. French historian Maurice Vaïsse has therefore argued, perhaps a bit optimistically, that "Loin de marquer une rupture militaire entre la France et l'Otan, ces accords mettent fin à l'incertitude et constituent un cadre réaliste pour la cooperation militaire dans le secteur Centre-Europe."[48] By agreeing to NATO's Harmel Report of 1967 the French not only showed some procedural flexibility, but a common political framework of both defense and détente towards the Soviet Union was put in place.

Despite the tension between Washington and Paris, in the foreseeable future de Gaulle clearly saw a role for the United States in Europe, stressing at his meeting with Senator Frank Church in May 1966 that "Tant qu'il y a la réalité majeure de la Russie puissante, il n'y a pas d'autre solution que l'appui américain pour que l'Europe ne soit pas dominée par elle. C'est pourquoi on a conclu l'Alliance atlantique et c'est pourquoi il faut la maintenir."[49]

Thus, after a number of years of escalating tension between the two countries, in de Gaulle's last two years American–French relations were to improve somewhat. The huge student–worker demonstrations and riots in Paris and other cities following May 1968 undermined both de Gaulle's self-confidence and the French economy. In November a currency crisis occurred when France lost one billion dollars in three weeks. De Gaulle still refused to devalue the franc, but since he wanted to protect it as best he could, it made little sense to continue his fierce attacks on the dollar. (The devaluation came instead in 1969 under Pompidou.) Paris and Washington basically agreed that the solution was for Bonn to revalue the mark, but to little avail since the German government disagreed.

The Soviet/Warsaw pact invasion of Czechoslovakia in August 1968 showed that the "Yalta system," as de Gaulle liked to call it, was stronger than he had thought. Moscow kept its allies in check, which made it much more difficult to transcend the traditional bloc system in Europe than de Gaulle had hoped, and this in turn underlined the need for an American role in Europe for many years still. Although the general himself continued to speak out against the United States, French policies were now modified, particularly at the levels below de Gaulle himself.[50]

The election of Richard Nixon as President of the United States in 1968 further stimulated the American–French rapprochement. Nixon and Kissinger both admired the French President as a person; they were less enthusiastic about European integration than their predecessors; they also held a much more relaxed view about the French nuclear deterrent. All this benefitted the relationship. Soon the Nixon administration was even to support the further development of the French *force de frappe*, putting a most troublesome issue in an entirely new light. The fact that the United States and North Vietnam opened negotiations about a ceasefire and a political solution for Vietnam, and did this in Paris, certainly helped too. Germany's increasing independence was also to cause a certain uneasiness both in Washington and in Paris that helped bring them somewhat closer together.[51]

De Gaulle and Nixon were to meet twice. The meetings were cordial, but despite the partial normalization most of the underlying differences remained: the French position in NATO, the role of the dollar, the war in Vietnam. Particularly in the Johnson years American policymakers frequently expressed the hope that after de Gaulle had left the scene, France would resume a more friendly course. The US should operate on the assumption that de Gaulle's leadership of France was temporary, and that he would be succeeded by a government "more responsive to public opinion, hence more favorable to NATO, to a United Europe and to the United States."[52] On 27 April 1969 Charles de Gaulle lost a referendum on some minor constitutional changes. The next day he resigned.

Notes

1. Arthur M. Schlesinger, Jr., *A Thousand Days: John F. Kennedy in the White House* (Boston: Houghton Mifflin, 1965), 875–88. See also Leopoldo Nuti, "Italy and the Cold War," *Journal of Cold War Studies*, 4:3 (Summer 2002), 2–23; Willy Brandt, *Erinnerungen* (Memoirs) (Frankfurt: Propyläen, 1989), 70–5.

2. US Department of Commerce, *Historical Statistics of the United States: Colonial Times to 1970*, 2 (Washington DC, 1975), 872–4.

3. *Historical Statistics of the United States*, 2, 870; Bureau of the Census, *Statistical Abstract of the United States, 1995* (Washington, DC: Government Printing Office, 1995), 809. See also Pells, *Not Like Us*,190. For French policies, see Kuisel, *Seducing the French*, 176–84.

4. Pells, *Not Like Us*, 160.

5. Duke and Krieger, *US Military Forces in Europe*, 233.

6. This project is best analyzed in Georges-Henri Soutou, *L'Alliance incertaine: Les rapports politico-stratégiques franco-allemands, 1954–1996* (Paris: Fayard, 1996), 82–109.

7. Irving M. Wall, *France, the United States and the Algerian War* (Berkeley: University of California Press, 2001).

8. Christopher S. Thompson, "Prologue au conflit: les premières impressions et l'anné 1940," in Institut Charles de Gaulle, *De Gaulle en son siècle. 4: La sécurité et l'indépendance de la France* (Paris: Plon, 1992), 239–53. The best general biography of de Gaulle is Jean Lacouture, *De Gaulle*. The French edition of this biography is in three volumes, the abridged English one is in two. Most relevant here is vol. 1 *De Gaulle: The Rebel, 1890–1944* (New York: Norton, 1990), parts III and IV.

9. Maurice Vaïsse, *La Grandeur politique étrangere du général de Gaulle, 1958–1969* (Paris: Fayard, 1998), ch. 2. See also Charles de Gaulle, *Lettres, notes et carnets* (Paris: Plon, 1980), de Gaulle to Alphand, 10 Dec. 1958, 147.

10. Alain Peyrefitte, *C'était de Gaulle* (Paris: Fayard, 1994), 352.

11. Jasmine Aimaq, *For Europe or Empire? French Colonial Ambitions and the European Army Plan* (Lund: Lund University Press, 1996), 190.

12. A collection of fine analyses of French–American relations under de Gaulle is found in Robert O. Paxton and Nicholas Wahl (eds.), *De Gaulle and the United States: A Centennial Reappraisal* (Oxford: Berg, 1994). See also Erin R. Mahan, *Kennedy, de Gaulle, and Western Europe* (Houndmills: Palgrave, 2002). For the Cuban crisis in particular, see Maurice Vaïsse (ed.), *L'Europe et la crise de Cuba* (Paris: Armand Colin, 1993).

13. *FRUS*, 1961–3, XIII, Memorandum of conversation Kennedy–de Gaulle, 1 June, 1961, 312–13.

14. For contemporary American analyses of de Gaulle, see *FRUS*, 1961–1963, XIII, Telegram from Bohlen to the State Department, 16 Feb. 1963, 758–60; NA, POL FR-US, Memorandum from Read to McGeorge Bundy, Talking points paper for the president's meeting with Couve de Murville, 1–2, 6; NA, POL FR-US, Memorandum from Bohlen to the secretary of state, 13 Dec. 1963. For de Gaulle's fears in 1945, see NA, 751.00/5-1245, Telegram from Matthews to Dunn, 1–3. For later historical analyses, see Eckart Conze, "Hegemonie Durch Integration? Die amerikanische Europapolitik und de Gaulle," *Vierteljahrshefte für Zeitgeschichte*, 14 (April 1995), 307; Lacouture, *De Gaulle: The Ruler, 1945–1970*, 61–3, 363–86, 471–4; Frédéric Bozo, *Two Strategies for Europe: De Gaulle, the United States and the Atlantic Alliance* (Lanham: Rowman & Littlefield, 2001), 187–232; Stanley Hoffmann, *Decline or Renewal? France*

Since the *1930s* (New York: Viking, 1974), 308, 310, 312, 350–1, 356–7; Georges-Henri Soutou, "France" in Reynolds, *The Origins of the Cold War in Europe*, 96–120, particularly 98, 100–4.

15. Quoted in Alfred Grosser, *The Western Alliance: European–American Relations Since 1945* (London: Macmillan, 1980), 209.

16. Much of the rest of this section follows my *"Empire" by Integration*, 58–63.

17. Wall, *France, the United States and the Algerian War*. For a more balanced account, see Matthew Connelly, *A Diplomatic Revolution: Algeria's Fight for Independence and the Origins of the Post-Cold War Era* (Oxford: Oxford University Press, 2002).

18. Wall, *France, the United States and the Algerian War*, 155–6; Connelly, *A Diplomatic Revolution*, 169.

19. Merrit and Pachula, *Western European Perspectives on International Affairs*, 254–5; Institut Français d'Opinion Publique, *Les Francais et de Gaulle* (Paris: Plon, 1971), 268.

20. For a summing up of these efforts at compromise, see Constantine A. Pagedas, *Anglo-American Strategic Relations and the French Problem 1960–63: A Troubled Partnership* (London: Frank Cass, 2000), 56–69. See also Vincent Jauvert, *L'Amérique contre De Gaulle: Histoire secrète 1961–1969* (Paris: Seuil, 2000), 243.

21. The best account of this process is now Alan S. Milward, *The Rise and Fall of a National Strategy 1945–1963: The United Kingdom and the European Community*, 1 (London: Frank Cass, 2002.)

22. Milward, *The Rise and Fall of a National Strategy*, 310–11, 315–16. In addition to my own account in *"Empire" by Integration*, 60–3, see also Giauque, *Grand Designs & Visions of Unity*, 158–85.

23. Those parts of this section that follow my *"Empire" by Integration*, 63–80 will generally not be documented again here.

24. Giauque, *Grand Designs & Visions of Unity*, 126–57; Lundestad, *"Empire" by Integration*, 63–4; Jeffrey W. Vanke, "An Impossible Union: Dutch Objections to the Fouchet Plan, 1958–62," *Cold War History*, 2:1 (Oct. 2001), 95–112.

25. Marc Trachtenberg, *A Constructed Peace: The Making of the European Settlement, 1945–1963* (Princeton: Princeton University Press, 1999). For two good, although now perhaps slightly dated, articles by Frank Costigliola on these events, both of them somewhat harsh on Kennedy, see his "Kennedy, the European Allies, and the Failure to Consult," *Political Science Quarterly*, 110 (Winter 1995), 105–23 and "The Failed Design: Kennedy, de Gaulle, and the Struggle for Europe," *Diplomatic History*, 8 (Summer 1984), 227–51.

26. Milward, *The Rise and Fall of a National Strategy*, 463–83; Geoffrey Warner, "Why the General said No," *International Affairs*, 78:4 (Oct. 2002), 869–82; Soutou, *L'Alliance incertaine*, 230–2.

27. Giauque, *Grand Designs & Visions of Unity*, 202–11, esp. 209.

28. *FRUS*, 1961–3, XIII, Summary record of NSC Executive Committee meeting, No. 39, 31 Jan. 1963, 158, 161. Kennedy's fears about de Gaulle's actions were stimulated by intelligence reports. George Ball thus writes in his *The Past Has Another Pattern: Memoirs* (New York: Norton, 1982), 271 that "There were wild

rumors of a plan to pave the way for France, with Bonn's assistance, to negotiate with Moscow for a whole new European arrangement. We compared and supplemented our intelligence reports with bits and pieces gathered by the British. We looked at all possibilities of a Paris–Bonn deal with Moscow, leading toward a Soviet withdrawal from East Germany to be followed by some form of confederation betwen the two parts of that severed country. That would, of course, mean the end of NATO and the neutralization of Germany."

Along equally alarming lines Theodore C. Sorensen writes in his *Kennedy* (New York: Bantam Books, 1966, 643–4): "Thus Kennedy was briefly startled early in 1963 by a foreign intelligence report of doubtful authenticity. 'Rumors from regular and reliable sources' maintained that De Gaulle and the Soviet Union had made or were about to make a secret deal, calling for a demilitarized Central Europe, including all Germany, Greece and Turkey, the progressive withdrawal of American troops from Europe as well as Germany, and a recognition of the Oder-Neisse line.... Fortunately it [the report] proved groundless; but this possibility motivated many of Kennedy's inquiries in the round of meetings that followed."

29. Britain refused to bow to the United States in the pipe dispute, but in the end London and Moscow could not agree on the price. For this and the pipe dispute in general, see Alan P. Dobson, "Anglo-American Relations and Diverging Economic Defence Policies in the 1950s and 1960s," in Jonathan Hollowell (ed.), *Twentieth-Century Anglo-American Relations* (Houndmills: Palgrave, 2001), 143–65.
30. This is basically the story told in Frank Mayer, *Adenauer and Kennedy: A Study in German–American Relations, 1961–1963* (Basingstoke: Macmillan, 1996).
31. On this point I have especially benefited from conversations with Leopoldo Nuti.
32. *FRUS*, 1964–8, XIII, Letter from President de Gaulle to President Johnson, 7 March 1966, 325.
33. *FRUS*, 1964–8, XIII, Memorandum from Johnson to Rusk and McNamara, 4 May 1966, 376–7; Jauvert, *L'Amérique contre de Gaulle*, 246–7. For the open attacks on de Gaulle, see Douglas Brinkley, *Dean Acheson: The Cold War Years, 1953–71* (New Haven: Yale University Press, 1992), 228–35.
34. Bozo, *Two Strategies for Europe*, 155–7.
35. *FRUS*, 1964–8, XII, Telegram from Bohlen to Secretary of State, 11 June 1966, 122–4.
36. Thomas A. Schwartz, "Lyndon Johnson and Europe. Alliance Politics, Political Economy, and 'Growing Out of the Cold War'," in H. W. Brands, *The Wages of Globalism: Lyndon Johnson and the Limits of American Power* (New York: Oxford University Press, 1995), 49–51.
37. Beatrice Heuser, *NATO, Britain, France and the FRG: Nuclear Strategies and Forces for Europe, 1949–2000* (New York: St. Martin's Press, 1997), 47–52.
38. Kaplan, *The Long Entanglement*, 130–5. The quotation is from 131.
39. North Atlantic Council, *NATO Final Communiqués 1949–1974* (Brussels: NATO Information Service, n.d.), 199.
40. Frédéric Bozo, "Détente versus Alliance: France, the United States and the Politics of the Harmel Report (1964–1968)," *Contemporary European History*, 7:3 (1998), 343–60; Bozo, *Two Strategies for Europe*, 144–7, 160–3, 175–8.

190–2, 196–7, 221–32, 245–9; Helga Haftendorn, *NATO and the Nuclear Revolution: A Crisis of Credibility, 1966–67* (Oxford: Oxford University Press, 1996), particularly 320–85.

41. Parts of this section follow my *"Empire" by Integration*, 94–7.
42. Frances M. B. Lynch, "De Gaulle's Veto: France, the Rueff Plan and the Free Trade Area," *Contemporary European History*, 9:1 (2000), 111–35.
43. *FRUS*, 1961–3, IX, Rostow to Kennedy, 4 Feb. 1963, 161–2; ibid., Dillon to Kennedy, 11 Feb. 1963, 162–4.
44. Nelson, *A History of US Military Forces in Germany* (81) states that there were 370,170 US troops in Europe in 1962 and 318,628 in 1964. Gregory Treverton, *The Dollar Drain and American Forces in Germany: Managing the Political Economics of Alliance* (Athens: Ohio University Press, 1978), 4, sets these numbers at 419,000 in 1962 and 368,000 in 1964.
45. For a fascinating account of these questions, see Francis J. Gavin, "The Gold Battles within the Cold War: American Monetary Policy and the Defense of Europe, 1960–1963," *Diplomatic History*, 26:1 (Winter 2002), 61–94. See also Grosser, *The Western Alliance*, 231–7.
46. Zimmermann, *Money and Security*, chs. 8–9.
47. Vaïsse, *La Grandeur politique étrangère du général de Gaulle*, 397–407; Kuisel, *Seducing the French*, 154–71, 176–84.
48. Vaïsse, *La Grandeur politique étrangère du général de Gaulle*, 394. ("Far from marking a military rupture between France and NATO, these accords put a stop to the uncertainty and constituted a realistic framework for military cooperation in the Central European sector."); Bozo, *Two Strategies for Europe*, 188–92. For a different interpretation stressing change in the French–NATO relationship, see Soutou, *L'Alliance incertaine*, 297–9.
49. De Gaulle, *Lettres, Notes et Carnets*, 1966, 294. ("As long as there is the major reality of the mighty Russia, there is no other solution than American support so that Europe is not dominated. That was why we concluded the Atlantic treaty, and that is why we must maintain it.")
50. *FRUS*, 1964–8, XII, Telegram from Embassy in France to Department of State, 2 Sept. 1968, 160–2.
51. Vaïsse, *La Grandeur politique étrangere du général de Gaulle*, 407–12; Bozo, *Two Strategies for Europe*, 230–9.
52. *FRUS*, 1964–8, XIII, Circular telegram from Rusk to the US posts in the NATO capitals, 2 March 1966, 320. See also Frank Costigliola, *France and the United States* (New York: Twayne, 1992), 136–48; Thomas A. Schwartz, "Victories and Defeats in the Long Twilight Struggle: The United States and Western Europe in the 1960s," in Diane B. Kunz (ed.), *The Diplomacy of the Crucial Decade: American Foreign Relations during the 1960s* (New York: Columbia University Press, 1994), 134–6; Lloyd Gardner, "Lyndon Johnson and De Gaulle," in Paxton and Wahl (eds.), *De Gaulle and the United States*, 257–78.

5

The United States, Western Europe, and Out-of-Area Disputes, 1945–1975

Invitations Frequently Declined

The United States and the Western European countries certainly had their differences over various European questions: the initial role for the United States, the rearmament of West Germany, the exact combination of arms and diplomacy in relations with the Soviet Union, France's position within the Western alliance. These were all serious questions, but all debate still took place against the background of a Soviet threat that disturbed the entire "free world" and a NATO framework that had been established to deal with this threat. However, out-of-area, i.e. outside the area covered by core Article 5 of the NATO treaty, disagreements between the United States and many Western European countries were even more frequent and the common framework much weaker.

Until about 1960 the pattern was that the European colonial powers wanted the support of the United States in their efforts to hang on to their colonies, but outside the areas where Washington saw a Communist threat and therefore felt justified in taking a lead, it was reluctant to provide such support. After about 1960 the pattern was reversed with the United States increasingly asking for Europe's assistance in the global struggle against Communism. Now, however, with their colonies in the process of gaining independence, the Europeans were focusing more on European matters. To put this in invitational terms, it could be argued that before 1960 the Europeans invited the Americans into their troubled areas while after 1960 the United States invited the Europeans to support it in the struggle against Communism. Contrary to the situation in Europe, both sets of invitations were frequently declined.[1]

Still, even these disagreements, serious as some of them were, were limited by several factors. First, despite the different starting points of anti-colonial United States and colonial Western Europe, their views were far from diametrically opposed, and varied according to who called upon whom for support. Second, disagreements between Washington on the one hand and London, Paris, the Hague, and even other European capitals on the other were kept within bounds by the fact that rarely were the various European capitals united on these extra-European issues. Third, and probably most important, out-of-area disputes were clearly limited by the common awareness that however important these disputes might be, the situation in Europe took precedence. The common framework in Europe should not be endangered.

The United States and Western Europe: Allies of a Kind[2]

The United States definitely saw itself as an anti-colonial power—after all, it had been the first British colony to rebel against London's rule and establish an independent country. In hindsight, America's independence was in fact to be seen by historians as forming the line of division between the first and the second British Empire. The words of the American Declaration of Independence from 1776 that "We hold these Truths to be self-evident, that all Men are created equal, that they are endowed by their Creator with certain inalienable Rights, that among these are Life, Liberty, and the Pursuit of Happiness . . ." formed part of the American creed. Sooner or later colonialism would have to end. Americans had certainly not fought the Second World War over the protection of colonial empires. Colonies should be set free very much in the same way the United States was setting the Philippines free in 1946. In Washington's opinion, the end of such empires would both help to reduce tension, in that imperial rivalry had led to many international conflicts, and also end what was seen as one of the inherent characteristics of colonialism—the exploitation of other peoples—and instead promote international trade and economic growth. It was a most welcome side effect if decolonization were then to strengthen the international position of the United States, as it was clearly expected to do. Finally, during the Cold War America's long-term anti-colonial tradition was buttressed by pragmatic considerations emphasizing that any attempt to hold back the forces of self-determination was bound to strengthen the Soviet side.

This obvious starting point was tempered by many different factors. Thus, even Franklin D. Roosevelt, who clearly believed more strongly than most leading Americans that colonialism was doomed, thought it would take a considerable time for it to be eradicated: India should get its independence as soon as was practicable; at the other extreme "the headhunters of New Guinea" might need hundreds of years to be properly prepared for independence. It emerged that FDR's cherished concept of some form of international trusteeship replacing colonial rule, basically applied to yellow and black people who were not yet up to the standards independence required. It also gradually became evident that the trusteeship period was supposed to last rather long, some twenty or thirty years, and in some cases even up to fifty years.

While Roosevelt told Winston Churchill privately about the need to set India free, in the face of the strong reaction of the British Prime Minister he did this more and more reluctantly—as long as the British guided their colonies toward independence they could proceed more or less at their own pace. In fact publicly Roosevelt never spoke out for India's independence during the Second World War, and at Yalta explicitly exempted Great Britain from the trusteeship concept. Harry Truman was an even more cautious supporter of decolonization. The United Nations Charter in May 1945 merely stipulated that colonial powers had an obligation to help dependent peoples take "progressive" steps toward self-government "according to the particular circumstances of each territory and its peoples and their varying stages of advancement." As we shall see, the American position toward the colonial powers was also tempered by the fact that these powers were the closest allies of the United States in the struggle against Communism in Europe and that they were sometimes fighting nationalist movements that were perceived to be Communist led.[3]

On the other hand, the European colonial powers were definitely aware of the traditional position of the United States. Now that position was combined with an overwhelming military, economic, political, and cultural strength. This was something the various imperial capitals had to take into account. London certainly did so for, as Louis and Robinson have argued with relevance to Britain:

There were powerful reasons for the belief that the anti-colonial sentiment of the American public might yet provoke the United States government to interfere if the British did not continue with a progressive colonial policy. Above all, dependence on the United States was probably the one experience humiliating enough to convince the British psychologically that the age of empire was ending.[4]

Paris, Brussels, the Hague, and other imperial capitals might be less specifically influenced by this American dimension, but even they realized that the Second World War represented a watershed in colonial history; and while Churchill might argue that the Atlantic Charter was formally limited to the occupied territories, clearly a war fought for liberty and freedom could not but have consequences in all parts of the world.

Nevertheless, differences clearly remained between the United States and the colonial powers, and nowhere were the consequences of such differences more obvious than in American–Dutch relations. Holland was a much smaller ally than Britain and France and the independence movement in Indonesia was clearly non-Communist in nature, which made it natural for the United States to support it, though even here Washington waited until 1948–9 to really make up its mind. Then, when Dutch military actions made it evident that the country still had a long way to go before it would be prepared to grant

Indonesia its independence, the Truman administration threatened to with-hold economic and even military assistance and Holland gave up. Despite the unjustified pressure they felt the United States applied, the Dutch remained one of the most Atlantic-oriented European nations. As one of their leading foreign policy practitioners, Dirk Stikker, emphasized in the context of the dispute over Indonesia, his belief in Atlantic cooperation "never suffered, nei-ther then nor later, when I was to encounter even more difficulties. I remained a staunch and loyal friend of the United States."[5]

The Indian case, which occasionally had put such a strain on the Roosevelt–Churchill relationship, represented few problems after the war when Washington modified its criticism, largely because there was no longer a way back for Britain. Despite Churchill's rather romantic view of the British role in India, promises had been made which more or less guaranteed India's independence once the war was over. This was the price that had to be paid to keep India quiet in the face of Germany's efforts to conquer Britain and Japan's onslaught on the British empire in East Asia right up to the border of British India. Under the more progressive Labour government of Clement Attlee and in view of London's rapidly growing difficulties in holding on to its position in India, for however limited a period, the British pulled out in 1947. India and Pakistan and then Burma and Ceylon (Sri Lanka) were given their independence. The colonial dam had been broken, to a much more dramatic extent than almost any contemporary observer realized. What had been granted in India could not be held back elsewhere, not by the British and soon not by any other colonial masters.

The United States and Western Europe: East Asia

The changing nature of America's colonial policy was best illustrated in Indochina. FDR frequently mentioned French Indochina as an example of how colonial powers had failed in their mission to improve conditions for the local people. Therefore the region was a prime candidate for trusteeship status. Yet, at the end of his life Roosevelt had more or less given up; he saw no alternative to the return of the French once the Japanese had been defeated, but perhaps France alone could act as the trustee, with independence still as the ultimate goal.[6]

The Office of Strategic Services (OSS)—the wartime predecessor of the CIA—was maintaining contacts with Communist-nationalist leader Ho Chi Minh and his anti-Japanese Vietminh resistance. The Vietnamese in turn flirted openly with the Americans in an attempt to weaken the French, as could be seen in the opening words of the Vietnamese declaration of inde-pendence from September 1945, repeating directly the key phrase of the

American Declaration of Independence. The sudden collapse of the Japanese forces after the dropping of the two atomic bombs over Hiroshima and Nagasaki created a vacuum that only the Vietminh were ready to fill. However, with British forces and then the French themselves coming back to regain the control they had lost, war soon broke out. The United States supported the French in their desire to return, but Washington clearly hoped for some sort of agreed solution, starting with local autonomy, that over time could lead to independence for Indochina. The assumption was that some sort of third way could be found, nationalist but still anti-Communist. American policy was again heavily influenced by the fact that France was an important ally in Europe, which meant nothing was to be done which could make the precarious life of weak centrist governments in Paris even more miserable.

While in the first years after the Second World War the overall pattern was one of the United States wanting to reduce the role of the colonial powers in Asia and later in Africa too, one factor quickly modified or even reversed this policy, namely the prospect of Communists taking control of a territory. Developments in Vietnam signaled what was to come. Those in China in the late 1940s were even more crucial, although what was most remarkable at first was how little the United States did to stop Mao Zedong's Communists from winning the Chinese civil war. For although Washington did give some economic as well as military assistance to the Kuomintang, it was negligible compared with what was done in Western Europe to contain Communism. The reasons for this restraint were many: Chiang Kai-shek's corrupt and authoritarian government was obviously less acceptable than the effective and democratic ones generally found in Western Europe; the Soviet Union intervened to a very limited extent in China, a fact that clearly circumscribed the freedom of action even of the United States; China was too big for any one country to control. How much would the US in the end have to invest to prevent Mao from coming to power? It frightened policymakers that no one knew the answer to such a question. And, then, the resources of the United States, however vast compared to those of other Great Powers, were limited, and priority had to be given to Western Europe.

With the Marshall Plan and the emerging Atlantic military structure claiming what they did, the Truman administration felt it had little to contribute in China. The Republicans in Congress kept asking why, if intervention was right in Europe, it was not right in China. But China was not Europe. After the fall of the mainland, the administration was simply waiting for the fall of Taiwan. The US was not to intervene in the Chinese civil war. In fact, it was pulling its troops out from the Asian mainland, as could be seen in the US withdrawal in 1949 from South Korea, and as was explicitly stated in Secretary of State Dean Acheson's so-called perimeter speech of January 1950. However, signs of change could be noticed even before the North

Korean attack on South Korea on 25 June 1950. The famous NSC 68 document meant that Truman's well-established defense budget ceiling of 15 billion dollars was being abandoned. The pressure to assist Taiwan was rapidly escalating. The Western European allies who, following Britain's lead, recognized the new government in Beijing were being criticized. Britain shared overall anti-Communism with the United States, but due at least in part to its role in Hong Kong, Singapore, and Malaya, and the position of India, it had to show a more pragmatic attitude to East Asia's stabilization. Washington's decision to give economic and military assistance to Indochina was taken in May 1950. Paris had finally agreed to give a Vietnamese government under Bao Dai "independence." This made it easier for the United States to give such assistance, although it meant little real change since control still remained with the French.

With the outbreak of the Korean War American policy changed dramatically. Instead of the more or less continuous feuding across the 38th parallel, there was now a massive attack that reawakened memories in Washington of the lead-up to the Second World War in the late 1930s.[7] The Truman administration rushed US Air Force and Navy units to the scene followed, as quickly as possible, by the Army. At its peak 350,000 US troops were in Korea. The priority then became to attract international forces to support America's action.

All of America's allies in Europe were quick to condemn the attack on South Korea. With Great Britain in the lead quite a few of them, including France, also contributed troops or medical personnel under the United Nations banner to what was in reality an American-dominated operation. Britain, together with Canada, Australia, and other Commonwealth members, actually contributed a force of approximately 27,000 at any one time, and a total of 81,000 over the duration of the war. This was more than half of the non-US total. The Attlee government saw potential political gains (primarily from the United States) in contributing, which overrode the negative military consequences of diluting British forces elsewhere in Asia.[8]

There were clearly differences between London and Washington in their approaches to the Korean War. London was skeptical of the new policy toward Taiwan under which the United States would now be prepared to intervene militarily to stop an invasion from the mainland. Britain agreed to play down the difference over recognition of China, including its representation in the UN, but did not yield as far as the substance of the policy was concerned. With the fortunes of the war changing after General Douglas MacArthur's successful amphibious operation at Inchon, the British soon became concerned about the nature of the general's statements about China. This concern increased a great deal in November after the Chinese intervened massively in the war. Any expansion of the war to parts of China, including "hot pursuits" into Chinese airspace, was opposed by the European allies, who also encouraged the idea of a demilitarized zone in the north of North Korea instead of the UN allies pushing all the way up to or even beyond the Yalu river.

The meetings in Washington between Attlee and Truman on 4–8 December 1950 sprang in great part from British and European concern over the American leadership in Korea, not least because of Truman's statements about the possible use of nuclear weapons. It is difficult to judge exactly what the effect of the British role was. William Stueck's conclusion in his *The Korean War: An International History* is that in December 1950–January 1951 the British definitely played a role in persuading the Americans to back away from an expanded war against China. At the Truman–Attlee summit the Prime Minister took the lead in injecting a modicum of restraint into the highly charged climate in Washington. Yet, the British input was clearly limited; the chances of the United States actually using atomic weapons in Korea were small in any case, as were the chances of the US directly involving Chinese territory in the war. The British role could still be significant in that it strengthened the State Department against the Pentagon and Congress. As almost always in transatlantic debates, rarely was it a case of everybody in one capital against everybody in the other. The elites in the various capitals were normally divided, and often especially so in Washington, a fact that frequently gave the allies a disproportionate influence.[9]

American–European disagreements were also limited by the fact that, despite the military build-up in Korea and East Asia, there was firm agreement that Europe still held center stage, as stated in the preparations for the NATO meeting in New York in September 1950: "Western Europe remains the key area for the defense of the whole free world."[10] The attack in Korea could in fact be a diversion from the major Soviet attack in Europe, making the build-up there even more significant than in Asia. Four new US divisions were sent to Europe, to the consternation of the Republican right. Agreement was reached at the New York meeting that West Germany had to be rearmed, although it was to take years of discussion before a solution was found on exactly how this was to be done. An integrated NATO command was established in Europe under General Eisenhower and ambitious plans were drawn up for European rearmament, particularly in Lisbon in 1952—so ambitious that they were never put into effect.

This understanding on Europe's primacy was reflected also in the Truman–Attlee talks. Naturally the Europeans were concerned that America's very large role in Korea would limit what it could do in crucial Europe. That was why again and again the European allies insisted on the importance of additional US forces being sent to Europe, but this time under an integrated American-led NATO command. There was a parallel in some ways with what had happened during the Second World War, when although after the attack on Pearl Harbor the United States had to respond in Asia-Pacific, the main focus was still on Europe.

The war in Vietnam was also escalating. In December 1952 the North Atlantic Council expressed its "wholehearted admiration for the valiant and long continued struggle by the French forces and the armies of the Associated States against Communist aggression."[11] The deteriorating French position led to the United States taking on an ever larger burden. In 1954 Washington paid about 80 per cent of French war expenses in Vietnam and American military advisers were also sent in, but even these measures could not stop the Communist advance. Washington and Paris both wanted to prevent a Communist victory, France in large part to preserve its position in Indochina, the United States primarily to stop Communism. Washington had long thought it could win only if the French were prepared to give non-Communist nationalists their chance, but for their part the French, if they could not gain the victory, were preparing to pull out; yet, even then the US was reluctant to give up. In the spring of 1954 the situation came to a crisis at Dien Bien Phu where the French wanted a direct US intervention to prevent the fall of the French garrison. This was not to be. The Eisenhower administration, including the US Army, was against fighting yet another war on the Asian mainland. So were the British and the Democrats in the Senate. Eisenhower dropped the idea.

At the ensuing Geneva conference that resulted in the independence of Cambodia, Laos, and North and South Vietnam, new differences arose among the allies. The United States, in the person of Secretary of State John Foster Dulles, wanted to keep a certain distance from the whole Geneva settlement to which British Foreign Secretary Eden contributed so mightily. America's emphasis was on establishing a new defense organization, the South East Asia Treaty Organization (SEATO), and it worked hard to sign up members. But India and Indonesia had no desire to participate; Britain opposed the inclusion of Taiwan, France the inclusion of Laos, Cambodia, and the two Vietnams, which, according to the Geneva agreement, were to be neutral; as a result the SEATO members then became the three major Western powers, together with Australia, New Zealand, the Philippines, Thailand, and Pakistan. In South Vietnam, with France on the way out and the United States determined to stop a further Communist advance, Washington more or less selected anti-Communist nationalist Ngo Dinh Diem as the new leader. The elections in all of Vietnam that had been promised within two years were not held. Even Eisenhower was convinced that "had elections been held at the time of the fighting, possibly 80 per cent of the population would have voted for the Communist Ho Chi Minh as their leader rather than Chief of State Bao Dai." There was little reason to believe that much had changed by 1956, although Bao Dai had then been replaced by Diem. Britain chose to keep a low profile, but it clearly disliked Washington's decision to foil the elections and instead build up Diem.[12]

The United States was clearly doing more than simply replacing the European colonial powers in many different parts of the world, but Washington was generally happy to be playing the lead role. The Pacific was becoming more and more of an American lake. The US (to the extent that the Truman administration had been able to control its own supreme commander, General MacArthur) was calling the shots in critically important Japan, taking very little interference not only from the Soviet Union, but also from its European and Asian allies. In the remarkable ANZUS treaty of 1951 the United States had replaced Great Britain as the guarantor of the security of long-time dominions Australia and New Zealand. Most of the initiative for this dramatic development had come from the Australian side and it reflected the respective roles of the US and Britain in the Pacific during the Second World War.[13] The Philippines continued its close relationship with the United States even after it had achieved its independence in 1946. The US was the dominant Great Power in Taiwan and South Korea, increasingly also in Southeast Asia.

Competitive Cooperation: The Middle East

In the Middle East US supremacy was emerging much more gradually than in the Pacific. Britain's position was definitely stronger here—to begin with, the Middle East was closer to home; Britain's military and material interests were very significant indeed; and its position had been dominant here for decades, if not centuries. In the early years after 1945 the United States was happy to recognize Britain's leading role in the Middle East, although it wanted to be more than a "junior partner" that "blindly" followed the British lead.[14]

Still, the signs of change were there for everybody to see. Washington was playing an increasingly larger role in the region, while Britain had to admit it no longer had the resources to sustain its traditional position there. Many of the local actors also wanted the United States to be more involved for their own military, political, or economic reasons. Even in the interwar years the US had become the leading foreign power in Saudi Arabia with its huge oil reserves. In 1946–7 Great Britain had been forced by its economic crisis to pull out of Greece and Turkey. Its replacement by the United States was formally announced in March 1947 in the form of the Truman Doctrine. In 1948 Britain had given up in Palestine, hard-pressed as it was by its own economy, both Jewish and Arab resistance, and American and Soviet opposition. The United States and the Soviet Union competed to be the first to recognize the new state of Israel. The US won, becoming the leading outside power even in Israel, although this was a more gradual development than is often assumed.[15]

Of course, the United States and Britain could still cooperate, as they did in Greece and Turkey, in the Tripartite Declaration of 1950 with France to prevent conflict in the Middle East, and as they did in toppling radical nationalist Mohammed Mossadeq in Iran in 1953. (Though many in Britain felt that 1953 was a victory primarily for the United States in that, under the restored Shah, American oil interests in Iran were in a much better position than they had been before.)

The blend of Anglo-American conflict and cooperation was seen in the creation of the Baghdad pact in 1955. The United States was most interested in extending the anti-Soviet pact system into the Near East where there was a gaping hole between NATO, which in 1951–2 had come to encompass also Greece and Turkey, and SEATO, which went as far west as Pakistan. To a large extent Britain shared America's desire for pact extension, but London also had a strong interest in shoring up its own position in the region. This latter desire was at best only in part shared by the United States, since in many ways Washington saw the British role as detrimental, in that it polarized Arab politics and made some Arab countries more reluctant to sign up with the West. In addition there was the growing commercial rivalry between the two countries in the Middle East. In the end the United States only became an associate member of the Baghdad pact, which then included the United Kingdom, Turkey, Pakistan, Iran, and Iraq. Only the last two had not already signed up with the West, so this was a limited success indeed.

If it had committed itself more directly to the pact, Washington feared that it would have strained relations not only with Israel, but also with crucial Arab non-participants such as Egypt, Saudi Arabia, and even Jordan. The British felt betrayed by an America that wanted their support in combating Communism while at the same time undermining their influence in the Middle East. The French now played a rather limited role in the region. Their troops had been pulled out of Syria and Lebanon in 1946; the defeat in Indochina had strained relations with the United States, and even Britain; and now Paris was singularly focused on the war in Algeria which had started in 1954, a war which made close relations with most Arab countries difficult. As to the desirability of American–British–French discussions about the Middle East, Eden simply replied, "Not at all at the top level. They are our enemies in the Middle East."[16]

Despite frequent denunciations of neutrality in general, especially by John Foster Dulles, in practice the Eisenhower administration had a more nuanced policy. In Egypt in 1952 the United States had preferred reforming military men to old-fashioned King Farouk. Yet, the effort to cultivate the new leaders lasted only a few years. Soon both London and Washington disliked the drift of Gamal Abdel Nasser's policies: the arms deal with Czechoslovakia, the recognition of China, his stance toward Israel. Therefore they cancelled the loan they had promised earlier for the building of the Aswan dam.

Britain and the US both responded negatively to Nasser's nationalization of the Suez Canal in 1956. While the British started preparations for a military intervention in Egypt to take the Canal back and topple Nasser in combination with both the French, who were happy finally to get at the "source" of their problems in Algeria (support from Egypt), and the Israelis who had their own obvious reasons for attacking Egypt, Eisenhower was opposed to the use of force and tried instead to promote a diplomatic solution. Drawing parallels between Nasser and Hitler, Eden argued that "The seizure of the Suez Canal is...the opening gambit in a planned campaign designed by Nasser to expel all Western influence and interests from Arab countries." Eisenhower replied that "you are making of Nasser a much more important figure than he is." In the American President's opinion, the use of force would only make Nasser even more popular in the region than he already was. It might also "cause a serious misunderstanding between our two countries."[17]

The Eisenhower administration clearly believed that the British would not use force without first having secured Washington's agreement, particularly when the British themselves were divided internally on this issue. The British, on the other hand, thought that their closest ally would not oppose them if they used force after diplomatic means had failed to get the Egyptians out of the Suez Canal. After Israeli forces had attacked Egypt on 29 October, on 5 November the British–French invasion of Egypt started. The next day Eisenhower won reelection as President in a landslide. Eighteen hours later the British–French operation was abruptly halted twenty-three miles down the Canal from Port Said. There was no doubt what stopped it—Eisenhower had made his opposition most explicit—with a run on the pound and Western Europe being short on heating oil, Washington refused to shore up the pound or start emergency oil shipments before the operation stopped. The French were furious, but had little choice, integrated as their forces were with the British. In the UN Washington could be seen as cooperating at least indirectly with Moscow against London and Paris, a new combination indeed in the Cold War.

The Suez debacle had several important consequences for the Middle East and for allied relations. Britain had invaded Egypt, in collaboration with Israel, and this accelerated the reduction in Britain's role in the region which had been clearly visible even before Suez and of which the invasion itself had indeed been such an important sign. For the first time the Suez crisis also made the Soviet Union an important actor in the Middle East as the new-found friend of Arab radicals. Again the United States took it upon itself to fill the space left by Britain, resulting in the Eisenhower Doctrine of January 1957 under which the United States would give economic and military aid to Middle East governments that felt their independence threatened. Again the importance of Western Europe was underlined when the President stated that if the Soviets were able to dominate the Middle East, "Western Europe would be endangered just as though there had been no Marshall Plan, no North Atlantic Treaty Organization."[18] This was modeled on the Truman Doctrine, ten years later, in an even more important region.

The Suez experience represented a watershed in American–British relations. For the first time since the Second World War London had taken major military action directly contrary, as it turned out, to Washington's wishes. The results had been disappointing, to put it mildly, leading London to the conclusion that never again should Britain put itself in a similar spot. It was up to Harold Macmillan, who had beaten a hasty retreat from his earlier position as one of the Suez activists, to put the new policy into effect as in January 1957 he replaced a worn-out Eden as Prime Minister. As early as March he and Eisenhower held wide-ranging discussions in Bermuda to coordinate their foreign and defense policies.

This reexamination was to bear fruit for the British in the shape of increased nuclear assistance from the United States. (With the assistance came dependence, as the French, who were not given such an exemption from the restrictive 1954 McMahon Act, were to point out.) Even in the Middle East it took remarkably little time to improve the relationship. Britain still had its role to play with moderate Arab regimes. In 1958 London and Washington intervened in separate and not entirely coordinated ways in Lebanon and Jordan to protect moderate regimes against possible radical consequences after Egypt and Syria had formed the United Arab Republic and, even more important, the monarchy in Iraq had been overthrown. London wanted as much coordination with Washington as possible, but the Eisenhower administration was still somewhat reluctant to be seen as part of a British effort to protect its role in the Middle East. Washington was intervening against possible Communist gains; London against Arab nationalism. Nevertheless, the operations succeeded in keeping the moderates in power in Lebanon and Jordan, with de Gaulle complaining about being left in the dark, despite traditional French interests in Lebanon.[19]

The French drew exactly the opposite conclusion from the British as a result of Suez. The Americans had already shown that they could not be trusted in Indochina; now they had shown that they could not be trusted in the Middle East either. Why then should they be trusted in Europe? Paris felt that Washington had not even stood up sufficiently against the Soviet nuclear threats during Suez. Foreign Minister Christian Pineau stated that the Atlantic alliance was the principal victim of Suez. "If our allies had abandoned us in difficult, if not dramatic circumstances, they were capable of doing so again if Europe in turn felt itself threatened." The French now made the final decision to go ahead with the production of their own nuclear weapons.

The wounds of Suez were kept open by serious Franco-American differences over the war in Algeria, where France was struggling to maintain its territorial integrity, of which Algeria allegedly was a part, while the United States wanted the support of moderate Arabs against Communist expansion. This included the FLN fighting the French in Algeria and newly independent moderate states Tunisia and Morocco. The US also had strategic bases in Morocco and Libya to consider. As Eisenhower politely expressed it to a leading French general, "It would be difficult for the United States to openly express support for France against the Arabs in view of the anti-colonial tradition in the United States. To attempt to do this would only arouse a controversy in the United States that would not be useful to France."[20]

France was bitterly disappointed. Paris, once again, came out more strongly in favor of European integration, but now firmly on the Continental model. In French eyes the British too had failed their loyalty test. Suez was an important part of the background to the French decision to support the Rome treaties of 1957 establishing the European Economic Community and Euratom. Thus, all this had been done before de Gaulle came to power in 1958.

Back Yards of Different Sorts: Southern Africa and Cuba

In Africa south of the Sahara the United States was long happy to leave the initiative with colonial powers Britain, France, Belgium, and Portugal. Of all the regions in the world, this part of Africa was clearly least important from the point of view of US national interests. While colonialism would ultimately have to go even here, the Americans agreed that this would be in a rather distant future since the Africans still largely behaved like "children." The Eisenhower administration emphasized moderation on both sides. The Europeans were to undertake reform aiming at independence some time in the future; the Africans were to show patience. When independence came much more quickly than had been assumed, the US stressed the advantages of continued cooperation between the former colony and the old mother country.[21]

This policy was modified by the Kennedy administration, which emphasized the importance of good relations with the new countries. Attacks on their neutrality in the Cold War largely stopped, economic assistance increased, as did pressure on the colonial powers to complete the process of decolonization. Portugal's policies in Angola and elsewhere were of particular importance in this context. Still, even under Kennedy Africa was really of limited interest to American policymakers, except when Cold War aspects were clearly involved as happened in the Congo. There, again, the objective was to limit Soviet influence, in the form of support to Prime Minister Patrice Lumumba and, after the country more or less broke up, to various regional groups. In this perspective Washington's initial criticism of colonial master Belgium was soon toned down.[22]

Portugal remained an important ally, not least because of the still highly valued base rights in the Azores, which somewhat limited US criticism of its colonial policies in Africa. Differences with France south of the Sahara were few and relatively small compared to the situation in North Africa. France wanted to maintain control, even after the independence of its former colonies; the US wanted to keep Communism out. While French control certainly kept the Soviet Union out, Washington disliked the harsh treatment meted out to Sekou Toure's Guinea after he broke with the French *Communauté* in 1958. The first more serious dispute came in 1965 with pro-American Sese Seko Mobutu's second, and this time effective, coup in the Congo. A Belgian colony which the French had clearly sought to bring inside its *chasse gardée* (private hunting ground), had now instead come under "Anglo-Saxon" influence.[23]

As underlined by Under Secretary George Ball, America's recognition of Africa as a "special European responsibility" was balanced by an assumed European sense of "our responsibility in Latin America."[24] And, indeed, the Europeans did defer to the United States in Latin America. When in 1954 the CIA intervened successfully to overthrow the elected Arbenz government in Guatemala, the British and other West European allies supported Washington in the UN Security Council. Privately Eden complained about America's naval blockade against Guatemala because it threatened cherished British maritime transit rights; publicly he kept quiet on the ground that "the first priority must be given to the solidity of the Anglo-American alliance."[25]

Initially, with Britain in the lead, most European governments were skeptical of Washington's increasingly negative response to Fidel Castro's coming to power in Cuba in 1959. Macmillan rejected Eisenhower's repeated requests for an economic embargo of Cuba. Reminiscent of earlier debates concerning China, the British Prime Minister expressed "doubts as to whether economic hardship would encourage opposition to Castro, especially if it could be blamed on the Americans and mitigated by Russian help."[26]

When a truly major crisis occurred, such as during the Cuban missile crisis in October 1962, the West Europeans were quick to support the United States. In a moment of real danger, and therefore supreme secrecy, the American response to the installation of Soviet medium-range missiles on Cuba was determined by a small group within the Kennedy administration, the so-called ExComm. NATO as such was only brought in after the crisis was largely over. Within these confines, President Kennedy himself made a point of consulting British ambassador David Ormsby-Gore, a personal friend of his, and he also kept more closely in touch with Macmillan than with any of the other European leaders. The British Prime Minister was happy to be *primus inter pares*, in fact so much so that in his memoirs he wrote that "we were 'in on' and took full part in . . . every American move . . . during the crisis." This definitely represented a gross exaggeration of the role Britain had played. Somewhat more correctly, he also noted that "our complete calm helped to keep the Europeans calm...during the crisis."[27]

During the missile crisis itself General de Gaulle in Paris was uncharacteristically supportive of the United States, though, when briefed by former Secretary of State Dean Acheson, he did initially note the important difference between being consulted and being informed; it was clearly the latter that was being done. Still, he asked Acheson to "tell your President that France will support him...I think that under the circumstances President Kennedy had no other choice. This is his national prerogative and France understands." In the longer run, however, de Gaulle felt that the Cuban crisis had illustrated his well-known point about it being more or less inevitable that the United States would think first and foremost of itself. The Europeans could risk being abandoned or there could even be "annihilation without representation."[28]

The crisis was resolved when Khruschev agreed to withdraw the Soviet missiles from Cuba in return for an American non-invasion pledge of the island and, as became public knowledge only many years later, a secret agreement to withdraw American medium-range missiles from Turkey. After the Cuban missile crisis Washington became super-sensitive on the matter of Cuba. When Alec Douglas-Home, in his brief period as Prime Minister in 1963–4, agreed to sell British buses to Cuba, President Johnson apparently never contacted him personally again.[29]

Vietnam: Not Even a Platoon of Bagpipers

As we have seen, while at first the Europeans complained about the lack of support from Washington, gradually the US came to play the leading role not only in Latin America, but also in most of Asia, and even took an interest in certain parts of Africa. Much of America's involvement flowed from the anti-Communism that dominated US foreign policy in general. The Europeans shared the anti-Communism, but disliked being squeezed out of areas they had traditionally dominated. After having abandoned their colonies, it was not difficult for them to feel concern that an American anti-Communist campaign in the Third World could detract from America's crucial commitment to Europe. In the 1960s and 1970s Vietnam provided the supreme example of the United States asking for European support, of how strained transatlantic relations could become, but also of the bonds that in the end kept the two sides together.

The American build-up in Vietnam was rapid. In 1961, 692 US military advisers were there; by 1962 this number had jumped to 12,000, in 1965 to 190,000, in 1966 to 390,000, and by 1968 to 500,000. The problem was that this dramatic increase did not really improve the American position. The NLF (Viet Cong) and particularly the North Vietnamese were not only able to respond, but also to mount spectacular new offensives. To minimize the effects in America of the build-up the Pentagon had to draw down forces and equipment in Europe. From 1964 to 1972 the number of US troops in Europe dropped from 318,000 to 252,000; more than half of those removed were sent to Vietnam.[30] Time and again the Europeans emphasized their concern about the escalation in Vietnam and the resulting diminution of the US commitment in Europe.[31]

For military and, even more, for important political reasons, Washington pressed its allies to contribute troops. To show that the United States was not alone, it wanted as many flags as possible represented in Vietnam. Since the symbolism was so important, President Johnson suggested to London that a "platoon of bagpipers" would be sufficient. If British troops could not be introduced directly into Vietnam, then perhaps Thailand could be considered. Secretary of State Rusk argued that Europe and the United States could not preserve their security merely by holding a line across Europe. "Their common security is involved also in what happens in Africa, in the Middle East, Latin America, South Asia, and the Western Pacific. They have a vital common interest in the defeat of active aggression in Southeast Asia." Johnson threatened that a lack of support could have consequences: "it has been costly that Europe has tended to 'disassociate' itself from the Viet Nam problem... the concept of disassociation can cut both ways."[32] For Washington the result was disappointing. Some of its allies in Asia responded positively, with Australia, New Zealand, South Korea, Thailand, and the Philippines sending troops. The Europeans did not. The British had a small military mission in Vietnam, but no troops, not even bagpipers. West Germany gave significant economic assistance; others sent some money, medical aid, or educational assistance. That was all.

If the United States had been disappointed with the Europeans during the Korean War, this was an even bigger let-down. Privately the Europeans could acknowledge "the notion that US fidelity to its Far Eastern commitments is important to Europeans protected by the US commitment here." Publicly, to avoid further controversy there was not a single mention of the conflict in Southeast Asia in NATO communiqués during the period of American involvement.[33]

The American focus was sharpest on Britain. America's heavy obligations in Vietnam led Washington into a reevaluation of Britain's world role. Shifting noticeably from its previous position, Washington should now encourage London to do as much as possible wherever it could. From Suez to Singapore the United Kingdom actually carried the main burden. It should be strongly induced to continue doing so since the United States could not be "the gendarmes of the universe."[34] In December 1965 Rusk explained to Johnson that the United States needed to insist that the British government understand that "in many areas, (e.g. Middle East) the UK can perform political security functions that no other nation can take over." Consequently, "both UK and US interests would be damaged were the UK to withdraw from its long-established positions."[35] The days of undercutting Britain's role were definitely gone.

Still, support for the war was very limited in Britain. London had three main arguments against participating. First, Britain was already involved in a conflict of its own in the region where it supported Malaysia in the *Konfrontasi* with Indonesia, in turn backed by China. Prime Minister Wilson argued that this was London's contribution to the fight against international Communism. With General Suharto's successful coup in Jakarta in the fall of 1965 this conflict ended, however. Second, Britain's economic problems in general and its balance of payments problems in particular being what they were, it just could not do more in Vietnam. In fact, so difficult was Britain's position that the threat of devaluation was almost always present. Third, Britain had been the co-chairman of the 1954 Geneva conference. As such it felt it had a strong and continued responsibility to look for possible peaceful solutions to the conflict in Southeast Asia.[36]

But although no troops were forthcoming, the American pressure generally made Britain refrain from publicly criticizing America's policy in Vietnam. Once asked why he put up with Johnson's rudeness and why Britain did not take a stronger line against the war in Vietnam, Wilson gave an entirely candid reply: "Because we can't kick our creditors in the balls." On some critical occasions London even explicitly supported the American role, although rather grudgingly. Privately Wilson was aching to contribute to a peaceful solution to the dispute. In that context, in February 1965, after an American bombing raid against North Vietnam, Wilson and Johnson had a very brusque telephone conversation. The conversation reached a low point when Johnson told Wilson bluntly that "I won't tell you how to run Malaysia and you don't tell us how to run Vietnam."[37] Johnson made it clear he would not see Wilson if the latter decided to come to Washington to present his ideas. (They did meet two months later.) While Wilson was proud of his close relationship with Johnson and visited him in the US seven times, Johnson liked Wilson much less and actually never visited him in Britain.[38]

Despite Washington's financial assistance to maintain the pound and its new-found support for Britain's global role, Wilson's economic problems were just too great for him to fall in with American wishes. Public expenditure had to be cut, and defense could not be exempted. The Labour government's decision to abandon Britain's military role in that vast region of traditional British domination east of Suez had been largely made in

July 1967, but its implementation was speeded up by the devaluation of the pound in November 1967. Significant cuts had to be made in defense commitments elsewhere too, in what was the third major reappraisal of Britain's role after 1945. The first had come in Greece, Turkey, India, and Palestine in 1947–8; the second in the Middle East after Suez. Britain was coming to focus increasingly on Europe, as did the Conservatives when they came back to power in 1970, despite their criticism of Labour for "scuttling" from east of Suez.[39]

While George Ball saw a silver lining in Britain's problems in that they could finally make London focus much more sharply on its European role, LBJ and Rusk were very disappointed with these developments. Rusk stated that he was "profoundly dismayed" by the British withdrawal. It "represented a major withdrawal of the UK from world affairs, and it was a catastrophic loss to human society." Washington was now hoping that the Conservatives would win the elections coming up in 1970. They did, but little changed as far as Britain's policy east of Suez was concerned.[40]

There was little need for the French to show restraint toward the Americans—after all, when Paris had failed so miserably in Vietnam, why should Washington succeed? The Johnson administration spent a lot of energy trying to refute this historical parallel, which, of course, in the end turned out to be largely true. The two countries had virtually traded places: for France in the early 1950s, simply read the United States in the 1960s.

De Gaulle's criticism started early and was stepped up significantly in 1964 after he reestablished diplomatic relations with China. The general advocated "neutralization" as the solution, encouraged by the initial effects of the neutralization of Laos in 1962. On purpose he kept vague exactly what area was to be neutralized. It could be anything from South Vietnam alone to all of Southeast Asia, including Thailand. Johnson saw this as a cover for the American retreat he so strongly opposed.[41] US relations with France were becoming strained on all fronts at the same time. De Gaulle's escalating criticism of America's role in Vietnam was accompanied by France's withdrawal from the military structure of NATO. It proved a small consolation that, contrary to Britain, after the withdrawal from Algeria, France did not significantly reduce its overseas commitments during the 1960s.[42] At first, Johnson took de Gaulle's criticism surprisingly mildly, but as opposition to the war increased in the United States itself, LBJ became more concerned. Yet, there was not much he could do about de Gaulle and, as long as the latter was relatively isolated in Western Europe, the damage was significant, but still limited.[43]

Among the other NATO allies, Italy pursued a position rather close to that of Britain, or perhaps even a little more supportive, torn between its traditional bonds to the United States and opposition to the ever escalating American warfare, mixed with hopes of Italy possibly pursuing a diplomatic role to end the war. The last point reinforced the need to stay on good terms with Washington. Most of the smaller allies were rather more critical of the United States. When the Labor government in Norway recognized North Vietnam in 1971, President Nixon became furious; diplomatic relations were almost broken and various implied threats presented. Norway was the first NATO country to recognize the main enemy of the United States. Only neutrals Sweden and Switzerland had preceded it. Norwegian humanitarian aid was divided among North Vietnam, NLF, and South Vietnam. Condemnation of the American Christmas bombing of Hanoi in 1972 was widespread, even among traditional friends of the United States.[44]

On the other hand, West Germany went quite far in expressing understanding for the American position. While public opposition against America's warfare increased and Bonn's bonds with Paris argued in favor of a low profile, the Erhard and then even the Kiesinger–Brandt government still showed the strongest sympathy for Washington among NATO allies. Any military involvement, including the engineering troops desired by Washington, was excluded for a country that limited its role strictly to the NATO area. Bonn did, however, rank second only to Washington in extending economic assistance to Saigon, and its support for the US is understandable: West Germany was militarily dependent on the United States for its security. For decades the US had protected it, and West Berlin in particular, against Soviet "aggression." This feeling dominated the thinking of most of the German political establishment and of the older generation in West Germany, unlike the many younger people who were protesting in the streets. If the US pulled out of Vietnam, would it then come to pull out of Berlin as well? Meeting with de Gaulle in June 1965, Chancellor Erhard poignantly expressed the German line of reasoning about Vietnam:

the Americans are fighting there for reasons of treaties and solemn obligations. Should the Americans leave that area...there will be an inevitable reaction from the German people, because the Germans would say to themselves that just as the Americans were not able to hold South Vietnam, they would not be able to hold unto... Berlin if it were seriously threatened. It came down unavoidably to the question if one could generally trust America.[45]

The Soviet invasion of Czechoslovakia in August 1968 undoubtedly also tempered the will of many European politicians to criticize the United States. Under Nixon–Kissinger there was surprisingly little explicit criticism of US actions in Indochina from Wilson and Heath in Britain, from Brandt in Germany (though he was somewhat more critical than his predecessors had been), or even from Pompidou in France, not only in public but also in private conversations.[46] The demonstrators in the streets were making much of the leaders' case anyway; despite the increased American bombing, under Nixon the US troops were really on the way out of Indochina; the French were instrumental in setting up American–Vietnamese negotiations in Paris that in January 1973 led to a cease-fire; and, again, the focus of the European leaders was on the situation in Europe where there was no desire to weaken the American military role. In fact many feared that the United States would come to make undue concessions to Moscow in Europe to find a diplomatic way out of Vietnam.[47]

Out-of-Area and the Year of Europe

In the Middle East, at the public level in the US there was a deep sympathy for the state of Israel, particularly among Jews, but also among the wider American population. Among some diplomats, military leaders, and, most of all, American oil companies with interests in the Middle East a different attitude could be found. They wanted the United States to work closely with moderate Arab regimes. Eisenhower's lack of support for Israel had shown most clearly in his forceful reaction against the Israeli–British–French Suez expedition. Until 1962 the United States actually refused to provide Israel with arms; only after 1967 did it become Israel's major arms supplier.

Naturally Britain had been skeptical at first of a state where the Jews had worked so hard to get the British out. But with London's problems with Egypt growing rapidly in the 1950s, cooperation with Israel increased. The same happened in France. As its problems in Algeria only grew, Paris persuaded itself that radical Arab countries were the source of the problem. One answer was to step up cooperation with Israel, and in fact France was its major arms supplier until the United States took over that role. (In its very early days Israel had received crucial supplies from Czechoslovakia, reflecting Stalin's early hopes for Israel.)

Under Kennedy and even more under Johnson the American–Israeli relationship became much closer. Economic and military aid increased dramatically. So did Washington's political understanding of Israeli military actions, as reflected in the support for Israel's preventive war in 1967 (the Six-Day War) against alleged Egyptian and Jordanian military preparations. Two main reasons could be found for the change on the American side: first, as the Soviet Union became a more important actor in the Middle East and was able to work with more radical Arab governments, the United States responded by emphasizing its Israeli connection; second, because Jews played an important role within the Democratic party, it was more important for Kennedy and Johnson to hold on to the votes and the money of America's Jews than it had been for Republican Eisenhower, influenced more by military considerations and oil interests.

In Europe, on the other hand, de Gaulle had started his reevaluation of French policy before the 1967 war. With the war in Algeria finally over in 1962, it now became a concern to work closely with independent Algeria and other Arab states. The 1967 war itself, which resulted in a dramatic Israeli victory and its ensuing occupation of the West Bank, Old Jerusalem, the Golan Heights, the Gaza Strip, and Sinai, changed European notions of the Jewish state dramatically. For many Europeans it was no longer a tiny island of Holocaust survivors in a sea of hostile Arabs, but a regional superpower occupying important Arab lands. De Gaulle even spoke of the Jews as "an elite people, self-confident and dominating...", words that were not intended to be as negative as they sounded, but that certainly infuriated Israelis. Europe was also becoming increasingly dependent on Arab oil. In 1973 it received 70 per cent of its oil from the Persian Gulf while the United States imported only 35 per cent of its domestic requirements, and then from several different regions.[48]

This was the background to the very different American and European reactions to the Yom Kippur War of 1973 (October War for the Arabs). The transatlantic split encompassed three main issues: the military resupply of Israel, the American alert vis-à-vis the Soviet Union, and the Arab oil embargo against the West. When, after a few days of hesitation following the Arab attack to see how the war was actually developing, the United States started to rush military supplies to Israel, it wanted European cooperation. The Nixon administration took the view that arms to Israel "is just as much in the vital interest of West Germany and the other NATO allies as it is in our interest."[49] The European allies saw it differently; they banned any use of their territory or air space to facilitate the American resupply effort. Only Holland was willing to help, but it was hardly geographically relevant on its own. Crucial Portugal accepted American use of the Azores, but only after Nixon had threatened to "leave Portugal to its fate in a hostile world unless he [President Caetano] complied immediately with the US request." West Germany initially let the Pentagon use the American facilities in Germany, but after a few days requested that this be stopped. Britain, under pro-European Edward Heath, to Washington's anger, declined the use of US bases in Britain and on Cyprus. Kissinger noted with bitterness that "the Soviet Union had been freer to use NATO airspace than the United States, for much of the Soviet airlift to the Middle East overflew allied airspace without challenge."[50]

When the Israeli troops were in the process of crushing Egypt's army, the Soviet Union threatened to intervene unless the Israelis stopped. Washington responded by putting its troops on DefConIII status, the highest state of readiness in peacetime conditions. This was done without informing the European allies in advance, even allies where there was a large American troop presence. The Europeans expressed anger at such lack of consultation, but further military tension ended when on 24 October Henry Kissinger was able to negotiate a ceasefire in the Middle East. Then, however, the Arab members of OPEC declared an embargo against the United States and soon against Holland. As we shall later see, the embargo led to several different responses on the Western side. The energy conference convened in Washington in February 1974 highlighted these complicated cleavages, and the creation of the International Energy Authority (IEA) resolved few of the issues.

In his April 1973 address launching the Year of Europe, Kissinger wanted to bring the United States and Western Europe closer together after a period when the Europeans felt that Nixon–Kissinger had focused just too much on America's adversaries and too little on its friends. The story about the Year of Europe is told in the next chapter. What matters most in this context is Kissinger's argument in his initial speech that "The United States has global interests and responsibilities. Our European allies have regional interests." The comment caused great irritation in Europe. In fact, it was argued that the United States was in many ways much more self-contained than were most European countries. The Europeans, particularly the former colonial powers, had economic and cultural, and especially in France's case, even military ties that were relatively at least as important as those the United States had with its various partners in Asia and Africa. Still, as the British case illustrated so clearly, Europe's extra-European political and military commitments had been reduced and European governments now focused more and more on the building of a stronger Europe and on establishing a détente with the Soviet Union. For long the United States had favored this retrenchment, but as it was overburdening itself in Vietnam it was now regretting an outcome to which it had itself contributed so much.

Thus, there were frequent out-of-area differences between the United States and its European allies. Yet, the impact of these disputes was softened in several different ways. Rarely if ever were these differences between the United States on one side and all the European powers on the other. During the Suez crisis Washington actually received the support of most of the European capitals when it denounced the British–French action. During the Vietnam War, which came closest to a real dispute between the two sides of the Atlantic, the German in particular, but also the British government and even those of some of the smaller allies, agreed to refrain from public criticism that could harm the basic American–European relationship. In the Middle East differences between the United States and Western Europe widened, especially during and after the 1973 war, but then Europe's role in the region had become smaller than before and, again, on most Middle East issues there was no unified European position. Above all, for decades the situation in Europe was clearly what mattered most. The American–European debate about how détente with the Soviet Union was to be maintained in Europe when it was being challenged by so many conflicts between the United States and the Soviet Union outside of Europe will be told in later chapters.

Notes

1. For a case study very much in these terms, see Mark Atwood Lawrence, "Transnational Coalition-Building and the Making of the Cold War in Indochina, 1947–1949," *Diplomatic History*, 26:3 (Summer 2002) 453–80.
2. This title is taken from Thorne, *Allies of a Kind.*
3. For a useful recent addition to a rapidly growing literature, see David Ryan and Victor Pungong (eds.), *The United States and Decolonization. Power and Freedom* (Houndmills: Macmillan, 2000).
4. Louis and Robinson, "The United States and the Liquidation of the British Empire in Tropical Africa, 1941–1951," in Gifford and Louis (eds.), *The Transfer of Power in Africa*, 31–56. The quotation is from p. 47.
5. Dirk U. Stikker, *Men of Responsibility: A Memoir.* (London: John Murray, 1966) 113–52. The quotation is from p. 118.
6. Lloyd C. Gardner, "How We Lost Vietnam, 1940–54," in Ryan and Pungong (eds.), *The United States and Decolonization*, 121–39; Victor Pungong, "The United States and the International Trusteeship System," in ibid. 85–101.
7. Ernest R. May, *"Lessons" of the Past: The Use and Misuse of History in American Foreign Policy* (New York: Oxford University Press, 1973), 52–86.
8. Michael F. Hopkins, "The Price of Cold War Partnership: Sir Oliver Franks and the British Military Commitment in the Korean War," *Cold War History*, 1:2 (Jan. 2001), 28–46; Richard Whelan, *Drawing the Line: The Korean War, 1950–1953* (Boston: Little, Brown, 1990), 152–3; David Rees, *Korea: The Limited War* (New York: St. Martin's, 1964), 32–3.
9. William S. Stueck, *The Korean War: An International History* (Princeton: Princeton University Press, 1995), 136–42.
10. *FRUS*, 1950, III, Paper Prepared by the Tripartite Drafting Group of the Preliminary Conversations of the United States, United Kingdom, and France, 1 Sept. 1950, 1171.
11. North Atlantic Council, *NATO Final Communiqués 1949–1974*, 74–5.
12. Dwight D. Eisenhower, *Mandate for Change* (New York: Doubleday, 1956), 449.
13. For a short account of the origins of ANZUS, see R. J. O'Neill, "The Korean War and the Origins of ANZUS," in Carl Bridge (ed.), *Munich to Vietnam: Relations with Britain and the United States since the 1930s* (Charlton: Melbourne University Press, 1965), 99–113. For longer accounts, see J. G. Starke, *The ANZUS Treaty Alliance* (Melbourne: Melbourne University Press, 1991) and W. David McIntyre, *Background to the ANZUS Pact: Policy-Making, Strategy, and Diplomacy, 1945–55* (New York: St. Martin's, 1995).
14. Sherwood, *Allies in Crisis*, 58.
15. For relatively recent studies of the American–Israeli relationship, see Yaacov Bar-Siman-Tov, "The United States and Israel since 1948: A 'Special Relationship'?" *Diplomatic History*, 22 (Spring 1998), 231–62 and the commentaries on that article by Peter L. Hahn (263–72) and David Schoenbaum (273–83) in the same issue; Abraham Ben-Zvi, *The United States and Israel: The Limits of the Special Relationship* (New York: Columbia University Press, 1993).

16. For a short account, see Martin Thomas, "From Dien Bien Phu to Evian. Anglo-French Imperial Relations, 1954–1962," in Alan Sharp and Glyn Stone (eds.), *Anglo-French Relations in the Twentieth Century: Rivalry and Cooperation* (London: Routledge, 2000), 310–19.

17. H. W. Brands, *The Specter of Neutralism: The United States and the Emergence of the Third World, 1947–1960* (New York: Columbia University Press, 1989). He deals with Egypt on 223–303; Sherwood, *Allies in Crisis*, 74–6.

18. Sherwood, *Allies in Crisis*, 92.

19. Sherwood, *Allies in Crisis*, 88–98. For interesting accounts about the events in 1958, see Wm. Roger Louis and Roger Owen (eds.), *A Revolutionary Year: The Middle East in 1958* (London and New York: Tauris, 2002).

20. Charles Cogan, *Oldest Allies, Guarded Friends* (Westport: Praeger, 1994), 108–17. The quotation is from p. 110. See also Wall, *France, the United States, and the Algerian War*; Martin Thomas, "Defending a Lost Cause? France and the United States Vision of Imperial Rule in French North Africa, 1945–1956," *Diplomatic History*, 26:2 (Summer 2002), 215–47.

21. For a recent revisionist account stressing how limited US influence was in West Africa, see Ebere Nwaubani, *The United States and Decolonization in West Africa, 1950–1960* (Rochester: University of Rochester Press, 2001). Karl P. Magyar (ed.), *United States Interests and Policies in Africa* (London: Macmillan, 2000) argues that Vice President Richard M. Nixon's Africa tour in 1957 came to represent a partial turning point in Washington's policy toward Africa south of the Sahara. For a summing up of the opposite view, see Nwaubani, *United States and Decolonization*, pp. xv–xvi. Both of these accounts appear to exaggerate their points of view.

22. Douglas T. Stuart and William Tow, *The Limits of Alliance: NATO Out-of-Area Problems Since 1949* (Baltimore: Johns Hopkins University Press, 1990), 71–2.

23. Peter J. Schraeder, "Cold War to Cold Peace: Explaining US-French Competition in Francophone Africa," *Political Science Quarterly*, 115:3 (2000), 398–400; John Kent, "The United States and the Decolonization of Black Africa, 1945–63," in Ryan and Pungong, *The United States and Decolonization*, 168–87. For an analysis emphasizing the changes with Kennedy, see Richard D. Mahoney, *JFK: Ordeal in Africa* (New York: 1983).

24. Schraeder, "Cold War to Cold Peace," 399, citing George W. Ball, *The Disciples of Power*, page reference missing in Schraeder.

25. Stuart and Tow, *The Limits of Alliance*, 151–2.

26. Stuart and Tow, *The Limits of Alliance*, 152.

27. Harold Macmillan, *At the End of the Day, 1961–1963* (London: Macmillan, 1973), 216; Sherwood, *Allies in Crisis*, 120–2.

28. Sherwood, *Allies in Crisis*, 116–23.

29. Sylvia A. Ellis, "Lyndon Johnson, Harold Wilson and the Vietnam War: A *Not* So Special Relationship?" in Jonathan Hollowell (ed.), *Twentieth-Century Anglo-American Relations* (Houndmills: Palgrave, 2001), 189, 200–1.

30. Nelson, *A History of US Military Forces in Germany*, 81, 103. For much higher numbers, indicating far larger withdrawals, see Stuart and Tow, *The Limits of Alliance*, 77–8.

31. *FRUS*, 1964–1968, XIII, Telegram from Secretary of State Rusk to the Department of State, 14 Dec. 1965, 283.

32. Sherwood, *Allies in Crisis*, 26–7; Frank Costigliola, "The Vietnam War and the Challenge to American Power in Europe," in Lloyd Gardner and Ted Gittinger (eds.), *International Perspectives on Vietnam* (College Station: Texas A&M University Press, 2000), 147–8.

33. *FRUS*, 1964–1968, XIII, Telegram from the Mission to NATO to the Department of State, 18 Dec. 1965, 287. See also *FRUS*, 1964–1968, XIII, Telegram from the Mission to NATO to the Department of State, 17 Dec. 1966, 525–6; North Atlantic Council, *NATO Final Communiqués 1949–1974*.

34. *FRUS*, 1964–68, XII, Memorandum of conversation Rusk–Gordon Walker, 7 Dec. 1964, 477.

35. Jeremy Fielding, "Coping with Decline: US Policy toward the British Defense Reviews of 1966," *Diplomatic History*, 23:4 (Fall 1999), 646.

36. Wm. Roger Louis, "The Dissolution of the British Empire in the Era of Vietnam," *The American Historical Review*, 107:1 (Feb. 2002), 1–25; Matthew Jones, *Conflict and Confrontation in South East Asia, 1961–1965: Britain, the United States and the Creation of Malaysia* (Cambridge: Cambridge University Press, 2002).

37. The quotations are from Louis, "The Dissolution of the British Empire in the Era of Vietnam," 4, 14.

38. Ellis, "Lyndon Johnson, Harold Wilson and the Vietnam War," 180–4, 199–201; John W. Young, "Britain and 'LBJ's War', 1964–68," *Cold War History*, 2:3 (April 2002), 63–92.

39. Saki Dockrill, *Britain's Retreat from East of Suez: The Choice between Europe and the World?* (Houndmills: Palgrave, 2002).

40. *FRUS*, 1964–1968, XII, Memorandum of conversation Rusk–Brown, 11 Jan. 1968, 604; *FRUS*, 1964–1968, XII, Johnson to Wilson, 11 Jan. 1968, 608–9; *FRUS*, 1964–1968, XII, Paper prepared in the Department of State, undated, 618–24; *FRUS*, 1964–1968, XII, Notes of NSC meeting 587, 4 June 1968, 624–7; Louis, "The Dissolution of the British Empire in the Era of Vietnam," 3.

41. Fredrik Logevall, *Choosing War: The Lost Chance for Peace and the Escalation of the War in Vietnam* (Berkeley: University of California Press, 1999), 103–7.

42. Sherwood, *Allies in Crisis*, 129.

43. Logevall, *Choosing War*, 83–5, 95–9, 129–33.

44. Rolf Tamnes, *Oljealder 1965–1995* (Oil Age 1965–1995). Vol. 6 in *Norsk Utenrikspolitikks Historie* (The History of Norwegian Foreign Policy) (Oslo: Universitetsforlaget, 1997), 356–7.

45. Costigliola, "The Vietnam War and the Challenge to American Power in Europe", 150–2.

46. Henry A. Kissinger, *White House Years* (Boston: Little, Brown and Company, 1979), 424–5.

47. See Leopoldo Nuti's essay, "Italy and the Battle of the Euromissiles," in Olav Njølstad (ed.), *From Conflict Escalation to Conflict Transformation: The Cold War in the 1980s* (London: Frank Cass, forthcoming.)

48. Jean Lacouture, *De Gaulle. The Ruler: 1945–1970* (London: Harvill, 1991), 434–46. The quotation is from 443; Sherwood, *Allies in Crisis*, 142 states that the US imported only 5 per cent. However, Kissinger writes that in 1970 the US imported 35 per cent of what it consumed. For this, see his *Years of Renewal* (New York: Simon & Schuster, 1999), 665. I have followed the latter.
49. Sherwood, *Allies in Crisis*, 138.
50. Sherwood, *Allies in Crisis*, 138–42.

6

Conflict and Cooperation: American–Western European Relations (not) Redefined, 1969–1977

Redefinitions and Cooperation

In the late 1960s the wider framework for and the basic structure of the North Atlantic alliance was being challenged on virtually all fronts at the same time, causing the need for a reappraisal of relationships. In the Cold War with the Soviet Union and its allies, the confrontation continued, but now it was being combined with détente, i.e. cooperation on important military, political, and economic issues. In the American–European relationship, it was obvious that Europe was striking out more on its own. Not only France, but even loyal West Germany was developing its own policy, particularly toward the Soviet Union and Eastern Europe in the form of its *Ostpolitik*. Western Europe had also come to count for more than it had in the early years of NATO. With British membership in the European Community, the EC was beginning to rival the United States in importance, at least economically. In Southern Europe a democratic revolution was taking place.

On the other side of the Atlantic, even the Nixon administration was talking about the decline of the US and how it would now have to cooperate with the other economic centers of the world. Such self-doubts were greatly stimulated by the American withdrawal from Vietnam and the Communist takeover of South Vietnam. Also outside of Europe, the combination of the rise of the Organization of Petroleum-Exporting Countries (OPEC) and the volatility of the Middle East highlighted a growing energy problem that was to prove quite troublesome in Atlantic relations. The rise of Japan and the Pacific rim was also beginning to redefine the role and importance of Western Europe in the world. In 1979 trade across the Pacific was to be greater than across the Atlantic.

With all these redefinitions taking place at the same time, one can easily imagine the strain they imposed on American–European relations; and, indeed, many were the quarrels and debates, on relations with the Soviet

Union, on alliance questions, the Middle East, Vietnam, energy matters. Yet, this was nothing new, for there had always been quarrels and debates among the NATO members; but these were more structural now than they had been earlier, in the sense that they touched basic relationships not only single issues, however important. What was amazing, though, was how well even these more structural debates were contained within the alliance framework.

In a period when the United States felt it was in decline, it needed its crucial allies in Western Europe even more than before. For their part, the Europeans, while wanting to strike out more on their own, resisted anything that might reduce the role of the United States in Europe, and thus continued to issue their invitations to the United States to stay in Europe; in these years the emphasis was particularly on the need for the American troops to remain. Europe's dependence on America, especially militarily, endured. In fact, Western Europe did not really expect to be the equal of the United States; it did not even want to be. In this basic sense the American–Western European relationship was *not* redefined.

The United States, Western Europe, and Détente

There had been periods of détente even in the 1950s, the most significant of which occurred after the death of Stalin, resulting in the end of the Korean and then the first Vietnam War, neutralization of Austria, and "the spirit of Geneva" after the Geneva summit of 1955—the first such meeting since Potsdam in 1945. Suez and the Soviet crushing of the Hungarian uprising in 1956 largely ended that period of détente, and Berlin also remained a festering sore in East–West relations. The successful end to the Cuban missile crisis in 1962 was to introduce another, longer period of détente. A partial test-ban treaty was signed; nuclear weapons were banned in space and in Latin America; a non-proliferation treaty was concluded in 1968; and—by no means least important—negotiations started on limiting strategic arms that in 1972 resulted in the SALT I treaty. In the early 1970s summits between Richard Nixon and Leonid Brezhnev became yearly affairs.[1]

Détente could easily come to represent a challenge to the stability of American–European relations since, the Soviet threat declining, the allies might conclude that they did not really need each other that much any more. In Europe there was also the fear of superpower condominium, of Washington and Moscow dictating events together in the way they had allegedly done at Yalta. While the United States itself could occasionally act rather independently, it was very much on Washington's mind that the European process of détente with the Soviet Union and Eastern Europe had to be managed within the NATO framework. If not done right, Moscow could play the Western

European allies off against the United States and each other. De Gaulle could be a sign of what would follow in other countries.

As we have seen, Washington had long hoped that once de Gaulle left the scene French relations with the United States and with NATO would improve, but Kissinger was quickly to disabuse the Nixon administration of any such notion. In fact, on the very day the general stepped down Kissinger wrote President Nixon that while he thought short-term changes would be small, "Over the long term... French foreign policy may become more difficult for us to live with." With a weaker government, the role of the left might well be strengthened, to the detriment of French–American relations. So much for the optimism as to what would follow after de Gaulle.[2]

The United States had been able to use the debate around the Harmel Report to strengthen NATO and reduce the challenge from de Gaulle. NATO was both to provide deterrence and to take the lead on détente, and its policy on Mutual and Balanced Force Reductions (MBFR) should be seen in the same light. The United States was looking for ways to follow up Harmel, and since the prospects for mutual force reductions would be weakened by NATO reductions alone, in June 1968 NATO affirmed the proposition that "the over-all military capability of NATO should not be reduced except as part of a pattern of mutual force reductions balanced in scope and timing." MBFR would not only put pressure on the Soviet Union to reduce its forces; it would also deflect pressure on the United States to undertake unilateral withdrawals from Europe. Again, this put France on the spot as, on the one hand, force reductions were part of the process of détente that the French clearly favored while, on the other, making even this a NATO matter would in some ways force France back into the alliance. This time Paris chose to dissociate itself from NATO's statement, but not to veto it.[3]

The Soviet invasion of Czechoslovakia in August 1968 held up détente temporarily, but not for long. The invasion had to be condemned, but the Western response was weak. Since Czechoslovakia was situated firmly within the Soviet sphere, there was little that could be done militarily without risking a war. Politically, the Johnson administration, with the President himself strongly in the lead, was preoccupied with the upcoming strategic arms control negotiations with Moscow, and even after the invasion Johnson wanted to achieve something before his own term was over. Britain was struggling with economic problems and a reduced defense role; France was in the middle of huge student–worker demonstrations shaking the very foundation of de Gaulle's regime. Thus, despite Western protests against the invasion, remarkably quickly détente was back on track.[4]

Germany and Berlin were at the heart of the Cold War in Europe. Under Konrad Adenauer's long rule Germany had come to insist that a resolution of the German question be a precondition for any wider Cold War agreement in

Europe, and any resolution of the German matter had to be on Western terms: a unified Germany based on free elections with the freedom for united Germany to join NATO. Under Kennedy, Washington had become increasingly impatient with Adenauer's inflexible stand, a stand that in fact held détente hostage to a Soviet capitulation in Germany. Though the building of the Berlin Wall in 1961 further underlined the failure of Adenauer's policy, nevertheless, Erhard had introduced only a few changes to it.

In his eagerness to promote détente, from 1966 to 1967 Johnson refused to let finding a solution to the German problem stand in the way of détente. In fact, it ought to be the other way around; the solution of other European issues could facilitate a German compromise. The Great Coalition government from 1966 to 1969 with CDU's Kurt Georg Kiesinger as Chancellor and SPD's Willy Brandt as Foreign Minister finally started to modify West Germany's policy. It abandoned the Hallstein Doctrine that had prohibited the recognition of any government that recognized the Communist regime in East Germany (with the exception of the Soviet Union). Except for improved relations with Romania, the success was still limited. The Soviet invasion in Czechoslovakia was a definite setback.

In 1969 a SPD–FDP government was formed under Brandt's leadership. The new Chancellor saw it as impossible to wean the individual "satellites" away from Moscow's grip; therefore priority now had to be given to relations with the Soviet Union. Brandt was also willing to go much further than his predecessors in recognizing political realities in Eastern Europe as they were. This was to result in important new agreements with the Soviet Union, Poland, and East Germany, whose governments and frontiers were now recognized by West Germany. In return Bonn was able to achieve recognition of its close ties with West Berlin and increased human contact across the Iron Curtain. West Germany quickly became the most important trading partner of the Soviet Union and the Eastern European countries. This was *Ostpolitik*. At first it was extremely controversial even inside West Germany; in April 1972 Brandt survived a no confidence vote by the narrowest of margins. Gradually, however, it became a popular success that could not be revoked. *Ostpolitik* recognized the status quo in Eastern Europe, a long-sought Soviet objective. But by recognizing this status quo Bonn hoped to transform it, at least in the long run. Brandt's expressed objective was *Wandel durch Annäherung*— transformation by moving closer together.[5]

The American response to *Ostpolitik* was very mixed indeed. Nixon wanted Kiesinger to continue as Chancellor and even sent him a congratulatory message after the elections. Since the FDP was now prepared to support the SPD, Brandt, however, took over.[6] In content *Ostpolitik* could be seen as highly complementary to Nixon–Kissinger's own détente. It could in fact be argued that this policy constituted the very heart of détente in that it was even more important in changing the overall climate between East and West than were the many arms control agreements signed by Washington and Moscow. Many felt that *Ostpolitik* signaled the end of the Cold War in Europe.

On the other hand, there could be no hiding the fact that not only Washington, but also Paris and even London, were quite concerned about *Ostpolitik*. It was one thing for the United States, France, or Britain to pursue such policies; it was quite another matter for Bonn to do so—in fact, Bonn was seen as forcing the pace. It was ahead of Washington in its efforts at East–West reconciliation while, more than anyone, it ought to be leaving the initiative to the Americans. Privately Nixon could use the strongest of negative terms about Brandt though Kissinger's response was much more temperate; Nixon even complained that the State Department bureaucracy was pro-Brandt and pro-Socialist and "I *totally* [sic] disagree with their approach."[7]

Germany's history was so special. *Ostpolitik* brought back memories of Rapallo, of the Soviet Union and Germany, the two outcasts of interwar Europe, moving closer together, a policy that with some historical simplification could be said to have resulted in the Nazi–Soviet Non-Aggression Pact of August 1939. The new fear was that Moscow, by playing the strong cards it held in controlling former German territory in Poland and East Germany, would be able to persuade the West Germans to abandon their strong ties to NATO and the West. *Ostpolitik* could also create expectations among the Eastern Europeans that could be destabilizing for East–West relations. Riots and rebellions could not be excluded.

Brandt repeatedly stressed that his Eastern policy was firmly based on his Western loyalties, but initially this hardly put American fears to rest. A National Security Council document affirmed that while Washington should continue to give general support to the "avowed objectives" of *Ostpolitik*:

We should not conceal . . . our longer range concern over the potentially divisive effect in the western alliance and inside Germany of any excessively active German policy in Eastern Europe as well as our concern over the potential risks of a crisis that such a policy might create in relations between Eastern European states and the USSR.[8]

Later, when in January 1972 Brandt diplomatically thanked Nixon for his support of *Ostpolitik*, Nixon coolly corrected him and said that his decision was not to support Brandt's policy, only not to oppose him.[9]

In fact, at least temporarily, concern over *Ostpolitik* helped drive France and the United States closer together. Nixon and French President Georges Pompidou agreed that West Germany, despite its cultural and economic ties with the West, was always potentially drawn toward the East. "The East holds millions of Germans as hostages. This is why we must keep Germany economically, politically and militarily tightly within the European Community."[10]

Pompidou feared that in the long run *Ostpolitik* could lead to German unification and the military withdrawal of the United States from Europe.[11]
French–German relations were at their poorest under Brandt–Pompidou,
which was one explanation why France under Pompidou became willing to
let Britain enter the European Community. When West Germany was becoming so resurgent, it would be advantageous to have Britain inside the
Community to help France control it.

Wilson and Heath shared much of the same concern about Germany's new
policy, and the London Foreign Office was even more skeptical, for although
London welcomed *Ostpolitik* as such, it soon came to see it as an effort to
draw West Germany into the Soviet orbit. In the early 1970s the Conservative
government viewed détente with greater suspicion than virtually any other
leading Western government. This was in part explained by the expulsion in
1971 of 105 Soviet citizens from Britain for espionage and by the resulting
Soviet response. Yet, as so frequently, Europe was divided in its response to
Ostpolitik and, while the Great Powers were initially skeptical, many of the
smaller countries, particularly in Scandinavia, were great admirers of Brandt
and his policy.

After a shaky start, in 1971–2 Bonn was more in step with Washington,
Paris, and London. The results of *Ostpolitik* had been significant indeed; the
other capitals were also cooperating closely with Moscow now; the worst
fears about the policy had proved unfounded; Brandt had shown that he had
a basic loyalty to the West. In fact, *Ostpolitik* would not have worked if the
other Western capitals had not agreed to cooperate with Bonn in the Four-
Power negotiations on Berlin that were an important part of this very policy.
Yet, just as he told him, Nixon did not support Brandt in the 1972 elections;
he stayed neutral between the SPD and the CDU.[12]

So, even *Ostpolitik* did not lead to any real crisis in American–European
relations. At the wider EC level the Hague summit on 1–2 December 1969 was
quite constructive after some difficult years earlier in the 1960s, and the foundation was laid for the inclusion of Britain, Ireland, and Denmark from 1973.
(Norway in the end voted against joining.) European Political Cooperation
(EPC) was agreed upon in the foreign policy area; an effort was even made to
bring about greater currency cooperation; the CAP was solidified.

While the Europeans, now with the Germans in the lead, generally pushed
hard for détente in Europe, they were afraid of anything that smacked of
superpower condominium. For the French, Yalta was the supreme historical
example of what the superpowers could do. Allegedly they had then divided
Europe between themselves, at the expense of the Europeans.[13] For the
French in particular the Declaration on the Prevention of Nuclear War, the
result of the Nixon–Brezhnev summit of June 1973, brought back memories
of Yalta. The starting point for the declaration had been a Soviet offer of an

American–Soviet alliance against China. Nixon had not rejected this outright, but had negotiated away most of the substance. Yet, in Article IV the declaration stated that in case relations between the parties or between either party and "other countries" (read China) involve the risk of nuclear conflict, the two parties "shall immediately enter into urgent consultations with each other and make every effort to avert this risk." As the French Foreign Minister Michel Jobert argued, it was natural that the two superpowers tried to avoid confrontation. "But what could be more natural also than that everyone in the world worry about this entente and the sense of arbitration that it presupposes." To a considerable extent even the West Germans worried about the condominium aspect of the 1973 declaration. Kissinger himself in fact came to regret it: "the result was too subtle; the negotiations too secret; the effort too long; and the necessary explanations to the Allies and to China too complex to have the desired effect."[14]

If many Europeans were skeptical of the 1973 declaration, the United States had been even more skeptical of what in 1973 became the Conference on Security and Cooperation in Europe (CSCE). The idea of an all-European security conference had originated in Moscow in 1954. It was generally seen as a Soviet propaganda weapon, at least until in 1969 the Soviets dropped their objections to the United States taking part and no longer insisted that the dissolution of NATO be on the conference agenda. The Soviet purpose was to have the intangibility of Europe's borders, especially that between East and West Germany, recognized. Indirectly this could be seen also as recognizing Soviet supremacy in Eastern and Central Europe. Now the Western Europeans became willing to pursue the security conference idea, first "in principle," then also in practice. For Brandt this meshed almost perfectly with his *Ostpolitik*; for Pompidou it gave *Ostpolitik* that wider setting which he wanted; while Heath had been skeptical to the CSCE concept, Wilson saw it as his chance to side with the Europeans; for the smaller European allies cooperation was clearly preferable to military confrontation.

To a large extent the EC countries acted as one unit in the CSCE negotiations, an early breakthrough for the European Political Cooperation. EPC had been established in 1969–70, again on French–German initiative, in an attempt to coordinate the foreign policy stances of the EC member countries. This was, however, to be done on an intergovernmental basis of meetings between the heads of state or ministers of the members, not on the supranational basis of the European Commission. In the CSCE the EC countries pushed for the inclusion of human rights principles, somewhat to the consternation of a Nixon administration that did not think much could come out of this in relations with the Soviets.

Washington disliked the CSCE idea, but to avoid becoming isolated diplomatically it accepted a European security conference with certain "linkages." Western access to West Berlin should be guaranteed; limits on conventional forces negotiated (until the MBFR negotiations were finally started in 1973). Soon the Western side widened the agenda further: confidence-building measures were introduced and, most important, so were various measures dealing with human rights and the free movement of people. "Respect for human rights and fundamental freedoms, including the freedom of thought, conscience, religion or belief" was to be affirmed as one of ten principles guiding relations between the participating states. In addition, certain specific points were to be given a more concrete form in Basket III of the planned final act. As Kissinger writes, "In some respects, it was a case of multilateral diplomacy run amok."[15]

But the heart of the matter was that more and more the Western side was transforming the negotiations to its advantage. The West Germans had already recognized the existing borders through *Ostpolitik*, but were now able to add a point about the peaceful change of borders. The CSCE met for a formal summit in Helsinki in 1975 where the final act was signed. New meetings under the CSCE umbrella were held later. The provisions under Basket III were to prove a more potent weapon in the hands of Eastern bloc dissidents than almost anyone had expected. Soon "Helsinki monitoring groups" for human rights sprang up in the Soviet Union and Eastern Europe—Sakharov and Orlov in the Soviet Union, Charta 77 in Czechoslovakia, and even Solidarity in Poland are key names that could be mentioned in this context.

In a reversal of roles, the United States was now beginning to realize the potential of the Helsinki process while the Western European governments came to fear that a very active exploitation of human rights could have negative consequences on détente. In the end the whole Helsinki process became a perfect example of negotiations having consequences almost entirely different from those foreseen by the negotiating parties, not only by the main instigator, the Soviet Union, but also by the United States and even the West Europeans. As Robert Gates has argued, "The Soviets desperately wanted the CSCE, they got it and it laid the foundations for the end of their empire. We resisted it for years, went grudgingly, Ford paid a terrible price for going— perhaps reelection itself—only to discover later that CSCE had yielded benefits beyond our wildest imagination. Go figure."[16] On the whole, despite the many changes in position, the United States and the EC had been able to contain their disagreements rather well. As the favorable end result dawned on them, the outcome could not do other than strengthen relations between the United States and Western Europe.

Nixon–Kissinger's Reappraisal of European Integration, 1969–1976[17]

For more than two decades the United States had provided strong support for European integration. Despite the preoccupation with Vietnam, even the

Johnson administration seemed to operate under the assumption that the more supranational the integration, the better it apparently was. At the same time, however, in the 1960s the United States had become more and more insistent not only on European integration taking place within an Atlantic context, but also on American economic interests being safeguarded. Considerable tension thus existed in the American policy.

Some of this tension was to be resolved by the Nixon administration, despite European affairs not coming very high on the administration's list of priorities. In February 1970 Nixon in fact explicitly spelled out his foreign policy priorities. East–West relations, policies toward the Soviet Union, and China came first; then he listed policy toward Eastern Europe as it affected East–West relations. Only in fifth place did Nixon list "Policy toward Western Europe, but only where NATO is affected and where major countries (Britain, Germany and France) are affected."[18] In Nixon's own memoirs the EC (or any related item) does not even appear in the index. What he writes about his conversations with Western European leaders also largely deals with the Soviet Union, China, and Vietnam.

In their European policy Nixon and Kissinger gave strong priority to the Atlantic framework for European integration. US leadership in the Atlantic alliance was taken for granted even in what the administration saw as a period of American decline. Europe's support was necessary to strengthen Washington in its dealings with the Soviet Union, and Nixon–Kissinger fought with determination powerful Congressional pressure to reduce the number of American troops in Europe. The administration continued to push for a more open and Atlantic EC, and therefore wanted Britain to "join Europe."

In principle little of this was new, except perhaps that, because of this Atlantic priority, Washington was no longer to push for the most supranational forms of European integration. The formal rationale for the new policy was that the Europeans had to decide on their own what they wanted; the real rationale was that the United States had clearly become rather ambivalent about the whole objective of a united Europe.

The new attitude showed immediately. It flowed from a period of serious reflection by Kissinger before he took office, a fact that was obvious from his recommendations to Nixon on American policy toward Western Europe as early as 22 February 1969, i.e. only one month after the inauguration. The first two points were traditional: "1. Affirm our commitment to NATO; 2. Affirm our traditional support of European unity, including British entry into the Common Market." The somewhat newer point was the next one: "3. Make clear that we will not inject ourselves into intra-European debates on the form, methods and timing of steps toward unity." Earlier administrations, particularly Johnson's, had said as much, but they had still favored European supranationalism. The Nixon administration did not.

The administration generally adhered to its stated policy of leaving the initiative on European integration to the Europeans, with Washington stressing the overall Atlantic framework. Nixon–Kissinger did not directly oppose further integration or pursue an explicit policy of divide-and-rule. Good reasons still existed for the United States to be sympathetic to European integration. In his writings Kissinger had been particularly concerned about the political–psychological evils of European dependence.[19] Dependence could only be avoided if the Europeans developed greater unity. Yet the conclusion was clear: the United States should "leave the internal evolution of a united Europe to the Europeans and use its ingenuity and influence in devising new forms of *Atlantic* cooperation [emphasis in original]."[20]

The administration's ambivalence to the EC showed in the fact that it continued to meet with the national leaders and resisted pressure to meet also with the joint EC Commission, although some lower level contacts were established even with the latter. Kissinger explained that although the United States supported the idea of European unity, "if the price for this is that we cannot talk with our traditional European friends, then over time this could create a massive change in our relations." As so often, Nixon put it more graphically—since it would take some time before the Europeans would learn to act as a group, "we have to work with the heads of Government in the various countries and not that jackass in the European Commission in Brussels." (Presumably Nixon meant Commission President Sicco Mansholt.)[21]

J. Robert Schaetzel, US ambassador to the EC in the years from 1966 to 1972, and a true believer in European integration, became very frustrated with the new Nixon–Kissinger policy. He later complained about the Nixon years that "in its isolation in Brussels the United States Mission to the European Communities might as well have been located on the upper reaches of the Orinoco."[22]

There were four main reasons for Nixon–Kissinger's change of attitude. These reasons also further illustrate the nature of the change in policy.

1. If America was declining, it made little sense to build up the EC. The EC was already the economic rival of the US; it could potentially become its political and, in the more distant future, even its military rival. In Kissinger's analysis the earlier policy had allegedly overestimated the American influence on European integration. As he wrote before he became National Security Adviser, "the future of a united Europe depends more on developments in London, Paris and Bonn than to [sic] strictures from Washington."[23] The American policy might even have led to stalemate: "While not sufficient to bring about our preferred solution, our influence is strong enough to block approaches with which we disagree."

The impact of this point had to be considerably reinforced by the Nixon administration's analysis that the United States was declining and that various regional power centers were rising, particularly on the economic side. In 1971 Richard Nixon described the situation in 1947, when he entered Congress, in these rather glowing terms:

We were number one in the world militarily, with no one even challenging us because we had a monopoly on atomic weapons. We also at the time, of course, were number one economically by all odds. In fact, the United States was producing more than 50 percent of all the world's goods.

Now this was all changing. Looking five to ten years ahead, Nixon stated that:

instead of just America being number one in the world from an economic standpoint, the preeminent world power, and instead of there being just two super powers, when we think in economic terms and economic potentialities, there are five great power centers in the world today [the United States, the Soviet Union, Western Europe, Japan, and China].[24]

With America's relative strength reduced, there had to be more cooperation and less American dictation.

Even for Nixon–Kissinger basic reasons allegedly existed for promoting European integration. Yet, important as these reasons may have been, a tactical side was obviously creeping into the US support, since the remaining three points indicate that Nixon–Kissinger actually disagreed with much of the earlier policy.

2. The Nixon administration felt that the basic assumption underlying the previous policy—that the United States and Western Europe shared all basic interests—was simply not true. An integrated Europe might well adopt policies that the United States did not favor. Again, as Kissinger stated in his early analysis of the previous policy, "We have sought to combine a supranational Europe with a closely integrated Atlantic Community under American leadership. These objectives are likely to prove incompatible." The differences between the two sides of the Atlantic had already been reflected in monetary and trade policies: "A politically united Europe was more likely to articulate its own conceptions in other areas as well." On the political side Kissinger was undoubtedly influenced by the growing differences between the United States and Western Europe, including West Germany's emerging *Ostpolitik*. These differences were more central to him than economic issues that he tended to regard as rather pedestrian.

On the economic side, nevertheless, on many occasions it had been illustrated that the two sides of the Atlantic did not have identical interests. The joint EC policy, as reflected in for instance the Kennedy round trade negotiations, enhanced existing doubts in Washington about the wisdom of the established policy. Such doubts were now entertained not only by the economic departments, but more and more by members of Congress too, and clearly even by the President himself.

American foreign policy had so far been formulated primarily by the State Department. The economic departments, primarily Treasury, Commerce, and Agriculture, naturally paid much more attention to domestic economic interests than did State. But Presidents, normally backed by their National Security Advisers, still tended to support State, particularly since the economic departments often were divided. If all these economic interests, inside the administration and in Congress, were to come together, they would represent a most powerful coalition. All of them were clearly more skeptical to the EEC than was the State Department; Agriculture and Commerce for the harm done to their respective business clients, Treasury for the break with multilateralism which regional economic integration represented.

This coming together of the economic interests was to take place under Nixon, whose Republican administration was considerably more protectionist in its basic attitude than previous Democratic ones. For a decade de Gaulle had represented the main challenge to the American policy on European integration. With de Gaulle's resignation in 1969, with the EC relatively unified on tariff matters, and with the American economic situation increasingly strained, this was now changing.

The President's foreign policy report for 1970 stated, in tune with traditional US policy, that "We consider that the possible economic price of a truly unified Europe is outweighed by the gain in the political vitality of the West as a whole." The three economic departments expressed disagreement with this statement. Instead they wanted to emphasize the problems created by the EC, problems that would only become greater with membership for Britain and other EFTA countries supplemented by the association of the former British colonies. More and more Congress was weighing in on the side of the economic departments. In November 1970 Nixon sent Kissinger a note which expressed the new mood: "K—It seems to me that we 'protest' and continue to get the short end of the stick in our dealings with the Community." Agriculture was the prime example. "The Congress is simply not going to tolerate this too passive attitude on the part of our representatives in the negotiations."

Such pressure from the economic departments and from Congress had to be reflected in Nixon's foreign policy report for 1971. Compared with the 1970 report, in 1971 there was a noticeable shift toward underlining the many problems the EC would create for the United States, whereas for years it had been uncritically believed that a unified Western Europe would automatically lift burdens from the shoulders of the United States: "The truth is not so simple. European unity will also pose problems for American policy, which it would be idle to ignore." Agriculture and preferential trading arrangements with countries outside the EC were especially mentioned.

The United States was beginning to experience serious economic problems. It had long been running a balance of payments deficit, but from 1960 the federal budget had also been in the red. Normally this would have caused a devaluation, yet, due to the dollar's international position, Washington could continue its spending ways. More than three-quarters of trade among non-Communist countries and of central banks' reserves was in dollars. In the course of 1967–8, the most important currencies—the dollar, the pound, the franc, and the mark—all experienced crises, demonstrating that the foreign exchange market was effectively out of control. The introduction in 1968 of a system of special drawing rights (SDR) to stabilize the market and to reduce dependence on the dollar was only partly successful.

With low economic growth and inflation producing the new phenomenon of stagflation, America was in trouble. In 1971 the United States was for the first time since 1893 running a deficit not only in its balance of payments but also in its balance of trade. Secretary of the Treasury John Connally was telling the President that "The simple fact is that in many areas other nations are out-producing us, out-thinking us and out-trading us." As so often, Nixon's response was graphic: "We'll fix those bastards."[25] The fix came in the form of the Nixon–Connally economic measures of August 1971, whereby the convertibility of the dollar into gold was suspended (the equivalent of a dollar devaluation), a 10 per cent surtax was added on imported goods, and domestically a wage and price freeze was imposed. These measures signaled that finally the United States had decided to clean up its international financial act, and in doing so was paying far more attention to its more narrowly defined economic interests than it had done previously.

The 1972 foreign policy report attempted to strike some sort of balance, probably partly in response to much of the outside world's, certainly including Western Europe's, strong criticism of the August measures. On the one hand, the report reiterated Washington's strong support for the geographical enlargement of the Community represented by the possible membership of Britain, Ireland, Denmark, and Norway. On the other hand, the problems posed to the United States by the enlarged EC were certainly also mentioned, and, as we shall shortly see, these problems were not only economic.

In the analysis of Nixon–Kissinger, Atlantic cooperation worked well in the security field, but not in the economic one. On several occasions this discrepancy led the President to ask whether "Atlantic unity in defense and security [can] be reconciled with the European Community's increasingly regional economic policies?" He gave the answer himself—Europeans could not have it both ways: "They cannot have the United States participation and cooperation on the security front and then proceed to have confrontation and even hostility on the economic and political front." The conclusion was obvious: in return for the security provided by the United States, the Europeans ought really to become more conciliatory on the economic front; alternatively, the United States would do less on the security front.[26] Yet, there were clear limits to the kind of pressure the US should exert. Although in the economic arena Nixon was convinced the "European leaders want to 'screw' us and we want to 'screw' them," the overriding point was still that "We should not allow the umbilical cord between the US and Europe to be cut and Europe to be nibbled away by the Soviets."[27]

3. In promoting an integrated Europe, Washington could actually be pushing its best friends in Europe away from itself. An integrated Europe might come to be dominated by Gaullist ideas, clearly an undesirable outcome for the Nixon administration too. Somewhat less dramatic, but more likely than a Gaullist scenario, several countries in Europe followed the American lead quite closely, but if their policies were to be submerged in a European community the result could easily be greater distance toward the United States. In Kissinger's words, "A confederal Europe would enable the United States to maintain influence at many centers of decision rather than be forced to stake everything on affecting the views of a single, supranational body."

In line with this argument, Nixon again started referring to the "special relationship" with Britain, a term generally frowned upon by earlier administrations in Washington. For Nixon–Kissinger there was no point in ending the "special relationship." Quite on the contrary, the objective should be to bring as many countries as possible into special relationships with Washington. The Nixon administration, too, definitely wanted to get Britain into the EC, but a close relationship with the UK could still be maintained in a confederal structure, while this would be impossible in a federal one. The British were also skeptical toward supranationalism, an additional reason for Washington to be the same.

The paradox was that now, when the United States finally took a strong interest in the "special relationship," Britain was not really interested. Prime Minister Edward Heath was more strongly committed to British membership in the EC than any of his predecessors and was ready to accept the EC pretty much as it stood. His strategy to accomplish membership for Britain included putting some distance between the US and the UK, and, largely for this reason, the Nixon–Heath relationship remained somewhat distant.

Heath did succeed, however, in bringing Britain into the EC. Not only was he himself very pro-European, but British industrialists were also becoming ever more so. Even more important were the changes on the other side of the English Channel, where Georges Pompidou held a more flexible position on British membership in the EC than had de Gaulle. This reflected the new President's more pragmatic personality, but also, as we have already seen, his uneasiness over West Germany's growing independence. The Six became the Nine.

4. Finally, the new American policy was undoubtedly also influenced by the complex attitude Nixon and Kissinger had toward France in general and toward de Gaulle in particular. They were both actually great admirers of the French President, especially of his personal qualities, though they were less enamoured of his attitude to the United States. As we have seen, the Johnson administration had pursued a relatively calm policy in the face of de Gaulle's challenge to American leadership, but Nixon–Kissinger wanted to take this policy one step further.

A lower American profile on European integration could help improve relations with de Gaulle and with his successor President Pompidou. (De Gaulle retired only three months after Nixon had taken office.) Pushing for a supra-national Europe clearly disturbed relations with de Gaulle/Pompidou since they were against it and wanted a loose confederal structure. Nixon's initiation of secret American assistance to the French nuclear weapons project certainly also helped improve relations.

The Kennedy and particularly the Johnson administrations had expected that the problems between the United States and Western Europe would largely disappear when de Gaulle left the scene. The Nixon administration also assumed that its new policy would help improve relations, and in some respects relations did improve. Certainly the difficult issue of British membership of the EC was solved. Serious problems remained, however, as was most clearly seen in connection with the so-called Year of Europe (1973).

The Year of Europe was Nixon–Kissinger's most ambitious attempt to redefine and strengthen relations with Europe within the crucial Atlantic framework. After heavy emphasis on the Soviet Union, China, and Vietnam, Europe was again to be at the center of Washington's attention. In the speech launching the scheme Kissinger stated that "The alliance between the United States and Europe has been the cornerstone of all postwar foreign policy." In the agenda for the future, the National Security Adviser affirmed that the United States would continue to support the unification of Europe. "We have no intention of destroying what we worked so hard to build." For the United States, "European unity is what it has always been: not an end in itself but a means to the strengthening of the West." Washington would "continue to support European unity as a component of a larger Atlantic partnership." The Atlantic framework was essential, of course, but Kissinger's emphasis on European unity was really a bit strong in view of the administration's reevaluation on this point.

Kissinger thought Pompidou had encouraged him to undertake the reappraisal implied in the Year of Europe speech. If this was indeed so, he was soon disabused of the notion.[28] The new Atlantic Charter that Kissinger proposed irked the Europeans, and not only the French, by pointing out that while the United States had global responsibilities, the Europeans only had

more regional ones and by emphasizing the "linkage" between the maintenance of the American security guarantee and a European *quid pro quo* in the
economic sphere and with regard to military burden-sharing. In response, the
EC's draft agreement stressed the political equality of the EC and the US and
also refused to recognize any linkage between security and political and economic problems. It was in this context that Nixon presented his warning that
"the Europeans could not have it both ways."

The Year of Europe produced much heat, but little light. French–American
differences were substantial, even after de Gaulle. At the time of Pompidou's
death in April 1974, even Kissinger felt that US–French relations were at an
all-time low. He, who had so strongly accused earlier administrations of use-
less bickering with the French, ended up in the very same position.[29] As we
saw in Chapter 5, Washington and most European capitals disagreed on the
right policy toward the Middle East, a critical issue in 1973, the Year of
Europe. Even the British were skeptical about the scheme since they wanted
to prove themselves good Europeans, and in any case American leverage was
rapidly being reduced under the growing scandal of Watergate. There were
endless procedural wrangles. Should Washington negotiate with the three
main European capitals individually, with the Nine in the form of the
Commission, or with the country holding the EC presidency? The correct
answer seemed to be all of the above.

The debate more or less ended with the Declaration on Atlantic Relations
approved by the North Atlantic Council in Ottawa on 19 June 1974. This document was consensus-oriented, but still largely based on American ideas. The
American security guarantee to Europe was tied to the Europeans assuming a
fair share of the defense burden. The linkage so urgently requested by the
United States was also vaguely recognized by an expression of intent that the
American–European security relationship "be strengthened through harmonious relations in the political and economic fields." Washington's fear that the
Europeans would "gang up" on the Americans was to be avoided by the
Europeans consulting the Americans *before* they reached decisions on import-
ant matters of common interest.

At the same time, the United States made significant concessions to the
Europeans. For the first time Washington explicitly recognized that the
British and French nuclear forces were "capable of playing a deterrent role of
their own contributing to the overall strengthening of the deterrence of the
Alliance."[30] For Washington this meant formally giving up its long-held
policy of getting the two countries to give up their independent deterrents. In
this context it helped that Washington, London, and Paris had a common
desire to keep the European weapons out of the upcoming SALT II talks. In
fact, the Nixon administration was now willing to provide the French with
crucial nuclear information, mostly in the form of "negative guidance," letting

French scientists present what they were doing, and then telling them whether they were on the right track or not.[31]

After Nixon's resignation in August 1974, President Ford had more pressing matters to deal with than American–European relations. In his very few statements on Europe he tended to emphasize the role of NATO, not the EC. The EC, on its side, was preoccupied with the adaptation of its three new members. Still, US–European relations improved a great deal under Ford, for although Kissinger continued as Secretary of State, Ford was prepared to listen more to the Europeans than Nixon had been. That was natural in view of his more limited foreign policy experience, but his personality was also friendlier than Nixon's had been. The changes in government in Europe in the very same year also worked in a favorable direction in that the new men were all more pro-Atlantic than their predecessors had been. In Britain Wilson came back as Prime Minister after Heath; when Wilson resigned in 1976 new Prime Minister James Callaghan was even more Atlantic in orientation; in France the more centrist Giscard d'Éstaing succeeded Pompidou as President; in West Germany Helmut Schmidt became the new Chancellor after Brandt had to resign because of the Guillaume spy scandal.

France and NATO agreed on further military cooperation both in peacetime deployment of forces and wartime coordination in case of a Soviet attack. Even the French nuclear weapons were now seen in a wider European perspective than simply as a French *force de frappe*. A regular system of consultation was set up between Washington and the capital of the country holding the EC presidency. In 1975 regular meetings of the heads of government in the five leading industrialized countries began (the US, the UK, France, West Germany, and Japan).[32]

The energy issue was to become really important and bothersome in allied relations in the 1970s. The Arab embargo during the 1973 war stimulated entirely different reactions in the West. France and the United Kingdom tried to get around the embargo by making bilateral deals directly with the Arab oil producers. West Germany, Italy, and most other EC members favored a coordinated European response. The United States and Holland pressed for cooperation among all Western oil-consuming countries. The various positions clearly reflected the different extent to which they had been hit by the embargo and the respective optimism with which they thought they could deal with the Arabs. The United States also felt the obligation to assert its leadership on this issue, though the effect of the Arab embargo on the US was softened by the fact that it was much less dependent on imports than were the Western European countries; much of what it imported also came from non-Arab countries: Venezuela, Nigeria, and Iran. Despite these differences, the International Energy Agency (IEA) was formed in September 1974. France chose not to join.

Washington wanted the oil consumers to organize themselves before they started any dialogue with the oil producers. The Western countries ought first to agree on measures such as energy conservation, reserve stocks of oil, and a financial facility to strengthen the consumer nations. Ford–Kissinger were even willing to hint at the use of military action to soften the oil producers, particularly Western-oriented Iran and Saudi Arabia. France, at the other extreme, wanted to call an energy conference without any degree of advance coordination among the consumers, except that it wanted the EC represented as one unit. Gradually, however, the Germans and the British came to support the Americans. France then modified its position. A producer–consumer dialogue was to be started, but on the basis of Western agreement in the areas mentioned.

In the ensuing negotiations the United States managed to isolate OPEC from other Third World raw material producers who, on the one hand, were badly hit by the rise in oil prices, but, on the other, saw the possibility of similar cartels with regard to their own raw materials. OPEC solidarity was also beginning to crack. The price of oil held relatively steady. Then, however, the fall of the Shah in 1978–9 and the rapid cut-back in Iranian oil production strengthened OPEC once more. In 1973 the price of oil had quadrupled; in 1978–9 it doubled again. The IEA was never to be the instrument that the United States had hoped for, although it did limit the scramble for bilateral deals somewhat.[33]

The Southern Flank, Communism, and the United States

In 1974–5, within months of each other, three long-surviving authoritarian governments in Southern Europe collapsed. In April 1974 a revolution occurred in Portugal which ended the remnants of the Salazar regime going back to the late 1920s. Three months later the military government in Greece that had taken power in 1967 fell. In November 1975 General Franco in Spain died. The new governments that emerged were all democratic, but in Portugal the transition was rather more chaotic than in the other two countries.[34]

Portugal had been a founding member of NATO despite the Salazar regime; that was in large part due to the crucial role of the Azores in communications between North America and Western Europe. Although this role became somewhat smaller with the development of longer-range aircraft, the strategic significance of the Azores could be witnessed even during the 1973 war in the Middle East. As we have already seen, under Kennedy the role of the Azores precluded Washington from going too strongly against Portugal's colonial policy in Africa, a policy that remained wedded to the notion that the colonies were really not colonies, but integral parts of the mother country.

In Spain a dislike of the Franco regime, particularly under Truman, had not prevented the United States from developing close military relations with it.

Through the 1953 base agreement Washington in fact made Spain an indirect member of NATO. Spain too had an important strategic position, bordering both on the Atlantic and the Mediterranean. It could also serve as a rear base for operations and even as a potential fall-back area for NATO. All this made the US develop increasingly stronger military ties with Spain. Franco could certainly agree with the anti-Communist purpose of NATO; however, he had problems with Britain over Gibraltar and with Morocco over Spanish Sahara. While the Spanish Navy and Air Force were increasingly interested in cooperation with the United States and NATO, the Army remained more aloof. Washington clearly hoped to bring Spain into NATO sooner rather than later, but the staunch opposition of most of the European members, particularly Norway, Denmark, Holland, and Belgium, made it impossible for Spain to become a direct member. Even Britain and France were skeptical of Spanish membership.[35]

In Greece the United States had taken over Britain's traditional role as the country's protector in 1946–7. As we have seen, in 1951–2 the US had played a crucial, even imperial role in bringing Greece and Turkey into NATO in the face of the opposition of more or less all other members with the exception of Italy. The American role, i.e. the role of the CIA and the Pentagon, in the military coup in Greece in 1967 is still debated, despite Washington's general preference for democratic government.[36]

Thus, the United States generally maintained closer military–political ties with all three of these authoritarian governments than did most Western European governments. In the most sensitive case, Greece, Washington resumed military shipments despite the rather perfunctory nature of the promises made by the colonels in power in Athens. As the NSC concluded, the administration anticipated "further specific steps which we can cite as further evidence of progress toward full constitutional government. The Prime Minister can be told that the US takes at face value and accepts without reservation his assurances on moving toward parliamentary democracy."[37]

The major European governments were certainly also prepared to work with the governments in power, opposition to the three regimes being much stronger in the smaller countries, particularly in Scandinavia. The fall of the three flowed primarily from domestic factors, if that term is interpreted widely enough to include the increasing problems Portugal had in its colonies and the Greek colonels' failed attempt to bring about a union between Greece and Cyprus.

The Cyprus problem was to have very significant repercussions in Greek–Turkish relations, but much less so in relations between the United States and Western Europe. There had been frequent feuding between the majority of Greeks and the minority of Turks, especially after Cyprus became independent in 1959. In 1964 a UN peacekeeping force was sent to the island to maintain peace between the two communities. In 1974 a coup backed by the colonels in Athens ousted President Makarios and aimed at *enosis* (union) with Greece. Turkish forces then invaded the island and took control of about one-third of Cyprus, which led to the collapse of the military government in Greece.

On the Western side Britain initially had the lead as far as the troublesome Cyprus issue was concerned. The island, which had come under British rule in 1878, was formally annexed in 1914. Even after independence in 1959 London maintained two important military bases on the island. Britain led the talks between Greece, Turkey, and the two communities on Cyprus. Kissinger cooperated closely with the British Foreign Secretary, James Callaghan, but America's position was increasingly influenced by the strong Greek lobby in the United States. Congress soon cut off military aid to Turkey in response to its invasion of Cyprus, although the administration feared the consequences this would have for Turkey's cooperation with the United States vis-à-vis the Soviet Union, and Turkey did in fact close all US military installations except one air base. The American sanctions were only ended well into the Carter administration. No solution has yet been found to the Cyprus issue, but Kissinger gave an interesting summing-up of Washington's relative satisfaction with its own diplomacy: "the eastern flank of NATO, though strained, remained intact. Despite Greek displeasure with the executive branch and Turkish outrage with Congress, both countries remained in NATO and on friendly terms with the United States. Throughout, the Soviet Union was kept at arm's length."[38]

After the fall of Franco, Spain was welcome to join NATO, although the Northern Europeans wanted to be certain of the country's democratic orientation first. America's association with the previous dictators did, however, make significant parts of the population in Spain, as in Greece, skeptical toward both the United States and NATO. After considerable debate, in 1982 Spain chose to join after a referendum where 40 per cent voted against joining NATO, even in its adopted French form of association. The US continued the use of its bases in Spain, although the American presence was reduced.[39] In 1981 Greece and in 1986 Spain and Portugal also became full members of the European Community.

During the Cold War it had been standard US policy to insist on the exclusion of Communists from the government of any NATO country. After the Communists had left the governments of France and Italy in 1947, this line of policy had been successfully maintained, with the exception of the rule of a leftist bloc, including Communists, in the government of Iceland in 1956–8. In 1971–4 another leftist government came to power in Reykjavik. This government too wanted the American troops out of the country, but again the national assembly was too divided and popular support for the American presence too strong for this policy to be carried out. In Washington President Nixon had decided that the "retention of US military presence in Iceland shall continue as a primary US policy objective." In part to facilitate this objective the administration stayed neutral in Iceland's fishery dispute with Britain. No pressure should be exerted on Iceland "to reverse its announced decision to extend Iceland's fishing limits" to fifty miles. In 1974 the leftists lost the election and US–Icelandic relations were once again normalized.[40]

However, developments in Southern Europe were much more important than those in geographically isolated Iceland. While both the United States and the Western European countries were happy to see the Southern dictatorships fall, Washington was more uneasy than the Europeans about what could now happen in the three countries. Nixon–Kissinger always feared revolution and Communism within the Western sphere. (Allende had been overthrown in Chile in 1973.)

The unanticipated toppling of the Portuguese dictatorship on 25 April 1974 led to rapid changes of government. From April 1974 to July 1976 there were six of them; to Kissinger it looked like "all of them moved progressively to the left." The American Secretary of State was still "strongly opposed to any American encouragement of Communist participation in the government of a NATO country." The Western European leaders were also concerned about Portugal's drift to the left, and they too wanted the Communists out of the government, but there was considerable disagreement as to how best to achieve this objective. West Germany under Schmidt favored economic aid to encourage the moderates; France under Giscard was skeptical toward such aid; Britain under Callaghan favored aid coupled with covert support to the moderates. Kissinger did not see how "moderates could be strengthened by aid for radicals," but was still persuaded to support a program of 20 million dollars in loan guarantees. The close cooperation between European and Portuguese moderate Socialists may have particularly helped to contain the drift to the left. The elections were won by Socialists and moderates. A Communist coup attempt failed. Portugal gradually embarked on a center-left course.[41]

Nowhere in Western Europe was the Communist party stronger than in Italy. In elections in 1975 and 1976 the PCI captured more than a third of the vote and came in only a few percentage points behind the Christian Democrats who had dominated Italian politics since the crucial 1948 election. In Italy itself there was considerable pressure to include the Communists directly in the government. Internationally there was détente; the PCI had not only become increasingly independent of Moscow, particularly after the Soviet invasion of Czechoslovakia in 1968, but was also flirting with openly accepting Italy's membership of NATO; the Socialists had moved to the right and abandoned their anti-Americanism; Italy was badly in need of domestic reform; the opening to the Communists could represent a *compromesso storico*, a widening of the government's political basis in the same way the opening to the Socialists had done in 1963.

There was considerable disagreement within the Christian Democrats on this issue, which gave Washington more influence than it would otherwise have had. From 1948 until at least 1968 the United States had been providing the Christian Democrats with substantial covert financial assistance. In the 1960s and 1970s Washington supported reform-minded Christian Democrat Aldo Moro's center-left governments, but had at the same time apparently maintained contacts even with very right-wing elements in the Italian army.[42] Now, with the Nixon administration, Kissinger, who had opposed even the 1963 opening to the Socialists, was adamant. He rejected the analogy to détente. To him there was a crucial difference between managing a conflict with adversaries and including representatives of the adversary in an alliance of democracies. The US had a special responsibility "to maintain the cohesion of the Alliance. If we weakened on that issue, a rush to expediency would soon follow." President Ford spoke accordingly with Moro. Ford's position was supported by social democrats Callaghan in Britain and Schmidt in West Germany, and by more conservative Giscard in France.[43] While the Communists remained out of the government, an interesting new chapter was to be added to the story in the Carter years.

Conflict, but Still Primarily Cooperation

Many different structural forces were influencing the American–European relationship. Most importantly, Nixon's détente with the Soviet Union, Brandt's *Ostpolitik*, and aspects of Gaullism in France reflected the fact that the Soviet threat had diminished, which lessened the need for standing together and left more room for the various countries to establish their own separate policies.

Then, in the economic sphere, the relative balance between the United States and the European countries was shifting in favor of the Europeans. In 1945 the US had produced almost as much as the rest of the world together. As the world was recovering from the ravages of the Second World War, naturally that percentage had gone down. In 1950 the US produced around 40 per cent of the world's GNP; in 1960 this had declined further to around 30 per cent; in 1975 the figure stood around 25 per cent. From the time Britain joined the EC in 1973 the total production of the Community was as large as that of the United States, at least if measured at market prices. In 1950 the US had held 50 per cent of the world's international monetary reserves; in 1970 this percentage stood at 16. Nixon was acutely aware of how the role of the United States had declined militarily in relation to the Soviet Union and economically in relation to Western Europe and Japan. The Europeans certainly appreciated their strengthened position. Both sides of the Atlantic wanted changes: Washington wanted the European capitals to carry a larger share of the common burden in standing up to the Soviet Union; the Europeans wanted greater influence. These were difficult discussions that could easily get out of hand.

On the European side there was a shift away from Britain and toward France and West Germany. In the 1950s West Germany had surpassed both Britain and France in the size of its GNP. In 1960 the economies of France, Germany, and Britain had constituted respectively 17, 26, and 17 per cent of America's GNP; in 1975 the corresponding percentages were 22, 28, and 15.[44] Britain was the one country growing more slowly than the United States. With de Gaulle in France and *Ostpolitik* in West Germany these two countries were also definitely standing on their own feet politically. Thus, in that power in Europe was slowly shifting away from Britain in the direction of France and even more of West Germany (despite the restraints the latter still imposed on itself), it could be argued that the Atlantic was becoming wider on the European side.

It could also be argued that the Atlantic was becoming wider even on the American side, partly owing to some interesting population changes that were taking place inside the United States. Among its four main regions, the Northeast and the Midwest, the two regions traditionally most oriented toward Europe, were relatively declining in population compared to the South, facing Latin America, and the West, facing the Pacific. In 1960 the first two still had a combined population 13 million larger than the last two; twenty years later there were 10 million more in the South and West.[45] Such shifts were bound to have significant foreign policy consequences. One of them was that Washington would pay relatively less attention than it had done earlier to what was going on in Europe compared to the many other parts of the world.

The economic problems in the American–European relationship have already been discussed, and among these the EC's Common Agricultural Policy represented the biggest thorn in America's side. While even agricultural exports to the EC increased overall, exports of those goods the Europeans protected fell dramatically, and the EC's various preference agreements with countries outside Europe, especially former colonial areas, created additional problems. The enlargement of the EC in 1973 had definite political advantages, but extended at least relative discrimination of American products further.

The fact that the United States was gradually becoming even more of a global power than it had been in 1945 was also to reduce its relative emphasis on Western Europe. In the first years after 1945 the United States had concentrated almost exclusively on Western Europe. The war in Korea was to shift some of its focus to East and Southeast Asia. Suez was to signal a new role for the US also in the Middle East. The Cuban missile crisis was to make Washington take Latin America less for granted than it had done in the early years after the Second World War. The energy issue symbolized the rise of the oil producers to economic power. It was also to make the American economy much less self-sufficient than it had been. Traditionally US exports had amounted to 3–4 per cent of its GNP; imports had been about the same. From 1970 to 1980 exports increased from 6.6 per cent of US GNP to 12.9 per cent and imports from 5.9 to 12.1 per cent. Oil constituted a major part of the explanation for the rise not only in imports, but also of exports, in this case to the oil exporters.[46]

East Asia in particular was becoming increasingly important militarily, politically, and economically. The US had security treaties with Japan, South Korea, and Taiwan in addition to the members of ANZUS and the dissolving SEATO arrangement. It had a large troop presence in Japan, South Korea, and the Philippines. With the Korean War Japan had initiated a period of such rapid and sustained economic growth over several decades that the like of it had hardly been seen in economic history. In 1960 the Japanese economy had constituted 15 per cent of that of the US; in 1975 this percentage had increased to 33 and the rise continued. In 1968 Japan surpassed West Germany in GNP and thereby had the third largest GNP in the world. (It may well have had the second largest, due to the inflated nature of Western measurements of Soviet GNP at the time.)

Since Washington for political reasons was shutting Japan off from its traditional Chinese market and markets in Southeast Asia were not what the Japanese had hoped, the Japanese economy became relatively oriented toward exports to the United States. The US was ready to help, again in large part for political reasons.[47] In fact, Washington was to act as Japan's sponsor in international economic bodies after the Second World War. In 1953 it granted MFN status to Japan; in 1955 Japan was given membership status in GATT; in the mid-1960s it joined the OECD; in the mid-1970s it became a founding member of the G-5. Starting in the 1960s there was also rapid economic growth in Taiwan and South Korea. The result was that from 1979 onwards trade across the Pacific was larger than across the Atlantic. And developments were definitely pointing in the direction of continued faster growth in East Asia compared to Western Europe. And then there was the war in Vietnam.

With all these multifaceted developments exerting pressure on American–European relations, it might be asked what still kept the two sides of the Atlantic so close together. There were still the more traditional factors, and, more than anything, despite détente there was still the unifying fear of the Soviet Union. Every now and then the Kremlin would undertake some action that would strengthen Western solidarity. In 1968 there was the invasion of Czechoslovakia; later there were advances in the Middle East, even in southern Africa, as we shall see. Then the rise of *Ostpolitik* somewhat reawakened concern about Germany's role. The memories of the Second World War were still close for the contemporary generation of Western policymakers; West Germany's economic strength was growing quickly and so was its political independence.

Thus, despite the many differences between the United States and various Western European countries, the two sides of the Atlantic were after all moving in the same direction. Paris worried about the dangers of another American–Soviet Yalta; Paris and Washington were both concerned about Bonn's *Ostpolitik*; but the truth remained that all three capitals were cooperating more and more with Moscow. Détente was a common policy for all the NATO countries. West Germany was gaining in status and independence, but despite the fears of its allies it remained a most loyal member both of NATO and of the EC. The United States and France were frequently at odds, but Nixon–Kissinger were determined to show more understanding for the Gaullist tradition than their predecessors had done. Pompidou was in turn prepared to modify this tradition by augmenting cooperation with the US. When the Atlantic climate had turned rather sour, political changes took place in 1974 both in the United States and in Europe's major countries, changes that once again brought the different sides closer together.

The American–European economic relationship was flourishing, despite trade across the Pacific growing even faster than across the Atlantic. American investments in Europe were far larger than in Asia; they increased from approximately 4 billion dollars in 1957 to approximately 24 billion in 1970, or from 15 to 30 per cent of total US foreign investment. European investments in America also increased dramatically. Despite occasional French protests, most European countries competed to attract American companies. US imports from what later became the nine EC countries rose sharply during the 1960s. Despite the alleged horrors of CAP and the relative discrimination against certain other US exports to these countries, such exports also increased. In 1968 both imports and exports represented around 25 per cent of total US figures. After 1968 the volume of US imports from Western Europe declined relative to other regions while exports to Western Europe were better sustained.[48] The United States and Western Europe in general, and France in particular, were feuding over energy, but they were all becoming progressively more dependent on the importing of oil.

In addition to such more general factors, in the years 1969–77 two special factors brought the United States and Western Europe closer together. First, on the American side, there was, as we have seen, Washington's increasing concern as to whether the United States could fully maintain its established leadership position in the world. If America was in decline, then it might make sense to become more skeptical of a highly integrated rival in Europe, but it certainly made no sense to antagonize its allies; America was becoming more, not less, dependent on the latter and had to act accordingly. Concessions had to be made, and Western Europe and Japan obviously came first among America's allies. Second, on the European side, although Western Europe was definitely becoming more assertive, there was still general agreement that America had to maintain its military role in Europe. When the war in Vietnam and the reluctance of Congress threatened this role, the elites on both sides of the Atlantic mobilized heavily to reduce the danger.

In the 1970s there were many such references to America's decline, whether in the form of Nixon's five power centers (the United States, the Soviet Union, Western Europe, Japan, and China) or, later, Jimmy Carter's "malaise" that was affecting the United States. The symptoms were many and easy to see: the war in Vietnam, the Soviet military build-up, the economic strength of Western Europe and Japan, America's increased dependence on foreign energy, its balance of payments problem with the dollar no longer being convertible into gold, the devaluation of the dollar, various unilateral measures of protection, increased political division and bitterness inside the US itself culminating in Watergate, the resignation of Nixon, and the assertiveness of Congress.

In the Cold War, if the United States was in relative decline and the Soviet Union was on the rise, the logical response was for Washington to limit Soviet military growth as best it could. This was an important part of the background for Nixon–Kissinger's détente policy. Granting the Soviet Union equality with the United States, in various declarations of principle and in arms control agreements, could be seen as major concessions by the United States. In the light of America's decline this was just proper insurance against an even more disagreeable future. (And, after all, in the arms race the equality in quantity was combined with a lead for the US in quality.)[49]

The Nixon Doctrine reflected this new recognition of the limits as to what the United States could and should do. Although initially formulated in a rather off-hand manner, the Doctrine was to become a new point of reference for Washington. Its central thesis was that the United States

"will participate in the defense and development of allies and friends, but that America cannot—and will not—conceive all the plans, designs and programs, execute all the decisions and undertake all the defense of the free world. We will help where it makes a real difference and is considered in our interest."[50]

The Nixon Doctrine reflected the lessons of Vietnam; it was less relevant in relations with Western Europe. The aspect of military devolution was in fact rather limited here. The Nixon administration was clearly less willing than its predecessors to promote actively the unity of the European Community.

While less hostile than earlier administrations to the Gaullist tradition in France, it was quite skeptical of West Germany's greater efforts at independence. On the military side, the American nuclear guarantee and the troop presence remained firm. In Europe devolution appeared to mean primarily "burden-sharing;" that the Europeans should be doing more on their own and be paying more for the American troops in the form of ever new offset agreements.

Yet, the United States did clearly recognize the importance of its alliances; none more so than NATO. Kissinger's Year of Europe initiative represented Washington's somewhat belated recognition that new realities required new approaches. According to Kissinger, the first new reality was that "The revival of western Europe is an established fact, as is the historic success of its movement toward economic unification." The second was that "The East–West strategic military balance has shifted from American preponderance to near-equality..."

The devolution on the Western side was more clearly reflected in the regular economic summits that were initiated in the mid-1970s. Matters which Washington, and other capitals, had dealt with largely nationally or bilaterally were now discussed in a wider setting. The United States, the United Kingdom, France, West Germany, and Japan had started informal discussions about energy and other economic matters after the 1973 crisis. In 1975 these discussions were institutionalized in the form of annual economic summits. The original proposal for such a summit came from Giscard d'Éstaing, but Gerald Ford quickly agreed despite the skepticism of the US Treasury. Japan was included here as a matter of course in view of its rapidly rising economic strength. The US had even tied it to the Atlantic setup when Kissinger in his Year of Europe speech had stressed that "In many fields, 'Atlantic' solutions to be viable must include Japan." France objected and Japan was not really that interested, so this Atlantic idea had been dropped in favor of the new more general summit. Italy was then included after some discussion; in 1976 even Canada was added to the list, at US insistence and against the wishes of France. The G-5 had become the G-7. At the first meetings staff participation was strictly limited; later they became much bigger.[51]

On the European side, there was a desire for a stronger role for Europe, but for the Europeans the reappraisal of old policies definitely did not include the American military commitment in Europe. The Europeans complained about the drawing down of US forces in Europe as a result of the war in Vietnam when numbers declined from 306,000 in 1966 to 246,000 in 1970.[52] On this point there was not much they could do in addition to complaining, since the American answer was obvious: if the Europeans were willing to contribute in Vietnam, the United States could maintain more troops in Europe.

The most important challenge, however, came in the form of Congressional resolutions to reduce the number of American troops in Europe. The most dramatic such initiative bore the name of Senator Mike Mansfield, Senate majority leader, and he and his co-sponsors offered their resolutions repeatedly in the years between 1966 and 1973. They reflected détente, and even more the frustrations of Vietnam and of Europe's lack of support there; they also reflected the fact that added to the balance of payments deficit, the US now also had a balance of trade deficit and even an increasing federal budget deficit; to sound a different note, discipline in the American forces in Europe was becoming a major problem. With Western Europe so economically strong, why could it not do more militarily? In a way Mansfield was asking why the Nixon Doctrine should not be applied where regional security responsibilities could most easily be devolved: in Europe.

The Nixon administration fought the Mansfield resolutions tooth and nail. It enlisted not only the full force of the administration, but also the foreign policy establishment of all previous administrations back to Truman's. The Europeans lobbied as hard as they could against Mansfield's proposal to cut the American troop presence in Europe by 150,000, i.e. in half, and encourage the Europeans to pick up the slack, with more cuts to come later. Each time the resolution was defeated in the Senate by comfortable majorities, majorities that did not really reflect the concern felt in Washington and in all European capitals, concern so strong that this in itself became the main factor in Mansfield's defeat. It was argued that even drastic reductions in US forces in Europe would only produce small gains in the balance of payments.[53] Probably unwittingly, even the Soviet Union helped out when in 1971 Brezhnev proposed mutual and balanced force reductions. If the United States pulled out troops unilaterally, this would of course undermine any leverage it had to reduce the Soviet presence in Eastern Europe.

However, the Nixon administration felt it had to accept another Senate resolution, the Jackson–Nunn amendment, to stave off worse disasters. It required the President to reduce US forces in Europe by the same percentage that Europeans failed to offset America's balance-of-payments costs arising from the stationing of those forces. Nixon too could indeed become frustrated with the Europeans, as evidenced by his bitter comment that "the Europeans cannot have it both ways."

In the end the Europeans increased their payments sufficiently for the crisis to blow over. It certainly also helped that America was beginning to pull its troops out of Vietnam. In 1973 US forces in Europe stood at 264,000, clearly above the low number of 246,000 from 1970. The Eurogroup among the European NATO allies, which Britain had initiated with France as associate member, had been formed in 1968–9 to highlight and strengthen Europe's role, although in a clearly Atlantic context, but its impact was rather limited. More importantly, while in 1960 the United States bore 74 per cent of NATO's total expenditures and little had changed by 1970, in 1975 this percentage had declined to 60. In the 1970s Bonn alone agreed to pay more than 5 billion dollars in various agreements for offset payments, until Ford and Schmidt agreed to end this very controversial arrangement in return for Bonn doing more in other less specified ways. The declining percentage was in part due to the phase-out of the Vietnam War and a new exchange rate for the dollar. Still, the Europeans now contributed 90 per cent of NATO's ground forces, 80 per cent of the navies, and 75 per cent of the aircraft. The US balance of payments also improved somewhat. Yet, burden-sharing was to remain a constant theme within the alliance.[54]

Kissinger was basically right. The Europeans favored unity, but they feared that "the attempt to articulate a European identity within NATO might give the United States an excuse for reducing its military establishment in Europe."[55] West Germany and Italy especially reacted negatively to any reduction in the number of US forces stationed there. The French were particularly insistent on creating a European identity, but even they strongly disliked any reduction in the American military presence in Europe. While US troops were no longer welcome in France, even Paris wanted them to remain in West Germany because it gave France the protection it wanted. Like de Gaulle, Pompidou feared that sooner or later the Americans would withdraw militarily from Europe, as they had done after the First World War. European unity therefore had to be encouraged. But unlike de Gaulle, Pompidou was careful not to do anything that could actually encourage the Americans to leave. One reason he was so concerned about SALT and MBFR was that he feared that they could lead to a weakening of America's nuclear and conventional presence. Like London, Paris was insisting that not only their own nuclear weapons, but also the US forward-based systems in Europe, be excluded from the SALT negotiations. Washington agreed, so they were kept out.

When Pompidou declared publicly that he favored the American military presence in Europe, he showed how far he was willing to go in deviating from de Gaulle's public line. French historian Georges-Henri Soutou has even argued that the fear of the US leaving Europe was "en particulier l'obsession de Pompidou."[56] Only the Americans could really balance Soviet might. As far as practical military cooperation between France and NATO was concerned, the Ailleret–Lemnitzer agreement from 1967 was widened through the Valentin–Ferber agreement of 1974 and the Biard–Schulze agreement of 1978. France remained outside NATO's military structure but uncertainty, about what Paris would do once a war had broken out and France had then decided to cooperate with NATO, was greatly reduced through these agreements. Since French forces continued to be stationed in Germany, it was more or less inevitable that they would be involved in the case of hostilities.[57]

Thus, French policy vacillated between the twin fears of the two superpowers dictating developments in Europe as at Yalta or the United States abandoning Western Europe altogether. The consistent line was the emphasis on the importance of France's role. The revised French position made possible the statement from the NATO summit of June 1974 that "the contribution to the security of the entire Alliance provided by the nuclear forces of the United States based in the United States as well as in Europe and by the presence of North American forces in Europe remains indispensable."[58] In fact, although de Gaulle had made it difficult to state so publicly, on the twenty-fifth anniversary of NATO this was the crucial point on which there would seem to have been virtual unanimity in Western Europe from the time the organization was founded. From this flowed America's inevitable domination of Atlantic security affairs. While in so many other ways the American–European relationship was being redefined, in this basic sense there was no redefinition, now or in the next couple of decades.

Notes

1. For my analysis of the various periods of détente, see my *East, West, North, South: Major Developments in International Politics Since 1945* (Oxford: Oxford University Press, 1999), 81–109.
2. Memorandum from Kissinger to Nixon, 28 April 1969, as quoted in Jauvert, *L'Amérique Contre De Gaulle*, 260–1; for the earlier expectation that the United States would simply wait de Gaulle out, see Jauvert, pp. 250–3.
3. Bozo, "Détente versus Alliance," 358; *NATO Final Communiqués*, 209–10.
4. John G. McGinn, "The Politics of Collective Inaction. NATO's Response to the Prague Spring," *Journal of Cold War Studies*, 1:3, (Fall 1999), 130–8.
5. A good short summary of *Ostpolitik* is found in Gottfried Niedhart, "The Federal Republic's Ostpolitik and the United States: Initiatives and Constraints," in Kathleen Burk and Melvyn Stokes (eds.), *The United States and the European Alliance Since 1945* (Oxford: Berg, 1999), 289–311. See also Helga Haftendorn, *Deutsche Aussenpolitik zwischen Selbstbeschränkung und Selbstbehauptung* (Stuttgart: Deutsche Verlags-Anstalt, 2001), 173–218; Banchoff, *The German Problem Transformed*, 74–83; M. E. Sarotte, *Dealing with the Devil: East, Germany, Détente, and Ostpolitik, 1969–1973* (Chapel Hill: University of North Carolina Press, 2001).
6. Martin J. Hillenbrand, *Fragments of Our Time. Memoirs of a Diplomat* (Athens: University of Georgia Press, 1998), 279.
7. For a good, short account of the Nixon administration and *Ostpolitik*, see Bernd Schäfer, "German Ostpolitik and the Nixon administration, 1969–1973," Paper presented at the conference *NATO, the Warsaw Pact and the Rise of Détente*, 1965–1972, Dobbiaco, 26–28 Sept. 2002.
8. NA, NSC documents, National Security Decision Memorandum 91, 6 Nov. 1970, 2.
9. Richard Reeves, *President Nixon: Alone in the White House* (New York: Simon & Schuster, 2001), 417. For Brandt's own account of his *Ostpolitik*, see his *Erinnerungen* (Frankfurt: Propyläen, 1989), 168–260.

10. Reeves, *President Nixon*, 414.
11. Soutou, *L'Alliance incertaine*, 314–20.
12. Kissinger, *White House Years*, 411, 422, 529–34, 966; Dana H. Allin, *Cold War Illusions: America, Europe, and Soviet Power 1969–89* (London: Macmillan, 1995), 39–41; Cogan, *Oldest Allies, Guarded Friends*, 151–3.
13. This was the highly distorted Gaullist version of what had actually happened when Roosevelt, Churchill, and Stalin met in February 1945 at Yalta. Europe was divided as a result of the Allies' military operations, not as a result of decisions taken at Yalta. The future of Poland had in fact been perhaps the most hotly contested issue at Yalta. There was much to be said for Averell Harriman's comment that the only thing that was true about de Gaulle's version of Yalta was that he had not been present himself. In this context, however, the important thing is that the French version of Yalta was and still is widely believed not only in France, but also in the rest of Europe and even elsewhere.
14. Cogan, *Oldest Allies, Guarded Friends*, 161–2; Soutou, *L'Alliance incertaine*, 337.
15. For Kissinger's interesting account of the Helsinki process, see his *Years of Renewal*, 635–63.
16. Robert Gates, *From the Shadows: The Insider's Story of Five Presidents and How They Helped Win the Cold War* (New York: Simon & Schuster, 1996), 89. For a superior account of the Helsinki process, see Daniel C. Thomas, *The Helsinki Effect: International Norms, Human Rights, and the Demise of Communism* (Princeton: Princeton University Press, 2001.)
17. This section builds largely on my *"Empire" by Integration*, first 99–107, then 97–8.
18. Reeves, *President Nixon*, 171–2.
19. Lundestad, *"Empire" by Integration*, 16–18.
20. Henry A. Kissinger, "What Kind of Atlantic Partnership?", *The Atlantic Community Quarterly*, 7 (1969), 32.
21. *FRUS*, 1969–76, III, Memorandum of conversation Nixon and his advisers, 11 Sept. 1972, 265.
22. Schaetzel, *The Unhinged Alliance*, 60–1.
23. Kissinger, "What Kind of Atlantic Partnership," 32.
24. *The Public Papers of the Presidents of the United States: Richard Nixon, 1971* (Washington, DC, 1972), 804.
25. Reeves, *President Nixon*, 340–1.
26. For an interesting top-level discussion of US-EC economic relations, see Memorandum of conversation Nixon and his advisers, 11 Sept. 1972, 259–66; Ibid, Paper prepared in the Department of State, undated, 283–9.
27. *FRUS* 1969–76, III, Memorandum of conversation Nixon and his advisers, 11 Sept. 1972, 264.
28. Kissinger, *Years of Upheaval* (London: Weidenfeld and Nicolson, 1982), 129–31; Cogan, *Oldest Allies, Guarded Friends*, 158.
29. Kissinger, *Years of Renewal*, 605; Cogan, *Oldest Allies, Guarded Friends*, 156.
30. North Atlantic Council, *NATO Final Communiquées 1949–1974*, 319.
31. Richard H. Ullman, "The French Connection," *Foreign Policy*, no. 75 (Summer 1989), 3–33; Pierre Melandri, "Les États-Unis et la prolifération nucléaire: le cas

français," *Revue d'Histoire Diplomatique*, 3 (1995), 208–15; Soutou, *L'Alliance incertaine*, 357–67; Cogan, *Oldest Allies, Guarded Friends*, 169–70.

32. Kissinger, *Years of Renewal*, 692–7; Soutou, *L'Alliance incertaine*, 357–67; Hillenbrand, *Fragments of Our Time*, 333–7.

33. For Kissinger's interesting account of these developments, see his *Years of Renewal*, 664–700.

34. Short accounts of the changes in the three countries are found in Derek W. Urwin, *Western Europe Since 1945: A Political History* (London: Longman, 1989), 298–313. More interesting and more extensive is Sassoon, *One Hundred Years of Socialism*, 572–644.

35. Kissinger, *Years of Renewal*, 632–3.

36. For the different views even today, see, for instance, the differing accounts in William Blum, *The CIA: A Forgotten History* (London: Zed books, 1986), 243–50 and Stephen G. Xydis, "Coups and Countercoups in Greece, 1967–73 (with postscript)," *Political Science Quarterly*, 89 (Fall 1974), 507–38.

37. NA, NSC documents, National Security Council Decision memorandum 67, 24 June 1970.

38. Kissinger, *Years of Renewal*, 192–239. The quotation is from 238.

39. Smith, *NATO Enlargement During the Cold War* contains good short accounts of the accessions to NATO of Greece, Turkey, and Spain. For the Spanish story, see 127–161.

40. For a short account of US-Icelandic affairs, see Valur Ingimundarson, "The Role of NATO and the US Military Base in Icelandic Domestic Politics, 1949–99" in Gustav Schmidt, *A History of NATO* (Basingstoke: Palgrave, 2001), vol. 2, 285–302, esp. 295–7. The quotations are from NA, NSC documents, National Security Decision Memorandum 137, Policy Toward Iceland, 13 Oct. 1971.

41. Kissinger, *Years of Renewal*, 629–32; Urwin, *Western Europe Since 1945*, 301–3.

42. *FRUS*, 1964–1968, XII, 171–305, particularly 184–8, 236, 241–2, 245, 259–60, 279, 288–9, 295–302: NA, National Security Council documents, US Policy Toward Italy (NSSM 88), 11 June 1970.

43. Sassoon, *One Hundred Years of Socialism*, 579–80; Kissinger, *White House Years*, 921; Kissinger, *Years of Renewal*, 626–9.

44. These percentages are all presented and discussed in my *The American "Empire"*, 87–93, 202.

45. Bureau of the Census, *Statistical Abstract of the United States, 1989*, 20.

46. Lundestad, *The American "Empire"*, 89–90.

47. Lundestad, *The American "Empire"*, 73–4, 88–90.

48. United States Department of State, *1958–1980: US Trade With the European Community*, Special Report No. 84, 28 June 1981, 1.

49. This line of thinking in the Nixon administration is most clearly brought out in Robert S. Litwak, *Détente and the Nixon Doctrine: American Foreign Policy and the Pursuit of Stability, 1969–1976* (Cambridge: Cambridge University Press, 1984).

50. US President, *US Foreign Policy for the 1970s: A New Strategy for Peace* (Washington, DC, 1970), 5.

51. Robert D. Putnam and Nicholas Bayne, *Hanging Together: Cooperation and Conflict in the Seven-Power Summits* (Cambridge, Mass.: Harvard University Press, 1987), 11–44; Kissinger, *Years of Upheaval*, 151; Kissinger, *Years of Renewal*, 692–7.

52. Nelson, *A History of US Military Forces in Germany*, 81,103.

53. A short account of the Mansfield resolutions is found in Powaski, *The Entangling Alliance*, 88–91. For a longer account, see Phil Williams, *The Senate and US Troops in Europe* (London: Macmillan, 1985), esp. 119–234. The balance of payments problem and the offset agreements are covered in Treverton, *The Dollar Drain and American Forces in Germany*. See also Kissinger, *White House Years*, 394–6, 938–49; *FRUS*, 1969–76, III, Memorandum from Bergsten to Kissinger, 3 Dec. 1970, 119–20; ibid., Paper Prepared in the Department of the Treasury, 10 Sept. 1971, 179–88.

54. Kaplan, *The Long Entanglement*, 157–60; Nelson, *A History of US Military Forces in Germany*, 103; Kissinger, *White House Years*, 385–86; Denis Healey, *The Time of My Life* (London: Penguin, 1990), 316–17; *FRUS*, 1969–76, III, Paper Prepared in the Department of State, 28 July 1971, 163–5; *FRUS*, 1969–76, III, Telegram from Secretary Rogers to the Department of State, 10 Dec. 1971, 213–14.

55. Kissinger, *White House Years*, 386.

56. Soutou, *L'Alliance incertaine*, 314–67, esp. 326–7. See also his, "Le Président Pompidou et les relations entre les Etats-Unis et l'Europe," *Journal of European Integration History*, 6:2 (2000), 111–46; Michel Jobert, *Memoires d'avenir* (Paris: Fayard, 1974), 268; Kissinger, *White House Years*, 963; Powaski, *The Entangling Alliance*, 100–1.

57. Diego A. Ruiz Palmer, "La coopération militaire entre la France et ses alliés, 1966–1991: Entre le poids de l'héritage et les défis de l'apres guerre froid," in Melandri, Vaïsse, and Bozo, *La France et L'OTAN 1949–1996* (Brussels: Complexe, 1996, 576–82.

58. North Atlantic Council, *NATO Final Communiquées 1949–1974*, 319.

7

From Bad to Worse: The United States and Western Europe, 1977–1984

Jimmy Carter took over as President of the United States with the best of intentions. While continuing to improve relations with the Soviet Union and China, he would at the same time upgrade America's ties with its allies in Western Europe. This was not to be. By the end of the seventies Moscow had become so frustrated with Carter that the Soviet leaders actually preferred Ronald Reagan in the 1980 elections. US relations with some Western European countries, particularly West Germany, also reached a nadir.

Ronald Reagan was determined to reestablish the leadership role of the United States with regard to both the Soviets and the Western Europeans. The "evil empire" was to be defeated from a position of strength; the "free world" was to be united under America's firm leadership. Neither was to be. Relations with the Kremlin plummeted. With the partial exception of Margaret Thatcher's Britain, in Western Europe criticism of the United States flourished. The alleged traditional alliance system based on rather exclusive US leadership, which even in the past had not fully represented reality, could not be resurrected. The Reagan administration lacked the necessary insight. Even more important, no longer did the United States hold the kind of predominant position that made this possible.

Yet, even in these very difficult times for Atlantic relations most European leaders continued to issue at least some invitations to the Americans to increase their role militarily and economically, although these invitations were clearly more ambivalent now than before. Public opinion was becoming more skeptical of the United States, but still supported the main dimensions of the American role in Western Europe.

Jimmy Carter: Despite the Best of Intentions...

The Carter administration came to power believing in "trilateralism" between the United States, Western Europe, and Japan. Virtually all the leading members of the administration, including the internationally inexperienced former

Governor of Georgia, had been members of the Trilateral Commission. The new National Security Adviser, Zbigniew Brzezinski, had in fact directed the Commission in the early 1970s and had introduced Carter to its work. On 31 December 1974 Carter wrote Brzezinski that "The Trilateral Com experience has been a wonderful opportunity for me, and I have used it perhaps even more than you could know."[1]

The new President had criticized Nixon–Kissinger for their concentration on relations with the Soviet Union and China at the expense of loyal allies such as the Europeans and Japanese. While the Japanese had been the victims of various "Nixon shocks" concerning the opening-up to China and American economic measures, the Europeans had allegedly been treated in a similarly cavalier fashion. After the war in Vietnam, the traumatic Watergate experience, and the tribulations of the Year of Europe, relations had to be improved.

The presumption was that from this low point relations could only go upward—as indeed at first they did. Carter's trip to Europe in the spring of 1977, for the G-7 meeting and the NATO summit, was successful. The Europeans, who had had so many complaints in the Nixon–Kissinger years, but who had nevertheless come to appreciate many of the administration's qualities, were favorably surprised by the new leadership and the personal qualities of a President who had such a limited background in international affairs.

Nixon–Kissinger had decided that only if the Europeans themselves pushed directly for further European integration would the United States support this goal. Washington's all-important task was to protect America's national interests even more forcefully than before, whether they be the supremacy of NATO or concrete economic interests. The Carter administration, however, adopted an outwardly much more favorable attitude to the European Community. In April 1977 Carter himself proclaimed that "I strongly favor, perhaps more than my predecessors, a close interrelationship among the nations of Europe, the European Community, in particular."[2]

Whereas Ford–Kissinger had agreed to consult regularly only with the chairman of the European Council, representing the national governments, not with the supranational Commission President, in January 1978 Carter visited the European Commission in Brussels, actually the first such visit by a US President. He promised that Washington would give "unqualified support" to what the Community was trying to accomplish, welcomed the participation of the Commission President in the G-7 summits, and softened the American opposition somewhat to the Common Agricultural Policy of the (now) Nine. The Tokyo round in GATT was successfully completed in 1979, thereby improving the basic commercial climate between the US and the EC.

All these elements were important, and not only as symbols. There were relatively few trade disputes between the United States and the EC under Carter.

The most significant one concerned textiles. Yet, the Carter years were also quiet ones for the EC—in fact, the whole decade from 1973 to 1983 has been described, with only slight exaggeration, as "the stagnant decade" in EC developments—and, partly for this reason, the Carter administration actually came to spend little time on EC questions, as witnessed by the fact that in their memoirs the leading policymakers have left these matters virtually unnoticed.

On the personal level, Carter and British Prime Minister James Callaghan became quite friendly, as did Secretary of State Cyrus Vance and young British Foreign Secretary David Owen, which undoubtedly helped make America's relations with Britain the most satisfactory among the European allies in the Carter years. The personal relationship between Carter and French President Valery Giscard d'Estaing was also relatively warm, although it was probably warmer on the American than on the French side. Policy differences between France and the United States remained considerable, however, although Giscard, being a non-Socialist but not a Gaullist himself, was presumably even freer to modify the Gaullist legacy than Pompidou had been. This may have led to expectations in Washington, expectations that remained unfulfilled, in part because of the deteriorating American–German relationship. Giscard remained firmly within the Gaullist consensus in France's foreign policy.

American–Italian relations were defined by Italy's ever present concern with its status and therefore produced a very negative response to any Western meeting, such as the one in Guadelope in January 1979 between the US, the UK, France, and West Germany, from which Italy was excluded. In part to enhance its position Italy was to give unexpectedly firm support to the stationing of American intermediate range weapons in Italy. Equally important was the resolution of the lingering issue of the position of the Italian Communist party in Italian political life. In the 1976 national elections, the PCI received 34.4 per cent of the vote, compared to 38.7 for the Christian Democrats (DC). As the DC's will for reform diminished and political scandals increased, it was beginning to lose its hold over the electorate. The Italian Socialist Party and the smaller coalition partners were increasingly open to a coalition with the PCI. Even reformers within the Christian Democrats favored the *compromesso storico*, a PCI–DC coalition.

When Carter took over in January 1977, he wanted to move away from what he considered the rigidities of the Nixon–Kissinger era. In his early statements the new President underlined the right of the Italian people to decide their own future, the US intention not to interfere in domestic politics, and even a desire to establish better working relations with the PCI. In the end, however, even the Carter administration came down on the side of excluding the PCI from government participation. In January 1978 the State Department issued a clarifying statement where it affirmed that "Our position is clear; we do not favor such participation and would like to see Communist influence in any Western European country reduced." As so often, the break with the past was smaller than it seemed with the Carter administration, where there was often a gap between presentation and substance. Influenced in part by Washington the Christian Democrats decided against the *compromesso storico*. So did the Communists. The PCI began to lose votes and pulled back. In Italy the issue of Communist participation was postponed until the Cold War was over.[3]

Rather surprisingly, the American–German relationship was to present the main challenge to Atlantic harmony. West Germany had been, and still was, quite dependent on the United States for its security, but this dependence had been somewhat reduced by the improved East–West climate under détente. While Kennedy had felt that Adenauer had been too dogmatic and anti-Communist, Nixon had felt even more strongly that Brandt was just too impatient in his *Ostpolitik*. Under Helmut Schmidt the West Germans wanted to protect and expand on the benefits of *Ostpolitik*, but now in a period of renewed East–West tension.

While the new *Ostpolitik* gave the Eastern Europeans added room to maneuver, in some ways it circumscribed West Germany's own freedom of action, as Bonn now had a vested interest in the new relationships and became rather averse to anything that might endanger them. Therefore, when new crises developed outside of Europe, in Angola, Ethiopia, and Afghanistan, and even in Europe over deployment of American Intermediate Nuclear Forces (INF) and in Poland in 1980–1, Bonn tended to be opposed to Western responses that could impact negatively on the Eastern relationships. Chancellor Schmidt even attempted to assume some sort of mediating role between Moscow and Washington, though without much success since West Germany clearly did not have the leverage to do this under such difficult circumstances.[4] In terms of the pendulum swings vis-à-vis the Soviet Union, while the American pendulum swung from cooperation with high hopes under Nixon–Kissinger to disappointment under Carter and new confrontation under Reagan, the German pendulum remained stuck in a cooperative framework. Many European countries, particularly among the smaller ones, followed the Germans on this point.

Washington and Bonn disagreed on Germany's sales of nuclear reactors to Brazil and on the German interest in having Radio Free Europe leave Germany, a radio station that Schmidt viewed as a Cold War relic. As we have seen, in the Nixon–Ford years the Europeans had taken the lead on human rights issues in Eastern Europe and the Soviet Union, particularly in the Helsinki process. When Carter came to power, he changed Washington's policy and soon started pushing human rights quite aggressively. Now most European governments felt that this was taking a good thing too far, and that human rights should not threaten the overall policy of détente with Moscow.[5] As early as April 1977 Carter noted that Schmidt had "been quite obnoxious to me".[6] It was to get worse. Two issues in particular were to challenge German–American relations: the neutron bomb and the stationing of American INF in Western Europe.

Traditionally the United States had developed its own weapons with little regard for what the Europeans thought, regarding strategy and weapons development as national questions, even though they could have significant repercussions for their European allies (witness the crisis over the Skybolt missile that was only resolved with Kennedy's offer to Macmillan of Polaris). American strategy sooner (massive retaliation) or later (flexible response) became NATO's strategy; American weapons were soon transferred to Western Europe, whether with fairly broad support (tactical nuclear weapons) or with more selective acceptance (the IRBMs in 1956–8). For the Europeans this unilateralism had at least some advantages: for example, they did not have to get involved in American production and could avoid to some extent deployment decisions that would have been highly controversial in most European countries.

The enhanced radiation weapon (ERW), or neutron bomb, was intended to be a counterweight to the Soviet lead in tanks in Central Europe. It was claimed that because of lower blast and heat effects than tactical nuclear weapons, the neutron bomb would reduce civilian casualties and collateral damage, but soon the media were presenting it as the weapon that would kill "people and not property." In 1977 ERW was still only at the experimental stage, but, perhaps pushed by an early revelation in the press, Carter decided to move ahead with development of the weapon. Yet, while his advisers were strongly in favor of the new weapon, the President was actually quite skeptical and, since Europe was the most likely deployment area, he wanted the Europeans to support deployment.

Soon the difference between development and deployment was disappearing. The Europeans did not really want to be involved in an American *development* decision and, without a strong American lead, West Germany, the most likely area for *deployment*, would not agree to deploy without the support of other European allies. Callaghan, who had given early support, was becoming doubtful in the face of rapidly increasing public opposition in Britain to ERW. Holland, one of the few other countries where the weapon could be usefully stationed, came out against. Attempts were made to link the ERW to the growing Soviet threat from the new SS-20 missiles—the neutron bomb would be deployed only after arms control negotiations had been unsuccessful. Yet, Carter was uncomfortable with the new weapon, particularly if the Germans would not come out in support of it. For Schmidt it was getting politically more and more difficult to give such support; when he went as far as he could, this was not enough, and Carter, against the advice of all his major advisers, deferred production. Schmidt was furious, feeling that he had taken great political risks in supporting the administration only to have Carter pull the rug from under him. After this the relationship never recovered.[7]

The chaos of ERW was to influence NATO's Dual-Track decision of December 1979. Everything had to be done to avert a similar crisis. Again, German–American relations were at the heart of the matter. The roots of the INF decision went back to Secretary of Defense James Schlesinger's concern in 1973 about America's lack of flexibility in case of a nuclear war in Europe and his belief that such flexibility could be provided by developing intermediate range weapons. His thoughts were received with considerable sympathy in Congress and in NATO's Nuclear Planning Group in 1976 but, when Carter took over, the new administration expressed rather limited interest in nuclear modernization; its emphasis was rather on the conventional side.

Now the Europeans took over much of the initiative. They were becoming uneasy about the lack of resolve in the Carter administration and also about the Soviet deployment of modern SS-20 missiles to replace the old SS-4 and 5. (Until now the NATO discussion had not actually been influenced by the SS-20 question.) The question of the Euro-strategic balance was raised in a speech on 28 October 1977 in London by Chancellor Schmidt. SALT I had codified the strategic nuclear balance between the United States and the Soviet Union. As Schmidt stated, "In Europe this magnifies the significance of the disparities between East and West in nuclear tactical and conventional weapons." The German Chancellor hoped that the Soviet lead on the conventional side would be addressed in the MBFR negotiations, but that left a "grey zone", the imbalance in INF. After the withdrawal of the American IRBMs from Turkey and Italy in 1963, the United States actually had no such weapons in Europe. Schmidt's hope was that the INF imbalance could be dealt with in the ongoing SALT II negotiations, but if this could not be done NATO had to deal with the issue accordingly. That presumably meant deployment of an American counterweight to the SS-20s. The British took an even stronger, but quieter interest in INF to make credible every step on the ladder of nuclear deterrence.

For the Carter administration, since the US had more than enough strategic weapons to deter the Soviets, there was little need to balance the Soviet Union at the INF level too—it was for the Europeans, not for the Americans themselves, to doubt the value of America's strategic weapons. Yet, in great part for political reasons having to do with the ERW debacle, Washington came to favor a European-based nuclear counter. Leadership had to be exerted; there could be no repetition of the ERW failure to lead. Schmidt had appeared to ask for INF deployment in Western Europe so, egged on by Brzezinski and the joint chiefs of staff, Washington came out in support of 572 ground-based

Cruise missiles and Pershing Is to be stationed in Europe. Soon, at least the defense departments in key European countries were moving toward deployment, and in Guadeloupe in January 1979 Carter, Callaghan, Giscard d'Estaing, and a somewhat reluctant Schmidt agreed on INF deployment combined with negotiations with the Russians. The assumption was that the weapons had to be deployed first; only then would the Kremlin take negotiations seriously. For Schmidt, again, it was particularly important that West Germany not be the only country where the new weapons would be stationed.

In December 1979 the Thatcher government decided to purchase Trident missiles from the United States to replace the obsolescent Polaris. Much more important, in the same month NATO made its Dual-Track decision, the two tracks combining deployment of the 572 warheads and arms control. To bring about as wide European support as possible, NATO underlined its willingness to forego deployment if Moscow would dismantle its SS-20s. Giscard privately supported the decision, but refrained from doing so publicly. Holland, Norway, Denmark, and even Belgium were the most skeptical. The attitude of Holland and Belgium represented a disappointment in that some of the weapons were to be placed there. Still, since both Britain and Italy were willing to accept the weapons, the potential problem of West Germany being "singularized" was avoided.

While the Soviets responded by withdrawing their offer to negotiate on INF, the European peace movement was mobilizing rapidly against any preparations to deploy the new weapons. The mobilization was particularly intense in Germany, making it virtually impossible for Schmidt to take any lead on this issue. Soon the SPD with Brandt as party leader in fact became the activist in trying to find ways to avert INF deployment. With this, the strain between Washington and several European capitals increased sharply, particularly with Bonn, until in 1982 the FDP decided to switch from the SPD to the CDU and brought Helmut Kohl to power in Bonn.[8]

The introduction of Soviet–Cuban troops into Ethiopia, Vietnam's intervention into Cambodia, and the fall of the Shah in Iran all undermined Washington's willingness to cooperate with Moscow. The fundamentalist regime in Tehran was firmly anti-Soviet and anti-Communist, but it still undermined the American position in the Near East. The Carter administration was tilting toward Beijing and hardliner Brzezinski was definitely winning the battle with Vance over the President's foreign policy soul. In November 1979 US embassy personnel in Tehran were taken hostage by Iranian students and held in confinement for more than a year. A feeling was spreading in Washington that it was time that the United States again let its voice be heard, whether in the face of Communists, ayatollahs, or even lukewarm allies.

The attitude to defense spending illustrated how the President was changing. Carter had initially stated that he wanted to reduce American defense spending, but when he came to power this was modified to mean that the defense budget would increase less than it would have done if Ford had been elected. For NATO, the administration actually increased US forces in Europe by 35,000 and increased pre-stocking of equipment substantially. Soon it came to push the NATO allies hard for a 3 per cent general increase in defense spending but, although the 3 per cent was adopted as a NATO benchmark in 1978, spending in Europe did not increase that much. Allies who had not earlier followed the American lead on defense spending all that strictly were not going to do so now, when they considered the East–West climate in Europe so much better than during the height of the Cold War. In the United States, however, Carter announced a 5 per cent increase shortly before the Soviet invasion of Afghanistan; military preparations were undertaken particularly in the Persian Gulf area; the propaganda campaign against the Soviet Union was stepped up; tougher export control measures were being prepared.

Then in late December 1979 came the massive Soviet invasion of Afghanistan. Carter proclaimed that the invasion had made a more dramatic change in his opinion "of what the Soviets' ultimate goals are than anything they've done in the previous time that I've been in office." In the Carter Doctrine of January 1980 the President proclaimed that "any attempt by any outside force to gain control of the Persian Gulf region will be regarded as an assault on the vital interests of the United States. It will be repelled by the use of any means necessary, including military force."

A whole array of measures were prepared to respond to the new Soviet challenge, which was perceived by some as aiming for the Persian Gulf. The SALT II treaty was to be withdrawn from Senate consideration (it was probably already dead there anyway); the United States would boycott the 1980 Summer Olympics in Moscow; exports to China would include even weapons, as would support for the mujahidin in Afghanistan; a grain embargo would be instituted, export controls greatly tightened, peacetime registration for the draft introduced, etc. Since Carter had already recommended that the defense budget for 1982–6 be increased by 5 per cent, no further addition was made. Reagan's revised defense budget for 1981 actually added only 6.8 billion dollars.[9]

Initially, the European allies appeared to be responsive to Washington's pleas that they follow suit: they all condemned the Soviet invasion and expressed their "grave concern"; further, they agreed to review all economic and financial relations with Moscow and not to take advantage of the openings provided by the American boycott. As could be expected, Britain was the strongest supporter of the Carter administration: the defense budget was increased by 3.5 per cent; Thatcher encouraged the Olympic boycott; diplomatic and economic contacts with Moscow were reduced. Even this was less than Washington had hoped for. And when the British Olympic Committee recommended sending British athletes to Moscow, Thatcher yielded.

Both Brandt, the old Mayor of West Berlin and now leader of the SPD, and Chancellor Schmidt, who had been a solidly pro-Western Defense Minister under Brandt, had strong Cold War credentials, but the Carter administration soon came to feel that Bonn was behaving much too independently. This was particularly the view of "Polish" anti-Communist Brzezinski, who felt that Schmidt wanted to set himself up as some sort of mediator between the United States and the Soviet Union and feared that French and German policies had the effect "of stimulating Franco-German competition in a race to Moscow."[10] This was worse than under de Gaulle; then at least there had been no such race. These more structural differences were supplemented by the rapidly growing personal animosity between Carter and Schmidt, an animosity so strong that it was very rare in Atlantic relations. Carter naturally saw himself as the leader of the Western alliance; Schmidt came to regard him as a moralist who was both inexperienced and untrustworthy. In his memoirs he entitles the chapter on Carter "Jimmy Carter: Idealismus und Wankelmut" (Idealism and Vacillation).[11]

Although West Germany boycotted the Moscow Olympics and condemned the invasion, Schmidt was determined to keep the lines of communication open with Moscow at a time when Carter wanted to close them. The Chancellor did indeed see himself as a possible mediator between Washington and Moscow. In his opinion, the United States had a tendency to "globalize" East–West relations, when in fact peace in Europe should be decoupled from out-of-area tension. German trade with the Soviet Union seemed to continue in a normal way throughout 1980. The Soviets made it clear that deliveries of natural gas to Western Europe would be curtailed if sanctions were imposed.

France protested against the Soviet invasion, but made a point of stressing that this was done independently of Washington's policies. Giscard shared Schmidt's opinion of the American tendency to "globalize" East–West relations. The government endorsed the Olympic boycott, but the French Olympic Committee nevertheless decided to send athletes to Moscow. The French also maintained full diplomatic and economic relations with the Soviet Union and as early as May 1980 Giscard met Brezhnev in Warsaw for long talks, presumably to persuade the Soviet leader to withdraw from Afghanistan. In Washington some felt that French diplomacy had fallen to the level of being Moscow's "telephone operator." Soon the French were asking the Americans to end their economic embargo.[12]

American–European relations were also strained in several other ways. On the monetary side, the complicated SDR system did not prove a success, since in practice the dollar remained the currency all others were measured against, and many Europeans became increasingly irritated at being tied to a currency they did not have the slightest control over. Monetary cooperation had long been an objective of the EC, but the attempts in the 1970s to design a fluctuation margin within the new international floating currency system did not succeed. However, in 1978 Schmidt and Giscard agreed on the framework for a European Monetary System (EMS). In part the inspiration for this came from German–French frustration at the expansionist policies of the Carter administration, resulting in inflation and a declining dollar. But the EMS was only a very partial success as, under pressure from Carter and the left wing of the SPD, Bonn in fact soon agreed to more expansionist policies in an attempt to reflate the international economy. Only when Kohl came to power in 1982 was the habitual fiscal balance restored.[13]

On the very emotional issue of the American hostages in Tehran, the Carter administration felt that the Europeans responded too timidly. They were too interested in maintaining commercial and other contacts with Iran and put too little pressure on the ayatollahs to get the hostages out. A certain cooling of Washington's attitude to the EC could be noticed too after the EC's declaration in June 1980 calling for a Palestinian homeland and Palestinian participation in Arab–Israeli peace talks. This diverged from America's policy, which was still pro-Israeli despite Carter's successful personal effort to bring about peace between Israel and Egypt in 1978–9.

Western Europe's attitudes were not what the Carter administration had hoped for, but the starting points were just too different on the two sides of the Atlantic. The United States focused on what it interpreted as a whole series of Soviet advances and the direct challenge to the US that these advances seemed to imply; the Europeans, and especially the Germans, focused on the tremendous improvements that détente had brought in Europe in general and in Germany in particular, in the form of improved contacts at all levels. The Europeans were against anything that smacked of extending NATO's area of responsibility to the Gulf. Instead they were on the look-out for possible diplomatic solutions, even to the crisis over Afghanistan where, sooner or later, Moscow would come to realize that it had over-extended itself. Western Europe was not as dependent on the United States as it had been in earlier decades, both because of a diminished threat and the economic and even military strengthening of Western Europe. Confidence in America had also been undermined by the bickering in recent years. West Germany, traditionally the most loyal ally, was now the most problematical one.

Ronald Reagan as Leader of the "Free World"[14]

Ronald Reagan believed in America's strength and America's mission. The new President clearly did not see the United States as declining. In his first State of the Union address, he warned Congress and the nation: "Don't let anyone tell you that America's best days are behind her, that the American spirit has been vanquished." Again and again he reaffirmed his basic creed:

the undeniable truth that America remains the greatest force for peace in the world today...The American dream lives—not only in the hearts and minds of our countrymen but in the hearts and minds of millions of the world's people in both free and oppressed societies. As long as that dream lives, as long as we continue to defend it, America has a future, and all mankind has reason to hope.

True, in the 1970s under Nixon and Carter the United States had suffered setbacks, of which Vietnam, Iran, and Afghanistan were the most traumatic. "How did this all happen?" Reagan rhetorically asked—and supplied the answer: "America had simply ceased to be a leader in the world." America had to regain "the respect of America's allies and adversaries alike." Thus, the United States had to stand up to the Soviet Union and resume an unambiguous leadership role in Western Europe. If the United States provided the leadership, the allies would follow. Secretary of Defense Caspar Weinberger shocked his European counterparts when he told them that "If the movement from cold war to detente is progress, then let me say that we cannot afford much more progress."

The debate about style and leadership was closely related to the question of the content of Reagan's policies. The American defense budget soon increased dramatically. Reagan proposed 14 per cent real growth for 1982, and subsequently 7 per cent annually, as compared to the 5 per cent Carter had proposed for 1982–6. Although Congress reduced this largesse somewhat, most of it remained. The Europeans had nothing against Reagan's big increases in American defense spending, but most of them had clearly been unwilling to grant even the 3 per cent increase that Carter had insisted upon. American defense spending was considerably higher than European, but, the Europeans argued, there were good reasons for that. American spending had a tendency to go in peaks and troughs, whereas in Europe the increases tended to be small but steady. As a result, overall defense spending from 1970 to 1987 actually rose more rapidly in Europe than in the United States.[15]

The new firmness virtually precluded any reappraisal of the American commitment to the defense of Western Europe, which helped US–European relations. Not only would the nuclear guarantee remain; in fact, the Reagan administration saw such a need to deter the Soviets that some of its most prominent members talked openly about nuclear war-fighting and a few even about prevailing in a nuclear war. This kind of public nuclear strategic thinking was too much of a good thing for European leaders. Such talk seemed unnecessary to deter the Soviets; it only served to scare the European public. On the question of American troops in Europe, the Reagan administration modernized the troops fully and strengthened reinforcement capabilities.

While wanting the Europeans to do their part, Washington did not apply too much pressure to bring about a stronger European conventional effort. So, on the very important point of the American commitment to Europe, not only did Washington stand firm, but it actually took away much of the incentive for the Europeans to increase their conventional strength.

Reagan showed little interest in arms control. He wanted to negotiate from a position of strength; therefore the US had to build up its defense before it would negotiate seriously with the Soviets—or rather, only then could the Soviets be expected to make the necessary concessions. In March 1983 Reagan presented his Strategic Defense Initiative (SDI) which, in the President's ambitious version, was to be a shield that would protect the United States from any missile attack. SDI was quickly seen as a potential obstacle to the Strategic Arms Reduction Talks (START, as Reagan renamed the SALT talks), and many wondered about its "Fortress America" implications. And this crucial new element was introduced by the President without any consultations at all with the Europeans. (In fact on SDI Reagan consulted very few members even of his own administration.)

The Europeans had become frustrated, as had the Soviets, with what they saw as Carter's vacillation. Consultations were fine, but on difficult issues there also had to be leadership. Yet, for many what the new President seemed to offer—leadership without consultations—could be just as bad; the Europeans quite simply insisted on being consulted much more closely than in the days of clear-cut American domination.

While they became more concerned with Moscow's new expansionism, most European leaders still wanted to protect and if possible even to expand the benefits of détente. They favored a continuation of serious arms control negotiations with the Soviet Union, although they differed somewhat on what part of these negotiations should receive priority. Thus, while West Germany under Schmidt and most smaller NATO allies wanted nuclear reductions, the French were much more interested in conventional reductions. Although European fears of an American decoupling from Europe had formed an important part of the background for NATO's Dual Track decision of December 1979, the Reagan administration's casual public attitude toward nuclear weapons and toward arms control in general worried European governments and, even more, the general public.

The American attitude helped stimulate a rapid growth in European peace movements, especially in the "Arch of Angst," Britain, West Germany, the Benelux countries, and Scandinavia. When INF negotiations with the Soviets broke down, deployments of Cruise and Pershing missiles started in November 1983, which could be seen as a success for James Callaghan, Helmut Schmidt, and the other fathers of the Dual Track decision. However, no one seemed interested in claiming paternity any more. In fact, both Callaghan and Schmidt had left the scene and new and more radical leaders had taken over their parties, parties that in the past had been crucial in maintaining the relative NATO consensus. In Germany the SPD now refused to commit itself to any INF deployment; in Britain the Labour party wanted to do away even with Britain's own nuclear force. The change of attitude in the German SPD influenced views even in Holland, Denmark, and Norway. The latter two openly flirted with the idea of a Nordic nuclear-free zone until the Reagan administration made it perfectly clear that it would accept no such idea.

Yet, what could have become a deep crisis in Atlantic relations did not develop into one. The main reason was that not only the United States, but also the leading countries in Western Europe, moved in a more anti-Soviet direction. This was first noticeable in Britain where in the 1979 elections the Conservatives triumphed over a Labour party that was increasingly divided internally. Margaret Thatcher became the new Prime Minister, the first woman to head a government in the Atlantic world. (She had little interest in promoting other women, however.)

Thatcher was quickly to become President Reagan and the whole administration's favorite partner in Europe. Although she had her differences with the administration in Washington, she would rarely criticize the Americans in public. To her the Atlantic relationship was essential, though some of Reagan's statements on Western Europe were too ideological even for her taste: "a combination of exaggerated American rhetoric and the perennial nervousness of European opinion threatened to undermine the good transatlantic relationship that would be needed to guarantee that [INF] deployment went ahead." Outwardly she almost always supported Reagan, or, as she phrased it herself, in his first years Reagan "still had to face a largely skeptical audience at home and particularly among his allies. I was perhaps his principal cheerleader in NATO."[16]

Reagan and Thatcher shared the same outlook on the evils of the Soviet Union and Communism, and also on the role of government or, rather, its limited role. The two leaders got along very well indeed on a personal level. Reagan needed an intimate ally in Europe, whereas Thatcher could strengthen Britain's eroded position through the link to Washington. Thatcher showed how closeness to the United States could in some respects compensate for Britain's reduced economic strength compared with France and West Germany. Probably no two American–European leaders had been as close personally and politically as Reagan and Thatcher (although in terms of what a friendship actually accomplished, the Roosevelt–Churchill relationship during the Second World War was far more significant).

The biggest surprise was the change in French policies. In the 1981 presidential elections Socialist François Mitterrand triumphed over non-Socialist Giscard d'Estaing. Mitterrand was to prove much more pragmatic than his predecessor had been, for, despite the fact that throughout his long politic; career he had developed a strong personal animosity toward de Gaulle, he wa able to readjust French policies in the direction of working more closely wit the United States while at the same time remaining within the wider Gaulli: consensus on foreign policy.

This showed particularly on the crucial INF issue. In Mitterrand's opinio the Soviet SS-20 missiles had to be balanced by American ones, otherwise th fear of American *découplage* from Europe arose. So concerned wa Mitterrand about the opposition in Germany to INF that in January 1983 h spoke out in the German *Bundestag* in favor of deployment, and it was obvi ous that in Germany the French Socialist President preferred the CDU to th SPD. The fact that only the previous day Soviet Foreign Minister Andre Gromyko had descended on Bonn to promote the cause of the SPD made th impact of Mitterrand's speech even greater. Reagan was fulsome in his praise "Your Bonn speech reinforces the Alliance at the very moment when th European countries are revealing their impotence or at any rate their anxiet in the face of public opinion... Your speech is... of inestimable value." I fact, France was virtually the only country in Europe where large demonstra tions against INF deployment did not take place.[17]

On his first day in office Mitterrand learned about the covert nuclea cooperation between the United States and France; he expanded this relation ship while continuing to keep it secret. He also accepted the level of coopei ation that had developed in NATO and in fact extended it further, so that Frenc politicians and generals came to participate more freely in NATO context than at any time since the pre-de Gaulle years. France hosted a meeting of th Atlantic Council in 1983, the first such meeting in Paris after de Gaulle, an France participated fully in most planning meetings and joint exercises ii NATO. In his first nine months in office Mitterrand crossed the Atlantic n less than three times. Toward Moscow, on the other hand, he prescribed "disintoxication cure," breaking with the pattern of extensive consultation that had developed under Pompidou and Giscard. On his March 1984 trip t the United States Mitterrand was celebrated not only by Reagan, but also b many American intellectuals and artists.

All this was rather unexpected in Washington, as on the very day o Mitterrand's announcement of his government on 23 June 1981 the Reaga; administration had despatched Vice President George Bush to persuad Mitterrand that he should not include Communists in the governmen Mitterrand refused to heed the advice, seeing the inclusion of fou Communists as tactical, in the sense that it would come to weaken the party But Reagan did not take lightly to such a break with the principle of not includ ing Communists in the governments of NATO countries. As we have seen, th Carter administration had come out against Communist participation in th

Italian government. One reason for the confusion in the Carter years was that in France the US administration had been flirting with a more positive attitude to Communist participation, for whereas in Italy the Communists dominated politics on the left and the Christian Democrats were in a state of considerable confusion, in France the Socialists had become the dominant force on the left and Mitterrand's credentials in fighting Communism and Soviet influence were hardly open to doubt. Though still out of power, he could in time become a tempting partner for the United States. Yet, Carter could not square the circle and, naturally, the negative January 1978 statement applied both to France and to Italy.[18] But in the end Mitterrand was proved right. As members of his government, the French Communists lost much of their strength in the 1980s, unable to reconcile a revolutionary approach with the everyday compromises of government.

Washington had clearly developed a growing dislike for European Socialists and Social Democrats unwilling to stand up and be counted in Washington's struggle against "the evil empire." That was why Mitterrand was such a pleasant surprise. In 1982 the FDP abandoned a more and more divided SPD and instead brought the CDU under Helmut Kohl to power in West Germany. In 1983 the CDU triumphed in the elections and the Kohl–Genscher government continued. While the Reagan administration became rather skeptical of Foreign Minister Hans-Dietrich Genscher's willingness to explore compromises with Moscow, Reagan got along much better with Chancellor Kohl than he had with SPD moderate Schmidt, not to mention Carter's very strained relationship with Schmidt. Kohl remained firm on INF deployment, which began to be implemented in November 1983. The most difficult phase of the Reagan–Kohl relationship occurred in 1985 in connection with Kohl's insistence that Reagan visit the Bitburg cemetery where German soldiers who had died in the Second World War were buried. Reagan went, but combined it with a visit to the Bergen–Belsen concentration camp.[19]

Ideology remained a guide, but an imperfect one, to a country's closeness to Washington. As we have seen, the support the Reagan administration received on some key Cold War issues from Socialist President Mitterrand in France was one example of this. Italy, where the search for an agreement with the Communists at last came to an end, was another, when, for the first time since 1945, the leadership position in the ruling center-left coalition went to parties other than the Christian Democrats—first in 1981–2 to the Republican Giovanni Spadolini and then, from 1983 to 1987, to the Socialist Bettino Craxi. The new governments tried to introduce some dynamism into Italian foreign policy, although not at the expense of Italy's reputation in NATO. To the surprise of many, Italy was to reaffirm its support for the INF decision, including the deployment on Italian soil. This compensated for the increasing doubts about deployment in Holland and Belgium and alleviated West Germany's fear about being "singularized" on the continent.[20]

Yet, despite these positive developments in America's relations with its four main partners in Europe, the disagreements were still numerous, particularly outside of Europe, but to some extent within Europe too. In fact, in some ways, in their appraisals of Soviet intentions the differences between the two sides of the Atlantic had hardly been more pronounced, but they were softened by the differences that were to be found also among the Europeans. The respective reactions to the imposition of martial law in Poland in December 1981 revealed the various splits: West Germany under Schmidt, because of *Ostpolitik* and the furious INF debate, was reluctant to do anything at all; France under Mitterrand clearly condemned developments in Poland, but wanted to be rather selective in its response; Britain under Thatcher was the closest to Washington, but still wanted to maintain good relations with the other European powers. Sanctions were applied against Poland, but Washington not only wanted to go much further than the European capitals on this point, but also, and even more important, imposed sanctions against the Soviet Union. Reagan's declared intention was "to convey to those regimes how strongly we feel about their joint attempts to extinguish liberty in Poland."

The Reagan administration's sanctions included the suspension of oil and gas technology sales and high technology exports in general. In fact, in June 1982 Washington, without any consultation in advance, moved into the highly controversial area of extraterritorial rights when it prohibited the export of technology manufactured both by American subsidiaries and even by licensees of American firms in Europe. Unlike the Germans twenty years earlier, the Europeans now refused to yield to the United States. (The British had not yielded even in 1962–3, but the quantities involved then had been relatively small.)

All the governments involved, certainly including Thatcher's Britain, stood firm. They felt that Washington was trying to return to the economic coercion of earlier decades, and that it was doing so in a very crude and illegal form. Contracts had already been signed for deliveries to the Soviet Union. The planned 3,500 mile pipeline from western Siberia to seven Western European countries represented a huge commercial deal and really mattered for European energy supplies. Washington had come out strongly against this pipeline and argued that it made the Europeans dangerously dependent on Moscow's goodwill. The Europeans saw this as representing rather exaggerated scenarios as, by the end of the 1980s, Europe's dependence on Soviet natural gas would only rise on average from 15 to 20 per cent. The effort to regulate the activities of American companies abroad and even of European companies was seen as an infringement of European sovereignty, and many felt that the American position smacked of hypocrisy, in that Reagan's anti-Soviet view did not include a continuation of the grain embargo Carter had imposed after Afghanistan. After five months of quite bitter dispute, the United States did back down, guided by the new Secretary of State, George Shultz. Existing contracts were to be honored while future credits and exports to the Soviet Union were to be tightened.[21]

On SDI the Reagan administration received less support in Europe than it did on INF. If developed, SDI would break with the ABM treaty of 1972, a cornerstone in arms control diplomacy. True, Reagan was once again backed by Thatcher, who thought that SDI would not only strengthen America's defense, but would also represent a technological challenge the Soviets would probably be unable to handle, and thus would be forced to make the necessary concessions. Yet, at least initially, her enthusiasm was tempered because of her fear that Reagan actually saw SDI as something that could come to do away with nuclear weapons altogether. Mitterrand was firmly opposed. SDI would lead to a build-up of Soviet offensive weapons; it would give no added security to Western Europe; and the world would simply have to learn to live with nuclear weapons. It must also have counted that potentially SDI could come to make the French *force de frappe* less relevant if a similar system was developed on the Soviet side. In an attempt to prevent European technological involvement in SDI, the French President even proposed a European space project, EUREKA. Although EUREKA was no success, on SDI most European leaders definitely sided with Mitterrand rather than with Thatcher.[22]

Reagan's anti-Communist doctrine also received rather limited support in Western Europe. Under this doctrine the United States would support "freedom fighters" who were prepared to take up the struggle against Soviet–Communist regimes. It was not sufficient simply to contain Communist expansion; Communism should be rolled back. While Eisenhower's "roll-back" in the 1950s had referred to Eastern Europe, Reagan was primarily concerned with the Third World. While Eisenhower's means had been psychological–political, Reagan's would be both military and economic.

Thatcher was all for putting "freedom on the offensive." Only Britain appears to have joined the United States in militarily supporting the mujahidin in Afghanistan, although the rebels had the broad support of the European public in their struggle against the Soviet forces. Skepticism was more evident as far as the US role in the civil wars in Angola, Cambodia, and particularly Nicaragua was concerned. In Nicaragua Washington's objective was to undermine and preferably to overthrow the Sandinista government "in the defense of the Western hemisphere against Soviet–Cuban expansion." For the Europeans the issue was one both of principle and pragmatism. They held that military assistance to forces trying to overthrow a government ran counter to international law and viewed Reagan's policies as unlikely to succeed and possibly even as counterproductive. On the European left in particular the United States was seen as upholding the traditional order of army–church–landowners against more popular forces. Mitterrand's France maintained close ties with the Sandinistas and even with guerillas in El Salvador, although the French President made it clear to Reagan that for him personally such revolutionary enthusiasm was not a crucial element of his foreign policy. Even the Thatcher government pointed to the need for a "peaceful solution."[23]

However, Margaret Thatcher and even François Mitterrand were reluctant to waste American goodwill in the cause of Nicaragua and Central America, where Reagan felt strongly and British and French interests were limited. For Britain this was particularly the case after the Falklands (Malvinas) War in 1982, a war that added considerably to the closeness of the American–British relationship. After Argentina invaded the islands, the United States tried to mediate between Argentina and Britain, but when this failed it chose Britain. American military and intelligence assistance was invaluable for the British defeat of the Argentineans after an expedition halfway down the globe. Although the EC countries gave political support to Britain, it was America's aid that really mattered.

Washington's assistance in the Falklands War did not, however, prevent Thatcher from speaking up quite forcefully and in public against the American invasion of Grenada in the fall of 1983. Once again, the Reagan administration was afraid of a leftist revolution with Soviet–Cuban connections in the Western hemisphere. Thatcher saw things differently—since there was already a leftist government in power, the coup that so agitated the Americans did not really represent any big change. Even more important was the matter of international law: "This action will be seen as intervention by a western country in the internal affairs of a small independent nation, however unattractive its regime." And, perhaps most important, without consulting London Washington had invaded a member of the British Commonwealth. After the Falklands and with the American invasion being supported by Grenada's small neighbors, Reagan was surprised at Thatcher's strong reaction.[24]

Differences over the Middle East persisted, although Mitterrand narrowed such differences somewhat when he modified the pro-Arab position France had followed since the 1967 war. One problem for the Europeans was that, whereas they might still take a considerable interest in Third World matters, in most areas they had few means of really influencing the outcome. As we have seen, disagreement between the United States and Western Europe on so-called out-of-(NATO) area affairs was nothing new.

While Mitterrand had come to represent a pleasant surprise to Washington in his East–West policies, the initial economic climate was cold between the United States and France. The Socialist government undertook significant nationalization and tried to speed up economic growth by pursuing an expansionist fiscal policy. Despite Mitterrand's foreign policy changes, the economic question served to sharpen the public's attitude toward the United States and the Reagan administration. In September 1981, 43 per cent of the French were more afraid of the United States and its monetary policy than the USSR and its defense policy. One year later, 45 per cent of the French considered America's high interest rates and the appreciating dollar responsible for current international tension.[25]

It soon became evident, however, that such a radical policy would only undermine the French economy as long as more conservative European governments (including even West Germany, particularly after the fall of Schmidt) gave priority to the struggle against inflation. The French Socialists had to abandon expansionism and follow more conservative fiscal and monetary policies, but at least it meant that, on the basis of the new *franc fort* policy, economic cooperation with West Germany could be resumed. The French Socialist experiment had largely failed, at least on the fiscal side, but the French–German rapprochement was to make possible a considerable reinvigoration of the EC.

During the first years of the Reagan administration the suspension of interest in the EC that had characterized Washington in the Carter years continued. On more general economic issues, especially the Carter but also the Reagan administration wanted export-rich and inflation-low West Germany (and Japan) to pursue more expansionist policies. These countries, not the United States, or France for that matter, could provide engines of growth. The Germans and the Japanese made only small concessions to this view. European criticism of America's economic policies soon became stronger than the other way around. This criticism could occasionally appear somewhat contradictory. When the dollar was high, there was a tendency to complain that this reflected high interest rates, which in turn drew capital away from Europe and to the United States. When the dollar later began to slide, many feared that this represented an effort to undercut European competition.

The main European criticism, however, concerned the US budget and trade deficits. When Reagan took over after Carter, the yearly budget deficit stood at $79 billion. Under Reagan it ranged from $128 to $221 billion and the historical total nearly tripled. The trade deficit was so great that the United States shifted from being the world's largest creditor as late as 1982 to being its largest debtor in 1986. From 1984 the United States also ran rapidly increasing deficits in its trade with Western Europe.[26]

The Europeans complained time and again about the budget and trade deficits, and on this point, at least, Thatcher was firmly in line with other European leaders. The budget deficit drove up interest rates. The trade deficit stimulated protectionism and was really a sign of irresponsibility made possible only by the dollar's role as the world currency. No other debtor state could take up loans in its own currency and while itself running huge deficits still lecture Third World debtors about the importance of fiscal discipline. At the same time, however, the fact that several members of the EC had higher government debts (in relative figures) than had the United States did not stop them from criticizing Washington.

America's leadership role had rested on its economic and military strength. The early Reagan years buttressed the military position of the United States. Reagan was also able to instill a renewed patriotism in the American people. But on the economic side the indicators were mixed indeed. After the recession of 1981–2, economic growth continued for the rest of the Reagan presidency at a higher level than in Western Europe. On a worldwide basis the United States experienced no further decline in its production as a percentage of total world production. It remained at around 23 per cent of world production. But, no one could be certain what long-term effects the two deficits, which in part had fuelled the economic growth, would have on the American economy.

European Invitations Under Carter–Reagan?

On the American side in the late 1970s–early 1980s there was strong support for the US military role in Western Europe. Among opinion leaders more than 90 per cent favored the commitment of American troops if the Soviet Union invaded Western Europe or even West Berlin (77 per cent). The public was somewhat less enthusiastic, but 50 to 60 per cent still favored the use of US troops. This was higher than in the case of an invasion of Japan and also higher that the corresponding number had been during the Vietnam War.[27]

On the European side, what happened to the European invitations that had been such a prominent characteristic particularly of the early American–European relationship? Once the benefits of the American presence were taken for granted, cries about American interference became louder and more frequent, and they came not only from the minority on the far left which all along had protested against the American role. As Michael Howard argued with reference to the early 1980s, "[We] now assume that the dangers against which we once demanded reassurance only now exist in the fevered imagination of our protectors."[28]

Yet, in many areas it was evident that the Americans were in fact still invited to play important roles. In the strategic area, the leading European governments had not really modified their long-held view that America should be as clearly committed as possible. As we have seen, the INF deployment decision sprang from a complicated mixture of European worries about America's potential decoupling from Europe and Washington's drive for leadership. On INF both Britain and France were actually skeptical of the zero option since that would leave some empty steps on America's escalation ladder in Europe. Under Kohl West Germany was concerned that with no INF, the pressure to remove even short-range weapons would escalate, particularly in Germany itself, where these weapons were stationed. Whereas public opinion in many countries reacted against aspects of the American nuclear presence in particular, support for NATO as such and for the American troops in Europe remained strong and steady. The pressure for a Western "no first use" pledge of atomic weapons came from certain prominent Americans and from the European peace movement, not really from European governments or strategists.[29]

On the economic side American investments in Europe had increased very rapidly. As late as 1957 they stood at only $1.7 billion. This amount increased to $24 billion in 1970 and $149 billion in 1987. The slower economic growth of the 1970s and 1980s largely made fears about "the American challenge" go away and now in fact often stimulated competition for new US investment. Britain led with US investments of $44 billion in 1987, followed by West Germany with $24 billion, Switzerland with $20 billion, the Netherlands with $14 billion, and France with 11 billion dollars.

At this time, however, the shoe was on the other foot, in that in the 1970s and 1980s European investments in America increased even more rapidly than American investments in Europe. There was less talk of the Americans buying Europe than foreigners taking over America. Although much of the publicity concerned the Japanese, most of this investment was in fact European. In 1970, European investment in the United States stood at $9.5 billion, in 1987 at $178 billion. Britain led with $75 billion, followed by the Netherlands at $47 billion, West Germany at $19 billion, and Switzerland at 14 billion dollars. In comparison Japanese investment in the US came to $33 billion.[30]

In the late 1970s–early 1980s the furious debate about INF deployment and Reagan's strong anti-Communism increased skepticism toward the United States in many European countries, and criticism of many aspects of American foreign policy grew. So, now the people were indeed becoming more ambivalent toward the United States than were their governments. On more specific issues the skepticism about America could be considerable.[31]

In Britain there was support for the British deterrent, whereas the public was quite divided on the presence of American nuclear weapons. The most striking fact concerning Britain was that in 1981–2 public confidence in the United States declined much more dramatically than in other major European countries. In fact, in these years more people disapproved than approved of the American bases in Britain. Yet, the basic sympathy for NATO and for the American role in Europe remained. A study of attitudes even in the late 1970s and early 1980s revealed that in Britain "One reason for the high level of support for NATO is that both it and the United States are, according to a variety of polls, regarded as staunchly dependable."

In West Germany there might be occasional outbursts of sympathy for a united and neutral Germany, but on the whole confidence in the United States and in NATO remained strong. While in 1956–7 a majority would actually have welcomed the withdrawal of American troops from Europe, in the 1960s, 1970s, and early 1980s strong majorities tended to favor American troops in Europe. West Germans combined very firm support for NATO and the American troop presence as such with a growing criticism both of certain aspects of the Reagan administration's foreign policy and of particular aspects of the strong allied military presence in a country about the size of Oregon. As a matter of fact, in most years in the 1970s and 1980s West Germany recorded the most pro-American score in the polls taken (after Ireland, with its very special ties due to by far the highest emigration from Europe to the United States on a per capita basis).

In Italy too confidence in the United States and in NATO largely endured, although from a two-thirds majority of favorable opinion in the 1950s and 1960s, the US image declined to a low of 41 per cent during the mid-1970s. Italy also combined definite support for NATO and friendly feelings for the United States in general with negative attitudes to Reagan's early policy on détente and East–West contacts. In Spain and Greece, where the United States had been associated with the pre-democratic regimes, Washington was under pressure to reduce bases and personnel. In the Greek case the matter was postponed; in the Spanish one NATO agreed to fund a partial relocation to Italy. In many countries there was rising sentiment for "European defense," but little or no enthusiasm could be found for the higher defense spending that could make a more independent force more likely. In Holland, Denmark, and Norway support for membership of NATO and for the American security guarantee remained stable at a high level from decade to decade. In the 1980s, however, the skepticism toward Reagan's policies led to a marked decline in confidence in the United States in other respects.

The most remarkable thing about French opinion was, as we have seen, the strong criticism of US economic policies. In France strong neutralist leanings were combined with a conviction that the United States would defend Western Europe anyway in case of a Soviet attack. In 1985, 69 per cent of the French believed that in a war they could "count on" the United States, actually a higher percentage than in both West Germany (67) and Britain (56). While the percentage of the population who thought NATO essential was noticeably smaller in France than in other NATO countries, there was "net support" for NATO even in France.

Two additional observations should be made about France. First, there are strong indications that the "national security elite" had a rather sophisticated and more positive attitude to the United States than the rest of French opinion.

Few in this security elite bothered to explain to the public how closely the United States and France were actually working together in the early years of Mitterrand's reign. Second, while in most countries confidence in the United States declined, in France there actually appears to have been some rehabilitation of the American image in the late 1970s–early 1980s. This was probably due to the discovery among French intellectuals of the *gulag* and the Soviet threat in general at a time when many other Europeans felt that with détente the Soviet threat had receded somewhat, at least in a longer time perspective.

In sum, the overall picture was quite complex. Particularly among the governments of the four leading European powers, there was still an interest in maintaining and even in strengthening at least certain aspects of the American military presence in Europe. Many of the governments of the smaller European countries were much more ambivalent. On the economic side virtually every European government competed more and more for American investment. The Europeans generally maintained their friendly attitude to the United States as such, although not necessarily to Reagan's activist policies, but little remained of the urge to involve the Americans that had characterized the early decades of the Atlantic relationship.

Notes

1. Zbigniew Brzezinski, *Power and Principle: Memoirs of a National Security Adviser, 1977–81* (New York: Farrar, Straus, Giroux, 1983), 5.
2. This and the next two paragraphs follow my *"Empire" by Integration*, 108–9.
3. A fine account of the Italian Eurocommunist issue is found in Olav Njølstad, "The Carter administration and Italy: Keeping the Communists Out of Power Without Interfering," *Journal of Cold War Studies*, 4:3 (Summer 2002), 56–94. See also Brzezinski, *Power and Principle*, 312; Allin, *Cold War Illusions*, 118–31.
4. Thomas Banchoff, *The German Problem Transformed: Institutions, Politics, and Foreign Policy, 1945–1995* (Ann Arbor: University of Michigan Press, 1999), 95–6, 111–18.
5. For a fine account of the CSCE process, see Thomas, *The Helsinki Effect*.
6. Brzezinski, *Power and Principle*, 292.
7. For a recent German account of the neutron bomb controversy, see Haftendorn, *Deutsche Aussenpolitik zwischen Selbstbechränkung und Selbstbehauptung*, 274–5. See also Raymond L. Garthoff, *Détente and Confrontation: American–Soviet Relations from Nixon to Reagan*, Rev. edn. (Washington, DC: Brookings, 1994), 937–9; Olav Njølstad, *Peacekeeper and Troublemaker: The Containment Policy of Jimmy Carter, 1977–78* (Oslo: Institute for Defense Studies, 1995), 99–127.
8. For a superior account of the INF issue, see Leopoldo Nuti, "Italy and the Battle of the Euromissiles," in Njølstad (ed.), *From Conflict Escalation to Conflict Transformation*. See also Haftendorn, *Deutsche Aussenpolitik zwischen Selbstbeänkung und Selbstbehauptung*, 264–307; Garthoff, *Détente and Confrontation*, 939–74.

9. For the argument that there was great continuity from Carter to Reagan, see Olav Njølstad, "The Carter Legacy: Entering the Second Era of the Cold War," in Njølstad (ed.), *From Conflict Escalation to Conflict Transformation*.

10. Brzezinski, *Power and Principle*, 313–14.

11. Schmidt, *Menschen und Mächte*, 222–9.

12. A succinct account of Western Europe's response to Afghanistan is found in Minton F. Goldman, "President Carter, Western Europe, and Afghanistan in 1980: Inter-Allied Differences over Policy toward the Soviet Invasion," in Herbert D. Rosenbaum and Alexej Ugrinsky (eds.), *Jimmy Carter: Foreign Policy and Post-Presidential Years* (Westport: Greenwood, 1994), 19–34.

13. David P. Calleo, *Rethinking Europe's Future* (Princeton: Princeton University Press, 2001), 167–8.

14. A very early draft of this part of the chapter was presented in my "The United States and Western Europe Under Ronald Reagan," in David E. Kyvig (ed.), *Reagan and the World* (Westport: Greenwood Press, 1990), 39–66.

15. Lundestad, "Uniqueness and Pendulum Swings in US Foreign Policy," in Lundestad, *The American "Empire"*, 127–31; Eurogroup, *Western Defense: The European Role in NATO* (Brussels, May 1988), particularly 10–11, 18–19.

16. Margaret Thatcher, *The Downing Street Years* (New York: HarperCollins, 1993), 156–71. The quotations are from 157–8 and 171.

17. My analysis of French policy builds largely on Frédéric Bozo, "Before the Wall: French Diplomacy and the Last Decade of the Cold War, 1979–1989," in Njølstad (ed.), *From Conflict Escalation to Conflict Transformation*; Jolyon Howorth, "Renegotiating the Marriage Contract: Franco–American Relations Since 1981," in Sabrina P. Ramet and Christine Ingebritsen (eds.), *Coming in from the Cold War: Changes in US–European Interactions since 1980* (Lanham: Rowman & Littlefield, 2002), 73–96. The quotation is from 75.

18. Njølstad, *Peacekeeper and Troublemaker*, 84–5; Allin, *Cold War Illusions*, 132–3.

19. For an account of the Bitburg incident, see George Shultz, *Turmoil and Triumph: My Years as Secretary of State* (New York: Scribners, 1993), 539–60.

20. For the situation in Italy, see Nuti, "Italy and the Battle of the Euromissiles," in Njølstad (ed.), *From Conflict Escalation to Conflict Transformation*.

21. Helene Sjursen, *The United States, Western Europe and the Polish Crisis: International Relations in the Second Cold War* (Houndmills: Palgrave, 2003). For the participants' accounts of the pipeline dispute, see Shultz, *Turmoil and Triumph*, 135–45; Thatcher, *The Downing Street Years*, 251–6. For a more general account, see Alan P. Dobson, *US Economic Statecraft for Survival 1933–1991: Of Sanctions, Embargoes and Economic Warfare* (London: Routledge, 2002) 262–73.

22. On Thatcher and SDI, see Thatcher, *Downing Street Years*, 247, 450, 462–71. On Mitterrand and SDI, see François Mitterrand, *Réflexions sur la politique extérieure de la France: Introduction à vingt-cinq discours (1981–1985)* (Paris: Fayard, 1986), 61–6.

23. Evan Luard, "Western Europe and the Reagan Doctrine," *International Affairs*, 4 (1987), 563–74.

24. Thatcher, *The Downing Street Years*, 326–35.

25. Renata Fritsch–Bournazel, "France: Attachment to a Nonbinding Relationship," in Gregory Flynn and Hans Rattinger (eds.), *The Public and Atlantic Defense* (London: Rowen & Allenheld, 1985), 91–2. For a good short survey in English of French foreign policy in these years, see Samuel F. Wells, "Mitterrand's International Policies," *Washington Quarterly*, Summer 1988, 59–75.

26. Benjamin M. Friedman, *Day of Reckoning: The Consequences of American Economic Policy under Reagan and After* (New York: Random House, 1988), 19; Martin and Susan Torching, *Buying Into America: How Foreign Money is Changing the Face of our Nation* (New York: New York Times Books, 1988), 194; *Economic Report of the President, 1989* (Washington, DC, 1989), 427.

27. John E. Rielly, "The American Mood: A Foreign Policy of Self-Interest," *Foreign Policy*, 34 (Spring 1979), 76–85; Rielly, "American Opinion: Continuity, not Reaganism," *Foreign Policy*, 50 (Spring 1983), 86–99.

28. Michael Howard, "Reassurance and Deterrence: Western Defense in the 1980s," *Foreign Affairs*, 61:2, (1982/3), 319.

29. Flynn and Rattinger, *The Public and Atlantic Defense*, 375–6; William K. Domke, Richard C. Eichenberg, and Catherine M. Kelleher, "Consensus Lost? Domestic Politics and the 'Crisis' in NATO," *World Politics*, 34:3 (1982), 382–407.

30. Bureau of Census, *Statistical Abstract of the United States, 1989*, 777–80.

31. The following paragraphs have been taken from my "Empire by Invitation in the American Century," 200–3. See also Dumbrell, *A Special Relationship*, 32–8.

8

The End of the Cold War and Cooperation in the End, 1984–1993

In Reagan's first years Washington's hardline policies towards the Soviet Union had been met with concern in most Western European capitals. While there was broad understanding that the Soviet Union's expansion in the Third World and its arms build-up had to lead to Western countermeasures, the feeling was that many of Reagan's policies went just too far. But in 1984 Reagan changed dramatically and the emphasis was now on American–Soviet cooperation, particularly in arms control. "The evil empire" was out and before long, apparently, the new man in the Kremlin, Mikhail Gorbachev, could be trusted. The two leaders held spectacular summits. In Western Europe almost everybody appreciated the change in the East–West climate, but again there was concern. This time the concern was that Reagan would go too far in the direction of Soviet–American harmony, not to say hegemony. In US–EU relations the second Reagan administration took a dim view of what it saw as clear signs of a Fortress Europe developing.

Even George Bush thought that Reagan might have been too captivated by Gorbachev. Yet, after almost a year of reflection, the new Bush administration concluded that East–West cooperation was indeed to continue at full speed. The resulting benefits seemed incredible: the old Soviet-Communist system was swept aside in Eastern and Central Europe, Germany was unified, and the Soviet Union even disappeared. These were huge changes for the Americans as well as the Europeans to deal with, mostly for good, but potentially also for bad. US–EU relations improved markedly under Bush. But what should be the role of the United States in this Europe united from "the Atlantic to the Urals?" Paris's vision was of a much more limited role for America now than during the Cold War, but in this the French were to be largely disappointed. Britain and the now unified Germany were definite supporters of a continued strong role for the United States in Europe. So were many others.

Reagan and Gorbachev: The Lovefest[1]

During most of his first term Ronald Reagan condemned the Soviet Union in the strongest of terms and rearmed at a rather hectic pace. He did not meet with any of the rapidly changing Soviet leaders, although this may in part have been because, as Reagan stated, "they keep dying on me." Then, in 1983–4 American policy toward the Soviet Union began to change. In his last four years Reagan met five times with new Soviet leader Mikhail Gorbachev. An INF treaty was signed in December 1987; progress was made on other arms control matters, including agreement in principle on a 50 per cent reduction in strategic weapons; the regional crises in Afghanistan and Angola–Namibia were defused; contacts of all kinds between East and West expanded dramatically.

The change in the Cold War was to a large extent the result of policy changes made by Gorbachev, apparently primarily in an attempt to turn the Soviet economy around. To achieve economic reform defense expenditures had to be reduced substantially. This could best be done in cooperation with the West, although in December 1988 Gorbachev announced that the Soviet Union would unilaterally cut conventional forces by 500,000. In an economy with little or no growth, defense and other "imperial" expenses may have constituted as much as 20–40 per cent of Soviet GNP. Gorbachev was also increasingly influenced by various Western European ideas about international cooperation at the expense of the old notions of the inevitability of the class struggle, even at the international level.[2] Yet, for Gorbachev to succeed there also had to be change on the Western, particularly the American, side. This change had in fact started before Gorbachev came to power in 1985 and speeded matters up enormously.

Many factors appear to have modified the hardline policy of Reagan's first years. The United States had gone through a considerable military, political, and psychological build-up under Reagan, and the President could argue that the nation was now acting from the desired position of strength. With his unbounded optimism he certainly expected the United States to come out the winner in the struggle with the Soviet Union. On the other hand, the Democrats in Congress and a clear majority of public opinion wanted (as did Secretary of State George Shultz and apparently also Nancy Reagan) to combine "strength" and "peace", and not stress only the first element as Reagan had done in his first years. In addition, certain specific incidents in the fall of 1983 may also have stimulated Reagan's change of policy: the Soviet shooting down of a Korean airliner, the airing of the television movie "The Day After" about the effects of nuclear war, and the apparently dramatic Soviet reaction to a NATO training exercise (Able Archer).[3]

The European attitude was probably important too, particularly since the European interest in continued contact with the Soviet Union coincided with such strong currents on the American side. In addition, the outcome of the pipeline dispute meant that parts of Reagan's hard line had actually collapsed. A policy that did not have the support of Western Europe would be ineffectual, punish only American companies, and could even drive that wedge into NATO that was traditionally seen as one of Moscow's primary objectives.

The Europeans responded early and positively to Gorbachev. Margaret Thatcher had invited the rising star to London in December 1984 and the two leaders obviously enjoyed each other's company. Thatcher communicated to Reagan her conclusion that "This was a man with whom I could do business."[4] After he became general secretary, France was the first country Gorbachev visited officially, and Mitterrand too commented favorably to Reagan about the prospects for cooperation. Mitterrand's return visit to Moscow in July 1986 seemed to indicate that France was Moscow's favorite partner. The most noticeable disharmony was found in the Gorbachev–Kohl relationship: the Soviet leader evidently considered Kohl the lackey of the United States; Kohl responded by charging Gorbachev with using the propaganda methods of Joseph Goebbels.

With the unaccustomed American–Soviet "closeness," American–European relations also improved. Nevertheless, new problems were soon to develop. In periods of East–West tension most Europeans tended to see Washington as overly rigid and ideological. This was even more clearly the case under Reagan than in similar periods in the past, primarily the 1950s. Then, when Washington and Moscow began to cooperate, fears soon emerged that the superpower duo would cooperate at the expense of Europe's interests; the old "Yalta" fears were resurrected. Such European swings at least in part reflected Europe's state of dependency on the United States: America acted, Europe reacted. The American swings were policy swings; the European ones could be called dependency swings.

The Geneva summit in November 1985 was the first one since Carter and Brezhnev had met in Vienna in 1979. It did not lead to dramatic results, but showed that Reagan and Gorbachev had a sincere interest in improving relations; they also made a promising start at the personal level. However, the next one, in Reykjavik in October 1986, was to be very dramatic, when the two leaders came very close to agreeing to the elimination of all strategic nuclear missiles and even shared a vision of a world entirely without nuclear weapons. Only disagreement on SDI prevented agreement. After the initial disappointment the two leaders developed quite favorable opinions of each other.

Reykjavik was to meet the worst expectations of the Europeans. Virtually every European found something to be appalled by. The right and the center were shocked by Reagan's nuclear abolitionism. Margaret Thatcher felt "as if there had been an earthquake beneath my feet"; the US and Western Europe were "poised between a remarkable success and a possible catastrophe." She decided to fly to Washington to warn Reagan.[5] Kohl too was afraid that the American nuclear guarantee to Europe might disappear. This made him more interested in military cooperation with the French, in part, it is true, to bring France closer to NATO. For Mitterrand Reykjavik had very much the look of a potential Yalta.

Further to the left, as in Scandinavia, where many like Reagan favored the end of nuclear weapons, they were very disappointed by his insistence on SDI. Repeatedly Denmark and even Norway were to make their opposition to SDI clear in various NATO contexts, much to the annoyance of the Reagan administration.

But whether left or right, almost all Western European leaders were disturbed by the "casual utopianism and indifferent preparation" of the whole exercise. The United States had suggested the most dramatic changes in the nuclear commitment, one of the crucial elements in America's relationship with Europe, without even consulting the Europeans. The combined efforts of George Shultz, the joint chiefs of staff, and, on the European side, Margaret Thatcher and Helmut Kohl defused the crisis, but Reykjavik remained a symbol of what America could do if left entirely to itself.[6]

The Reykjavik summit did, however, stimulate talks on an INF agreement, and at their third meeting in Washington in December 1987 Reagan and Gorbachev signed a treaty that led to the dismantling of all land-based intermediate-range missiles, a goal that both Reagan in America and the peace movement in Europe had favored. When Gorbachev, to the surprise of many Western politicians and observers, accepted the idea, various politicians, including Thatcher and Mitterrand, defense experts, and military men in Europe were less than happy. They were opposed to the zero option, as were many in Washington, and had seen it as largely tactical. Dismantling the Cruise and Pershing missiles could lead to America's "decoupling" from Europe; it could stimulate Germany's neutralism; it undermined NATO's strategy of flexible response. The skeptics among the leading politicians had no choice, however, but to support the INF agreement, squeezed as they were between Reagan and the peace movement.[7]

The United States, with firm support from Britain and even from France, still wanted to modernize its Short-range Nuclear Forces (SNF) in Europe. In fact, many felt that this was doubly necessary after the INF agreement, since they feared that Western Europe was now in danger of becoming nuclear-free. Kohl, however, was under much pressure in Germany on this issue and became increasingly skeptical about the new installation of missiles of this type in Germany, where indeed they would be stationed. In the end he opposed deployment entirely. The Bush administration accepted his position; SNF were to be negotiated away for Soviet concessions; London and Paris were disappointed.

While in 1985–6 Thatcher and Mitterrand had been very supportive of American–Soviet cooperation, in 1986–7 they cooled considerably—Reykjavik and INF were not what they had hoped for. Britain and France were quite concerned about the status of their own nuclear forces and feared that they could be sacrificed as part of a wider disarmament deal. Although there was no question of Germany's unification at this stage, Thatcher and Mitterrand were also increasingly worried about the pace of Soviet–West German rapprochement and the extent to which Kohl and, even more, Foreign Minister Genscher were open to Soviet disarmament proposals. After a bumpy start the Soviet–West German relationship had improved quickly, so much so that by 1988 Bonn appeared to be Gorbachev's favorite European partner, which did not help matters much in London and Paris. After right-wing parties won the national assembly elections in 1986, Mitterrand had to accept a power-sharing arrangement with the center-right government under Jacques Chirac (cohabitation). Chirac's approach to the Soviet Union was assumed to be more conservative than Mitterrand's and this too slowed down the pace of Soviet–French détente.[8]

Despite such problems, cooperation with Moscow was indeed preferable to confrontation, nor was it really an option for the British and the French to stand aside from the escalating process of East–West friendliness. If France wanted to maintain the special Franco-German relationship, it had to make certain adjustments in favor of Bonn; for her part, Thatcher definitely wanted to protect the special relationship with Reagan. In Paris the Chirac government and the military were in fact more open to the United States and to NATO than was Socialist Mitterrand. SDI may have functioned as a negotiating lever in disarmament negotiations with the Soviets, as the European Great Powers wanted, and was not the obstacle to agreement many had feared. Gradually the machinery of allied consultation began to work better; on both sides of the Atlantic there was a certain amount of learning from mistakes.

In its last years the Reagan administration was also able to make amazing progress on various regional disputes. In both Afghanistan and Angola the Reagan Doctrine of rolling back Communist-dominated regimes could be seen as meeting with success: Gorbachev was pulling the Red Army out of the festering sore that had been Afghanistan; in Angola the Cuban troops were to be gradually withdrawn in return for the independence of Namibia from South African control. These successes also improved American–European relations and strengthened Washington's position in Europe.

On other Third World issues, however, success was more elusive and criticism from Western Europe remained strong. Central America in general and Nicaragua in particular were seen as a Reagan fiasco, although European sympathies with the Sandinistas were reduced as a result of their repression of the opposition in Nicaragua. Only Britain supported the American air strike against Libya in 1986 in response to Libyan president Qaddafi's support for terrorist acts; even Thatcher was ambivalent, but may well have wanted to return US services rendered over the Falklands. Many Europeans, especially in the southern countries, considered Quaddafi a big nuisance rather than a threat—France and Spain did not even grant the US use of their air space.

In Chad, however, the French, with American support, had sent in troops against the Libyans. The sight of an administration that made the fight against international terrorism a top priority actually trading arms to Iran for American hostages in Lebanon, and then using the profits to finance the Contras in Nicaragua against the will of Congress, undermined Reagan's credibility both with allies and the American public. The glimpses that Irangate provided of the policymaking chaos in Washington exceeded the worst expectations of many observers.[9]

Many Europeans thought Reagan's policies toward Nicaragua, Libya, and Iran too emotional and saw them as reflecting a certain itch to get even with rulers who had certainly offended America, but who did not really threaten its vital interests. In the bloody Iran–Iraq war between 1980 and 1988 Washington came to press hard for European support to protect shipping in the Persian Gulf. The United States was importing only a little oil from the Middle East, whereas the Europeans were importing a great deal (and the Japanese even more). Freedom of navigation had traditionally been an important principle, especially for the British. Several Western European states therefore did agree to send in naval ships to protect shipping—and in this way too at least indirectly to support Iraq over Iran.

The American aloofness from the United Nations in the form of the refusal to pay its dues in full and to accept the jurisdiction of the International Court of Justice on the Nicaraguan issue, and even the withdrawal from UNESCO, met with little support in Europe, with the exception of Britain's similar attitude to UNESCO. The whole US response to the world organization seemed to represent another of those American pendulum swings. No one had had higher hopes for the UN; unrealistic expectations in turn led to a serious backlash when they could not be fulfilled. Under Reagan the backlash reached new heights, particularly in Congress.

In direct US–EC relations, with the adoption of the Single European Act (SEA) of 1985–6, the EC took on new life. The troika of Mitterrand, Kohl, and Commission president Jacques Delors provided the EC with firm leadership. Britain under Thatcher actually supported the SEA from the perspective of the liberalization of trade. By 1992 the act aimed to establish the free flow of persons, goods, capital, and services, in other words a fully integrated market. Although the Reagan administration continued some of Washington's traditionally pro-integrationist rhetoric and thus welcomed the Single European Act, it apparently did not take it very seriously at first, reflecting the previous decade's experience with the EC of considerable talk but little action.[10]

As the act was in fact ratified in the national parliaments and fleshed out, articles about the danger of a "Fortress Europe" began to appear in the American press. The administration now expressed concern on several points, warning that "The creation of a single market that reserves Europe for the Europeans would be bad for Europe, the United States, and for the multilateral economic system."[11] Agriculture, as always, remained the single most difficult issue and came up in ever new variations, as for instance in the harm caused to US agriculture by the inclusion of Spain and Portugal in the EC in 1986. Greece had been included in 1981, so now the EC had twelve members. Washington viewed many of the SEA directives implementing the integrated market as protectionist and disputes broke out over banking, the standardization question, public procurement, preferences for the EC members, etc.

The more critical attitude was stimulated by the fact that in 1984 the United States, which had consistently been running a surplus in its trade with the EC, began to run deficits. There were protectionist elements on the European side, but the fact that the Reagan administration combined free trade arguments with a growing protectionism of its own did not help matters much. Economic disputes between the United States and the EC proliferated not only about the SEA directives, but also about current trade practices. Many of these disputes were commented upon by the President himself, and usually in rather negative terms.

In 1984 the French presented plans to revitalize the Western European Union, and in June the Defense Ministers of the seven members, France, Germany, the Benelux countries, Britain, and Italy, met for the first time since 1973. In October the Foreign and Defense Ministers adopted a Rome declaration underlining their determination "to make better use of the WEU framework in order to increase cooperation between the member states in the field of security policy and to encourage consensus." This was to be done "bearing in mind the importance of transatlantic relations."

Although the reactivation of the WEU received the public approval of the Reagan administration, more privately the administration was clearly afraid that the French initiative could impact negatively on the supremacy of NATO. In late March 1985 Richard Burt, the Assistant Secretary of State for European and Canadian affairs, therefore sent a letter to the seven WEU governments cautioning them that in particular they should not seek a common position on arms control matters outside the NATO framework—there was to be no "ganging up" on the United States. The American concern was only partly alleviated by the fact that the reactivation of the WEU did not go as far as the French had hoped.

All these developments made relations between the United States and the European Community the coolest ever, such that US support for the EC seemed largely ritualistic. Reagan's close relationship with Thatcher was to increase Washington's skepticism toward the EC further, as the British Prime Minister discovered that the enforcement of the Single European Act had much stronger elements of French dirigisme than she had expected.[12]

The Liberation of Eastern Europe, the Unification of Germany, and the New World Order

When Vice President George Bush took over as President in January 1989, he did not automatically want to continue Ronald Reagan's policies. Although Bush himself had a relatively optimistic view as to Gorbachev's intentions, key policymakers such as National Security Adviser Brent Scowcroft, Secretary of State James Baker, and Secretary of Defense Richard Cheney felt that Reagan might have gone too far in cooperating with the Soviet leader. They had all served in the Ford administration. They had seen détente falter and collapse then; the same might happen again. At worst they feared that Gorbachev might revitalize the Soviet Union and that then the Cold War contest might be renewed once more. Yet, after a period of study and analysis, the administration concluded that there was no alternative to continued cooperation with the Soviet leader, and with the American–Soviet summit in Malta in early December 1989 the dismantling of the Cold War was resumed. Many saw Malta as the end of the Cold War—an endless number of articles were written about its history "from Yalta to Malta."

The most important element in the dismantling of the Cold War was the sweeping aside of the entire Cold War structure in Eastern Europe. In that revolutionary half-year in 1989, from the free national assembly elections in Poland in June to the collapse of the Ceauşescu government in Romania in December, all the Communist governments fell. With Gorbachev in part trying to guide events, in part being guided by them, the threat of Red Army intervention rapidly receded. Then there was little holding the people back. Victory in one country stimulated the people in the other countries in the region. In this *annus mirabilis* those who had been the weakest party in the Cold War, the people of Eastern Europe, were to triumph. The pace of events was simply incredible.

The Western powers were really secondary actors in this process. They were generally afraid that these events would spiral out of control and cautioned both sides, certainly including the opposition, to show restraint. Still, they had some influence: the West served as an example of success, of what Eastern Europe could achieve; first *Ostpolitik* and détente and then the West's cooperation with Gorbachev had taken away much of the enemy image that had helped hold the Warsaw Pact together. The desperate economic situation in Poland and East Germany opened these countries up to pressure from the West; but, while George Bush was the prime instigator of restraint in most of Eastern Europe, he was to be much more out front in the unification of Germany, by many considered Bush's "finest hour."

While during the Cold War the Western powers had generally stuck to the ritual of favoring German unification, it was rather obvious that they were quite comfortable with the existing division. A divided Germany, with the major part firmly anchored to the West, was both a known and a safe quantity. No one could know what unification would lead to. Even under the best of terms it could destabilize Atlantic and European relations. But, then, no one expected that Germany would be unified.

During the night of 9–10 November the Berlin Wall came tumbling down, in part as a result of the general events in Eastern Europe, including East Germany, in part because of the increasing political and administrative chaos in East Berlin. On 28 November Helmut Kohl presented his ten-point program to the German Bundestag. In point four the German Chancellor argued that after free elections in East Germany, "confederative structures" were to be developed between the two German states, leading eventually to a federal system for all of Germany. Privately, at that time Kohl still thought that unification would take five to ten years; he did not want to confront the issue of a united Germany's alliance membership, telling Bush that "They will remain in the (Warsaw) Pact and we, in NATO."[13]

In reality, however, the entire process would take less than a year with unification completed on 3 October 1990. Kohl's increasingly impatient diplomacy was crucial in this context. He insisted that the opening be used while Gorbachev was in power, since no one could be certain how long he would last. Even more important was the insistence of the East German population on simply joining West Germany as swiftly as possible. Interest in the SPD and in East German intellectual circles in negotiating an arrangement between the two German states met with little popular favor. Kohl promised the East Germans that their mark would be exchanged at a 1:1 rate with the West German one. In the East German elections of March 1990 the integration-eager CDU somewhat unexpectedly triumphed over the more reluctant SPD. In December 1990 in the first free all-German elections in nearly sixty years the people ratified the popularity of Kohl's policy in both East and West Germany.

Internationally, after some confusion even on the American side, the initially cautious Bush administration decided to follow the breakneck speed of the German Chancellor and, even more, the East German people. Washington definitely preferred Kohl's CDU to a SPD perceived as anti-nuclear and too friendly to the Soviet Union. Later Bush praised Kohl as "the consummate politician, perhaps the most skilled I have ever seen, and I admire him."[14]

Yet, on one crucial point Bush was quite explicit where not only Kohl and particularly Foreign Minister Genscher, but also members of his own administration, were more ambiguous: all of the new united Germany would have to be part of NATO. The decisive victory of the CDU over the SPD in the East German elections meant that any SPD ideas for a confederal Germany outside of NATO were rejected. To Washington neutrality was totally out of the question; even leaving the old East Germany out of NATO would be destabilizing and would only serve to strengthen neutrality in the western part. Feelers, even from Kohl, for a French solution for Germany in NATO, i.e. of Germany being a member of NATO but without foreign troops on its soil, were also discarded. One France in NATO was more than enough. The entire country would now be part of NATO. In the end the United States did agree to special limitations on the allied presence in the Eastern part, but it too became part of the NATO area.[15]

Both Britain's Margaret Thatcher and France's François Mitterrand were clearly skeptical of Germany's unification. Thatcher harbored strong anti-German feelings. Although she did not believe in the collective historical guilt of the Germans, she did believe in national character, meaning that the Germans could quite simply not be trusted. She wanted a democratic East Germany to maintain its own separate existence, if necessary in some sort of confederation with West Germany. In December 1989–January 1990 the British and French leaders tried to establish a common platform on this crucial transformation of European politics. As Mitterrand explained, at times of great danger France and Britain had always established special relations. "Such a time had come again." In December 1989 Mitterrand even visited Gorbachev in Kiev and the Communist leadership in East Berlin in an effort to slow down the rush towards unification. He told the East Germans that France and the German Democratic Republic (GDR) "still had much to do together." Both Thatcher and Mitterrand tried to take the initiative away from the two Germanies and instead place it with the four Great Powers that had occupied Germany after 1945.

However, with the dramatic events moving rapidly the way they were France and Britain could not come up with any real alternative. It was impossible to defeat the combination of the East German people, Kohl, and Bush. France gave up first. With the country's foreign policy having been based on cooperation with Germany, outright opposition to unification would mean a total break with this past. It would also endanger European integration, so now, instead of opposition, Mitterrand decided to use Germany's unification to push that integration to new levels. The French President apparently wanted US forces and nuclear weapons to remain in Germany; he was strongly opposed to Germany becoming neutral, although at this stage it was somewhat unclear in the President's mind exactly what should be the future of NATO.[16]

Soviet leverage was rapidly being undermined by what happened in East Germany and by Gorbachev's desire to attract Western economic support for his perestroika and to bring the Cold War to an end. The United States and West Germany were certainly more equal than the others in the complicated set of 2 (Germanys) + 4 (allied powers in Germany) that formally brought about unification, but even from Washington's point of view it was crucial that this arrangement precluded any bilateral deal between Moscow and Bonn.

The United States was able to secure all its most important objectives. As Zelikow and Rice have argued, "NATO remained; American troops and nuclear weapons stayed in Europe; and German power continued to be tightly integrated into the postwar structures." In a way the United States was the balancer of the whole process. Moscow was assured that its security interests would not be impaired, Germany's neighbors that the United States would still be on hand to provide a counterweight to ascendant German power, France and Britain that they really had no alternative to a united Germany in NATO. France did insist, however, that united Germany had to be even more firmly bound up than before with the European Community. Kohl, the European federalist, readily agreed. As we shall see, this led to the Maastricht treaty and the European Community being replaced by the European Union.

With the end of the Cold War and with the disappearance of the Soviet Union itself in December 1991, there was a great deal of uncertainty as to what would happen with NATO and with the American role in Europe. It was argued that no alliance had survived the disappearance of the threat against which it had been directed. How would the Germans react to having American troops on their soil when all the Russian troops would be gone in a few years' time?

The United States reduced the number of its troops in Europe from about 400,000 during the height of the Cold War to about 150,000. The decision was Washington's own, because there was little or no pressure from the European side for such a dramatic reduction. Britain was actually opposed; Germany was prepared to support whatever position the US developed, but Kohl asked Bush to "Remember Wilson in 1919."[17] This was a serious warning. Even France was uneasy about a reduction on this scale. In Washington too the joint chiefs were reluctant to undertake any really large-scale withdrawal, but the President simply insisted. The Soviet threat was gone, the Conventional Forces in Europe (CFE) agreement of November 1990 led to dramatic reductions in the number of Soviet troops in Europe—and America's large balance of payments deficit also counted. All US nuclear weapons were eventually to be withdrawn except a small number that remained on dual-purpose aircraft stationed in Europe. Again, this was another decision made in Washington rather than was something the European allies wanted, much less pressed for.

In Washington's eyes, NATO was to remain the crucial Atlantic organization, although in a reformed version whereby it would become more of a political body and somewhat less of a military one. The treaty would remain virtually unaltered, but its strategy was to be redefined with less emphasis on nuclear weapons and more on projecting conventional power even outside the traditional NATO area. It was foreseen in Washington that NATO might eventually enlarge geographically to the east.

Britain and France were against emphasizing the last resort function of nuclear weapons, since this meant the downplaying of one of their major Great Power assets. France did not really want to do away with the American nuclear guarantee or the American forces in Europe, but feared that the US itself would do this. NATO should continue as an insurance policy against the unexpected, protecting against a revived Russia and anchoring Germany in the new Europe.

In any case, whether the US left or not, Paris thought that new structures had to be developed. All the many new post-Cold War tasks should be handled by organizations other than NATO. The EU was to develop a stronger foreign policy and security identity; the Conference on Security and Cooperation in Europe was to become an important pan-European body, integrating the Soviet Union/Russia into the new security architecture. Mitterrand even proposed that a pan-European confederation be created with the Soviet Union in, but with the United States out. Any expansion of NATO's tasks outside the collective assistance of Article 5 was regarded by Paris as an artificial attempt to strengthen the Anglo-American position at Europe's expense. As one French official was quoted: "We don't want NATO to become a directorate for global security affairs, and we fear that US attempts to invent impossible missions for NATO will only fuel Soviet fears and pacifism in Europe."[18]

France did have considerable support from Spain and even Italy, but the American policy was supported, in full or at least in major part, by the UK, Germany, Holland, Denmark, and Norway. And the idea of a confederation without the US was a non-starter with virtually all the allies. Washington was prepared to leave more room for the EU, but found the CSCE "unwieldy and frustrating." Most important, the Bush administration feared that the French ideas would mean that gradually NATO would simply atrophy.[19] The London Declaration on a Transformed North Atlantic Alliance from July 1990 spelled out how "this Alliance must and will adapt." NATO was to remain the key Atlantic body. A fundamental revision of Alliance strategy was to be undertaken, including "new force plans consistent with the revolutionary changes in Europe." The political side was to be greatly strengthened, and as a sign of this they would invite Gorbachev to address the NATO Council and the Eastern Europeans to start diplomatic and military consultations. In return for this, the French got the strengthening of a European pillar within NATO. The London Declaration thus recognized that "the move within the European Community towards political union, including the development of a European identity in the domain of security, will also contribute to Atlantic solidarity."

Doubts about America's role in Europe soon began to fade. The Bush administration was determined that the United States would continue as the leader on the Western side with NATO remaining the crucial coordinating mechanism in Atlantic relations. The US had broad support in most European countries for its overall role. First, not even the Soviet Union wanted it to leave; in a Europe undergoing such revolutionary change Gorbachev—at least—came to see the US as in part a stabilizing force in Europe, as a power whose presence was still desirable. Second, the newly liberated Eastern and Central Europeans definitely wanted the United States to play an active role. The closer their connections with NATO (and they saw US nuclear weapons as the heart of the organization), and the greater US investment and economic support in their countries, the better. Third, and most important in this context, most Western European governments expressed a clear preference for a continued substantial American role.

Naturally Kohl's Germany was very appreciative of America's support for German unification. There was considerable talk about "a special relationship" developing between the United States and Germany, based on the closeness of their views and Germany's new importance after unification. Initial surveys of public opinion after unification suggested a weakening of support for NATO and the US troops in Germany, but this erosion soon stopped.[20]

In fact, the United States had several "special relationships." The old one with Britain certainly still counted, although Margaret Thatcher was quite offended by Washington's new emphasis on Germany. George Bush was not quite as admiring of the "Iron Lady" as Reagan had been. Thatcher had strongly rooted for Bush in the 1988 elections, but as she later explained,

with the new team's arrival in the White House I found myself dealing with an Administration which saw Germany as its main European partner in leadership, which encouraged the integration of Europe without seeming to understand fully what it meant and which sometimes seemed to underestimate the need for a strong nuclear defense.

She tried to convince the new administration that the ties of blood, language, culture, and values which bound Britain and America together "were the only firm basis for US policy in the West; only a very clever person could fail to appreciate something so obvious."[21]

From this rather unpromising start the Bush–Thatcher relationship improved a great deal. After John Major took over in November 1990 his style suited Bush better and the two developed an excellent rapport, so good in fact that in 1992 Major was accused of having worked to secure Bush's election over Clinton. On the troublesome Northern Ireland issue, Bush followed Major's lead.[22]

With regard to France, Bush was determined to improve relations with Mitterrand and to some extent succeeded. France admitted defeat on its pan-European construction as it did, at least temporarily, on its idea of a European SACEUR. Washington scotched this idea only after some hesitation, but the smaller European allies in particular were anxious to preserve the principle of SACEUR being an American. In June 1992 Mitterrand even stated that "Today, no other force than that of NATO [is] capable of ensuring the security of [the European] countries; so let us be realistic." Paris had come to accept that the United States and NATO would have larger roles than Mitterrand had foreseen after the dramatic events of 1989, and could perform other missions than simply the ones that fell under Article 5 of the NATO treaty, including peacekeeping. In January 1993 Paris also agreed that in a crisis even the newly established German–French military corps, where units from Belgium, Luxembourg, and Spain had been added to make this the Eurocorps, was to be placed under NATO command.[23] As we shall see, in return Washington would show a positive attitude to an invigorated EU and WEU.

The Gulf War was to strengthen American–European relations considerably. The two sides of the Atlantic agreed that Saddam Hussein's takeover of Kuwait, an internationally recognized country and a major oil producer located in the world's primary oil producing region, could not go unanswered. The United States had to take account of the threat to Saudi Arabia and potentially even to Israel; the Western Europeans were even more dependent on oil imports from the region than was the United States. Thatcher was particularly insistent on a strong response and warned Bush "not to go wobbly on me."

France had extensive contacts with Iraq and in the French government several ministers were opposed to cooperating with the United States in a military response. In the end, however, Mitterrand came down strongly on the American side. The United States would respond militarily whatever France did; Britain would also support the US whatever France did; if France did not participate, it would be shut out of the political arrangements made after the war; then Saddam Hussein's forces in Kuwait took French diplomats there hostage and destroyed the French embassy.[24] In Germany for constitutional, political, and historical reasons it was out of the question to participate militarily in an operation far outside the NATO area, but the Kohl coalition contributed ten billion dollars in cash to the American-led force. The United States was even able to gain the support of the Soviet Union and most Arab countries, and thereby to get a mandate from the UN for military action. On the Security Council even Cuba and Yemen voted in favor of such action.

The UN-sanctioned response to Saddam's incorporation of Kuwait was to establish a degree of military and even political cooperation that strengthened Atlantic ties significantly. Not only the British but also the French forces were closely integrated into the American-led military structure. This worked well, although the war underlined America's superiority in conventional weapons. The French and the British concluded that a drastic military reorganization had to be undertaken with the emphasis on the mobility of their conventional forces. The successful outcome of the short war against Iraq had to strengthen these new-found bonds further.

In the summer of 1991 the former Yugoslavia was falling apart. Slovenia and Croatia were determined to secede from a country where Serb nationalism under Slobodan Milosevic was becoming ever more pronounced. Serbia responded by going to war. The United States was determined to stay out of this conflict—in Secretary Baker's phrase, it allegedly had "no dog" in this war. Dealing with the end of the Cold War and then with the war against Iraq was more than enough even for the sole remaining superpower and the American presidential election was only a year away. The conflict in Yugoslavia conjured up memories of age-old feuds in the Balkans where the United States presumably had no major interests.

The European decision to take a lead in this matter made it easier for the Americans to stay out. The words of Jacques Poos, Foreign Minister of Luxembourg, the country that was holding the rotating presidency of the European Community, have become famous: "The hour of Europe has dawned." Yugoslavia was a case for sophisticated European diplomacy, not for crude American military might. Washington was somewhat miffed by European suggestions that the American role could be minimized, but was certainly willing to let the Europeans take the lead. Again, in the words of James Baker, in Washington there was an undercurrent "often felt but seldom spoken that it was time for the Europeans to step up to the plate and show that they could act as a unified power. Yugoslavia was as good a first test as any."[25]

The trouble was that the Europeans had difficulties agreeing on what to do. Germany, very uncharacteristically, took the lead and insisted on the diplomatic recognition of Croatia. The reasons for this unusual activism are still unclear. German Catholic interests were involved; there was a significant Croat presence in Germany; there were historical connections; ex-Yugoslavia could become a special interest for an increasingly active Germany.[26] Most other EU countries were against recognition. They feared that Croatia's recognition would lead to the independence of Bosnia; that could in turn trigger a Serb reaction and bring the war totally out of control. Faced with the threat of a unilateral German recognition, the other EU countries nevertheless decided to follow Genscher's lead. The United States opposed the EU decision, but Washington's central focus for months to come would still be on the peaceful dissolution of the USSR, and the US recognized Croatia a few months later. Much more was to follow, but in the Bush years the situation in ex-Yugoslavia had still not become a burning issue in Atlantic relations.

The United States and the EU: What Now?[27]

The atmosphere between the US and the EC was to improve under George Bush, despite the general continuity between the Reagan and the Bush administrations. An inter-agency study from the summer of 1989 concluded that the "accelerated political integration within the EC was unstoppable and that US opposition to the process would be both futile and counterproductive." Thus, in part the Bush policy consisted in adapting to the inevitable in the form of further integration, but it also represented a real change of heart.

While Reagan had tended to get personally involved in the economic disputes between the two sides of the Atlantic, Bush was much more focused on the overall political relationship. His statement that "what an absurdity it would be if future historians attribute the demise of the Western alliance to disputes over beef hormones and wars over pasta" could be seen as an indirect slap at his predecessor.

The change of heart under Bush was not only personal, but also had deeper political and economic causes. On the political side, the Cold War was coming to an end, although the administration was rather slow to declare it over. The liberation of Central and Eastern Europe in 1989 and the unification of Germany in 1990 reinforced Washington's sympathy for European integration. The liberation of Eastern Europe had to be buttressed financially and commercially and, with Reagan having run up huge budget and trade deficits, Washington now left much of the initiative for economic dealings with Eastern Europe to the EC.

A strong EC was seen as even more useful in integrating united Germany in Europe, for, while the United States encouraged German unification, with united Germany being bound to become the leading Western European power, its further integration in the EC as well as in NATO was seen as essential for continued stability. The EC was also valuable in the perspective of the American desire for burden-sharing, which was underlined by the Gulf War and the drawing down of American troops in Europe toward 150,000. If Washington was to do less in Europe and more in other parts of the world, the European capitals had to do more in Europe. Starting in 1989 Washington encouraged the Europeans to play a somewhat larger role away from home, even in a sensitive region for the US such as Central America—preferably on the economic side—but with rather limited success in this case.

On the economic side, the situation was improved by the working out of US–EC compromises on some of the many disputes related to the SEA, such as the banking directive, certain standardization procedures, etc. The fact that by the first quarter of 1990 the United States was again enjoying a surplus in its trade with the EC was important, particularly in view of the much larger trade problems the US was facing with Japan. It must also have helped that detailed analysis of the effects of the EC on American trade once more seemed to indicate that trade creation had considerably exceeded trade diversion in the enlargements of the EC. (Certain agricultural products again appear to have been the major losers.) If the SEA generated the expected extra growth, the assumption was that the extra trade created would continue to compensate for the diversion losses in the form of European products receiving preferences compared to American ones. American investment in the EC had increased from 18 per cent of total US investment abroad in 1960 to 38 per cent in 1988. And for this investment the single market was undoubtedly a great advantage. No longer would American corporations have to deal with the intricacies of many different national bureaucracies jealous of their own rules and regulations.

Still, economic disputes continued to arise between the United States and the EC, and even Bush had to protect American economic interests, as witnessed by his early statement that "We're not to disarm unilaterally in agriculture." Some of the economic issues could be addressed in the Uruguay round in GATT. The Bush administration, like all previous administrations since Eisenhower, hoped that successful GATT negotiations would ensure easier access for American goods to the EC market. Agriculture remained the greatest bone of contention between the US and the EC. Ferocious battles were waged particularly with France over reform of the CAP and over "cultural production." Under Bush good progress was made in these negotiations, although the agreement itself was only completed under Clinton. Underneath all the sound and fury France was adapting to liberal norms and moving away from the dirigisme of the past.

In its early days the Bush administration tried hard to increase its influence at the EC table. Reminiscent of Kissinger's efforts in 1973, in view of the upcoming single integrated market, Secretary of Commerce Robert Mosbacher advocated "a seat at the table at least as an observer" because he wanted "to engage the EC in a broadened dialogue at all levels." The EC responded negatively, as it had in 1973. It was difficult enough to work out unified positions within the EC without the United States taking direct part even in the initial discussions.[28]

The administration then tried to reach its goal of consultation in more normal ways. To facilitate an improved climate it proposed the setting up of additional machinery for regular consultations with the EC, a proposal which was then formally adopted in the November 1990 Transatlantic Declaration. The point of the Declaration was for the US and the EC to reaffirm their determination to strengthen their partnership. In more direct terms, the US objective was to establish "a more united European Community, with stronger, more formal links with the United States." In the end common goals were indeed stated, although again in rather vague terms. The Declaration represented another attempt to contain structural changes and political and economic differences within new formulations and elaborate new machinery for consultations.

In Washington the assumption was still that the United States would act as the undisputed leader, despite the relative rise of Western Europe. This assumption could be expressed with surprising bluntness, at least as much bluntness as in the heydays of US domination, as when Under Secretary of State Lawrence Eagleburger in 1989 stated that regardless of how big the EC got, or what issues European governments devolved to common decision-making, the need for a strong American voice in Western affairs would not be diminished. In fact, "the President will remain the preeminent spokesman for the free world in the decade ahead."

When the Bush administration felt that the supreme role of NATO, and of the United States, was threatened it spoke out forcefully. In March 1991 it thus presented the so-called Dobbins démarche to European capitals (also called the Bartholomew démarche, after the State Department officials who presented its content to the various European governments). Deputy Assistant Secretary of State for European Affairs James Dobbins made it plain that while the United States would welcome a stronger European voice in NATO, it was most uneasy about the development of a WEU which was not closely connected to NATO. This was the same issue that had made Richard Burt intervene in 1985 and looked like the dispute from 1973–4 over again. A European security "caucus" within the alliance, a caucus possibly based on the WEU, was not acceptable. No "ganging up" against the United States would be tolerated. On important matters the United States indeed had to be consulted *before* the Europeans reached agreement. In November 1991, vaguely reminiscent of Dulles's "agonizing reappraisal," the President himself expressed these feelings in public when he declared that the American role in the "defense and affairs" of Europe would not be made superfluous by a European Union. "If our premise is wrong—if, my friends, your ultimate aim is to provide independently for your own defense, then the time to tell us is today."

On more concrete defense issues, the strong words occasionally being used by the Bush administration could not hide the fact that it often had difficulties in coming up with clear-cut positions. In principle the administration favored an invigorated WEU, but only as long as the WEU was NATO's European "pillar" and not part of a European Community "bloc". The good side about the WEU was that it could help in burden-sharing, particularly outside the NATO area. The bad side was that a strong WEU could lead to greater European independence and even threaten the supreme role of NATO. Fortunately for Washington there was opposition to such independence even inside the WEU/EC.

On a related issue, the Eurocorps that originated in 1988–9 when France and Germany established a joint military unit, the administration was not really able to develop a unified position. The military leaders tended to see the corps in a more favorable light than did the diplomats, who again feared for the preeminence of NATO, and of the United States. Washington did, however, give approval to the talks that were going on between Britain and France about military nuclear cooperation, although it is unclear what this meant since the talks were top secret and not only the British but even the French were cooperating with the United States in this sensitive field.

On the Maastricht agreements of 1991–2 formally proclaiming a European Union (EU), with an Economic and Monetary Union (EMU) to be gradually set up later, the Bush administration indicated strong support for further integration. After the Maastricht meeting the President welcomed "the historic steps toward economic and political union" and proclaimed that:

The United States has long supported European unity because of our strong conviction that it was good for Europe, good for the Atlantic partnership, and good for the world. I have made clear from the very outset of this administration my view that a strong, united Europe is very much in America's interest. A more united Europe offers the United States a more effective partner, prepared for larger responsibilities.

Again, the administration calculated that developments toward a monetary union were probably inevitable and therefore Washington should in no way be seen as obstructing further progress on this point. On the substance side, good arguments could be found on both sides of the issue. Thus, a monetary union would undoubtedly help the many American corporations already inside the EU and greatly reduce the troublesome issue of competitive devaluations, but it could also threaten the central role of the dollar in international finance. These conflicting considerations led to a rather low American profile on the concrete issues involved. On the EU's Common Foreign and Security Policy (CFSP) however, apparently more of a distant construction than the EMU, integration for Washington had, as always, to be reconciled with the preeminent role of NATO.

Stumbling to Success

In the Reagan–Bush years the world was being rapidly transformed. This came on top of the slower changes that had been going on for decades. Some of the main premises behind American–European cooperation—the Soviet threat, America's strength, Europe's weakness, and Europe being the central arena in the Cold War—had all changed rather dramatically compared to the founding years of the Atlantic relationship. In most European countries the Soviet leader Gorbachev was now more popular than the American President, whether Reagan or Bush. With the events of 1989–91 the Soviet threat ended, as did the Soviet Union itself.

Despite the rapid growth of the United States after 1983, in long-term perspective its economic strength had declined compared with that of Europe. After a lot of talk about "Eurosclerosis," in the mid-1980s the EC was becoming more dynamic again. Spain and Portugal became new members. The Single European Act established the goal of sweeping away all the many small barriers that still inhibited the movement of people, goods, services, and capital within the Community, and also strengthened political cooperation within the EC.

A European pillar was being created within the Atlantic community. The United States had traditionally supported European integration; it still did. At the same time, however, it was becoming increasingly concerned about protecting American political and economic interests. On the financial and investment side, one could almost talk about a reversal of roles between the United States and Europe. The United States was now borrowing from Europe, not lending. Finally, the rather icy "long peace" that had prevailed in Europe during the Cold War was now apparently being replaced by true cooperation from the Atlantic to the Urals, whereas conflicts were still found in many other parts of the world. These new conflicts demanded much of Washington's attention. Economically the focus in America shifted from the relatively stagnant Atlantic to the rapidly flourishing Pacific.

Despite all the changes, not only did the organizations of the American–European relationship remain, with NATO at the center, but the basic early characteristics of the relationship were also maintained, somewhat modified but not really by much. The US nuclear guarantee endured, as did the American troops, however reduced in number at the end of the Cold War. At Yalta Franklin Roosevelt had predicted their withdrawal within two years. Eisenhower had repeatedly stressed that "the boys" would have to be brought home. They still remained.

Despite America's relative decline, Reagan had tried to exert a leadership even more emphatic than Eisenhower's in the 1950s and Kennedy's in the early 1960s. That effort had failed, but the leadership role continued. In fact, Washington was still being invited to play a substantial role in European affairs, although the invitations were now more ambiguous than in the early period.

No systematic redefinition of privileges and burdens took place. The United States still wanted to be the leader, but it also wanted to cut its expenses. It wanted "hegemony on the cheap." The Europeans wanted more influence, but were hesitant about taking on new burdens. In many small ways the relationship was being redefined on a daily basis, but the discrepancy between altered premises and remaining characteristics was so large that, at least from a logical point of view, it seemed that a more comprehensive redefinition had to take place sooner rather than later.

Yet, politics is only in part logic. NATO had weathered many a crisis in the past. To some extent it survived because of historical and bureaucratic momentum and inertia. But that was only part of the story. The Europeans still wanted insurance against surprises, wherever they might come from, and such insurance the United States could provide. It came now, as in the early days, in the form of the nuclear guarantee and US troops. The merging of the growing British and French nuclear forces could possibly establish a credible European deterrent, but that remained a distant prospect. In fact, despite the goals of the SEA, in 1992, when the SEA was to come into force, Britain was once again outside the European Monetary System, after having been on the inside for only a couple of years. When currencies could not be tied together, how could the supreme weapon of defense?

On the American side, the two growing deficits were bound to lead to new rounds of debate on burden-sharing and on the future size of the American military presence in Europe. Nevertheless, the fact remained that the troops were not only a trigger for the American nuclear deterrent; they were also the symbol of America's close relationship with Western Europe. A total withdrawal of troops could reduce expenditures; it would also be a clear sign of America's reduced interest and position in Europe.

Reagan learned the hard way that there was no easy solution for American–European problems. The past could not be recreated, particularly a past that had never existed. In his policies toward Western Europe, Reagan ended up by "muddling through." That was what most of his predecessors had done as well. Bush expected less than his predecessor and by the disappearance first of the Soviet empire and then of the Soviet Union itself actually got much more than he could ever have dreamed about. In fact, as late as 1 August 1991 Bush had warned the Ukrainian parliament against the dangers of "suicidal nationalism," definitely not his finest hour.

Whether in the long run this stunning success would make American–Western European problems smaller or bigger remained to be seen. In the short run, however, it was becoming increasingly evident that not only would NATO continue after the end of the Cold War, but so also would America's leadership in Europe. In the debate with Paris over Washington's post-Cold War role, Washington had definitely triumphed, not least because most Western European countries favored such an outcome. In this sense the Americans were still invited to play an active role in Europe. And the newly liberated Central and Eastern Europeans were even more insistent on such an outcome than were the Western Europeans.

What was absolutely certain, though, was that the founders of the post-war American–European relationship would have been amazed by the permanence of the system they had created in the years after 1945. In this perspective, perhaps a more appropriate phrase than "muddling through" would be "stumbling to success."

Notes

1. A first draft of this section was presented in my "The United States and Western Europe Under Ronald Reagan," in Kyvig, *Reagan and the World*, 51–62.
2. I have written about Gorbachev's motives for change in my " 'Imperial Overstretch,' Mikhail Gorbachev, and the End of the Cold War," *Cold War History*, 1:1 (Aug. 2000), 1–20.
3. The importance of the incidents is argued in Beth A. Fischer, *The Reagan Reversal: Foreign Policy and the End of the Cold War* (Columbia: University of Missouri Press, 1997). These incidents may have been important enough, but that certainly does not discount the influence of the other factors mentioned here.
4. Thatcher, *The Downing Street Years*, 463.
5. Thatcher, *The Downing Street Years*, 471–2.
6. Michael Howard, "A European Perspective on the Reagan Years," *Foreign Affairs*, 66:3 (1987/8), 479–82; Soutou, *L'Alliance incertaine*, 391–2.
7. Thatcher, *The Downing Street Years*, 770–4.
8. See the chapters by Frédéric Bozo on France, Sean Greenwood on Britain, and Hans-Hermann Hertle on Germany in Njølstad (ed.), *From Conflict Escalation to Conflict Transformation*.
9. For an inside account of this chaos, see Shultz, *Turmoil and Triumph*, 783–859.
10. The preceding and the following paragraphs are based on my *"Empire" by Integration*, 110–11.
11. Speech by Deputy Secretary of the Treasury Peter McPherson to the Institute of International Economics, 4 Aug. 1988.
12. Geoffrey Howe, *Conflict and Loyalty* (London: Macmillan, 1994), 407–10, 457–8, 533–5.
13. Philip Zelikow and Condoleezza Rice, *Germany Unified and Europe Transformed: A Study in Statecraft* (Cambridge, Mass.: Harvard University Press, 1995), 123. For the fall of the Wall the best account is Hans-Hermann Hertle, *Der Fall der Mauer: Die Unbeabsichtigte Selbstauflösung des SED-Staates* (Opladen and Wiesbaden: Westdeutscher Verlag, 1999).
14. George Bush and Brent Scowcroft, *A World Transformed: The Collapse of the Soviet Empire* (New York: Knopf, 1998), 57–64. The quotation is from 64.
15. Zelikow and Rice, *Germany Unified and Europe Transformed*, 176, 180, 186–7, 195–6, 207, 211, 214–15, 277–9; Bush and Scowcroft, *A World Transformed*, 252–5.
16. For a fascinating account, see Thatcher, *The Downing Street Years*, 790–9. See also Charles G. Cogan, *The Third Option: The Emancipation of European Defense, 1989–2000* (Westport: Praeger, 2001), 18–25.
17. Bush and Scowcroft, *A World Transformed*, 271.
18. Holly Wyatt Walter, *The European Community and the Security Dilemma, 1979–92* (Basingstoke: Macmillan, 1997), 170–1.
19. James A. Baker, III, *The Politics of Diplomacy: Revolution, War, and Peace 1989–1992* (New York: Putnam, 1995), 173–4.
20. John S. Duffield, "NATO's Functions after the Cold War," *Political Science Quarterly*, 109:5 (1994/5), 783–4.

21. Thatcher, *The Downing Street Years*, 768–9, 782–4. The quotations are from 768, 784. See also Bush and Scowcroft, *A World Transformed*, 83–4.
22. John Major, *The Autobiography* (London: HarperCollins, 1999), 224–34.
23. Rachel E. Utley, *The French Defense Debate. Consensus and Continuity in the Mitterrand Era* (London: Macmillan, 2000), 159–78; Cogan, *The Third Option*, 52–5.
24. I am grateful to my research assistant Dag Axel Kristoffersen for having examined relevant French books and articles on this point.
25. Baker, *The Politics of Diplomacy*, 636–8. See also David Halberstam, *War in a Time of Peace: Bush, Clinton, and the Generals* (New York: Simon & Schuster, 2001), chs. 8–14.
26. Simon Duke, *The Elusive Quest for European Security: From EDC to CFSP* (London: Macmillan, 2000), 204–7.
27. This section follows my *"Empire" by Integration*, 111–17.
28. Youri Devuyst, "European Unity in Transatlantic Commercial Diplomacy," in Eric Philippart and Pascaline Winand (eds.), *Ever Closer Partnership? Policy-Making in US-EU Relations* (Brussels: Peter Lange, 2001), 291–4.

9

America's New Strong Role in Europe, 1993–2001

With the end of the Cold War, the position of the United States was considerably enhanced: militarily, since the Soviet Union had now disappeared, no one could threaten America's vast; economically, in the 1990s the rapid growth of the United States was to coincide with Japan's ever growing problems; ideologically, America's market system and democracy reigned supreme. On the more negative side, the resulting celebration of the United States bred arrogance at home and opposition abroad. In fact, the strongest restraint on US power appeared to be the reluctance of the American people to remain truly involved in the affairs of the outside world. In some ways America's position at the end of the Cold War could be compared with that in 1945, but while relatively stronger militarily, the economic basis was not as sound now with the big deficits in the federal budget and, even more serious, in the balance of payments. For good and ill, increased globalization also made even the United States more interdependent with the rest of the world now than in the first decades after 1945.

Many expected the role of the United States in Europe to shrink now that the Soviet–Communist threat had gone. Western Europe presumably did not need the US in the same way it had during the Cold War; now a strengthened EU could manage much more on its own. Indeed, in some ways the American role did decline; thus, the number of US troops in Europe was drawn down even further under Clinton than had already been done under Bush, and there was much talk in Washington about Asia and the Pacific replacing Europe and the Atlantic as the focus of America's interests.

Yet, the big surprise was *how little* the American role in Europe changed. The unification of Germany and Western Europe's participation in the Gulf War under US leadership had set the pattern under Bush. Now, under Clinton, America's lead was to be most clearly seen in the wars in ex-Yugoslavia and in the process of NATO expansion. NATO did not collapse when its raison d'être, the Soviet Union, the enemy against which it had been directed, disappeared and the Warsaw Pact was dissolved. On the contrary, NATO took in new members from among the former Pact members and some of the disputes that had plagued NATO for decades were now being softened—thus, France was moving closer to NATO again. In return the Clinton administration was showing a more open attitude than had that of Bush to European integration in the form of monetary and defense cooperation.

In fact, with so many signs of change in Washington, European governments and publics were renewing their invitations to the United States to stay involved in Europe. In Western Europe the invitations were weaker and more ambivalent now than in the early years after the Second World War, but still clear enough. In Central and Eastern Europe, finally free from Soviet control, the invitations to the United States were indeed quite similar to those the Western Europeans had extended almost fifty years earlier. Thus, in the end the lead of the United States in matters of European high politics continued in rather unexpected ways.

Re-emerging US Leadership in Europe, I: Ex-Yugoslavia

William Jefferson Clinton, the new President, at first almost seemed to make a point of stressing his lack of interest in foreign affairs. Bush had allegedly lost the election because he had been too preoccupied with the outside world— "It's the economy, stupid" was the conclusion of the campaign. To Clinton the domestic side was what counted and only those parts of foreign policy which directly affected the state of the American economy were to be given priority. In this context, ratification of the North Atlantic Free Trade Area (NAFTA) and the transformation of GATT into the more powerful World Trade Organization (WTO) were crucial. With more support from Republicans than from Democrats, Clinton was able to get both measures through Congress.

On the economic side Washington continued to emphasize the importance of Asia and the Pacific over Europe and the Atlantic. The primacy of the Pacific over the Atlantic in trade was indeed growing. In 1979 trade across the Pacific had for the first time exceeded trade across the Atlantic; in 1996 US trade with Asia stood at 570 billion dollars, compared to 270 billion with Europe. Despite Japan's increasing economic and political problems starting in the early 1990s, many Asian economies were still booming compared with the relatively more lethargic European ones.

Gradually, however, it became evident that the political concerns of the Old World could not be shoved aside and of these the situation in Bosnia was the most urgent. Bosnia had declared its independence in March 1992; it was recognized by the United States and the EU countries in April; soon afterwards war broke out between its three peoples, Serbs, Croats, and Bosnian Muslims. UN troops, largely from European countries, were sent in for "peacekeeping" and humanitarian missions. They were not to take sides in the conflict.

Initially the Clinton administration, like its predecessor, was not interested in the United States taking any lead in the complex situation in ex-Yugoslavia. This was a European problem that the Europeans ought to handle. The aloof attitude was reinforced by the Republicans after they took control of both houses of Congress in the 1994 elections. Yet, in reality, when differences developed between the United States and the EU countries, Washington was not prepared to defer to the European capitals. This became evident in the very first weeks of the Clinton administration. Cyrus Vance, working for the UN, and David Owen, for the EU, had developed a plan for the division of Bosnia into ten "cantons," each controlled by one of the three groups. In the United States the plan was attacked as a sell-out to the Serb aggressors and Vance was greatly disappointed when Warren Christopher, his deputy in the State Department in the Carter years and now the Secretary of State under Clinton, went against the plan. Washington thus undercut the EU's work for a political solution to the situation in Bosnia. The search had to start all over again.

Early on the Clinton administration had invented "assertive multilateralism" as its foreign policy slogan—it was soon dropped. Instead the United States wanted to underline its right to intervene unilaterally if necessary—a new, more informal slogan emerged: "multilateral when you can, unilateral when you must." In ex-Yugoslavia the administration slowly came to favor a policy of "lift and strike." The "lift" part referred to the US being opposed to the UN policy of a weapons embargo applying to all the parties in the conflict. Islamic states had secretly violated this policy by giving support to the Muslims in Bosnia. The US knew about this, but did not object, and later gave covert assistance itself to the Muslims and the Croats. The "strike" part referred to the desire to punish the Bosnian Serb aggressors by conducting bombing campaigns against them. Despite this apparent activism, the American military had no desire to intervene and were completely opposed to the introduction of US ground troops. The military had been burnt by Vietnam; they suspected that in the end the politicians would have no will to take American casualties in the Ballkans.

The EU countries pursued a different policy altogether. They provided the mainstay of the UN forces in Bosnia and supported the UN sanctions. The Europeans were against taking sides in the Bosnian civil war. That would make their forces part of the war; it would mean war with the Bosnian Serbs supported by Serbia. Bombings should only be authorized by the UN for the protection of the UN troops, not by NATO for more political purposes; such bombings inevitably resulted in the Serbs taking UN troops hostage. In a situation of developing chaos and fighting, the pressure for withdrawal increased in most EU countries.

Although the European troops in Bosnia under the UN flag were being humiliated, little was being done about it, since Washington and the European capitals were directly at odds—in fact, the US was violating the UN embargo, first covertly, then openly. Many talked about "NATO's darkest hour." The French, under President Jacques Chirac, argued strongly for a more decisive policy, threatening to withdraw their troops if it were not adopted. The Clinton administration had given its consent to help move the UN troops out if need be, an operation of considerable risk. Washington now decided that if it could be facing a serious risk anyway, it was better to do this for some constructive purpose instead of simply "implementing a failure." Serb actions, such as the shelling of Sarajevo and the killings of about 8,000 Muslims in Srebrenica, strongly increased the sentiment for intervention against the Bosnian Serbs.

NATO, i.e. largely US, bombings of Bosnian Serb positions started "the largest military action in NATO history." The US had taken over leadership in Bosnia, on this point most strongly supported by France, and then Britain. Even more important than the bombing for the favorable outcome was probably the Croat offensive against the Serbs in retaking the Krajina part of Croatia, an operation that was much more successful than even the Clinton administration had thought likely. The Muslims were also showing greater strength than before. Under strong US leadership, particularly from Assistant Secretary of State Richard Holbrooke, a diplomatic solution was then hammered out in Dayton, Ohio. Bosnia was to remain one country, but the Croat–Muslim and the Serb parts were to have very substantial autonomy. The division of territory between the two parts was largely unchanged compared with the Vance–Owen plan, despite their proposed ten-part structure being changed to a two-part one in Dayton.[1]

Potentially even more explosive than Bosnia was the situation in Kosovo, which the Serbs were strongly committed to maintaining as part of what remained of Yugoslavia; the Albanian Kosovars, by far the largest part of the population there, were just as determined to secede, and the emerging Kosovo Liberation Army (KLA) was prepared to do almost anything to attract Western support.

When in 1998–9 the Serbs committed new atrocities in Kosovo and when at Rambouillet in France Yugoslav President Slobodan Milosevic refused to agree to the Contact Group's (the US, the UK, France, Germany, Italy, and Russia) rather harsh conditions for a diplomatic solution, war again broke out. Although the United States was to depict the Kosovo war largely as an American undertaking, initially Britain and France (who had been co-chairmen at Rambouillet) were at least as eager to respond to Serb actions.

Differences among the allies over Kosovo were definitely smaller than over Bosnia, but in the conduct of the war itself American–European differences were still noticeable, reflecting earlier military experiences and national values. The United States wanted to act as decisively as possible once it started to use force; the French in particular wanted to build up gradually and save the best targets as a warning of what could come. Washington wanted to strike directly at Milosevic and the central leadership; the European capitals favored striking at the Serb forces actually undertaking the ethnic cleansing. The US wanted to succeed without using ground troops; the Europeans were prepared to take greater risks with their troops.[2]

The situation was saved by the fact that after seventy-seven days Milosevic gave up. What was most remarkable was that NATO, due to its waging the war exclusively from the air and leaving the ground fighting to the KLA, did not suffer a single casualty. Despite a cumbersome system of warfare by NATO committee, Washington, London, and Paris were calling most of the shots, a procedure that could be painful enough. The Clinton administration was desperately afraid that American losses would undermine whatever limited support there was for the Balkan war. By far the largest part of the air war was carried out by the US Air Force, since the Europeans, with only the partial exception of Britain and France, had limited capabilities as far as stand-off precision bombing was concerned.

Politically, under the official surface of solidarity, marked differences existed. The Greeks were quite sympathetic to the Serbs for historical and religious reasons and also because of their antipathy towards the Albanians; the Italians felt they carried too much of the burden since most of the air operations originated there and they were receiving large numbers of Albanian refugees; opposition in Germany and other countries too was significant. The very difficult question of a land invasion was avoided only by the Serbs seeking a political solution, and the Russians and the EU being instrumental in finding one. Formally Kosovo actually remained part of Yugoslavia, but in reality it was governed by NATO and the Albanians, however divided the latter were.

Despite the tension across the Atlantic, in the end NATO was successful. That was a great blessing for the American–European relationship—but the wars in Bosnia and Kosovo had illustrated most explicitly the extent to which the Europeans were still dependent on the United States for fighting a war, even a limited one, on their own very doorstep. The British and the French had made useful contributions, but hardly more.

In a longer-term perspective, on the European side the change in Germany was quite important. After sixteen years of Kohl rule, a SPD–Green coalition under Gerhard Schröder took over after the elections in September 1998. In opposition the SPD, not to mention the Greens, had furiously opposed any deployment of German forces outside the NATO area. Now, not only did the Red–Green government support the war, but German forces were operating militarily as peacekeepers in Bosnia, and in Kosovo German Tornado strike aircraft actually fired shots in combat. No longer would Germany simply pay its way out of military responsibilities. Schröder seemed determined to make

Germany a more normal country. In EU matters that would mean greater influence and relatively smaller financial contributions for Germany, none of which was much to the liking of Paris.[3]

US Leadership, II: NATO's Enlargement and Reform

The United States was also to show firm leadership on the question of NATO's possible enlargement, now that the end of the Cold War had brought up the question of what was to be the relationship between existing NATO members and the Central and Eastern European countries, which now had the freedom to make their own foreign policy choices. In 1993, with the Clinton administration in the lead, NATO decided on the Partnership for Peace concept. Those Central and Eastern European countries that wanted to could have a military–political connection with NATO, but they would not fall under the Article 5 commitment of the members having to come to their assistance in case of an attack against them.

Then, in 1994 the administration gradually moved toward favoring the admission of some of these countries into NATO as full members with the same protection as the other member states. Clinton made speeches in Brussels, Prague, and Warsaw which made it clear that membership was only a question of "when," not "whether," but with the US military largely against, only in December did Washington come out united in favor of this policy. The German Defense Minister Volker Rühe and the NATO Secretary General Manfred Wörner had been early supporters of this line, as had researchers at the RAND Corporation and Republican Senator Richard Lugar. National Security Adviser Tony Lake and later Richard Holbrooke were the driving forces inside the administration. The motives for the American decision to enlarge NATO were many: strategic (finding a new rationale for NATO after the end of the Cold War, strengthening NATO's and America's position in Central and Eastern Europe); political (strengthening democracy and avoiding nationalistic rivalry in the region); economic (orders for military equipment from the new NATO members); domestic (the votes of the Poles and other Central and Eastern Europeans living in the US, and the general public's support for NATO enlargement.) The strong interest of Poland, under Lech Walesa, and the Czech Republic, under Vaclav Havel, certainly also had a major influence.[4]

On NATO enlargement the initial response of the Western Europeans was rather tepid; they feared Russia's opposition to such a move. Gradually, however, the Clinton administration won over the support of the Kohl government in Germany and the Major government in Britain. Berlin was still grateful for America's role on unification and Washington's upgrading of its relations with Germany. In London Conservative John Major undoubtedly preferred Republican George Bush to Democrat Bill Clinton. There were significant Anglo-American differences over Bosnia and in Northern Ireland Clinton was no longer letting Britain define America's policy, as became clear when Sinn Fein leader Gerry Adams was allowed to enter the US. Yet, even Major concluded that "Our instincts and outlook were more often in tune with North America than with Western Europe."[5] Many of the smaller NATO countries also supported enlargement.

Mitterrand's France was initially skeptical about bringing new members into NATO, since this would serve to reinvigorate the alliance, and thereby US leadership, in a way Paris did not want. In the end, however, it was left with little choice if it wanted to strengthen its own position in Eastern Europe. Russia was strongly against NATO enlargement, although President Boris Yeltsin weakened his case when at a crucial time, in August 1993 during a visit to Warsaw, he very unexpectedly announced that Russia could accept Poland's membership of NATO. Soon, however, he reverted to the expected opposition.

In effect, the United States was to decide which Eastern and Central European countries were to become members of NATO during this first round. Washington insisted on only three new members, Poland, the Czech Republic, and Hungary, while France and the Southern Europeans favored the inclusion also of at least Romania. In the critical NATO meeting Germany backed the United States over France. The US prevailed; in 1999, when NATO celebrated its 50th anniversary, the three countries formally joined. It was a triumph for Washington and NATO that they were able to combine this expansion with Russia's reluctant acceptance of it in the form of the NATO–Russia Founding Act.

The end of the Cold War could be seen as a victory for de Gaulle's vision for Europe; the continent had in some ways been unified "from the Atlantic to the Urals." There was little celebration in Paris, however. Its emphasis on the EU and the CSCE had lost out to Washington's strong preference for NATO. Reluctantly new (from 1995) Gaullist President Jacques Chirac had to conclude that "more Europe tomorrow means more NATO today." The US was just too strong, so strong that the French had invented a new term for it; the US was the world's "hyperpower." (The term actually sounded more neutral in French than in English.) Then, on 5 December 1995, Chirac proclaimed that France might be rejoining NATO's military structure.

There were many reasons for this surprising change. Events after 1989 had firmly indicated that the United States still had an important role to play in Europe. Lingering doubts about developments in Russia and the unification of Germany provided a continued need for the American "pacifier"; in the Gulf War and the war in Bosnia the United States and France had come to be close partners both politically and militarily, and this strengthened interest in a normalization in NATO as well. Moreover, France had little backing from its European partners in challenging the United States, and its dream of leading a much more independent Europe was "the rest of Europe's nightmare."[6] Militarily Europe simply was not yet up to the task of taking over from the United States in Europe. In fact, on the military–technological side Europe was falling increasingly behind the US. Domestically in France it was easier for Gaullist Chirac, with rather Atlanticist Eduard Balladur as Prime Minister, to take this step than it would have been for Socialist Mitterrand. This was the French version of the "only Nixon could go to China" argument; many on the center-right were also more relaxed about the American position in Europe than were the left.

Not that there was any shortage of Franco-American quarrels. Outside of Europe Chirac declared that "The United States has the pretension to want to direct everything, it wants to rule the whole world." And it was true that Clinton was becoming increasingly ambitious in his foreign policy. Taking direct aim at France, the President had even pointed out that "The time has passed when Africa could be carved into spheres of influence or when outside powers could view whole groups of states as their private domain." The United States and France clashed over Rwanda and Zaire, where Washington wanted new governments while Paris held on to the existing ones. The United States clearly won. In Algeria the United States was more open to a negotiated solution between the government and the Islamic-led insurrection than was France; in the Middle East the traditional differences continued between a US friendly to Israel and a France much more sympathetic to the Palestinian/Arab cause. Washington forced francophone Boutros-Ghali out as Secretary General of the United Nations and had him replaced by Kofi Annan.[7]

The French rapprochement towards NATO could be seen as a triumph for the United States, both in terms of revenge on de Gaulle and of French recognition of a crucial role for the US in Europe even after the end of the Cold War. In return, however, Chirac insisted on a stronger role for Europe, and for France within NATO. Despite Clinton's more open attitude to Europe's integration compared to Bush, the resulting disputes between Washington and Paris about the new command structure for NATO revealed a firm American position. America would not yield its hold on NATO's Southern Command which supervised US ground forces in Bosnia and the American sixth fleet in the Mediterranean. The result was that France did not join NATO's military integrated structure after all, but only took up its seat on the main military–political bodies in SHAPE.

After the end of the Cold War in Europe the United States increasingly wanted to change NATO into more of a global organization. The saying was that "NATO had to go out of area or it would go out of business." With the fall of the Soviet Union, the traditional problems of the alliance had largely been solved. The burning issues were now found elsewhere (ex-Yugoslavia, the Middle East, Iraq, even East Asia). However, the Europeans, almost without exception, were against such a development. They did not see themselves as intervening around the world. They emphasized the importance of finding diplomatic solutions to any conflict before military means were used. Any military intervention ought to be sanctioned by the United Nations. Many Europeans saw a lingering Russian threat and wanted to concentrate on Europe. They accepted that NATO was enlarged and that its role was extended to the Balkans, but that was about it.

The outcome of the revisions of NATO's strategy in 1991 and 1999 was that NATO remained a regional organization whose role was confined to "the Euro-Atlantic region." In 1999 Russia had become NATO's partner. The global challenges that had been merely mentioned in 1991 were underlined in 1999 (terrorism, weapons of mass destruction, etc.). Some limited opening was provided for the American view that NATO could intervene in out-of-area missions without the explicit support of the UN. In principle NATO could undertake any operation it wanted to, and not simply limit itself to Article 5 operations as the French had long insisted upon, but the preference was clearly for larger operations which other organizations could not undertake.

The Clinton Administration and the EU[8]

The overall tone of the Clinton administration towards the European Union was only to be firmly set by the President himself in Brussels in January 1994. There he proclaimed his support for the EU and for Europe's development of stronger institutions of common action. The US encouraged not only the EMU but, in principle, also looked favorably on the EU's commitment to develop a Common Foreign and Security Policy and on the Western European Union's intention to assume a more vigorous role. Thus, Clinton soon saw himself as more pro-European than his predecessors. In the President's own words, his administration, unlike earlier ones, has "not viewed with alarm ... the prospect that there could be greater European security cooperation between the French and the Germans and between others as well."

While leaving the initiative almost entirely with the Europeans, the administration did express support for both the widening and the deepening of the European Union. Washington strongly favored the inclusion of the Central and Eastern European countries in the EU. The prospect of membership would "help lock in democratic and market reforms" in these countries. The US distanced itself from the British view of stressing only the widening and largely opposing the deepening. Secretary of State Warren Christopher thus proclaimed that President Clinton "has been a strong supporter of deeper European integration, reaffirming the commitment made, in earlier years, by President John Kennedy." The line thus went from Kennedy to Clinton, while the Presidents in between presumably had more mixed records.

The Clinton administration's support for further European integration was important as such. But how was this approach to be reconciled with the traditional emphasis on the supremacy of NATO? Under Clinton the Europeans were given more leeway in defining their own posture than had been the case under Bush. The shift was seen in the Eurocorps question. After agreement had been reached in January 1994 that NATO would have "first call" on all units for missions under Article 5 of the NATO treaty, the heart of the treaty, Washington's fears of the corps subsided substantially.

The Bush administration had reluctantly come to support the concept of a "European defense identity." In July 1990 in London NATO had taken the position that such an identity would in principle contribute to alliance solidarity. The NATO summit in Rome in November 1991 endorsed this idea somewhat more strongly, although it too clearly underlined the essential role of NATO. But Clinton was willing to go further. At the NATO meeting in Brussels in January 1994 the alliance members gave their

full support to the development of a European Security and Defence Identity which, as called for in the Maastricht Treaty, in the longer term perspective of a common defence policy within the European Union, might in time lead to a common defence compatible with that of the Atlantic Alliance. The emergence of a European Security and Defence Identity [ESDI] will strengthen the European pillar of the Alliance while reinforcing the transatlantic link and will enable European Allies to take greater responsibility for their common security and defence. The Alliance and the European Union share common strategic interests.

Although the stronger formulation was in part due to the more determined input of the EU countries, it also reflected the change on the American side from Bush's traditional Cold War insistence on NATO's supremacy to Clinton's added focus on the Europeans doing more for their own defense. A "grand bargain" was struck whereby the United States would support ESDI while the Europeans would accept that this ESDI be built within the wider NATO structure. The most specific result of the administration's more positive attitude to European defense was the American proposal for Combined Joint Task Forces (CJTF) within NATO. The CJTF concept was first discussed by the NATO Defense Ministers in Travemünde, Germany, in October 1993. The "grand bargain" was endorsed in principle by the alliance in Brussels in January 1994 and spelled out in greater detail and approved by the NATO Foreign Ministers in Berlin and the Defense Ministers in Brussels in June 1996.[9]

CJTF meant that specifically designated forces from some (or all) of the NATO countries, or possibly even from the wider Partnership for Peace states, could be put together for operations, particularly outside the NATO area ("Non-Article 5 missions," in NATO parlance) while still drawing upon NATO infrastructure. As the saying went, these forces would be "separable, but not separate" from NATO. In more understandable terms, under such an arrangement European forces could be put into action without any direct American contribution of troops, while still making use of NATO assets, such as command-and-control systems, and possibly even national assets such as US transport aircraft, etc. This appeared to mean that the WEU, or even the EU, would be able to act on its own, although within a NATO context.

The Clinton administration's more forthcoming attitude could be explained by the fact that the Cold War was now definitely over, so Washington could presumably be more relaxed about the specific forms of European integration. The EU could do a useful job in integrating the Central and Eastern European countries in a democratic and market-oriented system. The administration's initial concentration on domestic affairs and its ensuing desire to take some of the traditional load off the United States certainly also counted. If America was to do less (and it was), it was natural to encourage the Europeans to do more. The American forces in Europe were to be drawn down by an additional 50,000 to 100,000. In 2000 they actually stood at a total of 117,600 for all of Europe, 69,200 of which were in Germany and 11,100 in Bosnia and Kosovo.[10]

In part Clinton's flexibility reflected a desire to forestall even greater independence on the part of the EU/WEU. The administration was sympathetic to the WEU, especially after it came to clearly accept the supremacy of NATO, but was opposed to the WEU being fused with the EU, which could easily lead to European "caucusing" or "ganging up", as the phrases went, against the United States. In practice it could also result in NATO guarantees being given to "neutral" EU countries that were not members of the WEU. The United States still supported with "enthusiasm" membership for Sweden, Finland, and Austria in the EU since with their new and open orientation they could serve as US allies in liberalizing the EU's markets and trade. The three countries entered the EU as of 1 January 1995, increasing the number of members to fifteen. Norway again voted "no" in a referendum. If, on the other hand, all EU members joined NATO, such a fusion of the EU and the WEU might be acceptable to Washington.

Time and again the Clinton administration emphasized the supremacy of NATO. In the words of Warren Christopher, "The first principle is that NATO is and will remain the anchor of America's engagement in Europe and the core of transatlantic security." The administration's proposal that at least some of the Central and Eastern European countries join NATO meant that these countries would be admitted to American-dominated NATO before they entered the European Union.

The most dramatic change in the Atlantic security picture appeared to take place when Britain joined France in the St. Malo Declaration of December 1998. While in the past London had always refused to do anything that could be seen as weakening the Atlantic defense priority, it now joined Paris in concluding that the EU "must have the capacity for autonomous action, backed up by credible military force, the means to decide to use them, and the readiness to do so... [which require] strengthened armed forces that can react rapidly to the new risks."

Why had the Blair government, that had taken over after Major as a result of Labour's victory in the 1997 elections, decided to change British policy? First, there was a tactical aspect to the statement in that Blair wanted to do something "European" to compensate for Britain's non-membership in EMU. A Franco-British link could also provide a counterweight to the Franco-German axis which had been so important for so long, but which was now showing signs of faltering. Britain could cooperate militarily with France while maintaining close relations with fellow Social Democrat Schröder's Germany in other fields. With the Socialists having won the elections for the national assembly in 1997, President Chirac had to appoint Lionel Jospin as Prime Minister. With cohabitation France's freedom to maneuver was further reduced.

Second, there was the American dimension. America might in the future come to reduce its role in Europe even more than it had already done. On a more short-term basis, the war in ex-Yugoslavia had underlined the military weakness of the Europeans, even of Britain and France, a fact that had led to considerable criticism in Washington. British–French cooperation might enhance European capabilities and thus remedy this situation somewhat.

Third, but perhaps most important of all, the change was smaller than it might seem in that the St. Malo Declaration also included references to "our respective obligations in NATO." Under Blair Britain's relations with Clinton's America were to remain very close indeed, as could be witnessed both on the personal and political level (the war in Kosovo, the continued bombing campaign and sanctions against Iraq, the breakthrough in 1998 for a negotiated solution in Northern Ireland). Britain was indeed struggling mightily to combine "the special relationship" with a pro-European stance.

The St. Malo Declaration made it possible for the EU to proclaim a European Security and Defense Policy (ESDP). ESDP was to be firmly based on intergovernmentalism, so unlike the federalist EDC of the 1950s. France and Britain were both opposed to supranationalism. France had consistently favored as strong a European dimension as possible, including defense. If France and Britain were able to agree, then the solution was almost by definition acceptable to Germany, particularly since Germany was now, after a prolonged debate which was ultimately resolved by its Supreme Court, finally able to send its armed forces outside traditional NATO territory. Italy was a strong supporter of European federalism, including a defense component, as were the Benelux countries, and could easily sign on to the new understanding. The strongest hesitation was expressed by Denmark and the former neutrals who feared that the EU was about to form a military bloc, but even Finland and Austria were clearly prepared to go along.

On this basis, in December 1999 in Helsinki the EU decided to take over the WEU. It set the headline goal of constituting a rapid reaction force of up to 60,000 troops by 2003, to be capable of deployment within sixty days and of being kept deployed for at least one year. The force had to be prepared to undertake the full range of the so-called Petersberg tasks (humanitarian and rescue missions, peacekeeping, and crisis management, including even peacemaking), but it was obviously too small to become a serious competitor to NATO. Javier Solana became the EU high representative for the Common Foreign and Security Policy, a choice favored by Washington since he had been serving as NATO's Secretary General.[11]

On the whole, however, the Clinton administration was rather ambivalent about this new development, and Congress was outright skeptical. Several US policymakers made statements about ESDP being in line with previous policy on European integration, and that this was what the United States actually wanted but, as always, the condition was that ESDP did not break with the supremacy of NATO. America's concern was expressed through the "three D's": the European defense initiative must not "decouple" the United States from Europe; it must not "duplicate" NATO structures and capabilities; and it must not "discriminate" against NATO members that did not belong to the EU (Turkey, Iceland, and Norway and the Central European countries that would become members of NATO). The US military were largely against the ESDP, since they feared it would only serve to complicate command structures in NATO and weaken NATO solidarity.

The European countries had 2 million men and women under arms, compared with 1.4 million in the US. They still had trouble fielding 40,000 peacekeepers in the Balkans. Because of rotation needs 60,000 would actually mean 200,000 troops. This might be difficult enough even on paper, but the real question remained how effective these forces would be in practice. European defense was only slowly moving away from its Cold War territorial orientation with the emphasis on conscription. In the new world of out-of-area intervention highly trained and very mobile forces were needed, and they could hardly be ordinary conscripts.

Despite the rhetorical flourishes of the French in particular about Europe finally becoming independent and in some ways the equal of the United States, it was difficult to foresee how any large-scale EU mission could be undertaken without American backing. Naturally NATO was to have first call on its own resources if it wanted to undertake some action. If for some reason it did not want to do this and the EU were then to act using NATO resources, the necessary decision would presumably still have to be taken by the NATO Council. Even with a European head of the CJTF the NATO chain of command would probably have to be respected, and of course the US still had full control over its national resources. Since all this clearly meant many different forms of American approval, it was highly problematic for the Europeans really to act alone. On top of it all, Turkey, with some sympathy from the US, insisted on having influence even on an EU force since it feared what the Greeks could be up to. This delayed negotiations between NATO and the EU significantly.

In the more relaxed international climate the Europeans had great difficulties in building up their own national resources, such as precision guided missiles, satellites, strategic sea and air lift, etc. In fact most of them were reducing their defense forces considerably. This was particularly true in Germany and most of the smaller European countries; somewhat less so in Britain and France. Although the reductions made it impossible to take on the new tasks required if Europe were to become more independent, in a comparative perspective the cuts were understandable as long as the Americans reduced their defense expenditures even more. But after Washington started increasing its defense budgets again in 1997, the Europeans were in some respects coming to rely even more on the Americans than before.[12] Similarly, while the American defense industry was quickly rationalized with only three huge companies left (Boeing–McDonnell Douglas, Lockheed–Martin, and Raytheon Hughes), the European process was slower and often divided between Britain and the Continent.

On the economic side, under Clinton too, many trade disputes disturbed relations between the United States and the European Union. Now these disputes concerned not only agriculture, as always, but also telecommunications, movie and television quotas, financial services, arms sales, US dislike of the EU's preferential trade agreements with former colonies, particularly the banana agreement, compensation to the US for the enlargement of the EU to include Austria, Finland, and Sweden, etc. Washington also signed "open skies" airline agreements with the separate countries, and not with the EU Commission as the latter wanted. In 1996–7 the attempts by Congress, half-heartedly supported by the Clinton administration, to apply US economic sanctions against foreign, including European, companies doing trade with Cuba (the Helms–Burton Act) led to harsh comments from the European side. The same applied to Washington's efforts to apply sanctions against trade with Iran and Libya (the D'Amato Act). The Americans, on the other hand, objected to the EU's "critical dialogue" with Iran; were skeptical toward French–German satellite cooperation, at least in part for business reasons; and also insisted that the markets of Eastern Europe be kept open for American goods and not more or less taken over by the West Europeans.

However, with the significant exception of the extraterritoriality parts of the two acts which the Clinton administration finally agreed to suspend, on the whole such economic disputes now played less of a role in determining the overall climate than they had done even under Bush. Despite considerable disagreement, especially between the United States and France, the US and the EU were able to complete the crucial Uruguay GATT round, thereby also establishing the new World Trade Organization. This achievement over-shadowed lingering disputes over agriculture and cultural quotas, at least temporarily.

With Washington now concentrating on opening up the Japanese and to some extent even the Chinese market, it could ill afford major disputes with the EU as well. Despite Congress's ratification of the WTO and NAFTA, Washington was also becoming less free-trade oriented, as could be witnessed in the follow-up negotiations to the WTO agreement between the US and the EU. The differences between the United States and the European Union were still the most important factor behind the delay in launching a new WTO round of negotiations, although the dissatisfaction of the developing countries with the failure of the developed countries to live up to their obligations under the earlier round certainly also counted.

At first the Americans had not taken the prospects of a European monetary union very seriously. Even in Europe there was great uncertainty as to who would be able to live up to the strict criteria laid down at Maastricht and thereby qualify as members of EMU from the start in 1999. But as the time for a common European currency approached, Washington and the American business community were waking up. The administration was "marginally positive" to EMU. The tentative conclusion appeared to be that despite the challenge the euro could come to represent to the dollar, the new currency could stimulate growth and thereby also further American economic interests. Naturally, the euro would also be of great benefit to the many American cor-porations already in Europe, as they would no longer have to deal with a wide variety of European currencies.[13]

Christopher's speech on 2 June 1995 urging the development of "a broad-ranging transatlantic agenda for the new century" could be seen as the Clinton administration's attempt to reformulate the basic creed of cooperation and to develop a machinery of consultations even beyond that of the Transatlantic Declaration from 1990. It led to the New Transatlantic Agenda, including the Joint US–EU Action Plan signed by Clinton, Spanish Prime Minister Felipe Gonzalez (on behalf of the European Council), and President Jacques Santer of the EU's Commission at the half-yearly US–EU summit in Madrid in December 1995.

The most striking new concept being discussed was the idea of a Transatlantic Free Trade Agreement (TAFTA), based on the model of the NAFTA agreement with Canada and Mexico. The Clinton administration first stated that it intended to give this idea "the serious study it deserves." It faced serious obstacles, however: growing protectionism in the United States, Washington's new emphasis on markets in Asia, divided opinions in Europe with France in particular being opposed, the unresolved relationship between such a vast free trade area and global trade liberalization. So, already by the December 1995 summit the free trade agreement was largely dropped in favor of a more loosely worded joint US–EU study "on ways of facilitating trade in goods and services and further reducing or eliminating tariff and non-tariff barriers." Nothing much was to come of these ideas.

New European Invitations to the United States

In the 1990s there was no substantial change in US evaluations of Western Europe. American leaders and the public both continued to have strong sympathy for the European countries; despite a change in favor of East Asia, Western Europe was still generally regarded as more important; the drop in the leaders' commitment to NATO in 1990 proved largely temporary.[14]

Still, as viewed from Europe, with the end of the Cold War the American presence in Europe could no longer be taken for granted. America's interest in European affairs appeared to be declining compared to what it had been during the Cold War. The implication seemed to be that now the Europeans would have to handle their own affairs. With this kind of attitude in Washington, it was rather obvious that if the Europeans really wanted the Americans to remain closely involved in European matters, they had better tell them so. The old invitations had to be renewed.[15]

And this is exactly what happened, as in country after country the invitations to the United States were in fact renewed. The motives for the new invitations varied: lingering fear of Russia; concern about the position of united Germany or about the effects of new regional crises in the Persian Gulf, in Bosnia, in Kosovo, or elsewhere; economic interest; the need to have the US as Europe's ultimate arbiter.

No European government really wanted the Americans to leave Europe. This applied to countries great and small. In Iceland, where since the Second World War the Americans had had an important but controversial air base, and the US Air Force now suggested they might pull out all the fighter jets, the Icelandic government persuaded the Americans to retain a small presence. In Norway, where the US had a comprehensive system of Collocated Operations Bases (COB, really pre-positioning of equipment) and now wanted to dismantle most of them, the Norwegian government convinced the Clinton administration to keep more than it had initially wanted if Norway agreed to pick up more of the expenses. In Germany, where fears had been expressed that the American troops might have to leave since the Red Army had left, the emphasis was now on the Americans staying. The most paradoxical change took place in France. As we have seen, Chirac announced that France might rejoin NATO's integrated military structure, although in the end France only joined NATO's Military Committee and certain other bodies, not the integrated command as such. Yet, it was symptomatic that when push came to shove in the dispute over the Southern Command even France's closest ally, Germany, abandoned the French. Nothing was to be done which could lead to a reduced American interest in Europe. And Spain now became fully integrated in NATO's military command.

In relations between the United States and the EU, interesting developments took place. In earlier years it was the Americans who had taken the initiative to deepen the American–European relationship. This had been seen in Kennedy's famous interdependence speech in 1962 and in Kissinger's Year of Europe initiative in 1973. The November 1990 Transatlantic Declaration was a more balanced effort with the Germans taking the initiative, but in close cooperation with Washington. The initiative, however, behind the New Transatlantic Agenda and the Joint Action Plan between the United States and the EU signed in Madrid in December 1995 was clearly European.

As early as November 1992 Chancellor Helmut Kohl had felt the need to commit the Americans more strongly to Europe. He was quickly supported by other Europeans, certainly including the Spanish and even the French. Under the New Transatlantic Agenda the US and the EU were to work together in some 100 different policy areas. A very elaborate system of consultation was set up between the two sides of the Atlantic. The Europeans wanted to guard against the domestic emphasis of the Clinton administration after the end of the Cold War, the signs of the United States reducing its role in Europe, and Washington's apparent concentration on Asia. Like the earlier efforts, this new scheme, while quite useful in practical terms, did not really change overall political realities.

The attitudes of the European publics toward the United States and NATO were strikingly friendly even after the end of the Cold War. By 1991 NATO had recovered most of the support it had lost in the early 1980s. In Britain favorable attitudes to NATO remained at about 70 per cent; German attitudes fluctuated more, but support for NATO never fell below 60 per cent; in both countries the public still looked to NATO rather than to such organizations as the OSCE, WEU, or EU to deal with European security problems. Among the smaller countries, Denmark, Norway, and the Netherlands continued to fully back NATO. Italy, while still strongly favoring NATO, was becoming somewhat more European in its security orientation. In France the public looked more to the EU, but the remarkable swing toward a more positive attitude to NATO and the United States continued into the 1990s. In 1993–5 French support for NATO stood at about 60 per cent. In Spain, a relatively new member of NATO where the US was in some ways still connected with the Franco regime, support was at a lower level, around 40 per cent. In Greece—with its strained relations with Turkey, its Orthodox Serb sympathies, and America's history of cooperating with the right—skepticism of the United States and, somewhat less, of NATO was probably the highest of any member country.

Virtually all the Central and Eastern European countries wanted to become members of NATO. For most of them the reason was quite obvious, although it was rarely stated in public: NATO membership was really a concerted invitation to the United States to protect them against a renewed threat from Russia. Membership in the EU could then help in solving their economic problems. Clearly, since the Russian threat had presumably disappeared, only the more general emphasis on becoming part of the West could be openly expressed. An important effect of the debate on membership of NATO and also the EU was that the Central and Eastern Europeans now had to put their houses in order—i.e. democratic reform had to expedited and potential border and ethnic problems solved. They would not become members otherwise. Even the Foreign Ministers of former "neutrals"—the term was now clearly out of favor—Finland and Sweden wrote that "We wish to emphasize the value of continued strong US involvement" in the Nordic and Baltic areas.

Some of the Central and Eastern European publics had somewhat larger problems than their governments in going directly from the Warsaw Pact to NATO. In 1996–7 among the ten countries Poland, Rumania, Slovenia, Estonia, Latvia, Lithuania, Hungary, the Czech republic, Bulgaria, and Slovakia an average of 53 per cent supported membership of NATO for their respective countries, while 17 per cent had not made up their minds, and 10 per cent were against joining NATO. For rather obvious historical reasons, Romania and Poland were at the high end with 76 and 65 per cent respectively. For almost equally obvious historical reasons, Bulgaria and Slovakia were at the low end, both with 27 per cent.

On the economic side, the European competition for American investment continued with dramatic force in the 1990s. Both in 1990 and in 1998 about half of all direct US foreign investment took place in Europe, and the total amount increased from 215 billion dollars to 489 billion, out of a total of 980 billion. (In the much-touted Asia/Pacific region US investment had increased even more in relative terms, but in absolute terms it only rose from 64 billion to 162 billion dollars.) It also helped US–European relations that America's transactions with Western Europe continued to be much more balanced than its transactions with Japan. Thus, in 1998 out of a total US current account deficit of 220 billion dollars, 75 billion was with Japan and 31 billion with all of the EC countries.[16]

In the 1990s Europe remained culturally as attached to the United States as it had ever been, as measured in everything from the popularity of American movies and television programs to the increase in sales of Coca Cola in Central and Eastern Europe. On the surface, France would seem to be an exception to this rule in that politicians there frequently spoke very negatively about the United States and public opinion polls revealed that the French public were rather lukewarm to the US as such. Yet, American movies and companies were doing quite well even in France. When Disney wanted to establish a Euro Disneyland and European countries again competed furiously to win the investment, France was the winner. While the Paris Disneyland was condemned by some Frenchmen as "a cultural Chernobyl," it quickly became the single most frequented tourist destination in France and then in Europe with more than 12 million visitors in 2001. After some initial problems the theme park also began to succeed financially.[17]

Notes

1. Halberstam, *War in a Time of Peace*, chs. 15–31. Many of the central actors have already written their memoirs about Bosnia and Dayton. On the American side, see Richard Holbrooke, *To End a War* (New York: Random House, 1998). On the European side, see David Owen, *Balkan Odyssey* (New York: Harcourt Brace & Company, 1995); Carl Bildt, *Uppdrag Fred* (Mission Peace) (Stockholm: Norstedts, 1997); Thorvald Stoltenberg, *De tusen dagene: fredsmekler på Balkan* (The Thousand Days; Peace Mediator in the Balkans) (Oslo: Gyldendal, 1996).

2. For an interesting account of these differences, see Wesley K. Clark, *Waging Modern War: Bosnia, Kosovo, and the Future of Combat* (New York: Public Affairs, 2001), 448–56. See also Joyce P. Kaufman, *NATO and the Former Yugoslavia: Crisis, Conflict, and the Atlantic Alliance* (Lanham: Rowman & Littlefield, 2002).

3 For a succinct account of these developments, see Josef Joffe, "Where Germany Has Never Been Before," *The National Interest*, 56 (Summer 1999), 45–53.

4. For three good accounts of the process of NATO enlargement, see Ronald D. Asmus, *Opening NATO's Door: How the Alliance Remade Itself for a New Era* (New York: Columbia University Press, 2002); Joseph M. Goldgeier, *Not Whether But When: The US Decision to Enlarge NATO* (Washington, DC: Brookings, 1999); George W. Grayson, *Strange Bedfellows: NATO Marches East* (Lanham: University Press of America, 1999). For the Russian angle, see also Strobe Talbott, *The Russia Hand: A Memoir of Presidential Diplomacy* (New York: Random House, 2002).

5. Major, *The Autobiography*, 455–7, 473–5, 496–9. The quotation is from 578.

6. See e.g. Dominique Moïsi, "The Trouble with France," *Foreign Affairs*, 77:3 (May/June 1998), 94–104. The quotations are from 98.

7. For a good survey of these disputes, see James Petras and Morris Morley, "Contesting Hegemons: US–French Relations in the 'New World Order,' " *Review of International Studies*, 26 (2000), 49–67. The quotations are from 58 and 66.

8. This part follows my *"Empire" by Integration*, 117–25.

9. The "grand bargain" is the expression of former US NATO Ambassador Robert E. Hunter. For his account of the NATO–EU process, see his *The European Security and Defense Policy: NATO's Companion—or Competitor?* (Santa Monica: RAND, 2002), particularly 13–19.

10. Michael O'Hanlon, "Come partly home, America: How to Downsize US Deployments Abroad," *Foreign Affairs*, 80:2 (March/April 2001), 5.

11. For two good accounts of these developments by Martin Walker, see his "The New European Strategic Relationship," *World Policy Journal*, 16:2 (Summer 1999), 23–30 and his "Europe: Superstate or Superpower?," *World Policy Journal*, 17:4 (Winter 2000/1), 7–16. See also Hunter, *The European Security and Defense Policy*, 29–70; Jolyon Howorth, "Britain, France and the European Defence Initiative," *Survival*, 42:2 (Summer 2000), 33–55.

12. For studies of recent defense expenditures in the US and Europe, see Keith Hartley and Todd Sandler, "NATO Burden-Sharing: Past and Future," *Journal of Peace Research*, 36:6 (1999), 665–80; Malcolm Chalmers, "The Atlantic Burden-Sharing Debate—Widening or Fragmenting?" *International Affairs*, 77:3 (2001), 569–85.

13. For a fine account of the American attitude to EMU, see Elizabeth Pond, *The Rebirth of Europe* (Washington, DC: Brookings, 1999), 183–9.

14. John E. Rielly, "America's State of Mind," *Foreign Policy*, 66 (Spring 1987), 39–56; Rielly, "Public Opinion: The Pulse of the '90s," *Foreign Policy*, 82 (Spring 1991), 79–96; Rielly, "The Public Mood at Mid-Decade," *Foreign Policy*, 98 (Spring 1995), 76–93; Rielly, "Americans and the World: A Survey at Century's End," *Foreign Policy*, 114 (Spring 1999), 97–114.

15. The rest of this section follows my "Empire by Invitation in the American Century," 203–6.

16. Bureau of Census, *Statistical Abstract of the United States, 2000* (Washington, DC: Government Printing Office, 2000), 781, 783, 786.

17. Andrew Lainsbury, *Once Upon an American Dream: The Story of Euro Disneyland* (Lawrence: University of Kansas Press, 2000); Nathalie Meistermann, "Disneyland Paris: New Day, Old Woes," *International Herald Tribune*, 16–17 March 2002, 9.

10

Transatlantic Drift: The Present and the Future

George W. Bush and 11 September

In the 2000 election most Western Europeans preferred Al Gore to George W. Bush. As so often, Europe went with the known quantity, and although it had taken a while for trust and reciprocity to develop under the Clinton–Gore administration, toward the end the American–European relationship functioned relatively well. It helped that the Democrats in Washington had faced left-of-center governments in London (Tony Blair) and Berlin (Gerhard Schröder) as well as in most of the smaller European countries. In Paris cohabitation continued with Gaullist President Jacques Chirac and Socialist Prime Minister Lionel Jospin. Sympathy for Bush was strongest in conservative-led Rome (Silvio Berlusconi) and Madrid (José Maria Aznar).

After Bush was elected President, there was a move to the right in Western Europe too. Right-of-center governments were formed in Norway, Denmark, Portugal, Holland, Turkey, Finland, and even in France after the elections there in June 2002, but this strengthened Atlantic relations only marginally— right-of-center did not mean the same thing in the United States and in Western Europe, or even necessarily inside Western Europe for that matter. In Britain Labour was reelected in a landslide in June 2001 while in Germany the SPD–Green coalition just scraped home in the September 2002 elections.

When George W. Bush took over as President with the most limited of mandates, Europe did not really know what to make of him. Like Bill Clinton he was inexperienced in international affairs and initially he wanted to concentrate on his domestic agenda of tax cuts and educational reform. He inherited little of his father's foreign policy experience, but many of his father's key advisers, including Vice President Richard Cheney, Secretary of State Colin Powell, and even National Security Adviser Condoleezza Rice. In his somewhat laid-back attitude, his cowboy-inspired language, his emphasis on religion, and, most important, his deep conservative nationalism, he appeared to resemble Ronald Reagan more than his father.

While traditional isolationism had long been dead, the new administration insisted that America's interests should come first. Of course national interest comes first in every country, but in pointing this out Bush wanted to distinguish his policies from those of his predecessor who allegedly had made a fetish of multilateralism. Such unilateralism was nothing new in American foreign policy. With its traditional sense of mission, its tremendous power, and its isolated geographical position the United States was one of the few countries that could really adopt such a policy. Moreover, the United States was not used to having its sovereignty limited by international bodies; it was used to dominating them. More and more even Bill Clinton had been forced in the same unilateralist direction, but he always managed to give the Europeans the impression that he was adopting this course most reluctantly. Most of the blame presumably went with the Republican-dominated Congress. That also explained America's skepticism toward the United Nations, including its refusal to pay its dues for membership and for peacekeeping operations.

The debate about national missile defense went back to the Nixon, or even the Eisenhower administration, and billions had been spent on relevant research even under Clinton, but Bush made Missile Defense (MD) his number one priority. A system was to be developed and then deployed as soon as possible and the 1972 ABM treaty was to be abrogated if the Russians did not agree to the necessary revisions. When they did not, Washington moved ahead as stated. The threat from certain "rogue" states was seen as rising; the relevant technology had been improved; military–industrial circles, backed by many Republicans, were pushing hard for development and deployment. The administration was prepared to increase the defense budget significantly, for both MD and other purposes.

The 1997 Kyoto Protocol on global climate change had no chance of passage in the United States even under Clinton, but Bush made his opposition to it explicit and in rejecting it long delayed presenting any alternative to limit the world's pollution. When this alternative was finally presented, it impressed few outside the United States. At the very end of his term Clinton had come out in favor of the 1998 Rome Statute of the International Criminal Court, but again Bush made his opposition most explicit. Clinton had already rejected the Ottawa Convention against land-mines; the Republican-led Senate had ratified the Chemical Weapons Convention, but only with amendments that actually undermined it; in October 1999 the Senate had rejected the Comprehensive Test Ban Treaty, despite the support it had from the Clinton administration and from important allies, in Europe and elsewhere. The Bush administration now rejected a crucial verification protocol to the 1972 Biological Weapons Convention. It also rejected a proposed UN convention to reduce the illicit trafficking in small arms and light weapons. On the economic side, the predominant free trade ideology was being increasingly challenged, although more from the labor unions and the Democrats than from business and the Republicans. A whole array of unilateral sanctions had been imposed on many different countries, but the Bush administration scrapped many of them.[1]

Except on the economic side where protectionist measures were taken in Europe as well, the Europeans basically supported all these various treaties and conventions. Unilateralism hardly existed as an option for Europe—the European countries did not have the power and were too dependent on each other and the outside world for that. The routines of international cooperation and the limits of sovereignty had become well established through their own extensive integration. On the question of "rogue states" Europe generally believed in dialogue while America preferred sanctions and isolation.

Tony Blair was still trying to act as America's best friend in Europe, despite his temporary problems in adjusting from Clinton to Bush. In Iraq the US and the UK still stood closely together against Saddam Hussein. Britain, Italy, and Spain showed somewhat more sympathy for the administration on MD than did most other European countries. Britain's role in Europe was limited by its staying out of EMU and chances of membership were not exactly increased by the fact that since the 1990s its economic record was rather better than that of France and Germany. In 2003 its GNP was thus larger than that of both France and Italy.[2] Yet, on ICC and most arms control issues the European position remained largely unified and this included Britain. On Kyoto the EU members were firm in their support of the protocol, but it was questionable whether they would actually be able to adhere to the rather ambitious goals they had agreed to there.

While in general the new administration emphasized America's national interests, in Europe Washington was actually prepared to act in a more cooperative manner. Here, and in Japan, the United States still had its strongest and closest allies. NATO gave the United States a unique instrument with which to guide developments in Europe. There were grandiose statements of common interest, such as in Warsaw in June 2001 when President Bush affirmed: "We share more than an alliance. We share a civilization.... The unity of values and aspirations calls us to new tasks ... our transatlantic community must have priorities beyond the consolidation of European peace."

In a rephrasing of his father's goals, Bush reaffirmed as his objectives "a Europe whole, free, and at peace." The "whole and free" part referred to the new role of Central and Eastern Europe. Nearly all these countries now wanted to become members of NATO and the EU. The President believed that "All of Europe's new democracies, from the Baltic to the Black Sea and all that lie between, should have the same chance for security and freedom—and the same chance to join the institutions of Europe—as Europe's old democracies have." For the Eastern and Central Europeans, America's guarantees would give security against a Russia that might be revitalized in the future. For the Americans, NATO expansion was bound to strengthen America's role in Europe.

More specifically in relation to Western Europe the President stated in Brussels that "It is in NATO's interest for the European Union to develop a rapid reaction capability." A European force integrated with NATO would present more options when NATO itself did not want to be engaged. Despite its very significant arms build-up, even the United States did not have enough resources to do everything. If Washington were to deal with those areas where its direct military force was most needed, then it had to turn peacekeeping activities in areas close to Europe over to the Europeans. The Europeans drew the obvious conclusion from this that the Pentagon wanted to pull all US forces out of the Balkans, to which they were strongly opposed and clearly feared a United States merely on the sidelines there. The State Department sided with the Europeans, pointing out that the Americans and the Europeans had gone into Bosnia and Kosovo together; they should leave together. The compromise became that Washington would adhere to the "in together, out together" policy, while at the same time gradually decreasing the number of American soldiers there. Even before the Bush administration came in, the Europeans accounted for more than 80 per cent of the 65,000 NATO forces in the Balkans.

With tension building in the Middle East between Israelis and Palestinians, the EU was working hard, first, to involve Washington in mediation and, then, to encourage a more generous attitude from the newly elected conservative Sharon government in Israel. The Bush administration saw it differently: under Bill Clinton the United States had become much too involved in the peace process, without success, although in its very last days it had appeared to have come quite close. Only the two parties themselves could bring about peace and Yasser Arafat clearly had to rein in terrorist elements before any renewed peace efforts should be undertaken.

On the economic side a whole array of disputes threatened American–European relations. On the long-lasting banana issue, where WTO had ruled in favor of the US, a temporary solution was found. No solutions were found for hormone-treated beef, where WTO had also ruled in favor of the US, and the question of foreign sales corporation tax codes, where WTO had supported the EU. So here the plaintiffs were already applying sanctions against the defendant. Disputes about genetically modified products, aircraft, steel—potentially the biggest dispute of them all—and even other products were also under way. Anti-trust legislation was becoming the hot new issue. US legislation was generally based on protecting the consumer while the EU was more concerned with protecting the competitors. The EU Commission had been unable to block the merger between American companies Boeing and McDonnell Douglas, but in 2001 it effectively stopped the proposed merger between General Electric and Honeywell. On the positive side, in November 2001 in Doha the WTO members, with the US and the EU in the lead, were finally able to agree to start a new round of global trade talks.

On 11 September 2001 Arab terrorists from the al-Qaeda network hijacked four American planes and flew them into the World Trade Center in New York and the Pentagon in Washington, DC. About 3,000 were killed, mostly Americans. The United States was in utter shock. The American mainland had not been attacked since 1814. Now it had been struck at its very heart. 11 September thus became a defining date in American history. Those who expected to remain the friends of the United States had to stand up and be counted in the now vastly enhanced American-led war on terrorism. Bush proclaimed what was to be called the Bush Doctrine: "We will make no distinction between those who planned these acts and those who harbor them."

Europe's response was swift and firm. For the first time in its history NATO invoked its famous Article 5. The terrorist acts were defined as an attack on the United States and all members thus had an obligation to come to its assistance. While everybody had expected that Article 5 would first be used in Europe, it was actually the United States itself that was attacked, on its own territory. The EU was also strong and unanimous in its condemnation of the attacks. So were the UN Security Council and General Assembly, and even the Organization of Islamic States.

It was obvious to the Bush administration that in the fight against terrorism it needed as broad support as it could possibly get. It made no sense to fight terrorism in one country alone. Now Washington finally paid the money it owed the UN. The NATO allies offered not only their general support, but also specific assistance in the form of intelligence sharing, overflight rights, replacing American troops in less sensitive spots (backfilling), etc. Tony Blair made it particularly clear that the UK would cooperate with the US to the extent that Washington would let it do so. President Chirac was the first foreign leader to visit Washington and New York after the air strikes and he expressed his "total support" for the United States. The newspaper *Le Monde*, generally rather skeptical toward the US, was the first in Europe to declare that "We are all Americans." In Germany Gerhard Schröder announced his "unlimited solidarity" and he indicated that Germany actually expected to be asked for its military assistance.[3] Even Vladimir Putin's Russia became part of the coalition against terrorism, leading to its close cooperation with the United States, its associate membership in NATO, and, even more surprisingly, American bases in several former Soviet Republics in Central Asia.

Afghanistan and Iraq

Thus, there seemed to be reason to believe that Atlantic harmony had been reestablished after some uneasy months under the new administration in Washington. Yet, interesting differences soon surfaced in the various responses to 11 September. First, for most Americans the terrorist acts represented a huge shock from which many would never fully recover. Foreign and domestic policies were dramatically changed. For most Europeans, not the target of the attacks and historically somewhat more used to war and terrorism, 11 September, however tragic, was not really an event that redefined history in the way it did in the United States. Europe condemned the attacks; various security measures were taken, but then gradually life moved on as before.

Second, while NATO invoked Article 5, with the exception of Britain (in addition to Australia and Canada), the United States hesitated a good deal before asking the European countries for significant military assistance. The advantages in getting such assistance were seen as outweighed by the need for Washington to have exclusive control over the operations against the Taliban government and the al-Qaeda network in Afghanistan. There was to be no repetition of the cumbersome NATO procedures for warfighting that had been practiced in Kosovo; in fact there was to be no role at all for NATO. Only slowly and in relatively limited ways did other NATO allies become involved militarily.

Third, while European leaders and public opinion were firm in their condemnation of the terrorist acts, many were afraid that the Bush administration would go too far in its response. Bombing Afghanistan was acceptable, particularly since the operation, coordinated with the rapidly reinforced Northern Alliance on the ground, met with unexpectedly quick success. When the President himself suggested that the operations could be widened particularly to Iraq, but possibly also to Iran and North Korea, the members of "the axis of evil", most Europeans became quite concerned that the United States would take its war too far.

There was an increasing suspicion in Europe that Washington was not considering its NATO allies quite as necessary as before. The attacks on 11 September, followed by America's military success in Afghanistan, gave rise to a new nationalism. America was strong; no one could defeat it. Now the military and the public were willing indeed to take casualties in the fight for America's honor and security and against international terrorism. The fear of casualties, more than anything, had restrained the United States in the 1990s. Now it would assemble ad hoc coalitions of the willing instead of relying on NATO as such. As was stated so frequently by the Bush administration, the mission determined the coalition; the coalition could not determine the mission. With the new conflicts far from Europe, NATO was quite simply less relevant. Militarily, the high-tech revolution in US military capabilities also lessened America's need for assistance from its NATO allies, although local bases were still highly appreciated. These, however, were not generally found in Europe, but in the regions concerned.

After the rapid triumph in Afghanistan, the focus was soon transferred to Saddam Hussein and Iraq. Although Saddam had been quickly defeated in the Gulf War in 1991, he had not only remained in power, but also failed to respect the many UN resolutions designed to prevent him from becoming a threat to his neighbors again. Now the Bush administration was determined both to remove him from power and the alleged weapons of mass destruction from Iraq's arsenal. America's determination appeared to flow from the success in Afghanistan, from the connection that was more or less automatically made between terrorism and Saddam (despite little direct evidence of such a connection), from the long-standing dispute with Iraq, and from America's new willingness to use its power, particularly in a country so close to Afghanistan and to the crucial Middle East.

Strong forces inside the administration wanted the United States to take on Iraq without involving the United Nations or NATO. Cooperation with Britain and with various local Arab governments would suffice. In September 2002 President Bush did decide, however, to ask for the support of the United Nations. This meant that the objective of overthrowing Saddam had to be played down and priority given to removing weapons of mass destruction and living up to the many UN resolutions that had been passed against him. Public opinion polls in the US at first revealed great support for military action against Iraq, particularly if such action was supported by the UN, but then this support eroded slightly.

In London Blair quickly decided to work closely with Bush even on this matter. St. Malo had not really meant such a change in British foreign policy after all. In return for his military and political support Blair might be able to have some influence on how Washington proceeded. He insisted that the UN deal with Iraq. He was also opposed to "regime change" in Baghdad and wanted to focus only on Saddam's weapons of mass destruction. Yet, public opinion in Britain was increasingly skeptical of Blair's attitude; the Labour party was badly divided on the issue and straddling the gap between Washington and Labour's left wing promised to be a high-wire act for Blair. On other issues the differences between London and Washington remained. In addition to Kyoto and the International Criminal Court, their views on the Middle East diverged. Blair favored a balanced solution to the Israeli–Palestinian conflict; Bush largely favored Israel.

To go directly against Washington on an issue so grave to Bush risked a strong American response. Even the future of NATO could be affected. It could also mean that Washington and London would simply proceed on their own and that other European capitals would be left facing the consequences, if the two, as expected, went on to victory in a military campaign. Then others might well be excluded from the regional settlement that would follow.

Such considerations were initially influential with the French, with their pragmatic realism and their economic interests in Iraq. When Bush chose the UN route over unilateral action, Chirac responded by supporting tough UN inspections of Iraq's military facilities and, presumably, concerted action if weapons of mass destruction were discovered. Negotiations in the Security Council were conducted primarily between France and the United States, since even Russia and China would not risk diplomatic isolation on an issue so crucial to Washington.

There was considerable sympathy for the American–British position in the governments of Italy, Spain, Portugal, Holland, Denmark, Ireland, and most of the Central and Eastern European countries. Most of these Western European countries had traditionally been close to the United States and decidedly Atlantic in their orientation. The Central and Eastern European countries saw the United States as their main protector and did not want to do anything that could slow down their integration into NATO. Many countries were also increasingly frustrated by the French tendency more or less automatically to assume that Paris was the spokesman for the EU. Almost at any cost Blair, Berlusconi, Aznar, and their supporters wanted to avoid an Atlantic division on an issue so serious to the Bush administration as Iraq.

France and Germany were increasingly skeptical toward America's possible use of force against Iraq. Within the EU they were supported by Belgium, Greece, and former neutrals Austria, Sweden, and Finland. On the whole this group favored diplomacy and international law over action, particularly unilateral action. They wanted to give the UN inspectors in Iraq the time they needed to complete the inspection process, at least as long as progress was made. Most Europeans did not share the optimism of the Americans about what would come after a military operation against Iraq. Washington thought in terms of democratic potential; many European capitals in terms of the West against Arabs. Particularly in France, leaders also had to be aware of the likely response in their own large and poorly integrated Muslim populations.

The French–German position had the support of public opinion in virtually every European country, even including Britain. In fact, polls in every European country revealed a great deal of skepticism toward the Bush administration. Large majorities stated that they did not believe that the United States was taking the allies' interests into account either in the war on terrorism or in its policy toward Iraq. When the Bush administration announced a new strategic doctrine emphasizing preemption over deterrence this was perceived in Europe as very negative. What right did the United States have to attack other countries before it had been attacked itself? As the crisis over Iraq developed in 2003, majorities in most European countries no longer had confidence even in the United States as such.[4]

Germany's response was the biggest surprise. In the 1990s its position had seemed to become more and more like that of any other Great Power, and less and less influenced by its guilt about the Second World War, as could be seen in Berlin's slowly escalating commitment from Bosnia to Kosovo and then to its military assistance in Afghanistan. No longer was there a Cold War dividing

Germany with the resultant need for West Germany to seek protection from the United States and NATO. United Germany was now situated right in the center of a more and more united Europe. Still, somewhat surprisingly, in the run-up to the German elections Chancellor Schröder made it emphatically clear that Germany would be offering no military or even economic contribution to any military campaign against Iraq, even if this campaign was supported by the UN. This attitude appeared to have made the difference in the close SPD–Green victory in the September 2002 elections. Relations between Washington and Berlin quickly became frigid.

This was the first time a German election had been won by a party emphasizing its distance from the United States. For groups on the left this skepticism toward the US may indeed have been important. It was probably equally significant that many Germans felt that the normalization of the country's foreign policy had been proceeding too quickly. The lesson after 1945 had indeed been learnt. Thus, after the elections even the CDU initially indicated some support for the policy of no German participation in military action against Iraq. As the relationship between Bush and Schröder continued to sour, the CDU moved closer to Bush, despite the continued popularity of Schröder's position inside Germany.

Turkey, which would be important in any military campaign against Iraq, was in a particularly delicate position. While it was very dependent on the United States militarily, politically, and economically, there was very little support at the mass level for its participation in a war against Baghdad. Elections had ended in a big victory for what had been a fundamentalist-inspired party. After considerable French–German resistance NATO agreed to give Turkey defensive assistance against a possible attack from Iraq. In the end, however, Ankara decided that it would not take part in an American-led intervention in Iraq.

Although no "smoking gun" (in the form of weapons of mass destruction) was really found by the UN weapons inspectors, Washington nevertheless prepared for military action against Iraq. Criticism of the Bush administration increased dramatically in Europe. France decided to veto any UN ultimatum to Saddam Hussein. It was supported on the Security Council by Russia and China. Several of the non-permanent members with Germany in the lead were of the same opinion. This did indeed look like the ganging-up against the United States which Washington had thought so unlikely and which so strikingly demonstrated how international relations had changed after the end of the Cold War. Chirac discovered that in speaking out against an American-led invasion he received not only almost unanimous support inside France, but also broad support from Arabs and even worldwide. France became the champion of those who wanted to restrain the American "hyperpower." Never before had France gone so directly against the United States on a matter of such importance to Washington. This opened up a big divide between Paris and Washington and also inside the EU.

A crisis was also developing over North Korea. It turned out that, contrary to the 1994 understanding with the United States, the North Koreans had maintained a nuclear program that possibly included the development of nuclear weapons. Western inspectors were thrown out and Pyongyang threatened to resume missile tests. Yet, in response to this second "axis of evil" country the United States relied on diplomatic and economic means. The military crisis with Iraq was enough; none of America's Asian allies favored a military response; North Korea was much stronger militarily than Iraq and could easily destroy Seoul from its territory. The European powers played only a secondary role in Korea, but here too they emphasized the need for a diplomatic, not a military, solution.

In Central and Eastern Europe the pace of events was almost incredible. After Poland, Hungary, and the Czech Republic had been admitted to NATO in 1999, in November 2002 Estonia, Latvia, Lithuania, Slovakia, Slovenia, Romania, and Bulgaria were invited to become members. NATO would then have twenty-six member countries. The first five, in addition to Poland, Hungary, the Czech Republic, Cyprus, and Malta, were also invited to become members of the EU; it would then have twenty-five members. Romania, Bulgaria, Croatia, and possibly even Turkey would follow later.

Before the new members were to be admitted in 2004, the EU would have a proper constitution, which was expected to strengthen the supranational element of the EU in many new areas. Veto powers would be diminished and the EU Commission strengthened, otherwise it would simply be impossible to operate an organization of twenty-five members. Yet, it remained to be seen how strong this federal element would be in foreign and defense matters where France, Britain, and many of the smaller countries were not willing to go very far.

The United States still clearly preferred that NATO be the dominant security organization in Europe. The Bush administration was much more afraid of the EU becoming an independent force than its predecessor had been. Washington's proposal in 2002 for a rapid reaction force of 20,000 within NATO was clearly intended to shift the momentum away from the EU's military plans, or even to tie the EU force closer to NATO. While it was uncertain what US "assets" the EU force would be able to draw on, the NATO force would clearly be able to draw on US and NATO assets such as airborne early warning stations, satellite data, and air and sea lift. Washington wanted NATO, not the EU, to intervene in major crises even outside the Euro-Atlantic area of the 1999 NATO strategy. The implication was clear: if NATO did not modernize in this way, the organization would become even less relevant to

Washington. The American command in Europe also wanted to move many of the American troops in Europe from Germany to Hungary, Romania, and Bulgaria. There they would be closer to the projected scene of action in the Middle East and Western Asia. Closer to home, Washington and the EU capitals agreed that the European role ought to be strengthened in the Balkans. The EU would take over from NATO its small peacekeeping program in Macedonia and from the UN the policing program in Bosnia. The EU also indicated it wanted to take over the much larger job of peacekeeping in Bosnia. The 2,500 US troops still remaining in Bosnia and Croatia would then presumably leave.

On 20 March the American–British forces attacked Iraq in what was to be an impressive display of military might. In the Security Council the Bush administration had underestimated the will of Paris, Moscow, and Beijing to stand up to Washington; then it underestimated Turkey's independence. In the war itself Iraq's resistance was not very convincing. The offensive progressed quickly, and, at least for the moment public opinion in America and, now that war had begun, even in Britain supported the war. In most of the rest of Europe public opinion continued to be against. It remained to be seen what exactly would be the future of NATO and the EU's Common Foreign and Security Policy.

The Future: Drifting Even Further Apart?

Historians are experts at analyzing the past—they are not experts at predicting the future. The future rarely represents simply an extension of the past and the present. Even for social scientists there are almost always too many variables to take into account in predicting the future, and the strength of the various variables is hardly ever known in advance. There are many examples of how wrong even the best of scholars may be when they venture into the prediction business. Thus, in *Rise and Fall of the Great Powers* Paul Kennedy predicted the fall of the United States. No sooner was the book out than the Soviet Union collapsed, not the United States. Then in *Preparing for the Twenty-First Century* Kennedy forecast that the twenty-first century would belong to Japan.[5] Again, no sooner was the book out than Japan entered into a prolonged period of economic and political stagnation. There it still remains. These days nobody is predicting that the future belongs to Japan.

Political science realists have long predicted that the close cooperation between the United States and Western Europe is bound to end. Two of their maxims would seem particularly appropriate. First, alliances do not survive the disappearance of the threat against which they were directed. Second, when one power becomes much stronger than its rivals, the rivals will "gang up" against this "hegemon." The Soviet threat has disappeared and the United States is definitely in a class of its own. Thus, the world should be balancing against the United States. Were they true, either of these maxims would be sufficient to forecast the end of American–European cooperation; together they would seem to project near historical inevitability.[6]

Political science liberals pay more attention to ideology and practical needs than to the alleged dictates of power politics. In the liberal view there have always been elements of strain in Atlantic relations; there might be even more strain in the future, but since the United States and the European Union are based on the same ideals of democracy and free markets and since they need each other politically, economically, and culturally there is little reason to believe that they will drift apart. As Joseph Nye has written about US–European relations, "it is more likely that they will fundamentally resemble the current state of relations rather than be radically different."[7]

The implications of the present study are clearly that the liberals have the strongest case. As we have seen, in the history of Atlantic relations after 1945 there has almost always been a crisis of one sort or another. Not a decade has passed, in fact hardly a year has passed, without one issue or another disturbing relations. In this sense NATO never had its "golden years" dominated by peace and harmony. Yet, compared to all other alliances in history, NATO was in a class of its own as far as successful cooperation is concerned.

Then, in the 1990s when realists, and many others, expected Atlantic cooperation to be seriously challenged, the big news was how little change there actually was. There was very little balancing against the United States. It was simply too powerful, too flexible in its approach, too distant geographically, and the potential balancers too divided for that.[8] The US remained a crucial actor in Europe. In many ways it still dominated events here from the unification of Germany to NATO enlargement and the war in ex-Yugoslavia. When the US indicated that it might be reevaluating its role in Europe, the Europeans in fact expressed their strong preference for America's continued strong role. That ever troublesome ally France moved closer to NATO and the United States. In modified form the invitations the Europeans had issued to the United States in the first years after the Second World War were now reissued. And Washington accepted these invitations since it so clearly realized that NATO was in its own definite interest. In George W. Bush's words, NATO remained "history's most successful alliance."

There were many reasons for the continued vitality of Atlantic cooperation. Contrary to what many thought, some of NATO's original rationale still remained. In Lord Ismay's terms, the Soviet Union was gone, but no one could be entirely certain about the future of a Russia that still had abundant supplies of nuclear weapons. Germany was no immediate threat to anyone, but it now had a population and an economy much bigger than any of its EU partners. Might it not follow a more national(ist) path in the future? Despite many American–European disagreements, many European politicians and foreign policy experts still saw the United States as the ultimate pacifier in Europe. And the US definitely had its own reasons for remaining in Europe. At the very deepest level, in the long-term future only the EU, not Russia, China, or Japan, probably had the basic economic strength to challenge the United States.

Then there were all the new challenges that the NATO allies faced in ex-Yugoslavia, the Middle East, and the Gulf, from international terrorism, etc. For the foreseeable future neither the United States nor the European Union threatened the vital, or even important interests of the other.[9] In recent political science the most significant finding seems to be not the threadbare maxims of realism, but the liberal insistence on the strong relationship between democracy, trade, and peace. Democracies quite simply do not go to war against each other and this is particularly so when they also trade heavily with one another.[10] All this would strongly appear to suggest that the likelihood of US–EU rivalry and conflict is quite limited.

Still, there is every reason to be cautious. It is far from obvious that the future will be merely a continuation of the past. Without arguing that conflict will entirely replace cooperation, a certain drifting apart seems very likely. In effect, it is already occurring. The signs that have clearly been there to see for a long time multiplied under George W. Bush. The run-up to the war against Iraq hastened the process of drift a great deal, despite the division inside the EU. In fact, a divide is opening up between the two sides of the Atlantic both at the leadership and the public opinion level. No longer are the differences tied to one or a few particular issues; now they are related to several broad sets of questions.

I see the following eight points as the primary reasons for concern about the continued close relationship between the United States and Western Europe:

1. The Cold War *is* over.
2. Unilateralism is growing stronger in the United States.
3. The EU is slowly but steadily taking on an ever stronger role.
4. Out-of-area disputes are becoming increasingly frequent and they have been notoriously difficult to handle for the two sides of the Atlantic.
5. Redefinitions of leadership and burdens are always difficult to do.
6. Economic disputes are proliferating.
7. Even cultural disputes are becoming increasingly numerous.
8. Finally, demographic changes are taking place, particularly on the American side of the Atlantic, that in the long run are likely to challenge the existing relationship.

Some of these issues are more divisive than others, but the sum of them is bound to affect significant change.

1. The fact that the Cold War is over has taken some of the cohesion out of NATO. The lingering suspicion about Russia and the new challenges are hardly likely to measure up to the old and constant fear about Soviet intentions. In the long run the traditional momentum working in NATO's favor is likely to peter out. In fact, NATO is already being redefined with the emphasis moving away from its military side to more general political functions. This process will continue with the addition of the many new members in Central and Eastern Europe. To exaggerate an important point, NATO could become "an OSCE with an integrated military structure."

This process is likely to accelerate with new generations assuming leadership roles on both sides of the Atlantic. Those who matured during and immediately after the Second World War have already disappeared from the scene. Helmut Kohl was probably the last of that generation. Born in 1930, he fondly recalled that his first dark suit, the one he wore on the night of his prom, had come out of an American CARE package, as had his wife-to-be Hannelore's gown.[11] Today the German government is dominated by "1968ers" who were out there in the streets protesting *inter alia* against the United States. Schröder himself was head of the Social Democrats' youth wing when it still described itself as Marxist, and acted as a defense lawyer to a member of the terrorist Red Army Faction.[12] The Bushes, the Blairs, the Chiracs, and the Schröders of today have less emotional and more pragmatic reasons for supporting Atlantic cooperation. Yet, they all experienced the Cold War and still see that period as the more or less automatic historical framework for thinking about international relations. The next generation of leaders may not have even that framework.

It is possible that terrorism or some other new threat could become as important in holding the two sides of the Atlantic together as the Soviet threat was during the Cold War. Major terrorist incidents in Europe would undoubtedly lead to responses there similar to those we have seen in the United States after 11 September. Barring that, however, the responses to terrorism are already developing along different lines in America and in most of Europe. 11 September will remain a huge event in American thinking; a much smaller one in European.

In addition, while the United States is emphasizing military means in combating terrorism, most European governments want to address what they see as the political and economic causes of the problem. As Bulgarian political scientist Ivan Krastev has stated, "The Americans feel they are engaged in a war, the Europeans feel they are engaged in preventing one." In fact, the single most disturbing finding for Atlantic cooperation in the flood of polls taken on both sides of the Atlantic in 2002 was probably that a majority of Europeans (55 per cent) thought that US policies contributed to the terrorist attacks on New York and Washington, DC.[13]

2. Although unilateralism has always been part of America's foreign policy, it has definitely been gaining strength in recent years. It would seem that the stronger unilateralism becomes, the greater the chances of conflict with Washington's European allies. The reasons for its strength are many. While in some historical periods unilateralism, and particularly its feebler variant of isolationism, has been associated with weakness, in recent years it springs from America's domination. The Soviet Union has collapsed; the United States is clearly the world's only superpower militarily; in the 1990s it witnessed stronger economic growth than other Great Powers; the military triumphs of the Gulf War, ex-Yugoslavia, and Afghanistan have finally chased the memories of Vietnam and Somalia away. If the twentieth century belonged to America, the twenty-first will allegedly be even more American.

America's military power is colossal. It now spends more on defense than the next fifteen to twenty industrialized countries together, or more than 40 per cent of what the entire world spends.[14] Americans are clearly willing to spend substantially more on defense than are Europeans, and huge new increases in US defense spending have been announced. With its vast lead, particularly in the new technologies, the United States is presumably freer to go it alone; with its global concerns its allies will be different from event to event; even these allies apparently have less to offer now and they have large problems in keeping up with America's new way of warfare.

America is uniquely powerful, but now it also feels itself to be uniquely vulnerable. The sense of vulnerability after 11 September may make the US appreciate allies, but it also drives it to dominate. As Julian Lindley-French has argued, this is reinforced by a political culture that "seems to see security as a series of zero-sum absolutes: one either has it or one does not." Missile defense and the war against terrorism are now presumably to give America its security back. Europeans, with their entirely different geography and history, find such an ambition difficult to grasp. They have never felt really secure; they never controlled their surroundings in the way Americans did.[15]

Yet, at the same time, terrorism is only the newest and most dramatic example that globalization has finally begun to challenge the sovereignty even of the United States. The outside world is intruding more and more on the United States, and Congress and the public are often responding negatively to this, thus strengthening unilateralism further. Internationally all kinds of conferences are held and measures adopted that the United States has to address, but cannot really dominate on its own. Many Americans find it puzzling that the United States is voted down in many international forums when it is so powerful and, most Americans automatically assume, its intentions are so good. Economically the US is much more dependent on exports and imports than it used to be and new organizations such as the WTO have more "bite" than the older ones. The same globalization is taking place in the environmental and cultural fields.

Inside the United States there has been a swing to the right. Although the supporters of unilateralism are many and varied, the particular strength of America's unilateralism in the 1990s obviously also had much to do with the Republican control of Congress after 1994 and of the presidency after 2000. While the public may not necessarily be so unilateralist in orientation, it is simply not particularly interested in foreign policy, and gone are the leaders in Congress who took such a strong interest in foreign affairs; the new leaders generally have their eyes sharply focused on domestic perspectives.

Again, it is difficult to predict what strength unilateralism will have in the future. The United States could come to see that many different global concerns, terrorism being only the most prominent one, require broad international cooperation. If the US is to lead effectively, it must reorient itself toward the global community and not automatically assume that the American standard is the world standard.[16] Yet, at the moment trends would appear to point firmly toward the US remaining "number one" among powers, to its being increasingly influenced by global forces to which many of its citizens will respond negatively, and probably also to domestic considerations taking precedence over foreign policy ones for both political leaders and voters. If the US is to set global norms all by itself, this will reduce its international legitimacy fundamentally. Such a development may, in fact, make it a more traditional imperial power, no longer the special "empire" of the present account.[17]

3. On the European side integration is progressing steadily, if often slowly. Historically the EU has been able to combine widening and deepening. It has widened from the EEC of six to the EC of nine and then twelve to the EU of fifteen; in 2004 it will most likely be adding ten new members. It has deepened by evolving from the Coal and Steel Community to the treaties of Rome, to the single integrated market, the common currency, and the European Security and Defense Policy. The progress in the last decade has been particularly impressive. The pattern has often been the same: ambitious goals have been established, goals that many felt were just too ambitious, but they were still largely reached, if not by all then certainly by most of the members.

The EU has far to go before it has really developed a common foreign and defense policy. Underneath the constant meetings and consultations there are still diverging national interests, which have been on full display recently in the different responses to the situation over Iraq. But slowly mechanisms are being developed and interests redefined. A common foreign economic policy has long been in existence; increasingly development assistance is coordinated and together the EU countries are by far the world's leading foreign aid donor. Not only humanitarian assistance, but also crisis management and peacekeeping, the so-called Petersberg tasks, are becoming EU matters. Slowly the EU is beginning to take on even more difficult security tasks.[18]

Many impatient people, such as Americans and journalists for example, have made a habit of underestimating the force of European integration, since progress has tended to be so slow and accompanied by so many acrimonious meetings. If and when the EU is truly able to develop a common foreign and defense policy, then this is bound to change the US–EU relationship dramatically. The EU has a population that is already almost a hundred million larger than that of the US and a gross national product somewhat larger than that of the US, depending on exactly how GNP is calculated. The upcoming EU constitution will undoubtedly strengthen the EU's supranational nature in many fields and improve coordination even in foreign and security policy. In fact, if the Europeans really accepted American exhortations about increased military capabilities, this could come to mean that there might be little or no need for the American forces in Europe. Not to mention what would happen if the EU countries developed a military strength commensurate with their economic position.

Yet, these are big "ifs". The EU has shown great willingness to develop the institutions necessary for a common policy; less progress has been made on the common policy itself and particularly on the means to carry out this policy. The conflict over Iraq has shown how deep the rift is between Britain and the Atlantic-oriented members of the EU on the one side and France, Germany, and their supporters on the other. The EU is divided right down the middle, but the fact that public opinion in almost every European country is so skeptical toward the Bush administration in general and to its Iraq policy in particular is a sign that fundamental change may be under way in Atlantic relations.

In defense, the crucial question remains how willing the EU countries will be to establish the defense needed. In the late 1980s–early 1990s defense expenditures in Europe actually fell less than in the United States, but compared with the European objective of a more independent defense this was still not very satisfactory. With defense expenditures rising sharply in the United States after 1997 and particularly after 11 September, with few indications that Europe will reverse its own expenditure policies, the Europeans are in some ways becoming more, not less dependent on the United States. This was also the lesson of the wars in ex-Yugoslavia and in Afghanistan. In several crucial fields of warfare the Europeans still rely almost entirely on the United States.

True, if the national armed forces of the EU members were truly integrated, the needed increase in defense spending would be somewhat smaller. But again, while there is definitely movement in this direction the process is still slow. With the EU countries feeling a continued need for 100,000 US troops in Europe, European independence in foreign policy is bound to be limited. The conclusion has to be that so far the Europeans have found it easier to continue to rely on the United States than to increase their own defense budgets.[19]

What, then, is happening to the European invitations to the United States? The Europeans clearly do not want any dramatic reduction in the American position and are afraid of the repercussions of any significant weakening in America's military role. Thus, when the US military suggested that they move many of their troops from Germany to Eastern Europe, the German government reacted negatively and saw this as punishment for its stand on Iraq. American investment in the troubled economies of Europe is still highly desired, as are most aspects of American popular culture.

Nevertheless, the emphasis is now definitely on what the Europeans can and must do for themselves, not what the Americans can do for them. Comfortable majorities (65 per cent) in European countries want the EU to become a superpower like the United States, although one generally cooperating with the US.[20] In fact, some argue, particularly in the United States, that the Europeans are so busy organizing themselves that they are not able to give the attention to the outside world that its many problems deserve. European governments understand they have to cooperate much more closely if the EU is not to lose its foreign policy credibility. With Paris and to some extent Berlin in the lead they are more and more defining themselves also vis-à-vis the Americans. Tony Blair's Britain views the situation differently, but London too sees the need for a stronger Europe. Only in that way can Blair enhance his leverage with the Americans.

Although the concrete new contributions may still be meager and the Europeans badly divided, the varying degrees of distance from the Bush administration will probably shift the focus somewhat away from Atlantic to European cooperation. In the past there have been several instances when public opinion in one or more countries was skeptical to Washington's policies. Now public opinion in almost every European country, however proAmerican its government, is highly skeptical to the Bush administration in general and its Iraq policy in particular. Such a situation has never existed before; most likely it will have serious ramifications for the future.[21] After the bitter battles over Iraq, the upcoming EU constitution is likely to strengthen this process of European definition.

4. Although there is still a feeling that the two sides of the Atlantic are facing some of the same threats and vulnerabilities, the new conflicts no longer

occur within the traditional NATO area. True, in 1999, at its fiftieth anniversary, NATO's strategy, not the treaty itself, was redefined at Washington's insistence to include the entire "Euro-Atlantic" region. Military cooperation in the Gulf War and, once it really got started, to some extent even in Afghanistan after 11 September also went fairly well. Still, the historical truth is that for the alliance it has generally been easier to cooperate on matters close at hand than on those far away. Out-of-area frequently meant conflict within the alliance, and Europe has tended to dislike America's focus on non-European crises, at least since the Vietnam War. Even in rather close at hand ex-Yugoslavia, in the early 1990s Atlantic relations were very strained until Washington took charge and sorted matters out at Dayton.

Now virtually all conflicts are out-of-area. Here the United States will generally be more activist than the Europeans. As the Bush administration does not tire of stating, the mission determines the coalition; it is not the other way around. In other words, NATO is no longer the more or less automatic framework of cooperation for Washington. Afghanistan and Iraq illustrate what we are talking about. In Afghanistan Uzbekistan's role was clearly more important than that of most NATO allies.[22] If the Europeans are not interested or able to act, Washington will act alone. In Iraq Secretary of Defense Donald Rumsfeld pointed out that the United States was prepared to act even without the support of Britain. Yet, if Europe does not behave in the desired way, Washington will lose even more confidence in Europe and NATO's role will be further reduced.

As already mentioned, the American definition of security is much more absolutist than the European one. Washington wants to eradicate threats many European capitals are prepared to live with, and its vast military arsenal gives Washington options the Europeans quite simply do not have. Most Europeans emphasize the options they do have: diplomatic negotiation and economic instruments.

The Middle East has been the most difficult and most constant issue in American–European relations. Polls revealed that this was still true in 2002.[23] Despite the work of the so-called Middle East Quartet of the US, the EU, the UN, and Russia, differences between the first two appear to be growing rather than becoming smaller. In 2002–3, in the constant hostilities between Israelis and Palestinians, a Republican administration that has very close connections with American oil interests, traditionally more sympathetic to the Arabs, is actually bringing the United States closer to Israel than almost any previous administration, and this is the Israel of Ariel Sharon and not the more moderate Rabin, Peres, or Barak. After 11 September Washington viewed the Palestinian *intifada* as connected to terrorism and repeatedly criticized Yasser Arafat for not doing enough to control the situation, and then almost abandoned him altogether. The Europeans, on the other hand, while disapproving of their means, saw the Palestinians as underdogs deserving a viable state of their own and the Israelis as occupiers of Arab land conquered in the 1967 war. Arafat was after all the elected leader of the Palestinians. These differences may well have had something to do with the Europeans being more dependent on Arab oil than were the Americans, but probably had even more to do with different notions of social and political justice, and with the Jewish lobby and the Christian right being stronger and having more sympathy from the rest of the population in the United States than in Western Europe.

5. While the economic and even the military balance between the two sides of the Atlantic has changed dramatically since the Atlantic system was set up, the relationship as such has not really been redefined. In 1945 the United States was producing almost as much as the rest of the world added together; now the EU is producing as much as the United States. In 1945 the United States was the world's largest creditor; now it is running increasingly bigger balance of payments deficits. While militarily the EU is still dependent on the US, with the Cold War over this dependence is after all smaller than it used to be. Now the EU countries are preparing, however slowly, to take on new tasks that will reduce their dependence further.

Repeated attempts have been made to redefine the Atlantic relationship. The most explicit efforts were made by Kennedy, Kissinger, and George H. Bush. The point was always that in return for greater influence the Europeans should be paying more toward the common defense. These efforts met with limited success, although in everyday matters events were moving in the desired direction anyway. The Europeans *were* becoming more influential and they *were* paying somewhat more, at least in a long-term perspective.

Yet, it could be argued that as far as the basic situation is concerned little has actually changed. Sooner or later there has to be a true redefinition of the American–European relationship. The United States has never had a truly balanced relationship with Western Europe. Under isolationism the US stayed away because it feared that the New World would inevitably be corrupted by the Old. After the Second World War the United States was so strong that it did not need to worry about being unduly influenced by the Europeans; influence went almost entirely in the other direction. Even in the more balanced state of affairs today, America remains the undisputed leader. It is impossible for Europe to be equal to the United States as long as it is militarily dependent on it.

The jury is still out on whether it will actually be possible for the US and Western Europe to have a truly balanced relationship. Slowly the day is approaching when we shall be able to find out. In America 52 per cent want the US to be the only major force in the world, and only 33 per cent welcome the idea of EU superpower status.[24] While many have argued that a balanced relationship will be more harmonious than the existing one, it should be noted that American–British relations only became special when after 1945 Britain became so clearly inferior to the United States. Before 1940, when Britain was relatively so much stronger, there was no special relationship.

6. There have always been economic disputes between the United States and various European countries but, with the end of the Cold War and the globalization of the world economy, such disputes have taken on added prominence and importance. During the Cold War military–political considerations almost always took precedence over economic ones. Globalization increases the number of potential conflicts dramatically as we can see from the flood of issues both large and small. America's steel duties are only the most recent example. For the most obvious electoral reasons the Bush administration, allegedly strongly in favor of free trade, imposed restrictions on foreign steel that brought protests from all corners of the world. As the saying goes, "all politics is local politics." Agriculture is the most contentious issue of all on both sides of the Atlantic. With globalization bringing so much change, the protection of jobs has become a crucial concern for voters in most countries.

With globalization the separation between foreign and domestic matters is rapidly being wiped out; tax, anti-trust, and environmental legislation being good examples. On the one hand, many Europeans now see globalization and Americanization as one and the same phenomenon, and they do not necessarily like it, particularly in France.[25] On the other hand, many Americans, still somewhat less affected by globalization, but also less used to foreigners intruding in their affairs, are also responding negatively. For these persons it is simply not acceptable that various international institutions, the WTO, the ICC, or a Kyoto protocol, should determine the actions of the United States.

Nevertheless, if there ever was a time when an Atlantic economic community existed, that would seem to be today. The economies of America and Europe are so inextricably linked that this would appear to argue strongly against the economic disputes growing out of control. Exports between the United States and the European Union are also much more balanced than in the case of China and Japan where the US runs large and, to many Americans, irritating deficits. Investment is even more important than trade. Here, in relations with nearly every Western European country the sales of American affiliates in that country far surpass the value of American exports. In 1998 US affiliate sales from Britain amounted to 224 billion dollars compared to 39 billion in goods exported to Britain, a ratio of almost 6 to 1. In fact, in nearly all developed nations US affiliate sales surpass exports by a wide margin. The many American companies in Europe represent 50 per cent of America's total affiliate sales.[26]

It is difficult to balance the proliferating economic disputes against the undoubted fact that economically the United States and the European Union are becoming more and more dependent on each other. Judging from the media and political debate, it would seem that conflict drives out cooperation, but for the politicians and business leaders in charge the calculations must after all be more balanced than such a simple observation would seem to indicate. The general downturn in the economy in the United States and Western Europe in 2001–3 could, however, come to threaten Atlantic relations in that it strengthened protectionism and made the necessary free trade compromises more difficult. The outcome of the new WTO Doha round will be very important in this context.

7. A cultural split is arguably developing between the United States and Western Europe when, traditionally, culture has been a field of cooperation. Under the impact of America's cultural hegemony Europeans did not become Americans, but they did become somewhat more like Americans than they had been in the past. This could be easily seen in so many fields: movies, television, popular music, literature, clothing, etc. More and more the English language became the lingua franca, first for scientists and then more and more for tourists and people in general. Today even some of France's biggest corporations are using English as their business language.

Now, rather suddenly, Americans are increasingly blamed by Europeans not for what they do, but for who they are. America is allegedly morally retrograde in that it does not respect international law abroad and at home practices the death penalty while being violently opposed to abortion and having a gun culture most Europeans find senseless. It is socially retrograde in that it does not care much about the plight of the poor, the inner cities, and public infrastructure. It is culturally retrograde in that it "gorges itself on fatty fast food, wallows in tawdry mass entertainment, starves the arts and prays only to one God, which is Mammon." In opposition to all this stands Europe with its alleged tolerance, community, taste, and manners.

Obviously much of this is caricature. Until recently unemployment was generally almost twice as high in major European countries as in the United States; most of the new vulgar television concepts have been developed in Europe, not in the United States; although the European TV industry and to some extent even the movie industry is becoming stronger, American popular culture remains almost as popular in Europe as it has ever been; America is strong even in high culture, everything from its world-leading universities to literature and music, etc.[27] The American response was obvious. If Europe is so superior to the United States, why then is it still so dependent on America, in everything from security to economic policies and cultural activities? Yet, the point is not who will win the debate, but the fact that Europeans and Americans appear to be moving apart even culturally.

Deeper down there *are* significant differences between the two sides of the Atlantic. On the whole Americans are more religious and moral(istic) than Europeans; Americans do see the world more in terms of good and evil, black and white, while Europeans frequently see things as ambiguous and grey; Americans do define security in more absolutist terms than Europeans do and the methods they have to protect their security are different; socialism and social democracy have a long and honorable history in Europe, in America they have hardly existed; the experiences of the two sides with war and terrorism are different; Americans are allegedly from Mars and Europeans from Venus, etc.[28]

Yet, on the other hand, these differences have not prevented cooperation between the two sides in the past and on the whole the United States and Western Europe are still closely bound together even culturally. Compared to the differences with most of the rest of the world, it could indeed be argued that one common Atlantic culture exists, characterized by democracy, relatively free markets, Christianity, and a high-consumption popular culture.

8. Finally, as we saw in Chapter 6, demographic changes are taking place particularly in the United States that threaten to make the Atlantic wider. The 2000 census revealed the extent of these changes, and showed that the relative strength of America's four main regions is definitely shifting. In 1970 the Northeast and the Midwest still had a total population 8 million bigger than the South and the West. In 1980 the South and the West had 10 million more inhabitants. In 2000 they had 46 million more. The South is by far the most populous region with 100 million people.

Such a dramatic shift has already produced dramatic political consequences. From the American Civil War to John F. Kennedy almost all of America's Presidents came from the Northeast and the Midwest. After Kennedy they have all, with the exception of the non-elected Gerald Ford, come from the South or West. We know what happened when the Democrats nominated their traditional liberal and usually European-oriented candidates from the Northeast and the Midwest. They all lost: Humphrey (1968), McGovern (1972), Mondale (1984), and Dukakis (1988). While Al Gore won the popular vote in 2000, he lost his home state of Tennessee. You have to be quite conservative to win in the South and the (mountain) West. The domestic consequences in the form of America's move to the right have become rather obvious. The consequences of the population shift have been less dramatic in foreign policy, but more and more the separation between foreign and domestic policy is being blurred. And, while the Northeast and the Midwest have been directed primarily toward Europe, in the South the focus is relatively more on the Western hemisphere and in the West on the Pacific/East Asia.

This regional development is being reinforced by the slow but steady decline in the number of Americans of European descent. The percentage of non-Spanish speaking Americans of European ancestry declined from 76 in 1990 to 69 in 2000. In California this group made up 90 per cent of the population in 1950; today they are a minority, 47 per cent. Hispanics now constitute 12.5 per cent, blacks 12 per cent, and Asian-Americans 4 per cent of America's population. With present immigration and fertility rates these trends are likely to accelerate in the future. It would be surprising indeed if over time these developments do not have significant foreign policy consequences in the direction of weakening America's relative interest in Europe.

It could be argued that these shifts in America are being complemented with similar shifts in Europe. The Atlantic is becoming wider on this side too in that European leadership will slowly be drifting away from Britain and France and toward Germany. United Germany's population is 23–25 million larger than that of France, Britain, and Italy. Its GNP is one-third larger (1.9 trillion dollars as compared with 1.1–1.4 trillion for the other three).[29] Slowly Germany is also taking on a political position of leadership; it is also becoming much more independent of the US than it used to be. The eastward shift is being strongly reinforced by the fact that while during the Cold War the Eastern European countries were being shut off from Western Europe, most of them are now in the process of joining both NATO and the EU.

On the other hand, despite all these shifts on the whole Americans and Europeans continued to like each other. When in 2002 Americans were asked to measure their warmth toward various countries, the leading European countries came out significantly higher than countries in other parts of the world, with the exception of Canada. Europeans on the whole continued to express warm feelings toward the United States.[30] This changed with Iraq, particularly in American–French and American–German relaions. Still the climate of especially German–American relations may improve again. And most important, the Central and Eastern Europeans, who will steadily count for more in European politics, are bound to be quite sympathetic to the United States. After decades under Soviet domination they are eager to cooperate with the United States militarily, economically, and culturally.

No one can predict the future. If history repeated itself, historians might be experts on the future, not only the past. But history does not really repeat itself; only historians do. Several of the eight points just discussed are ambiguous, and it is far from obvious in what ways they will actually work themselves out. Undoubtedly, many other points will also be relevant in such a discussion. Were I to hazard a guess, I would certainly not be predicting any direct confrontation between the United States and Western Europe as such, but rather a conflict with some European countries and a general continued slow drifting apart between the two continents.

As Mark Twain said, "history never happened the way it was supposed to. Historians exist to correct this defect." History is kind to historians. We rearrange the past and we predict the future. When we get it wrong, we just try again. Politicians may not get that many chances.

Notes

1. For a good short account of recent American unilateralism, see Stewart Patrick, "Don't Fence Me In: The Perils of Going It Alone," *World Policy Journal*, 18:3 (Fall 2001), 2–14. For a larger collection of essays, see Stewart Patrick and Shepard Forman (eds.), *Multilateralism & US Foreign Policy: Ambivalent Engagement* (Boulder: Lynne Rienner, 2002).
2. The World Bank, *World Development Report 2003* (New York: Oxford University Press, 2003), 234–5.
3. For a good account of the European response to 11 September, see Philip H. Gordon, "NATO After September 11," *Survival*, 43:4 (Winter 2001–2), 89–106.
4. *Aftenposten*, "Mister smaken på Amerika," ([Europe] Loses the taste for America), 28 March 2003, 26.
5. Paul Kennedy, *The Rise and Fall of the Great Powers: Economic Change and Military Conflict from 1500 to 2000* (New York: Random House, 1987); idem., *Preparing for the Twenty-First Century* (New York: Random House, 1993).
6. For the hard version of this realism, see John Mearsheimer, *The Tragedy of Great Power Politics* (New York: Norton, 2001). For a softer version, see Walt, "The Ties That Fray," 3–11.
7. Joseph S. Nye, Jr., "The US and Europe: Continental Drift?" *International Affairs*, 76:1 (2000) 51–9.
8. For an excellent anthology dealing with this question, see G. John Ikenberry (ed.), *America Unrivaled. The Future of the Balance of Power* (Ithaca: Cornell University Press, 2002).
9. This important point is strongly argued in Robert D. Blackwill, *The Future of Transatlantic Relations* (New York: Council on Foreign Relations report, 1999).
10. The most recent and most powerful statement about this relationship is found in Bruce Russett and John Oneal, *Triangular Peace: Democracy, Interdependence, and International Organization* (New York: Norton, 2001).
11. Joffe, "Where Germany Has Never Been Before," 45–6.
12. *The Economist*, 7 Dec. 2002; a survey of Germany, 18–23.
13. Craig Kennedy and Marshall M. Bouton, "The Real Trans-Atlantic Gap," *Foreign Policy*, 133 (Nov.–Dec. 2002), 70.
14. *The Economist*, 9 March 2002, 32. These percentages have increased even further since this article was written. Now the United States may well be spending as much on defense as the rest of the world added together.
15. Julian Lindley-French, *Terms of Engagement: The Paradox of American Power and the Transatlantic Dilemma post-11 September* (Paris: The European Union Institute for Security Studies, Chaillot Papers, May 2002), 27–31, 77–8. The quotation is from 77.

16. Joseph S. Nye Jr., *The Paradox of American Power: Why the World's Only Superpower Can't Go It Alone* (Oxford: Oxford University Press, 2002).

17. For an analysis already seeing the United States in these terms, see Andrew J. Bacevich, *American Empire: The Realities & Consequences of US Diplomacy* (Cambridge, Mass.: Harvard University Press, 2002).

18. For an optimistic account of what the EU has achieved and could achieve in the future, see Charles A. Kupchan, *The End of the American Era: US Foreign Policy and the Geopolitics of the Twenty-First Century* (New York: Knopf, 2003).

19. Michael Clark and Paul Cornish, "The European Defence Project and the Prague Summit," *International Affairs*, 78:4 (Oct. 2002), 777–88; Presentation by former Deputy SACEUR Rupert Smith before the Norwegian Atlantic Committee, 5 September, 2002.

20. Kennedy and Bouton, "The Real Trans-Atlantic Gap," 68, 70.

21. See for instance Fareed Zakaria, "Why America Scares the World and What to Do about It," *Newsweek*, 24 March 2003, 14–29.

22. For an account of the Afghan war, see Bob Woodward, *Bush At War* (New York: Simon & Schuster, 2003.)

23. Kennedy and Bouton, "The Real Trans-Atlantic Gap," 68–70.

24. Kennedy and Bouton, "The Real Trans-Atlantic Gap," 70.

25. See e.g. "Putting the Brakes on," *The Economist*, 4 Aug. 2001, 25–6.

26. Joseph Quinlan and Marc Chandler, "The US Trade Deficit: A Dangerous Obsession," *Foreign Affairs*, 80:3 (May/June 2001), 87–97, particularly 94–5.

27. Josef Joffe, "Who's Afraid of Mr. Big?," *The National Interest*, 64 (Summer 2001), 43–52. The quotation is from 44. See also Anthony J. Blinken, "The False Crisis Over the Atlantic," *Foreign Affairs*, 80:3 (May/June 2001) 35–48; Suzanne Kapner, "American TV Losing out in Global Ratings War," *International Herald Tribune*, 2 Jan. 2003, 1.

28. Robert Kagan, *Of Paradise and Power: America and Europe in the New World Order* (New York: Knopf, 2003). For another recent analysis along these lines, see, for instance, "Living with a Superpower," *The Economist*, 4 Jan. 2003, 18–20.

29. *World Development Report 2003*, 234–5.

30. Kennedy and Bouton, "The Real Trans-Atlantic Gap," 68.

BIBLIOGRAPHY

In the bibliography I have listed primarily books and articles mentioned in the foot-notes. Only certain standard works have been listed in addition. A complete list of books and articles used would have been very much longer.

Sources

Documents on Western Europe in the US National Archive (NA) for the period 1945–1968.

Foreign Relations of the United States (*FRUS*), the volumes on Western Europe, 1945–1968.

North Atlantic Council, *NATO Final Communiqués 1949–1974* (Brussels: NATO Information Service, n.d.).

Public Papers of the Presidents of the United States, 1945–2000. (Washington, DC: Government Printing Office, 1950–2002).

US Department of Commerce, Bureau of Census, *Historical Statistics of the United States: Colonial Times to 1970*, 2 vols. (Washington, DC, 1975).

——*Statistical Abstract of the United States* (Washington, DC: Government Printing Office, 1989–).

Literature

Adler, Emanuel, and Barnett, Michael (eds.), *Security Communities* (Cambridge: Cambridge University Press, 1988).

Adler, Selig, *The Isolationist Impulse: Its Twentieth-Century Reaction* (London: Collier-Macmillan, 1957).

Aldrich, Richard J., *The Hidden Hand: America and Cold War Secret Intelligence* (London: John Murray, 2001).

Allin, Dana H., *Cold War Illusions: America, Europe, and Soviet Power 1969–89* (London: Macmillan, 1995).

Ambrose, Stephen, *Eisenhower: The President* (New York: Simon and Schuster, 1984).

——*Nixon: The Triumph of a Politician 1962–1972* (New York: Simon and Schuster, 1989).

Aimaq, Jasmine, *For Europe or Empire? French Colonial Ambitions and the European Army Plan* (Lund: Lund University Press, 1996).

Arenth, Joachim, *Johnson, Vietnam und der Westen: Transatlantische Belastungen 1963–1969* (Munich: Olzog, 1994).

Aronson, Lawrence, and Kitchen, Martin, *The Origins of the Cold War in Comparative Perspective: American, British and Canadian Relations with the Soviet Union, 1941–48* (Houndmills: Macmillan, 1988).

Art, Robert, "The United States and the NATO Alliance: Managing the Unsolvable," in *The 1980s: Decade of Confrontation? The Eighth National Security Conference 1981. Proceedings* (Washington, DC, National Defense University Press, 1981).

Asmus, Ronald D., *Opening NATO's Door: How the Alliance Remade Itself for a New Era* (New York: Columbia University Press, 2002).

Athanassopoulou, Ekavi, *Turkey, Anglo-American Security Interests 1945–195.* (London: Frank Cass, 1999).

Bacevich, Andrew J., *American Empire: The Realities & Consequences of U.S Diplomacy* (Cambridge, Mass.: Harvard University Press, 2002).

Baker, James A., *The Politics of Diplomacy: Revolution, War, and Peace 1989–199.* (New York: Putnam, 1995).

Ball, George, *The Past Has Another Pattern: Memoirs* (New York: Norton, 1982).

Banchoff, Thomas, *The German Problem Transformed: Institutions, Politics, and Foreign Policy, 1945–1995* (Ann Arbor: University of Michigan Press, 1999).

Bar-Siman-Tov, Yaacov, "The United States and Israel since 1948: A 'Special Relationship?' " *Diplomatic History*, 22 (Spring 1998), 231–62.

Ben-Zvi, Abraham, *The United States and Israel: The Limits of the Special Relationship* (New York: Columbia University Press, 1993).

Berghahn, Volker R., *America and the Intellectual Cold Wars in Europe* (Princeton Princeton University Press, 2001).

Bergsten, C. Fred, "America and Europe: Clash of Titans?" *Foreign Affairs*, 78:2 (1999), 20–34.

Betts, Richard, *NATO's Midlife Crisis* (Washington, DC: Brookings Institute, 1989).

Bildt, Carl, *Uppdrag Fred* (Mission Peace) (Stockholm: Norstedts, 1997).

Bischof, Günter, and Dockril, Saki (eds.), *Cold War Respite: Geneva 1955* (Baton Rouge: Louisiana University Press, 2000).

Blackwill, Robert D., *The Future of Transatlantic Relations* (New York: Council on Foreign Relations report, 1999).

Blinken, Anthony J., "The False Crisis over the Atlantic," *Foreign Affairs*, 80:3 (2001) 35–48.

Blum, William, *The CIA: A Forgotten History* (London: Zed books, 1986).

Borstelmann, Thomas, *The Cold War and the Color Line: American Race Relations in the Global Arena* (Cambridge, Mass.: Harvard University Press, 2001).

Bozo, Frédéric, "Détente versus Alliance: France, the United States and the Politics of the Harmel Report (1964–1968)," *Contemporary European History*, 7 (1998) 343–60.

——*Two Strategies for Europe: De Gaulle, the United States and the Atlantic Alliance* (Lanham: Rowman & Littlefield, 2001).

——"Before the Wall: French Diplomacy and the Last Decade of the Cold War, 1979–1989," in Olav Njølstad (ed.), *From Conflict Escalation to Conflict Transformation: The Cold War in the 1980s* (London: Frank Cass, forthcoming).

Brands, H. W., *The Specter of Neutralism: The United States and the Emergence of the Third World, 1947–1960* (New York: Columbia University Press, 1989).

Brandt, Willy, *Erinnerungen* (Memoirs) (Frankfurt: Propyläen, 1989).

Brett, Teddy, Gilliat, Steve, and Pople, Andrew, "Planned Trade, Labour Party Policy and U.S. Intervention: The Successes and Failures of Post-War Reconstruction," *History Workshop*, Spring 1982, 138.

Brinkley, Douglas, *Dean Acheson: The Cold War Years, 1953–71* (New Haven: Yale University Press, 1992).

Brogi, Alessandro, *A Question of Self-Esteem: The United States and the Cold War Choices in France and Italy, 1944–1958* (Westport: Praeger, 2002).

Brown, Michael E., "Minimalist NATO: A Wise Alliance Knows When to Retrench," *Foreign Affairs*, 78:3 (1999), 204–18.

Brzezinski, Zbigniew, *Power and Principle: Memoirs of a National Security Adviser, 1977–81* (New York: Farrar, Straus, Giroux, 1983).

——*Game Plan: How to Conduct the U.S.—Soviet Contest* (New York: Atlantic Monthly Press, 1986).

Bullock, Alan, *Ernest Bevin: Foreign Secretary, 1945–1951* (London: Heinemann, 1983).

Burk, Kathleen, "War and Anglo-American Financial Relations in the Twentieth Century," in Fred M. Leventhal and Roland Quinault (eds.), *Anglo-American Attitudes From Revolution to Partnership* (Aldershot: Ashgate, 2000).

——"The Marshall Plan: Filling in Some of the Blanks," *Contemporary European History*, 10 (2001), 267–94.

Bush, George, and Scowcroft, Brent, *A World Transformed: The Collapse of the Soviet Empire* (New York: Knopf, 1998).

Calleo, David P., *Beyond American Hegemony: The Future of the Western Alliance* (New York: Basic Books, 1987).

——*Rethinking Europe's Future* (Princeton: Princeton University Press, 2001).

Calvocoressi, Peter, *The British Experience, 1945–1975* (Harmondsworth: Pelican, 1979).

Chalmers, Malcolm, "The Atlantic Burden-Sharing Debate—Widening or Fragmenting?" *International Affairs*, 77 (2001), 569–85.

Clark, Michael, and Cornish, Paul, "The European Defence Project and the Prague Summit," *International Affairs*, 78 (2002), 777–88.

Clark, Wesley K., *Waging Modern War: Bosnia, Kosovo, and the Future of Combat* (New York: Public Affairs, 2001).

Club, Edmund O., *China and Russia: The Great Game* (New York: Columbia University Press, 1971).

Cogan, Charles, *Oldest Allies, Guarded Friends* (Westport: Praeger, 1994).

——*Forced to Choose: France, the Atlantic Alliance, and NATO—Then and Now* (Westport: Praeger, 1997).

——*The Third Option: The Emancipation of European Defense, 1989–2000* (Westport: Praeger, 2001).

Cohen, Eliot, "The Long-Term Crisis of the Alliance," *Foreign Affairs*, 61:2 (1982), 325–43.

Cole, Wayne S., *Roosevelt and the Isolationists 1932–45* (Lincoln: University of Nebraska Press, 1983).

Commission on Neutrality Policy, *Had There Been a War...: Preparations for the Reception of Military Assistance 1949–1969* (Stockholm: Fritzes, 1994).

Connelly, Matthew, *A Diplomatic Revolution: Algeria's Fight for Independence and the Origins of the Post-Cold War Era* (Oxford: Oxford University Press, 2002).

Conze, Eckart, "Hegemonie Durch Integration? Die amerikanische Europapolitik und de Gaulle," *Vierteljahrshefte für Zeitgeschichte*, 45 (April 1995), 307.

Costigliola, Frank, "The Failed Design: Kennedy, de Gaulle, and the Struggle for Europe," *Diplomatic History*, 8 (Summer 1984), 227–251.

Costigliola, Frank, *France and the United States* (New York: Twayne, 1992).
—— "Kennedy, the European Allies, and the Failure to Consult," *Political Science Quarterly*, 110 (Winter 1995), 105–23.
—— "The Vietnam War and the Challenge to American Power in Europe," in Lloyd Gardner and Ted Gittinger (eds.), *International Perspectives on Vietnam* (College Station: Texas A & M University Press, 2000), 147–8.
Daalder, Ivo H., "Are the United States and Europe Heading for Divorce?" *International Affairs*, 77, (2001) 553–67.
Dedman, Martin J., *The Origins and Development of the European Union 1945–95: A History of European Integration* (London: Routledge, 1996)
Devuyst, Youri, "European Unity in Transatlantic Commercial Diplomacy," in Eric Philippart and Pascaline Winand (eds.), *Ever Closer Partnership? Policy-Making in US-EU Relations* (Brussels: Peter Lange, 2001).
Deutsch, Karl W. et al., *Political Community and the North Atlantic Area: International Organization in the Light of Historical Experience* (Princeton: Princeton University Press, 1957).
Dimbley, David, and Reynolds, David, *An Ocean Apart: The Relationship between Britain and America in the Twentieth Century* (New York: Random House, 1988).
Dobson, Alan P., *Anglo-American Relations in the Twentieth Century: Of Friendship, Conflict and the Rise and Decline of Superpowers* (London: Routledge, 1995).
—— "The USA, Britain, and the Question of Hegemony," in Geir Lundestad(ed.), *No End To Alliance. The United States and Western Europe: Past, Present and Future* (Houndmills: Macmillan, 1998). 134–63.
—— "Anglo-American Relations and Diverging Economic Defence Policies in the 1950s and 1960s," in Jonathan Hollowell (ed.), *Twentieth-Century Anglo-American Relations* (Houndmills: Palgrave, 2001), 143–65.
—— *US Economic Statecraft for Survival 1933–1991: Of Sanctions, Embargoes and Economic Warfare* (London: Routledge, 2002).
Dockrill, Saki, *Britain's policy for West German Rearmament 1950–1955* (Cambridge: Cambridge University Press, 1991).
—— *Britain's Retreat from East of Suez: The Choice between Europe and the World?* (Houndmills: Palgrave, 2002).
Domke, William K., Eichenberg, Richard C., and Kelleher, Catherine M., "Consensus Lost? Domestic Politics and the 'Crisis' in NATO," *World Politics*, 34 (1982), 382–407.
Duchêne, François, *Jean Monnet: The First Statesman of Interdependence* (New York: Norton, 1994).
Dudziak, Mary L., *Cold War Civil Rights: Race and the Image of American Democracy* (Princeton: Princeton University Press, 2000).
Duffield, John S., "NATO's Functions after the Cold War," *Political Science Quarterly*, 109:5 (1994/5), 783–4.
—— *Power Rules: The Evolution of NATO's Conventional Force Posture* (Stanford: Stanford University Press, 1995).
—— "The North Atlantic Treaty Organization: Alliance Theory," in Ngaire Woods (ed.), *Explaining International Relations Since 1945* (Oxford: Oxford University Press, 1996), 337–54.

Duggan, Christopher, and Wagstaff, Christopher (eds.), *Italy in the Cold War: Politics, Culture and Society 1948–58* (Oxford: Berg, 1995).

Duke, Simon, *The Elusive Quest for European Security: From EDC to CFSP* (London: Macmillan, 2000).

—— and Krieger, Wolfgang (eds.), *U.S. Military Forces in Europe: The Early Years, 1945–1970* (Boulder: Westview, 1993).

Dumbrell, John, *A Special Relationship: Anglo-American Relations in the Cold War and After* (Houndmills: Macmillan, 2001).

Eisenberg, Carolyn Woods, *Drawing the Line: The American Decision to Divide Germany, 1944–1949* (Cambridge: Cambridge University Press, 1996).

Eisenhower, Dwight D., *Mandate for Change* (New York: Doubleday, 1956).

Eizenstat, Stuart, "Are the U.S. and EU Listening to Each Other?" *European Affairs*, 2:4 (2001), 35–43.

Ellis, Sylvia A., "Lyndon Johnson, Harold Wilson and the Vietnam War: A *Not* So Special Relationship?" in Jonathan Hollowell (ed.), *Twentieth-Century Anglo-American Relations* (Houndmills: Palgrave, 2001), 189–201.

Ellwood, David W., *Rebuilding Europe: Western Europe, America and Postwar Reconstruction* (London: Longman, 1992).

Eriksen, Knut Einar, and Pharo, Helge, *Kald krig og internasjonalisering 1949–1965, Norsk utenrikspolitikks historie 5* (Cold War and Internationalization 1949–1955, The History of Norwegian Foreign Policy, 5) (Oslo: Universitetsforlaget, 1997).

Eurogroup, *Western Defense: The European Role in NATO* (Brussels, May 1988).

Featherstone, Kevin, and Ginsberg, Roy H., *The United States and the European Union in the 1990s: Partners in Transition* (Basingstoke: Macmillan, 1996).

Fielding, Jeremy, "Coping with Decline: U.S. Policy toward the British Defense Reviews of 1966," *Diplomatic History*, 23:4 (Fall 1999).

Fischer, Beth A., *The Reagan Reversal: Foreign Policy and the End of the Cold War* (Columbia: University of Missouri Press, 1997).

Flynn, Gregory, and Rattinger, Hans (eds.), *The Public and Atlantic Defense* (London: Rowen & Allenheld, 1985).

François-Poncet, Jean, "Europe and the United States: The Lessons of a Crisis," *Atlantic Quarterly*, 1:2 (1983), 105–15.

Freedman, Lawrence, "The Atlantic Crisis," *International Affairs*, 58 (1983), 395–412.

Friedman, Benjamin M., *Day of Reckoning: The Consequences of American Economic Policy under Reagan and After* (New York: Random House, 1988).

Fritsch-Bournazel, Renata, "France: Attachment to a Nonbinding Relationship," in Gregory Flynn and Hans Rattinger (eds.), *The Public and Atlantic Defense* (London: Rowen & Allenheld, 1985), 91–2.

Fursdon, Edward, *The European Defence Community: A History* (London: Macmillan, 1980).

Gaddis, John, *The Long Peace: Inquiries into the History of the Cold War* (New York: Oxford University Press, 1987).

—— *We Now Know: Rethinking Cold War History* (Oxford: Oxford University Press, 1997).

Galtung, Johan, and Gleditsch, Nils Petter, "Norge i verdenssamfunnet" (Norway in the World Comunity), in Natalie Rogoff Ramsøy and Mariken Vaa (eds.), *Det norske samfunn* (The Norwegian Society) (Oslo: Gyldendal, 1975).

Gardner, Anthony Laurence, *A New Era in US–EU Relations?: The Clinton Administration and the New Transatlantic Agenda* (Aldershot: Avebury, 1997).

Gardner, Lloyd C., "Lyndon Johnson and De Gaulle," in Robert Paxton and Nicholas Wahl (eds.), *De Gaulle and the United States: A Centennial Reappraisal* (Oxford: Berg, 1994).

—— "How We Lost Vietnam, 1940–54," in David Ryan and Victor Pungong (eds.), *The United States and Decolonization: Power and Freedom* (Houndmills: Macmillan, 2000). 121–39.

Garthoff, Raymond L., *Détente and Confrontation: American-Soviet Relations from Nixon to Reagan*. Rev. edn. (Washington, DC: Brookings, 1994).

Gates, Robert, *From the Shadows: The Insider's Story of Five Presidents and How They Helped Win the Cold War* (New York: Simon & Schuster, 1996).

Gaulle, Charles de, *Lettres, notes et carnets* (Paris: Plon, 1980).

Gavin, Francis J., "The Gold Battles within the Cold War: American Monetary Policy and the Defense of Europe, 1960–1963," *Diplomatic History*, 26:1 (2002), 61–94.

Gearson, John P. S., *Harold Macmillan and the Berlin Wall Crisis, 1958–62: The Limits of Interest and Force* (Basingstoke: Macmillan, 1998).

Giauque, Jeffrey Glenn, *Grand Designs & Visions of Unity: The Atlantic Powers and the Reorganization of Western Europe, 1955–1963* (Chapel Hill: University of North Carolina Press, 2002).

Goldgeier, Joseph M., *Not Whether But When. The U.S. Decision to Enlarge NATO* (Washington, DC: Brookings, 1999).

Goldman, Minton F., "President Carter, Western Europe, and Afghanistan in 1980: Inter-Allied Differences over Policy toward the Soviet Invasion," in Herbert D. Rosenbaum and Alexej Ugrinsky (eds.), *Jimmy Carter: Foreign Policy and Post-Presidential Years* (Westport: Greenwood, 1994), 19–34.

Gordon, Philip H., *France, Germany, and the Western Alliance* (Boulder: Westview, 1995).

—— "NATO After September 11," *Survival*, 43:4 (2001/2), 89–106.

Graebner, Norman, *America as a World Power: A Realist Appraisal from Wilson to Reagan* (Wilmington: Scholarly Resources, 1984).

Greenwood, Sean, "Helping to Open the Door? Britain in the Last Decade of the Cold War," in Olav Njølstad (ed.), *From Conflict Escalation to Conflict Transformation: The Cold War in the 1980s* (London: Frank Cass, forthcoming).

Grayson, George W., *Strange Bedfellows: NATO Marches East* (Lanham: University Press of America, 1999).

Grosser, Alfred, *The Western Alliance: European-American Relations Since 1945* (London: Macmillan, 1980).

Haftendorn, Helga, *NATO and the Nuclear Revolution: A Crisis of Credibility, 1966–67* (Oxford: Oxford University Press, 1996).

—— *Deutsche Aussenpolitik zwischen Selbstbeschränkung und Selbstbehauptung* (Stuttgart: Deutsche Verlags-Anstalt, 2001).

Hahn, Walter F., and Pfaltzgraff, R. L. (eds.), *Atlantic Community in Crisis: A Redefinition of the Transatlantic Relationship* (New York: Pergamon Press, 1979).

Halberstam, David, *The Best and the Brightest* (New York: Random House, 1972).

—— *War in a Time of Peace: Bush, Clinton, and the Generals* (New York: Simon & Schuster, 2001).

Hanhimäki, Jussi M, *Containing Coexistence: America, Russia, and the "Finnish Solution," 1945–1956* (Kent: Kent State University Press, 1997).

—— *Scandinavia and the United States: An Insecure Friendship* (New York: Twayne, 1997).

Harper, John Lamberton, *American Visions of Europe: Franklin D. Roosevelt, George F. Kennan, and Dean G. Acheson* (Cambridge: Cambridge University Press, 1994).

Hartley, Keith and Sandler, Todd, "NATO Burden-Sharing: Past and Future," *Journal of Peace Research*, 36:6 (1999), 665–80.

Healey, Denis, *The Time of My Life* (London: Penguin, 1990).

Heller, Francis Howard, and Gillingham, John R. (eds.), *Nato: The Founding of the Atlantic Alliance and the Integration of Europe* (Basingstoke: Macmillan, 1992).

—— —— (eds.), *The United States and the Integration of Europe: Legacies of the Postwar Era* (New York: St. Martin's, 1996).

Hertle, Hans-Hermann, *Der Fall der Mauer: Die Unbeabsichtigte Selbstauflösung des SED-Staates* (Opladen and Wiesbaden: Westdeutscher Verlag, 1999).

—— "Germany in the Last Decade of the Cold War," in Olav Njølstad (ed.), *From Conflict Escalation to Conflict Transformation: The Cold War in the 1980s* (London: Frank Cass, forthcoming).

Heuser, Beatrice, *Transatlantic Relations: Sharing Ideals and Costs* (London: Royal Institute of International Affairs, 1996).

—— *NATO, Britain, France and the FRG: Nuclear Strategies and Forces for Europe, 1949–2000* (New York: St. Martin's Press, 1997).

Hillenbrand, Martin J., *Fragments of Our Time. Memoirs of a Diplomat* (Athens: University of Georgia Press, 1998).

Hitchcock, William I., *France Restored. Cold War Diplomacy and the Quest for Leadership in Europe 1944–1954.* (Chapel Hill: University of North Carolina Press, 1998).

—— *The Struggle for Europe: The History of the Continent since 1945* (London: Profile Books, 2003).

Hobsbawm, Eric, *Age of Extremes: The Short Twentieth Century 1914–1991* (London: Michael Joseph, 1994).

Hoffmann, Stanley, *Decline or Renewal? France Since the 1930s* (New York: Viking, 1974).

Hogan, Michael, *The Marshall Plan: America, Britain, and the Reconstruction of Western Europe, 1947–1952* (Cambridge: Cambridge University Press, 1987).

Holbrooke, Richard, *To End a War* (New York: Random House, 1998).

Hopkins, Michael F., "The Price of Cold War Partnership: Sir Oliver Franks and the British Military Commitment in the Korean War," *Cold War History*, 1:2 (Jan. 2001), 28–46.

Howard, Michael, "Reassurance and Deterrence: Western Defense in the 1980s," *Foreign Affairs*, 61:2, (1982/3), 319.

Howard, Michael, "A European Perspective on the Reagan Years," *Foreign Affairs*, 66:3 (1987/8), 479–82.

Howard, Michael Eliot, "An Unhappy Successful Marriage: Security Means Knowing What to Expect," *Foreign Affairs*, 78:3 (1999), 164–75.

Howe, Geoffrey, *Conflict and Loyalty* (London: Macmillan, 1994).

Howorth, Jolyon, "Britain, France and the European Defence Initiative," *Survival*, 42:2 (2000), 33–55.

—— "Renegotiating the Marriage Contract: Franco-American Relations Since 1981," in Sabrina P. Ramet and Christine Ingebritsen (eds.), *Coming in from the Cold War: Changes in U.S.–European Interactions since 1980* (Lanham: Rowman & Littlefield, 2002), 73–96.

Hunter, Robert E., *The European Security and Defense Policy: NATO's Companion— or Competitor?* (Santa Monica: RAND, 2002).

Ikenberry, G. John, "American Power and the Empire of Capitalist Democracy," *Review of International Studies*, 27 (2001), 191–212.

—— (ed.), *America Unrivaled: The Future of the Balance of Power* (Ithaca: Cornell University Press, 2002).

Ingimundarson, Valur, *The Struggle for Western Integration: Iceland, the United States, and NATO during the First Cold War*, 3/1999 (Oslo: Institute for Defense Studies, 1999).

—— "The Role of NATO and the US Military Base in Icelandic Domestic Politics, 1949–99," in Gustav Schmidt (ed.), *A History of NATO*, 2 (Basingstoke: Palgrave, 2001), 285–302.

Institut Français d'Opinion Publique, *Les Français et de Gaulle* (Paris: Plon, 1971).

Ireland, Timothy P., *Creating the Entangling Alliance: The Origins of the North Atlantic Treaty Organization* (Westport: Greenwood Press, 1981).

Isaacson, Walter, and Thomas, Evan, *The Wise Men: Six Friends and the World They Made* (New York: Simon and Schuster, 1986).

Jacobs, Seth, " 'Our System Demands the Supreme Being': The U.S. Religious Revival and the 'Diem' Experiment, 1954–55," *Diplomatic History*, 25 (2000), 589–624.

Jackson, Ian, *The Economic Cold War: America and East-West Trade, 1948–63* (Houndmills: Palgrave, 2001).

—— " 'Rival Desirabilities': Britain, East–West Trade and The Cold War, 1948–51," *European History Quarterly*, 31:2 (2001), 256–87.

Jackson, Robert J., *Continuity of Discord: Crisis and Responses in the Atlantic Community* (New York: Praeger, 1985).

Jauvert, Vincent, *L'Amérique contre De Gaulle: Histoire secrète 1961–1969* (Paris: Seuil, 2000).

Joffe, Joseph, "European-American Relations: The Enduring Crisis," *Foreign Affairs*, 59:4 (1980/1).

—— "Europe's American Pacifier," *Foreign Policy*, 54 (Spring 1984), 64–82.

—— "Where Germany Has Never Been Before," *The National Interest*, 56 (1999), 45–53.

—— "Who's Afraid of Mr. Big?," *The National Interest*, 64 (2001), 43–52.

Johnston, Andrew M., "Mr. Slessor Goes to Washington: The Influence of the British Global Strategy Paper on the Eisenhower New Look," *Diplomatic History*, 22:3 (1989), 361–98.

Jonas, Manfred, *Isolationism in America, 1935–1941* (Ithaca: Cornell University Press, 1966).

Jones, Matthew, *Conflict and Confrontation in South East Asia, 1961–1965: Britain, the United States and the Creation of Malaysia* (Cambridge: Cambridge University Press, 2002).

Jones, Joseph M., *The Fifteen Weeks: An Inside Account of the Genesis of the Marshall Plan* (New York: Harcourt, Brace & World, 1955).

Jobert, Michel, *Memoires d'avenir* (Paris: Fayard, 1974).

Kagan, Robert, *Of Paradise and Power: America and Europe in the New World Order* (New York: Knopf, 2003).

Kaiser, Karl, "Die Krise der europäisch-amerikanischen Beziehungen," *Europa-Archiv*, 29 (1974), 387–98.

Kaplan, Lawrence S., *The Long Entanglement: NATO's First Fifty Years* (Westport: Praeger, 1999).

Kapner, Suzanne, "American TV Losing out in Global Ratings War," *International Herald Tribune*, 2 January 2003, 1.

Kaufman, Joyce P., *NATO and the Former Yugoslavia: Crisis, Conflict, and the Atlantic Alliance* (Lanham: Rowman & Littlefield, 2002).

Kennedy, Craig, and Bouton, Marshall M., "The Real Trans-Atlantic Gap," *Foreign Policy*, 133 (Nov.-Dec. 2002), 66–70.

Kennedy, Paul, *The Rise and Fall of the Great Powers: Economic Change and Military Conflict from 1500 to 2000* (New York: Random House, 1987).

—— *Preparing for the Twenty-First Century* (New York: Random House, 1993).

Kent, John, "The United States and the Decolonization of Black Africa, 1945–63," in David Ryan and Victor Pungong (eds.), *The United States and Decolonization: Power and Freedom* (Houndmills: Macmillan, 2000), 168–87.

Kahler, Miles, and Link, Werner, *Europe and America: A Return to History* (New York: Council on Foreign Relations Press, 1996).

Kelleher, Catherine McArdle, *Germany & the Politics of Nuclear Weapons* (New York: Columbia University Press, 1975).

Kindleberger, Charles P., *The World in Depression, 1929–1939* (Berkeley: University of California Press, 1973).

—— "Hierarchy versus Inertial Cooperation," *International Organization*, 40 (1986), 841.

Kissinger, Henry, *The Troubled Partnership: A Re-appraisal of the Atlantic Alliance* (New York: McGraw-Hill, 1965).

—— "What Kind of Atlantic Partnership?" *The Atlantic Community Quarterly*, 7 (1969), 32.

—— *White House Years* (Boston: Little, Brown and Company, 1979).

—— "Something is Deeply Wrong in the Atlantic Alliance," *The Washington Post*, 21 Dec. 1981, A21.

—— *Years of Upheaval* (London: Weidenfeld and Nicolson, 1982).

—— *Years of Renewal* (New York: Simon & Schuster, 1999).

Kleiman, Robert, *Atlantic Crisis: America Confronts a Resurgent Europe* (New York: Norton, 1964).

Kuisel, Richard, *Seducing the French: The Dilemma of Americanization* (Berkeley: University of California Press, 1993).

Kupchan, Charles A., *The End of the American Era: US Foreign Policy and the Geopolitics of the Twenty-First Century* (New York: Knopf, 2003).

Kurth, James, "The Next NATO: Building an American Commonwealth of Nations," *The National Interest*, 65 (Fall 2001), 10–11.

Lacouture, Jean, *De Gaulle: The Rebel, 1890–1944* (New York: Norton, 1990).

——*De Gaulle: The Ruler 1945–1970* (London: Harvill, 1991).

Lainsbury, Andrew, *Once Upon an American Dream: The Story of Euro Disneyland* (Lawrence: University of Kansas Press, 2000).

Larres, Klaus, *Churchill's Cold War: The Politics of Personal Diplomacy* (New Haven: Yale University Press, 2002).

——"[Review of] Thomas Banchoff, 'The German Problem Transformed'," *Journal of Cold War Studies*, 4:2 (Spring 2002), 113–18.

Lawrence, Mark Atwood, "Transnational Coalition-Building and the Making of the Cold War in Indochina, 1947–1949," *Diplomatic History*, 26 (2002) 453–80.

Lees, Lorraine M., *Keeping Tito Afloat: The United States, Tito, and the Cold War* (University Park: Penn State University Press, 1997).

Leffler, Melvyn P., *A Preponderance of Power: National Security, the Truman Administration, and the Cold War* (Stanford: Stanford University Press, 1992).

Lieber, Robert J., "No Transatlantic Divorce in the Offering," *Orbis*, 44:4 (2000), 571–84.

Lindley-French, Julian, *Terms of Engagement: The Paradox of American Power and the Transatlantic Dilemma post-11 September* (Paris: The European Union Institute for Security Studies, Chaillot Papers, 2002).

Lipson, Charles, *Standing Guard: Protecting Foreign Capital in the Nineteenth and Twentieth Centuries* (Berkeley: University of California Press, 1985).

Litwak, Robert S., *Détente and the Nixon Doctrine: American Foreign Policy and the Pursuit of Stability, 1969–1976* (Cambridge: Cambridge University Press, 1984).

Logevall, Fredrik, *Choosing War: The Lost Chance for Peace and the Escalation of the War in Vietnam* (Berkeley: University of California Press, 1999).

Louis, William Roger, "The Dissolution of the British Empire in the Era of Vietnam," *The American Historical Review*, 107:1 (2002), 1–25.

——and Bull, Hedley (eds.), *The "Special Relationship": Anglo-American Relations Since 1945* (Oxford: Clarendon Press, 1986).

——and Owen, Roger (eds.), *A Revolutionary Year: The Middle East in 1958* (London and New York: Tauris, 2002).

——and Robinson, Ronald, "The United States and the Liquidation of the British Empire in the Tropical Africa, 1941–1945," in Prosser Gifford and William Roger Louis (eds.), *The Transfer of Power in Africa: Decolonialization 1941–1951* (New Haven: Yale University Press, 1982).

Lowe, Peter, "Waging Limited Conflict: The Impact of the Korean War on Anglo-American Relations, 1950–1953," in Dale Carter and Robin Clifton (eds.), *War and Cold War in American Foreign Policy, 1942–62* (New York: Palgrave Macmillan, 2002), 133–55.

Luard, Evan, "Western Europe and the Reagan Doctrine," *International Affairs*, 4 (1987), 563–74.

Lucas, Scott W., "Mobilizing Culture: The State–Private Network and the CIO in the Early Cold War," in Dale Carter and Robin Clifton (eds.), *War and Cold War in American Foreign Policy* (Houndmills: Palgrave, 2002).

Lundestad, Geir, *America, Scandinavia, and the Cold War, 1945–1949* (New York: Columbia University Press, 1980).

—— "The United States, the Marshall Plan and Corporatism," in *Maktpolitik och Husfrid: Studier i Internationell och svensk historia tilägnade Gøran Rystad* (Power Politics and Domestic Peace: Studies in International and Swedish History Dedicated to Gøran Rystad) (Lund: Lund University Press, 1991).

—— "Empire by Invitation? The United States and Western Europe, 1945–1952," *Journal of Peace Research*, 23 (1986), 263–77.

—— *The American "Empire" and Other Studies of US Foreign Policy in a Comparative Perspective* (Oxford: Oxford University Press, 1990).

—— "Uniqueness and Pendulum Swings in US Foreign Policy," in *The American "Empire" and Other Studies of US Foreign Policy in a Comparative Perspective* (Oxford: Oxford University Press, 1990), 127–31.

—— "The United States and Western Europe Under Ronald Reagan," in David E. Kyvig (ed.), *Reagan and the World* (Westport: Greenwood Press, 1990), 39–66.

—— "American–European Cooperation and Conflict: Past, Present and Future," in Geir Lundestad (ed.), *No End to Alliance. The United States and Western Europe: Past, Present, Future* (Houndmills: Macmillan, 1998)

—— *"Empire" by Integration: The United States and European Integration, 1945–1997* (Oxford: Oxford University Press, 1998).

—— "Introduction," in Geir Lundestad (ed.), *No End to Alliance. The United States and Western Europe: Past, Present, Future* (Houndmills: Macmillan, 1998)

—— *East, West, North, South: Major Developments in International Politics Since 1945* (Oxford: Oxford University Press, 1999).

—— "Empire by Invitation in the American Century," *Diplomatic History*, 23:2 (1999), 189–217.

—— " 'Imperial Overstretch': Mikhail Gorbachev and the End of the Cold War," *Cold War History*, 1:1 (2000), 1–20.

Lynch, Frances M. B., "De Gaulle's Veto: France, the Rueff Plan and the Free Trade Area," *Contemporary European History*, 9 (2000), 111–35.

McGinn, John G., "The Politics of Collective Inaction: NATO's Response to the Prague Spring," *Journal of Cold War Studies*, 1:3 (1999), 130–8.

McIntyre, David W., *Background to the ANZUS Pact: Policy-Making, Strategy, and Diplomacy, 1945–55* (New York: St. Martin's, 1995).

Macmillan, Harold, *At the End of the Day, 1961–1963* (London: Macmillan, 1973).

Magyar, Karl P. (ed.), *United States Interests and Policies in Africa* (London: Macmillan, 2000).

Mahan, Erin R., *Kennedy, de Gaulle, and Western Europe* (Houndmills: Palgrave, 2002).

Mahoney, Richard D., *JFK: Ordeal in Africa* (New York, 1983).

Maier, Charles S., "The Two Postwar Eras and the Conditions for Stability in Twentieth-Century Western Europe," *American Historical Review*, 86:2 (1981), 327–52.

—— "Empires or Nations? 1918, 1945, 1989...," in Carl Levy and Mark Roseman (eds.), *Three Postwar Eras in Comparison: Western Europe 1918–1945–1989* (Houndmills: Palgrave, 2002).

Major, John, *The Autobiography* (London: HarperCollins, 1999).

Malmborg, Mikael af, "Sweden—NATO's Neutral 'Ally'? A Post-Revisionist Account," in Gustav Schmidt (ed.), *A History of NATO: The First Fifty Years*, 3 (Houndmills: Palgrave, 2001), 295–303.

May, Ernest R., *"Lessons" of the Past: the Use and Misuse of History in American Foreign Policy* (New York: Oxford University Press, 1973).

—— "The American Commitment to Germany, 1949–1955," in Lawrence S. Kaplan (ed.), *American Historians and the Atlantic Alliance* (Kent: Kent State University Press, 1991), 52–80.

Mayer, Frank A., *Adenauer and Kennedy: A Study in German–American Relations, 1961–1963* (Basingstoke: Macmillan, 1996).

Mearsheimer, John, *The Tragedy of Great Power Politics* (New York: Norton, 2001).

Mee, Charles L., *The Marshall Plan: The Launching of the Pax Americana* (New York: Simon and Schuster, 1984)

Meistermann, Nathalie, "Disneyland Paris: New Day, Old Woes," *International Herald Tribune*, 16–17 March 2002, 9.

Melandri, Pierre, "Les États-Unis et la prolifération nucléaire: le cas français," *Revue d'Histoire Diplomatique*, 3 (1995), 208–15.

Merrit, Richard L., and Puchala, Donald J. (eds.), *Western European Perspectives on International Affairs* (New York: Praeger, 1968).

Middlemas, Keith (ed.), *Orchestrating Europe: The Informal Politics of the European Union 1973–95* (London: Fontana, 1995).

Miller, James Edward, *The United States and Italy 1940–1950: The Politics of Diplomacy and Stabilization* (Chapel Hill: University of North Carolina Press, 1986).

Millis, Walter (ed.), *The Forrestal Diaries* (New York, Viking, 1951).

Milward, Alan S., *The Reconstruction of Western Europe, 1945–51* (Berkeley: University of California Press, 1984).

—— "Conclusions. The Value of History," in Alan S. Milward et al., *The Frontier of National Sovereignty: History and Theory 1945–1992* (London: Routledge, 1993), 182–201.

—— *The European Rescue of the Nation-State* (London: Routledge, 1992).

—— *The Rise and Fall of a National Strategy 1945–1963: The United Kingdom and the European Community*, 1 (London: Frank Cass, 2002).

Mitterrand, François, *Réflexions sur la politique extérieure de la France: Introduction à vingt-cinq discours (1981–1985)* (Paris: Fayard, 1986).

Moïsi, Dominique, "The Trouble with France," *Foreign Affairs*, 77:3 (1998), 94–104.

Moores, Simon, " 'Neutrals on our Side': US Policy towards Sweden during the Eisenhower Administration," *Cold War History*, 2:3 (April 2002), 29–62.

Morgenthau, Hans, "The Crisis of the Alliance," in Karl H. Cerny and Henry W. Briefs (eds.), *NATO in Quest of Cohesion* (New York: Praeger, 1965).

Nash, Philip, *The Other Missiles of October: Eisenhower, Kennedy, and the Jupiters 1957–1963* (Chapel Hill: University of North Carolina Press, 1997).

Nelson, Daniel J., *A History of U.S. Military Forces in Germany* (Boulder: Westview, 1987).

Niedhart, Gottfried, "The Federal Republic's Ostpolitik and the United States: Initiatives and constraints," in Kathleen Burk and Melvyn Stokes (eds.), *The United States and the European Alliance Since 1945* (Oxford: Berg, 1999), 289–311.

Ninkovich, Frank A., *The Diplomacy of Ideas: U.S. Foreign Policy and Cultural Relations 1938–1950* (Cambridge: Cambridge University Press, 1981).

Nixon, Richard M., "The time to Save NATO," *Atlantic Community Quarterly*, 6 (1968/9), 479–84.

Njølstad, Olav, *Peacekeeper and Troublemaker: The Containment Policy of Jimmy Carter, 1977–78* (Oslo: Institute for Defence Studies, 1995).

—— "The Carter Administration and Italy: Keeping the Communists Out of Power without Interfering," *Journal of Cold War Studies*, 4:3 (2002), 56–94.

—— "The Carter Legacy: Entering the Second Era of the Cold War," in Olav Njølstad (ed.), *From Conflict Escalation to Conflict Transformation: The Cold War in the 1980s* (London: Frank Cass, forthcoming).

Norris, Robert S., Arkin, William M., and Burr, William, "Where They Were," *The Bulletin of Atomic Scientists*, Nov./Dec. (1999), 26–35.

Nuti, Leopoldo, "Italy and the Cold War," *Journal of Cold War Studies*, 4:3 (Summer 2002), 2–23.

—— "Italy and the Battle of the Euromissiles," in Olav Njølstad (ed.), *From Conflict Escalation to Conflict Transformation: The Cold War in the 1980s* (London: Frank Cass, forthcoming).

Nwaubani, Ebere, *The United States and Decolonization in West Africa, 1950–1960* (Rochester: University of Rochester Press, 2001).

Nye, Joseph S., "The US and Europe: Continental Drift?" *International Affairs*, 76:1 (2000) 51–9.

—— *The Paradox of American Power: Why the World's Only Superpower Can't Go It Alone* (Oxford: Oxford University Press, 2002).

O'Hanlon, Michael, "Come Partly Home, America: How to Downsize US Deployments Abroad," *Foreign Affairs*, 80:2 (2001), 2–8.

O'Neill, R. J., "The Korean War and the Origins of ANZUS," in Carl Bridge (ed.), *Munich to Vietnam: Relations with Britain and the United States since the 1930s* (Charlton: Melbourne University Press, 1965).

Osgood, Robert, *NATO: The Entangling Alliance* (Chicago: University of Chicago Press, 1962).

Owen, David, *Balkan Odyssey* (New York: Harcourt Brace & Company, 1995).

Pagedas, Constantine A., *Anglo-American Strategic Relations and the French Problem 1960–63: A Troubled Partnership* (London: Frank Cass, 2000).

Palmer, Diego A. Ruiz, "La coopération militaire entre la France et ses alliés, 1966–1991: Entre le poids de l'héritage et les défis de l'après guerre froid," in Pierre Melandri, Maurice Vaisse, and Frederic Bozo (eds.), *La France et l'OTAN 1949–1996* (Bruxelles: Complexe, 1996), 576–82.

Palmer, A. W., *A Dictionary of Modern History 1789–1945* (Harmondsworth: Penguin Books, 1965).

Palmer, John, *Europe without America? The Crisis in Atlantic Relations* (New York: Oxford University Press, 1987).

Patrick, Stewart, "Dont Fence me in: The Perils of Going it Alone," *World Policy Journal*, 18:3 (2001), 2–14.

—— and Forman, Shepard (eds.), *Multilateralism & U.S. Foreign Policy: Ambivalent Engagement* (Boulder: Lynne Rienner, 2002).

Paul, Septimus H., *Nuclear Rivals: Anglo-American Atomic Relations, 1944–1952* (Columbus: Ohio State University Press, 2000)

Paxton, Robert O., and Wahl, Nicholas (eds.), *De Gaulle and the United States: A Centennial Reappraisal* (Oxford: Berg, 1994).

Pells, Richard, *Not Like Us: How Europeans have Loved, Hated, and Transformed American Culture since World War II* (New York: Basic Books, 1997).

Petras, James, and Morley, Morris, "Contesting Hegemons: US–French Relations in the 'New World Order'," *Review of International Studies*, 26 (2000), 49–67.

Peyrefitte, Alain, *C'était de Gaulle* (Paris: Fayard, 1994).

Pfaff, William, "The Coming Clash of Europe with America," *World Policy Journal*, 15:4 (1998/9), 1–9.

Poggiolini, Ilaria, "Italy," in David Reynolds (ed.), *The Origins of the Cold War in Europe: International Perspectives* (New Haven: Yale University Press, 1994).

Pond, Elizabeth, *Beyond the Wall: Germany's Road to Unification* (Washington, DC: Brookings, 1993).

—— *The Rebirth of Europe* (Washington, DC: Brookings, 1999).

Powaski, Ronald E., *The Entangling Alliance: The United States and European Security, 1950–1993* (Westport: Greenwood Press, 1994)

Pungong, Victor, "The United States and the International Trusteeship System," in David Ryan and Victor Pungong (eds.), *The United States and Decolonization: Power and Freedom* (Houndmills: Macmillan, 2000), 85–101.

Putnam, Robert D., and Bayne, Nicholas, *Hanging Together: Cooperation and Conflict in the Seven-Power Summits* (Cambridge, Mass.: Harvard University Press, 1987).

Quinlan, Joseph, and Chandler, Marc, "The U.S. Trade Deficit: A Dangerous Obsession," *Foreign Affairs*, 80:3 (May/June 2001), 87–97.

Rees, David, *Korea: The Limited War* (New York: St. Martin's, 1964).

Reeves, Richard, *President Nixon. Alone in the White House* (New York: Simon & Schuster, 2001).

Reid, Escott, *Time of Fear and Hope: The Making of the North Atlantic Treaty 1947–1949* (Toronto: McClelland and Stewart, 1977).

Rielly, John E., "The American Mood: A Foreign Policy of Self-Interest," *Foreign Policy*, 34 (1979), 76–85.

—— "American Opinion: Continuity, not Reaganism," *Foreign Policy*, 50 (1983), 86–99.

—— "America's State of Mind," *Foreign Policy*, 66 (1987), 39–56.

—— "Public Opinion: The Pulse of the '90s," *Foreign Policy*, 82 (1991), 79–96.

—— "The Public Mood at Mid-Decade," *Foreign Policy*, 98 (1995), 76–93.

—— "Americans and the World: A Survey at Century's End," *Foreign Policy*, 114 (1999), 97–114.

Reynolds, David, "Britain," in David Reynolds (ed.), *The Origins of the Cold War in Europe: International Perspectives* (New Haven: Yale University Press, 1994).

Rimington, Stella, *Open Secret: The Autobiography of the Former Director-General of MI5* (London: Hutchinson, 2001).

Risse-Kappen, Thomas, *Cooperation Among Democracies: The European Influence on U.S. Foreign Policy* (Princeton: Princeton University Press, 1995).

Riste, Olav, *Norway's Foreign Relations—A History* (Oslo: Universitetsforlaget, 2001).

Rodman, Kenneth A., *Sanctity versus Sovereignty: The United States and the Nationalization of Natural Resource Investments* (New York: Columbia University Press, 1988).

Romero, Federico, "Interdependence and Integration in American Eyes: From the Marshall Plan to Currency Convertibility," in Alan S. Milward et al., *The Frontier of National Sovereignty: History and Theory 1945–1992* (London: Routledge, 1993), 155–81.

Rothwell, Victor, *Britain and the Cold War 1941–1947* (London: Jonathan Cape, 1982).

Russett, Bruce, and Oneal, John, *Triangular Peace: Democracy, Interdependence, and International Organization* (New York: Norton, 2001).

Ryan, David, and Pungong, Victor (eds.), *The United States and Decolonization: Power and Freedom* (Houndmills: Macmillan, 2000).

Sandars, C. T., *America's Overseas Garrisons: The Leasehold Empire* (Oxford: Oxford University Press, 2000).

Sarotte, M. E., *Dealing with the Devil: East, Germany, Détente, and Ostpolitik, 1969–1973* (Chapel Hill: University of North Carolina Press, 2001).

Sassoon, Donald, *One Hundred Years of Socialism: The West European Left in the Twentieth Century* (New York: The New Press, 1996).

Schaetzel, Robert J., *The Unhinged Alliance: America and the European Community* (New York: Harper & Row, 1975).

Schäfer, Bernd, "German Ostpolitik and the Nixon Administration, 1969–1973," Paper presented at the conference *NATO, the Warsaw Pact and the Rise of Détente, 1965–1972*, Dobbiaco, 26–28 Sept. 2002.

Schein, Martin (ed.), *The Marshall Plan: Fifty Years After* (New York: Palgrave, 2001).

Schlesinger, Arthur M., *A Thousand Days: John F. Kennedy in the White House* (Boston: Houghton Mifflin, 1965).

—— "America and Empire," in Arthur M. Schlesinger, *The Cycles of American History* (Boston: Houghton Miffin, 1986).

Schmidt, Helmut, *Menschen und Mächte* (Berlin: Siedler, 1987).

Schoenbaum, Thomas J., *Waging Peace and War: Dean Rusk in the Truman, Kennedy and Johnson Years* (New York: Simon and Schuster, 1988).

Schraeder, Peter J., "Cold War to Cold Peace: Explaining U.S.–French Competition in Francophone Africa," *Political Science Quarterly*, 115 (2000), 398–419.

Schwarz, Hans-Peter, *Adenauer: der Staatsmann: 1952–1967* (Stuttgart: Deutsche Verlags Anstalt, 1991).

Bibliography

Shultz, George Pratt, *Turmoil and Triumph: My Years as Secretary of State* (New York: Scribner's, 1993).

Schurman, Franz, *The Logic of World Power: An Inquiry into the Origins, Currents, and Contradictions of World Power* (New York: Pantheon, 1974).

Schwabe, Klaus, "The Origins of the United States' Engagement in Europe, 1946–1952," in Francis Howard Heller and John R. Gillingham (eds.), *Nato: The Founding of the Atlantic Alliance and the Integration of Europe* (Basingstoke: Macmillan, 1992).

——"Do Personalities Make a Difference?" in Kathleen Burke and Melvyn Stokes (eds.), *The United States and the European Alliance since 1945* (Oxford: Berg, 1999).

Schwartz, Thomas Alan, *America's Germany: John J. McCloy and the Federal Republic of Germany* (Cambridge, Mass.: Harvard University Press, 1991).

——"Victories and Defeats in the Long Twilight Struggle: The United States and Western Europe in the 1960s," in Diane B. Kunz (ed.), *The Diplomacy of the Crucial Decade: American Foreign Relations during the 1960s* (New York: Columbia University Press, 1994).

——"Lyndon Johnson and Europe. Alliance Politics, Political Economy, and 'Growing Out of the Cold War'," in H. W. Brands(ed.), *The Wages of Globalism: Lyndon Johnson and the Limits of American Power* (New York: Oxford University Press, 1995).

Senate Committee on Armed Services, *NATO: Can the Alliance Be Saved?* Report of Senator Sam Nunn, 97th Congress, 2nd Session, 1982.

Serfaty, Simon, *Stay the Course: European Unity and Atlantic Solidarity* (New York: Praeger, 1997).

Servan-Schreiber, Jean Jacques, *Le Défis américain* (Paris: Denoël, 1967).

Shlaim, Avi, *The United States and the Berlin Blockade, 1948–49: A Study in Crisis Decision-Making* (Berkeley: University of California Press, 1983).

Sherwood, Elizabeth D., *Allies in Crisis: Meeting Global Challenges to Western Security* (New Haven: Yale University Press, 1990).

Helene, Sjursen, *The United States, Western Europe and the Polish Crisis: International Relations in the Second Cold War* (Houndmills: Palgrave, 2003).

Skidelsky, Robert, "Imbalance of Power," *Foreign Policy*, 129 (March/April 2002), 46–55.

Smith, Mark, *NATO Enlargement During the Cold War: Strategy and System in the Western Alliance* (Basingstoke: Palgrave, 2000).

Smith, Michael, *Western Europe and the United States: The Uncertain Alliance* (London: Allen & Unwin, 1984).

Smyser, William R., *From Yalta to Berlin: The Cold War Struggle over Germany* (Basingstoke: Macmillan, 1999).

Sorensen, Theodore C., *Kennedy* (New York: Bantam Books, 1966).

Soutou, Georges-Henri, "France," in David Reynolds (ed.), *The Origins of the Cold War in Europe: International Perspectives* (New Haven: Yale University Press, 1994).

——*L'Alliance incertaine: Les rapports politico-stratégiques franco-allemands, 1954–1996* (Paris: Fayard, 1996).

—— "Le Président Pompidou et les relations entre les États-Unis et l'Europe," *Journal of European Integration History*, 6:2 (2000), 111–46.

—— "France and the Cold War, 1944–63," *Diplomacy and Statecraft*, 12:4 (Dec. 2001), 35–52.

Spaak, Paul-Henri, *The Crisis of the Atlantic Alliance* (Columbus: Ohio State University Press, 1967).

Starke, J. G., *The ANZUS Treaty Alliance* (Melbourne: Melbourne University Press, 1991).

Steel, Ronald, *The End of Alliance: America and the Future of Europe* (London: Viking, 1964).

—— "NATO's Afterlife," *The New Republic*, 2 Dec. 1991, 18–19.

Stenseth, Dagfinn, *Vitne til historien* (Witness to History) (Oslo: Damm, 2001).

Stikker, Dirk U., *Men of Responsibility: A Memoir* (London: John Murray, 1966).

Stoltenberg, Thorvald, *De tusen dagene: fredsmekler på Balkan* (The Thousand Days: Peace Mediator in the Balkans) (Oslo: Gyldendal, 1996).

Stromseth, Jane E., *The Origins of Flexible Response: NATO's Debate Over Strategy in the 1960s* (New York: St. Martins, 1988).

Stuart, Douglas T., and Tow, William, *The Limits of Alliance: NATO Out-of-Area Problems Since 1949* (Baltimore: Johns Hopkins University Press, 1990).

Stueck, William S., *The Korean War: An International History* (Princeton: Princeton University Press, 1995).

Tamnes, Rolf, *The United States and the Cold War in the High North* (Oslo: Ad Notam, 1991).

—— *Oljealder 1965–1995* (Oil Age 1965–1995), Norsk Utenrikspolitikks Historie (The History of Norwegian Foreign Policy), 6 (Oslo: Universitetsforlaget, 1997).

Thatcher, Margaret, *The Downing Street Years* (New York: Harper Collins, 1993).

Taylor, A. J. P., *The Struggle for Mastery in Europe 1848–1918* (London: Oxford University Press, 1974).

Thies, Wallace J., *Friendly Rivals: Bargaining and Burden-Shifting in NATO* (Armonk: M. E. Sharpe, 2003).

Thomas, Daniel C., *The Helsinki Effect: International Norms, Human Rights, and the Demise of Communism* (Princeton: Princeton University Press, 2001).

Thomas, Martin, "From Dien Bien Phu to Evian: Anglo-French Imperial Relations, 1954–1962," in Alan Sharp and Glyn Stone (eds.), *Anglo-French Relations in the Twentieth Century: Rivalry and Cooperation* (London: Routledge, 2000), 310–19.

—— "Defending a Lost Cause? France and the United States Vision of Imperial Rule in French North Africa, 1945–1956," *Diplomatic History*, 26 (2002), 215–47.

Thompson, Christopher S., "Prologue au conflit: les premières impressions et l'année 1940," in Institut Charles de Gaulle, *De Gaulle en son siècle. 4: La sécurité et l'indépendance de la France* (Paris: Plon, 1992), 239–53.

Thorne, Christopher, *Allies of a Kind: The United States, Britain, and the War Against Japan, 1941–1945* (Oxford: Oxford University Press, 1978).

Talbott, Strobe, *The Russia Hand: A Memoir of Presidential Diplomacy* (New York: Random House, 2002).

Torching, Martin, and Torching, Susan, *Buying Into America: How Foreign Money Is Changing the Face of the Our Nation* (New York: New York Times Books, 1988).

Trachtenberg, Marc, *A Constructed Peace: the Making of the European Settlement, 1945–1963* (Princeton: Princeton University Press, 1999).

Treverton, Gregory F., *The Dollar Drain and American Forces in Germany: Managing the Political Economics of Alliance* (Athens: Ohio University Press, 1978).

——*Making the Alliance Work: The United States and Western Europe* (Ithaca: Cornell University Press, 1985).

Ullman, Richard H., "The French Connection," *Foreign Policy*, 75 (1989), 3–33.

United States Department of State, *1958–1980: U.S. Trade With the European Community*, Special Report No. 84, 28 June 1981, 1.

Urwin, Derek W., *Western Europe Since 1945: A Political History* (London, 1989).

Utley, Rachel E., *The French Defense Debate. Consensus and Continuity in the Mitterrand Era* (London: Macmillan, 2000).

Vaïsse, Maurice (ed.), *L'Europe et la crise de Cuba* (Paris: Armand Colin, 1993).

——*La Grandeur politique étrangère du général de Gaulle, 1958–1969* (Paris: Fayard, 1998).

Vanke, Jeffrey W., "An Impossible Union: Dutch Objections to the Fouchet Plan, 1958–62," *Cold War History*, 2:1 (Oct. 2001), 95–112.

Walker, Martin, "The New European Strategic Relationship," *World Policy Journal*, 16:2 (1999), 23–30.

——"Europe: Superstate or Superpower?" *World Policy Journal*, 17:4 (2000/1), 7–16.

Wall, Irving M., *France, the United States and the Algerian War* (Berkeley: University of California Press, 2001).

——*The United States and the Making of Postwar France, 1945–1954* (Cambridge: Cambridge University Press, 1991).

Walt, Steven M., *Origins of Alliances* (Ithaca: Cornell University Press, 1987).

——"The Ties that Fray: Why Europe and America are Drifting apart," *National Interest*, 54 (1998/9), 3–11.

Walter, Holly Wyatt, *The European Community and the Security Dilemma, 1979–92* (Basingstoke: Macmillan, 1997).

Warner, Geoffrey, "De Gaulle and the Anglo-American 'Special Relationship' 1958–1966: Perceptions and Realities," in Pierre Melandri, Maurice Vaisse, and Frederic Bozo (eds.), *La France et l'OTAN 1949–1996* (Brussels: Complexe, 1996), 247–52.

——"Why the General said No," *International Affairs*, 78 (2002), 869–82.

Watt, D. Cameron, *Succeeding John Bull: America in Britain's Place 1900–1975: A Study of the Anglo-American Relationship and World Politics in the Context of British and American Foreign-Policy-Making in the Twentieth Century* (Cambridge: Cambridge University Press, 1984).

——"Britain, the United States and the Opening of the Cold War", in Ritchie Ovendale (ed.), *The Foreign Policy of the British Labour Governments, 1945–1951* (Leicester: Leicester University Press, 1984).

Wells, Samuel F., "Mitterrand's International Policies," *Washington Quarterly*, Summer (1988), 59–75.

Whelan, Richard, *Drawing the Line: The Korean War, 1950–1953* (Boston: Little, Brown, 1990).

White, Theodore H., *Fire in the Ashes* (New York: Harper & Row, 1953).

—— *In Search of History: A Personal Adventure* (New York: Harper & Row, 1978).

Wiebes, Cees, and Zeeman, Bert, "Benelux," in David Reynolds (ed.), *The Origins of the Cold War in Europe: International Perspectives* (New Haven: Yale University Press, 1994).

Williams, Geoffrey, *The Permanent Alliance: The European-American Partnership 1945–1984* (Leyden: A. W. Sijthoff, 1977).

Williams, Phil, *The Senate and US Troops in Europe* (London: Macmillan, 1985).

Willis, F. Roy, *France, Germany, and the New Europe 1945–1967* (Oxford: Oxford University Press, 1968).

Winand, Pascaline, *Eisenhower, Kennedy, and the United States of Europe* (London: Macmillan, 1993).

Woodward, Bob, *Bush At War* (New York: Simon & Schuster, 2003.)

World Bank, *World Development Report 2003* (New York: Oxford University Press, 2003).

Wyatt-Walter, Andrew, "The United States and Western Europe: The Theory of Hegemonic Stability," in Ngaire Woods (ed.), *Explaining International Relations Since 1945* (Oxford: Oxford University Press, 1996).

Xydis, Stephen G., "Coups and Countercoups in Greece, 1967–73 (with postscript)," *Political Science Quarterly*, 89 (1974), 507–38.

Young, Hugo, *This Blessed Plot: Britain and Europe from Churchill to Blair* (Houndmills: Macmillan, 1998).

Young, John W., *Britain and European Unity, 1945–1992* (London: Macmillan, 1993).

—— "Britain and 'LBJ's War', 1964–68," *Cold War History*, 2:3 (2002), 63–92.

Zakaria, Fareed, "Why America Scares the World and What to Do about It," *Newsweek*, 24 March 2003, 14–29.

Zeiler, Thomas W., *Free Trade, Free World: The Advent of GATT* (Chapel Hill: University of North Carolina Press, 1999).

Zelikow, Philip, and Rice, Condoleezza, *Germany Unified and Europe Transformed: A Study in Statecraft* (Cambridge, Mass.: Harvard University Press, 1995).

Zimmermann, Hubert, *Money and Security: Troops, Monetary Policy, and West Germany's Relations with the United States and Britain, 1950–1971* (Cambridge: Cambridge University Press, 2002).

INDEX